NEW PERSPECTIVES IN NORTH–SOUTH DIALOGUE

ESSAYS IN HONOUR OF OLOF PALME

NEW PERSPECTIVES IN NORTH–SOUTH DIALOGUE

ESSAYS IN HONOUR OF OLOF PALME

Edited by
KOFI BUENOR HADJOR

Published in association with
THIRD WORLD COMMUNICATIONS

I.B.TAURIS & Co Ltd
Publishers
London

Published in 1988 by
I. B. TAURIS & Co Ltd
3 Henrietta Street
Covent Garden
London WC2E 8PW

in association with Third World Communications

Designed & Typeset by Columns of Reading
Printed by T.J. Press, Padstow

British Library Cataloguing in Publication Data

New perspectives in north-south dialogue :
essays in honour of Olof Palme.
1. Developed countries. Economic relations with
developing countries.   2. Developing countries.
Economic relations with developed countries
I. Hadjor, Kofi Buenor   II. Palme, Olof,
1927-1986
337'09172'2

ISBN 1-85043-105-1

American Library of Congress Cataloguing in Publication Data applied for

For the people of Sweden
who produced
OLOF PALME

Olof Palme with fellow Swedes.

Contents

Acknowledgements

The idea of publishing a memorial volume in honour of Olof Palme took shape over a period of some months. Of course, we were all shocked and angered at his untimely death. But what also occurred to us was that, regardless of this tragedy, the issues with which Olof Palme was associated had to be kept alive.

It was at this point that the idea for the present collection of essays took off. Virtually everyone we canvassed for this project was enthusiastic and supportive, and an idea was turned into reality in a record period of time.

Those from the Third World do not forget their dead. We hope that this volume will remind generations to come of Olof Palme's contribution to the progress of North–South dialogue. We have attempted to focus on issues rather than personalities. The issues with which Olof Palme was involved retain a vital relevance for the present and the future. In fact, their resolution probably represents the most important challenge facing humanity today.

The publication of this volume is motivated by our certainty that a critical examination of Olof Palme's contribution will help stimulate the reactivation of a genuine North–South dialogue. We are grateful for the support and encouragement of the many individuals who have made this project possible. Special thanks are due to:

—— all the contributors who obliged us by writing such excellent essays for the volume;

—— Mathias Morsberg and Nils Daag of the Swedish Embassy in London, for introducing the project to the Swedish Government, who gave us practical support without which the project would have remained unrealizable;

—— our colleagues at Third World Communications—Laura Brako, Sharmini Brookes, Esha Durayappah, Judy Hirst, Joyce Mensah, Nnadozie Okpokiri, Richard Renwick, and Robert Wood—for their various crucial roles;

—— Farehk and Nayar Jahangir of Excellent Litho, whose enthusiasm for this volume was so great that they printed the pre-launch promotional material at purely cost price;
—— Cary Yageman for inputting the entire manuscript into the computer;
—— Pauline Tiffen for compiling the acronyms and abbreviations;
—— Linda Briggs for the initial editing;
—— Katarina Robinson for her publicity and promotional work; and
—— Carlos Ramirex for suggesting an appropriate title for the volume.

The speedy publication of *New Perspectives* owes much to our collaboration with I. B. Taurus, who worked hard to produce this book quickly from our text.

I also wish to express my special thanks to:

—— Basil Davidson, the noted historian, whose books have had such an influence on my journalistic work;
—— Immanuel Wallerstein, the renowned social scientist, who at McGill University taught me how to understand the dynamics of the world system;
—— Peter Worsley, the eminent critical anthropologist, whose retirement from Manchester University has been actively invested in furthering the progress of Third World Communications—and who personally translated Fidel Castro's essay for the present volume.

This trio has supported Third World Communications in countless ways since its inception. Without their crucial contribution, our publishing efforts would not have survived—and the Essays in Honour of Olof Palme would never have seen the light of day.

Finally, I would like to draw attention to the wider purpose of the present volume. Its aim is not merely to honour the dead, but to ensure the vital ideas live on—in practice, as well as in theory. To this end, all revenues received by Third World Communications from sales of *New Perspectives* will go towards establishing an Institute of Third World Studies in London, with the explicit aim of promoting the world view that Olof Palme stood for. The Institute will, amongst other things, sponsor original research into development issues, organize conferences, seminars, and other gatherings for Third World scholars, politicians, and activists, and regularly publish material on the Third World of a qualitatively new standard.

Thus *New Perspectives*, we are sure, marks an exciting new beginning in North–South dialogue. Our responsibility is not merely to mourn, but to *organize*. If the present volume stimulates the reader in this direction, it will have fulfilled its aim.

Kofi Buenor Hadjor
London, January 1988

Notes on Contributors

Kofi Buenor Hadjor (editor) is publisher/editor of Third World Communications. He studied at McGill, Stanford, and Oxford Universities. He was press aide in the publicity secretariat of the late-President Kwame Nkrumah of Ghana and represented Ghana on the Permanent Secretariat of the Cairo-based Afro–Asian People's Solidarity Organization. He has taught at several universities in Africa, Canada, and the USA. He was UNESCO'S Communications Advisor to the government of Tanzania, Director of the Tanzania School of Journalism, and editor of *New African*, a leading news magazine on Africa. His most recent publications include: *On Transforming Africa: Discourse with Africa's Leaders* (1987), *Kwame Nkrumah and Ghana: The Dilemma of Post-Colonial Power* (1988), *Africa Today: A Critical Perspective* (1988), and *On the Brink: Nuclear Proliferation and the Third World*, edited with Peter Worsley (1987). A forthcoming title to be published by Penguin is *Third World Key Terms: A Critical Vocabulary*.

A. M. Babu was a member of President Nyerere's Cabinet in Tanzania for eight years. He was educated in Zanzibar and as an external student at London University. He was active in political organization during the anti-colonial struggle in Africa, serving as President of the Umma Party in Zanzibar which later merged with the Afro–Shirazi Party. He was secretary of the Freedom Committee of the Pan African Freedom Movement for East and Central Africa. He became the first Foreign Minister and Minister of Trade in the post-revolution government of Zanzibar, and played an active role at UNCTAD I in Geneva in 1964. From 1979 to 1981 he was visiting lecturer in International Relations and Black Studies at San Francisco State University, and in Afro–American Studies at the University of

California, Berkeley. Since 1981 he has been Visiting Professor in Black
Studies at Amherst College. He is contributing editor to *Africa Now*
and *Pacific News Service*, and has published *African Socialism or
Socialism in Africa* (1981).

Willy Brandt fled Germany in 1933 and lived in exile in Norway and
Sweden during the Second World War. He first joined the Social
Democratic Party in 1931. He was Governing Mayor of West Berlin
from 1957 to 1966, when he became Vice-Chancellor and Foreign
Minister in the CDU/SPD coalition. From 1969 to 1974 he was
German Chancellor in the SPD/FDP government. He has been
President of the Socialist International since 1976 and from 1979–83
was a member of the European Parliament. He has received numerous
honorary degrees and foreign decorations, including the Nobel Peace
Prize in 1971 and the Einstein International Peace Prize in 1985. He
was Chairman of the Independent Commission on International
Development Issues, which produced two reports: *North–South: A
Programme for Survival* (1980) and *Common Crisis: North South:
Cooperation for World Recovery* (1983). He resigned as Chairman of
the SPD in 1987.

Gro Harlem Brundtland is Prime Minister of Norway and Chairperson
of the Norwegian Labour Party. Educated at the Universities of Oslo
and Harvard, she trained as a physician. She has held a number of
different governmental positions and is a member of the Parliamentary
Standing Committee on Foreign Affairs, Chairperson of the UN World
Commission on Environment and Development, and a member of the
Independent Commission on Disarmament and Security Issues (the
Palme Commission). Her publications include articles on preventive
medicine, school health, and growth studies.

Ingvar Carlsson is Prime Minister of Sweden. He received a degree in
Politics, Science and Economics from Lund University and also studied
at Northwestern University, USA. He joined the government in 1958 as
assistant to the Prime Minister in the Cabinet Office, and from 1961 to
1967 was Chairman of the Youth League of the Swedish Social
Democratic Party. He was Minister of Education and Cultural Affairs
from 1969 to 1973, and Minister of Housing 1973–76. He became
Deputy Prime Minister in 1982 and Prime Minister in 1986 after the
assassination of Olof Palme. He is co-author of the Social Democratic
Party's *The Future in the Hands of the People* and chairman of the
working group which presented the Social Democratic Party's
economic programme, *Future for Sweden* (1984).

Fidel Castro is Head of State and President of the Council of State of Cuba. He studied at the University of Havana and practised law. He was actively involved in the armed struggle against the Batista regime from 1953 until Batista fled in 1959, when Castro became Prime Minister of Cuba. He has received numerous international awards, including the Dimitrov Prize (Bulgaria) 1980, Order of Lenin 1972, 1986, and Gold Star (Vietnam) 1982. His publications include *Ten Years of Revolution* (1964), *History Will Absolve Me* (1968), and *Fidel* (with Frei Betto) (1987).

Basil Davidson began his studies on Africa in 1950 and has at various times been Visiting Professor at the Universities of Ghana, California at Los Angeles, and Edinburgh. He is Honorary Research Fellow of the Centre of West African Studies at the University of Birmingham, and an Honorary Doctor of the Open University and of the Universities of Ibadan, Edinburgh, and Dar es Salaam. He has written many works on African history, culture, and societies, including: *Old Africa Rediscovered* (1959), *Black Mother—the African Slave Trade* (1961, revised 1980), *The African Past* (1964), *The Africans, A Cultural History* (1969), *In the Eye of the Storm, Angola's People* (1972), *Can Africa Survive?* (1975), *Modern Africa* (1982), and *Africa* (television series) 1984.

Luis Escheverría was President of Mexico from 1970 to 1976. He submitted 'The Charter of Economic Rights and Duties of the States' adopted by the UN General Assembly, 12 December 1974, and was appointed Mexico's Ambassador in UNESCO. From 1977 to 1978 he was a member of UNESCO's Executive Council. He was President and Director General of the Center for Economic and Social Studies of the Third World in Mexico City (1976–80).

Anoushiravan Ehteshami was educated in Iran and Britain and has a degree in social sciences from Trent Polytechnic in Nottingham. Since 1983 he has been working on his Ph.D. at the University of Exeter on the subject of the role and impact of transnational companies in the developing countries, with special reference to Brazil, Iran, and South Korea. He lectures on a wide range of subjects including the Iranian Revolution, the Iran–Iraq war, Libya, and Central and South America. He is also on the editorial board of the *Third World Book Review*.

Andre Gunder Frank is Professor of Development Economics and Social Sciences at the University of Amsterdam and Director of its institute for Socio–Economic Studies of Developing Regions. He is a citizen of West Germany, but was educated in the USA, receiving a

Ph.D. in Economics from the University of Chicago with a dissertation on Soviet agriculture. He has taught economics, history, sociology, and other social sciences, especially Third World development at universities in the USA, Europe, and Latin America. His writings are associated particularly with the historical study of development and underdevelopment, and dependence, and have been published in 21 languages. His books include: *Capitalism and Underdevelopment in Latin America* (first published 1967), *Latin America: Underdevelopment or Revolution* (1969), *Sociology of Development and Underdevelopment of Sociology* (1969), *Dependent Accumulation and Underdevelopment* (1978), *Crisis in the World Economy* (1980), and *Crisis in the Third World* (1981).

Gunnar Fredriksson is the former Editor-in-Chief of the Swedish Social Democratic Party publications, *Stockhom Tidnigen* and *Afftonbladet*. He has written extensively on politics and development issues. His titles include studies of Thomas Paine and Bertrand Russell, as well as writings on India. He is currently a well-known columnist, writing on current affairs.

Frank Furedi is Chair of the Development Studies Department at the University of Kent at Canterbury. He is author of *The Soviet Union Demystified* and is currently working on a book on the subject of the Soviet Union in the Third World.

Rajiv Gandhi is Prime Minister of India and President of the Congress (I) Party. Educated in science and engineering at Trinity College, Cambridge, Gandhi, as a pilot, initially avoided a career in the world of politics—a world in which his grandfather, mother, and younger brother had already set an illustrious precedence. However, the death of his brother Sanjay in 1980 persuaded Gandhi to take an active role in politics, thereby aiding his mother at a time of intense internal and external parliamentary challenge. In June 1981 Gandhi won the seat previously held by his brother. He became General Secretary of the Congress (I) Party in 1983. The brutal assassination of Indira Gandhi on October 30, 1984 propelled Gandhi to the centre of Indian politics. Calling for new elections, Gandhi was elected with the largest mandate in India's history; his party won more seats in Parliament than ever before in the preceding seven general elections. He is Chairman of the Non-Aligned Movement and has been particularly active in promoting the policies and objectives of nuclear disarmament.

Fred Halliday was born in Ireland, and studied at the Universities of Oxford and London. He is the author of *Arabia without Sultans, Iran:*

Dictatorship and Development, The Making of the Second World War (1986), and, with Maxine Molyneux, *The Ethiopian Revolution*. Fred Halliday is Professor of International Relations at the London School of Economics, and contributing editor to *MERIP Middle East Reports*.

Judith Hart has a first-class degree in Sociology from the London School of Economics. She was a lecturer from 1946–59 and was elected Labour Member of Parliament for Lanark and Clydesdale in 1959. She was Joint Parliamentary Under-Secretary of State for Scotland from 1964 to 1966, then Minister of State at the Commonwealth Office (1966–67), Minister of Social Security (1967–68), and Paymaster General Cabinet Minister (1969). She was in the Ministry of Overseas Development 1969–70, 1974–75, and 1977–79, and Member of the United Nations Panel of Eminent Persons on Transnational Corporations, South Africa and Namibia, New York, 1985. She is Honorary Fellow at the Institute of Development Studies, University of Sussex. Her published works include *Aid and Liberation* (1979).

Neil Kinnock is Leader of the Labour Party of the UK and Leader of the Opposition. He obtained a BA degree in Industrial Relations and History and a Diploma in Education from University College, Cardiff and has been an MP since 1970. He was a member of the Public Expenditure Select Committee (1971–73) and of the Nationalized Industries Select Committee (1973–77). From 1977 to 1978 he was Chairman of the Welsh Group of Labour MPs, and in 1979 was appointed Chief Opposition Spokesman on Education, when he was elected to the Labour Party National Executive Committee. In 1980, 1981, and 1982 he was in the Shadow Cabinet and became Leader of the Labour Party in 1983. He is a Director of the 7:84 Theatre Company (a socialist community theatre group), Vice-President of Fair Play for Children and the Workers' Educational Association, and a member of the Socialist Educational Association and the Socialist Medical Association. His publications include *Wales and the Common Market* (co-author, 1972) and *Making Our Way* (1986).

Michael Manley was Prime Minister of Jamaica from 1972 to 1980 and is a politician, journalist, and trade unionist. He was educated at Jamaica College and the London School of Economics. He has been President of the People's National Party of Jamaica since 1969 and President of the Jamaica Workers' Union since 1984. He is Vice-President of the Socialist International and Chairman of the Socialist International Economic Committee. His work has received several recognitions, including the UN Special Award for Contributions to the

Struggle Against Apartheid in 1978 and the Juliot Curie Medal, the World Peace Council in 1979. His major publications include the *The Politics of Change* (1974), *A Voice at the Workplace* (1975), *Jamaica: Struggle in the Periphery* (1982), and *Global Challenge* (published by the Socialist International Economic Committee).

Maxine Molyneux was born in Karachi and grew up in India and Latin America. She studied at the University of Essex from where she obtained a Ph.D. in sociology and where she now teaches. She is author of *State Policies and the Position of Women in the Democratic Yemen*, *Women under Socialism*, and co-author (with Fred Halliday) of *The Ethiopian Revolution*. She is currently writing a comparative study of the policies of peripheral socialist states with respect to women and family. Her articles have appeared in *World Development*, *Monthly Review*, *New Left Review*, *Feminist Studies*, *Latin American Perspectives*, *Critical Social Policy*, and elsewhere.

Robert Mugabe is the Prime Minister of Zimbabwe. He studied at universities in South Africa and London and was a teacher from 1952. In 1960 he entered politics and was actively involved in the struggle for Rhodesian independence. He was co-founder of the Zimbabwe African National Union in 1963 and attended the Geneva Constitutional Conference on Rhodesia in 1976, the Malta Conference in 1978, and Lancaster House in 1979. He has received honorary doctorates from the Universities of Ahmadu Bello, Nigeria, and Edinburgh. He was given the Newsmaker of the Year Award (South African Society of Journalists) in 1980 and the International Human Rights Award (Howard University, Washington) in 1981.

Julius Nyerere was educated in Tanzania and Uganda (where he obtained a Teacher's Diploma) before winning a scholarship to Edinburgh University. He obtained an MA in 1952 and then taught history at St Francis' College near Dar es Salaam from 1953 to 1955. In 1954 he became Founder-President of the Tanganyika African National Union, (TANU), travelling the country campaigning for independence. In the first elections in which Africans had the vote, in 1958, he was elected as a member of the Legislative Assembly, and became Leader of the Opposition in Parliament. In 1961 he became the first Prime Minister of the first government of independent Tanganyika, was elected President when it became a republic in 1962, and from 1964 to 1985 was President of the United Republic of Tanzania (after Tanganyika and Zanzibar united). He is a founder member and Chairman of the Chama Cha Mapinduzi Party which was formed by a merger of TANU and the Afro–Shirazi party of Zanzibar in 1977. In 1981 he was given the Third World Award.

Thord Palmlund has been Director General of the Swedish Immigration Board since 1980. He was with NIB [the predecessor to the Swedish International Development Agency (SIDA)] from its start in 1962, and with SIDA from 1965 to 1969. During the 1970s he served in the Ministry of Foreign Affairs, and in 1978–79 as Under-Secretary of State for International Development Cooperation.

Robert Pollin teaches economics at the University of California, Riverside.

Timothy Shaw is Professor of Political Science and Executive Director of the Pearson Institute for International Development for African Studies at Dalhousie University, Halifax, Nova Scotia. He has a BA degree in Politics and Sociology from the University of Sussex, an MA from the University of East Africa in International Relations (1969) and a Ph.D. in Politics from Princeton University. His recent publications include: *Towards a Political Economy for Africa: The Dialectics of Dependence* (1985), *Nigeria: Africa's Major Power* (co-author with J. O. Ihonvbere), *Petroleum and Politics at the Semi-periphery: Towards a Nigerian Mode of Production* (co-author with J. O. Ihonvbere), and *Southern Africa in Crisis: An Analysis and Bibliography* (1986).

Oliver Tambo is Head of the External Mission of the African National Congress of South Africa. He studied at University College, Fort Hare, Cape Province. He was a secondary school teacher and, from 1951 to 1960, was a solicitor in Johannesburg. During this time he was twice banned from attending meetings (1954–56 and 1959–64) and in 1956 was arrested on treason charges, which were withdrawn the following year. He escaped to London in 1960 and has been actively involved in the fight against apartheid ever since.

Immanuel Wallerstein is Director of the Fernand Braudel Centre for the Study of Economics, Historical Systems, and Civilizations at the State University of New York at Binghampton. His works include *Africa: The Politics of Independence* and *Africa: The Politics of Unity*. The first volume of his *Modern World Systems* appeared in 1974 and the second volume (subtitled *Mercantilism and the Consolidation of the European Economy 1600–1750*) appeared in 1980. His most recent publication is *Historical Capitalism*. He is a regular contributor to *The Third World Book Review*.

Eduardo Zepeda teaches economics at the Metropolitan Autonomous University at Azcapotzalco, Mexico City and is a Ph.D. candidate at the University of California, Riverside.

List of Abbreviations

ACP	African, Caribbean and Pacific
ANC	African National Congress
CIA	Central Intelligence Agency
COMECON	Council for Mutual Economic Aid/Assistance (East European)
DAC	Development Assistance Committee
EEC	European Economic Community
ECOSOC	Economic and Social Council
EFTA	European Free Trade Association
FAO	Food and Agriculture Organization
GATT	General Agreement on Tariffs and Trade
GDP	gross domestic product
GNP	gross national product
IBRD	International Bank for Reconstruction and Development
ICDSI	Independent Commission on Disarmament and Security Issues
IDA	International Development Agency
IISS	International Institute for Strategic Studies
IFAD	International Fund for Agricultural Development
ILO	International Labour Organization
IMF	International Monetary Fund
MNR	Mozambique National Resistance
MPLA	Popular Movement for the Liberation of Angola

NAM   Non-Aligned Movement
NASA   National Aeronautics and Space Administration
NATO   North Atlantic Treaty Organization
NICs   newly industrializing/influential countries
NIDL   New International Division of Labour
NIEO   New International Economic Order

ODA   Official Development Assistance
OECD   Organization for Economic Co-operation and
               Development
OPEC   Organization of Petroleum Exporting Countries

PAICV   Partido Africano da Independencia da Capo Verde
PAIGC   Partido Africano da Independencia da Guine e Capo
               Verde
PLO   Palestine Liberation Organization
PRG   Provisional Revolutionary Government

RTA   retrospective terms adjustment

SADCC   Southern African Development Co-ordination
               Conference
SDI   Strategic Defence Initiative
SIDA   Swedish International Development Agency
SIPRI   Stockholm International Peace Research Institute
SWAPO   South West Africa People's Organization

TANU   Tanganyika African National Union

UNCTAD   United Nations Conference on Trade and Development
UNDP   United Nations Development Programme
UNESCO   United Nations Educational, Scientific and Cultural
               Organization
UNICEF   United Nations (International) Children's (Emergency)
               Fund
UNIDO   United Nations Industrial Development Organization
UNITA   National Union for the Total Independence of Angola

WHO   World Health Organization
WST   world system theory

ZAPU   Zimbabwe African People's Union

SECTION ONE

Tributes

1

A Tribute to Olof Palme

RAJIV GANDHI

I pay homage to Olof Palme, warm-hearted friend, far-seeing statesman, and herald of a more humane world. He earned respect as thinker and man of action. Politics is derisively called the art of the possible. Such people redeem politics. Olof Palme had a vision of human possibilities, and a grasp of how to realize them. He loved peace and worked for it. He had a deep feeling for the poor and downtrodden of all lands. The development of developing countries was one of his major concerns. He saw the link between the removal of poverty and the pursuit of peace. He contributed solidly to the search for an alternative to the strategy of balance of power.

The advent of nuclear weapons created a new situation in history, demanding new methods of thinking. He played a powerful role in publicizing and educating public opinion in Europe and elsewhere about what he called 'nuclear realities'. Leaders of nuclear weapon states have proclaimed that a nuclear war cannot be won and, therefore, must not be fought. But they continue to manufacture, test, and accumulate more and newer weapons. They advance novel justifications for doing so. They claim that the possession of nuclear weapons has kept peace in the world. This claim is patently unjustified. The peace that obtains can at best be called a grey peace. It is precarious and unstable. Relentless efforts are made to extend military presences to new areas. Tensions escalate. Support is given to one or the other side in most of the wars that smaller countries have fought.

What is significant is not that no nuclear weapons have been used since Hiroshima and Nagasaki, but that nuclear weapons of unbelievably greater destructive power are being produced and are positioned in various parts of the world. The confrontation is more intense. The danger of annihilation is greater. It will persist as long as nuclear weapons exist and there is a possibility of their use by design or error, by accident, or by malfunction.

Nuclear weapon states subscribe to the doctrine of deterrence. It is based on the belief that if the size of nuclear arsenals increases, the possibility of their use decreases. Deterrence is a perverse extension of the policy of confrontation. It assumes that bloc antagonism is a permanent feature of international relations, which must be fed as a matter of duty. Olof Palme likened it to a drug which must be taken in continuously increasing doses in order to be effective. Independent scientists have pointed out the unscientific basis on which the doctrine of deterrence rests. Their graphic scenarios of 'nuclear winter' should be a reminder of the danger of even a fraction of the present stockpiles of nuclear weapons being used.

Deterrence is now sought to be extended to outer space. That would deprive us of the use of one of the most promising common resources of mankind. It will also trigger, through chain reaction, an unprecedented arms race in both offensive and defensive weapons. It will ruin the chances of disarmament for all time to come. One is entitled to ask: If there are no winnable wars on earth, can there be winnable contests in outer space?

Most people still do not seem to realize the extent of the historical change brought about by nuclear weapons. Until Hiroshima, we all lived in a state of innocence. Even in the most terrible and long drawn-out of earlier conflicts, even when they extended over the seas and continents, there was a certainty of survival. We could be sure that although people and states were mortal, humankind is immortal. The nuclear weapon has deprived man of his immortality. It has made final extinction a possibility. Whatever has happened since has made the possibility an increasing probability.

This is the context in which the Six-Nation Five-Continent Peace Initiative was fashioned. It owes much to the vision of Olof Palme and Indira Gandhi. The six speak on behalf of all nations and peoples who feel threatened by the growing nuclear arsenals. The Declaration adopted by us in Delhi in January 1985 sought to focus the attention of the nuclear weapon powers and of the larger world on the dimensions of the problem and its implications for humankind as a whole. We have addressed ourselves to human security, not the security of this nation or that bloc. Our proposals are eminently practical and necessary: (i) a halt to the testing, production, and deployment of all nuclear weapons and their delivery systems; (ii) a comprehensive test ban treaty and, pending this, a moratorium on testing; and (iii) the prevention of an arms race in outer space by prohibiting the development, testing, production, and deployment of all space weapons. We are heartened at the worldwide response to these proposals. We shall continue our effort until it succeeds.

In a world where nuclear weapons are looked upon as a currency of power, the Six-Nation Initiative asserts the right of all peoples to their future. All nations of the world, and not only the handful of nuclear weapon states, have contributed to the making of civilization. On all of us is cast the responsibility to preserve it. Nobody has the right to wipe it out.

Olof Palme's vision was not confined merely to securing a world without nuclear arms. He also longed to see a world without want. He discussed the link between the two. Armaments, after all, are death-dealers. Resources allocated to armaments are giving to death what should belong to life. Disarmament would release massive resources for solving the economic and social problems of the world.

Olof Palme exploded many of the myths put forward by the merchants of military and monetary power. His was a voice of sanity raised against the politics of power and domination. The best way we can remember him is to carry forward the causes he espoused with such integrity and eloquence.

2

An Internationalist Vision

FIDEL CASTRO

I have rarely experienced such a sense of the unexpected and the unusual as I did at the moment when I received the news of the murder of Olof Palme.

Sweden, that peaceful democracy where the class struggle, though present, is mitigated by a high standard of living and the skilful tactics of social democracy, a country free from religious strife where national solidarity has been established over centuries, seemed an unlikely setting for such a crime, and Palme an unlikely victim. It was improbable, too, that this man, whose open, almost childlike smile was the most obvious outward sign of his strong personality, would have provoked anyone to criminal hatred. Without hazarding any guesses as to who might have been responsible—but whose identity is nevertheless quite clear to us—as I stated when we paid homage to our dear friend in the Swedish Embassy in Moscow, external forces were very probably involved in that crime.

These attributes of Palme's Sweden come back to my mind when I am asked to discuss, as a contribution to this international tribute offered to a great fallen leader, my ideas about the possibility of relationships between countries with different social systems and whose economies are at different stages of development.

Cuba bases her foreign policy on that very possibility. True, our closest politico–economic relationship is with countries with a socialist economic structure and with a political orientation similar to our own. But Cuban experience confirms that there can be a friendly political atmosphere despite these differences between countries with different and even antagonistic social systems, where relationships tend to be contradictory—as between developed industrialized countries and a developing country. Regular economic co-operation, too, can help us find ways of resolving the inequalities which separate us from the richer countries.

But one has to admit that international relations with countries

6

having different ideologies and different types of economy from our own are not identical in every case. To take an extreme example, we maintain normal relations, including promising economic relations, with Mrs Thatcher's Britain. It even happens that Conservative members of the House of Lords co-operate with Labour members to promote trade with our country. But one cannot deny that the present British government's support for apartheid—implicit in its refusal to condemn it—as well as its colonialist stance on the Malvinas issue and its participation in Mr Reagan's Strategic Defense Initiative (Star Wars) make stable relations between Cuba and Britain difficult.

The situation is quite different in the Swedish case. Here we have a country which is capitalist in structure but with its own distinctive features and marked by a more egalitarian distribution of income as a result of a long period of Social Democratic rule. The existence of finance capitalism in Sweden is obvious enough, but the absence of a colonial tradition—which inevitably always leaves its stamp—and the special kinds of economic relationships between Sweden and developing countries, which are the result of the considered foreign policy of the Social Democrats, have made it possible for Cuba, in her campaign in international institutions to induce the developed countries to change their economic policies and introduce at least a minimal element of justice into their dealings with the underdeveloped world, to point to Sweden as one of the examples which other capitalist countries might follow if they are to move towards more than just international relations of the kind we are calling for. Olof Palme contributed a great deal to the positive image which Sweden has today among Third World countries.

Swedish Social Democratic policy antedated Palme. But when our never-to-be-forgotten friend assumed the chief responsibility for the government of Sweden, he introduced into his country's foreign policy a heightened sense of awareness of international responsibility for development as a major responsibility for Swedes, given the backwardness that still prevails over vast areas of the world. This brought him very close to us, who speak for the world that is trying to develop itself.

Even before I got to know him personally, a positive relationship had grown up between us, based on his clear internationalist stand on peace, on the arms race, on co-operation for development, on racism, and on other issues. When we met for the first time, we saw him emerge at the top of the aeroplane steps with that characteristic smile. Our people instantly recognized him as a friend who would not be deflected by possible ideological differences.

During Palme's period in power, Cuba had very clear evidence of the friendliness of Swedish policy. Under the aegis of the Swedish Agency for International Development and other national agencies the Swedish contribution to Cuban development reached nearly $12 million a year. Experience showed us that this was not just Swedish co-operation but also Social Democratic co-operation, and that Palme's personal standards with regard to obligations about underdevelopment were central to that policy. This became evident during the interregnum following the defeat of the Social Democrats when a centre–right coalition was in power and when some parties in the coalition prevented Cuba from receiving this crucial aid, reducing it to an insignificant amount.

The specific influence of a progressive government and of the political leadership characteristic of Palme became very clear during his stay in Cuba. In the legendary Cuban city of Santiago, the scene of decisive revolutionary operations, Palme surprised the crowd which greeted him by his emotional statement, which he gave in excellent Spanish, that he had come to make his friendship visible by visiting them personally. But words are not the only vehicle of communication. His message went beyond that. It expressed the political attitudes which brought Palme and Sweden close to us: when he praised the heroism of Vietnam and the liberation of Portugal; when he quoted the words of Salvador Allende before his death, that it was the people who made their own history; and when he reaffirmed his total support for Chile. Cubans felt that neither differences of social system or of psychological characteristics separated them from this simple man whose enthusiasm was a refutation of the stereotype of the unemotional Nordic.

And in his speech he went further. He made his support for the New International Economic Order (NIEO) absolutely clear and spelled out his reasons. He praised the Charter of Rights and Duties of States which has still to be translated into action. Soon after, in a press interview, he emphasized the importance of the International Women's Conference in which he had just participated in Mexico. In a thousand different ways it became evident that in addition to the socialism of which we are so proud there are other kinds of international policy which justify ongoing co-operation between countries which, like Cuba and Sweden, work for peace, for the rights of all peoples, and for human progress.

On his last visit to the USA, Olof Palme avoided meeting Mr Reagan and made his disagreement with US foreign policy very open, making himself the spokesman for the so-called Western world by saying explicitly what others had only expressed half-heartedly and did not dare to say clearly.

That is why we saw him as a friend. Though he was a fine spokesman for Sweden he was devoid of any formality and protocol.

We talked to him both at official receptions and in more informal situations which we will never forget. We were better able to establish that intimacy in personal conversations in the early hours of the morning at Jose Marti airport in Havana than in more formal contexts.

Although we know that Palme has left a tradition and a spirit to his colleagues which will persist though he himself has gone, we are all certain that he stamped Swedish and Social Democrat politics with a style and decisiveness which will be difficult to replace: something that those who took advantage of his straightforwardness (which led him to walk through the apparently peaceful streets of Stockholm in the early hours of the morning with no protection other than the company of his wife) to commit a cowardly murder knew only too well. They have deprived humanity of one of the most noted figures of our century.

3

Champion of Justice and Peace

INGVAR CARLSSON

Address by the Prime Minister, Mr Ingvar Carlsson, at the funeral ceremony of Olof Palme at the Stockholm City Hall, 15 March 1986.

We are gathered today at the bier of Olof Palme. An abominable assassination has confronted us with the cold, grim face of death. We stand united in anger and grief. But death is at the same time a reminder of life. And Olof Palme's life is a poignant reminder of the chance life gives us, a reminder that life can be like a radiant smile, that the value of life is infinite.

With us today are friends from all parts of the world. They bear witness to the fact that the grief and sense of loss felt by us extend far beyond the borders of our country.

We always grieve when we lose someone, although we know that death is inevitable and comes to us all sooner or later. Most of us have said a last farewell to someone who has passed on after completing a long life's work. Death is the natural end and we are ready for it when it comes. But this is not the case here. Olof Palme's strength was unabated, he was full of great and vigorous enthusiasm. He also possessed the wisdom which only comes from long experience. Olof Palme seemed indispensable to us for a long time yet.

But suddenly he was cut down like a free and powerful bird killed in full flight. Many of his best years were thus taken from him, from us. This makes our grief harder to bear, more sombre and bitter.

A few days ago I received a letter from Siogrid Fernstrom from Forsbacka, who delivers newspapers. This is what she wrote:

> I have delivered newspapers for eighteen years. The early morning of 1 March was for me the hardest working day in all these years. Coming out at four o'clock on a cold dark winter's night, not long out of bed but alert and ready for two hours' work, then seeing the terrible news in extra large letters on the front pages of the two

10

newspapers I deliver was like seeing the ground disappear from underneath my feet. In spite of my state of shock this appalling news must be spread, and I, a link in the chain of distribution, must not fail my duty this morning. In my despair I thought of all the old age pensioners, who go early to bed and wake up early too, waiting for me. It hurt me so to have to bring this bad news in their loneliness.

I understand her message to be: We must not allow ourselves to be paralysed. We must find the strength to carry out our duties even on the hardest day of our lives. We must seek consolation so that we can overcome our grief. This is not easy, but it is necessary. We must go on, we must see the light and meet life. This is what Olof Palme himself would have done in our position: he who was always on the move, always proceeding to new tasks and new objectives.

We all have many different memories of Olof Palme. Some of them are of a physical nature, like his unruly hair which it seemed impossible to comb into place, the hopeless tie, the ceaseless dancing of his feet behind the rostrum when he made a speech.

Palme was close to us. Year after year we recognized his well-known figure in the streets, we heard and saw him on the radio and television—his vibrant voice, his face, a little more lined as the years passed, a little heavier and wiser, his piercing blue eyes. And we remember all the times we saw him almost jumping up on to the platform to make speeches all over the country, all the autographs he wrote, all the people he met and spoke to and never forgot, full of intuitive respect as he was. What the exaggerated picture of the polemicist highlighted by the television cameras did not convey was that Olof Palme's most faithful companions were laughter and cheerfulness. If humour is the most prominent characteristic of humanity, then Olof Palme was, in this respect too, profoundly human.

Other memories of Olof Palme vary from individual to individual. This is of course because, being human beings, we saw him with different eyes. But another reason is that he was a complex person. Olof Palme's words were unambiguous and compelling. His commitment was profound and genuine. It was above all the momentous issues facing mankind that fascinated and challenged his creative spirit. He moved people's hearts. But at the same time he was a practical politician, patient and well aware that democracy must hasten slowly. Politics to Olof Palme was not just a matter of will. It was also a day-to-day job that had to be done.

Olof Palme was a prominent champion of peace, but he was also a man who stood in the thick of debate and political struggle, and he was under heavier attack than most. Those of us who stood by his side sometimes wished that his adversaries would get to know him better and thus have the privilege of learning what the man was really like. For this man, who never shied away from a fight and, like Master Olof in Strindberg's play, refused to compromise with his conscience, was also a man of personal modesty, a good friend, and fond of his family.

As a speaker Olof Palme could spellbind his audience with his intensity and gift of expression. When among friends he often just sat listening. He was careful in his choice of words, but at the same time well aware of the possibilities of language, possibilities which he mastered better than most. When roused he was capable of rebukes that overstepped the conventional limits of diplomacy in a conscious attempt to provoke people into awareness and action.

But we also remember the gentle tone he used when speaking to children, who always liked to listen to him. Once, at the height of an election campaign, Olof Palme visited the Kryddgarden School in Malmo, a school with children from 35 countries; he spoke to the pupils and danced with them. A few days ago Elisabeth Zemljic, one of the girls who was present, told us about this meeting: 'It must have meant a lot to him. You could see how his face positively beamed. It was wonderful to see that a person like that, so famous all over the world, can still mean so much to children. Somehow I think that it was we children who really understood him best.'

It is perfectly natural that a prime minister should be well known in the capitals of the world. But Olof Palme was also known in many poor, remote villages. This was not due to his office, however. It was because of his views and acts, his courage in never flinching from plain language, the conviction that he was on the side of right and freedom. And in a way he found no difference between New York and Varnamo, or New Delhi and Storuman, or Maputo and Smedjebacken. There were differences of climate, language, and colour, of course. But there was no difference when it came to essentials: everybody has his dreams and aspirations. And as long as Olof Palme was able to help, no journey was too long and no place too insignificant.

Thus Olof Palme made the world the concern and the responsibility of us all. But, at the same time, surely no other Swede can have seen more of his own country and met a greater number of his countrymen than Olof Palme. When children from every municipality in the land paid their tribute to Olof Palme's memory by joining in song in today's service, they were sending greetings from the entire country which he loved so well and from the future he believed in.

But Olof Palme was not only a generous and versatile personality. He possessed great integrity; deep inside the public and private person were fused into one. Everyone who was close to him, his family, his friends, and colleagues, as well as some of his political adversaries, has experienced and often talked of Olof Palme's gentleness and sympathy, the interest he showed in so many of the lives he came in contact with. This side of Olof Palme was often absent from the official picture of him. But it is precisely here that we find the strongest driving force in his struggle for a better and more just society, a society where everyone is of equal value. And one can see that Palme's international involvement and his struggle for peace and solidarity across borders was based on this insight into the lives of those living in conditions of hardship.

Thus these many qualities and aspirations were combined in making up the personality and life achievement that we recognize as Olof Palme's. Our grief and sense of loss at the assassination of Olof Palme have brought us closer together. This can be seen everywhere. It can be seen that the streets are quieter, people now show more consideration and understanding. Sweden will never be quite the same again.

Olof Palme's life's work is also a legacy to be used by us to the best of our understanding and ability.

Olof Palme was a democrat. He respected other people's opinions, but above all he respected people themselves. This was why he could sit for hours and discuss things with young people at a meeting, or with people at their place of work or with people he met in the streets. He believed in progress, and he believed in the possibility of convincing people by argument. His belief in reason was a part of his optimistic view of humanity and his deeply rooted humanism.

Olof Palme was a champion of solidarity. He often expressed his views on solidarity with the words: 'It's not just a question of them and us. It's just us.' Injustices and class differences roused his indignation. And his impatience at the unavoidable slowness and ineffectiveness of the political process at times—all too often—was as marked as his passion for justice. He realized that in a just society people must work together.

Olof Palme's manifest solidarity with immigrants and refugees extended beyond merely opening Sweden as a place of refuge. He was keen that we should show generosity and make the same opportunities available to those who came here as to those born in the country. He was an implacable opponent of all forms of racism and hostility to foreigners. It is gratifying, at the same time as it fills us with a sense of obligation, to note that so many immigrants from various countries show such heartfelt sorrow at the death of a Swedish leader and prime minister.

Olof Palme was a champion of peace. Peace was in fact his most important task, since he regarded war as the greatest threat to mankind. And he used to tell the younger generation: 'You are really the first generation which cannot afford to fail at any price.' For a nuclear war will destroy all vestige of human life. Olof Palme was always talking about how we in Sweden come into the world and how the world comes into us. As soon as he got the chance he himself travelled immediately after the Second World War to the USA and later to Asia.

There was obviously a moral driving force behind Olof Palme's internationalism, his efforts for peace, and the freedom and independence of all nations. But there was also a national interest underlying this moral standpoint. The world does not only belong to the great and powerful. We, the smaller nations, also have a right to live, and to develop and preserve our identity. For this right to be a reality, certain principles are laid down in the UN Charter. This was how Olof Palme expressed it himself when speaking to the United Nations:

> When the integrity and independence of one small country are violated, this sends a vibration of anger and anxiety through the hearts and minds of citizens in other small countries. For them the rule of law and observance of our common commitments under the Charter are seen as imperatives for a future in peace and security.

To Olof Palme the arms race was a dire threat to the survival of the human race. The nuclear powers have usurped the right to decide matters of life and death, not only in their own countries, but also in all other countries. In a world that lives under the constant threat of destruction, where there are great conflicts, and where demands for more and increasingly advanced weapons are growing, Palme spoke with the voice of sense and reason.

The death of Olof Palme means that we Swedes have lost our principal spokesman on behalf of democracy, solidarity, and peace. But there is general support in our country for these values. And we have not lost the things he gave us, his inspiration and experience.

As a friend and colleague of Olof Palme I feel emboldened to express his appeal to those of us who are to continue his work:

> Develop Swedish democracy on the basis of explicit respect for the equal value and individuality of all people!
> Make sure that Sweden and the world, as far as this lies in our power, is characterized by justice, fellowship, and solidarity.
> May this nation never indulge in introspection. Be open to the world at large and try to contribute to peace and co-operation between peoples and nations.

The memory of Olof Palme will be with us for a long time to come, in the yearning of our finest moods—his light, the clarity of his thought, his articulate reason, and his warm sympathy.

Thank you, Olof. You will always remain in our hearts.

4

The Scandinavian Perspective on the North–South Dialogue

GRO HARLEM BRUNDTLAND

Introduction

Olof Palme's dream was of a world of free men and women, freed from hunger and poverty, freed from insecurity and injustice, freed from exploitation and degradation. He hoped that all men and women could live as confident and independent human beings in democratic societies. We must never stop striving towards the accomplishment of that dream. The striving itself counts; it is a never-ending struggle which piece by piece will lead us in the direction of fulfilling a dream. A 1000-mile journey always begins with a small step. Several steps have already been taken and our ability to continue may well be the ultimate test of our civilization.

The active support given by Olof Palme and Sweden to the liberation movements in the 1960s is probably one of Palme's most important political contributions to further North–South dialogue. Twenty years later this support may seem obvious. We must remember, however, that in the 1960s the liberation movements were considered of a dubious nature in the Western world, even far into the social democratic movement. Olof Palme took the lead in supporting the liberation and freedom of those Third World countries that did not benefit from peaceful decolonization within the UN framework. In the 1960s Palme's political leadership in this context was courageous and, as we know today, had far-reaching consequences. Olof Palme's political support of the global negotiations in the 1970s for a New International Economic Order (NIEO) was quite clear. But his personal involvement in this economic process was not as intense as it was in the liberation movement of Vietnam and South Africa.

I believe Palme's preference for the directly political issues rather than for the economic–political aspect of the NIEO was due to his personality. He was a truly political man. Olof Palme was brutally taken from us while engaged in efforts to create a better future. He was

15

also deeply involved in following up the work of the Independent Commission on Disarmament and Security Issues (ICDSI) of which he was a chairman, which published its *Common Security* report in 1982. I know that sincere hopes and expectations in all corners of the globe were vested in Olof Palme's leadership on these issues. He was intensely involved in getting an increasing number of countries to adhere to our proposals and ideas. He was keenly aware of the need to support and strengthen the international perspective and to bolster our key global institution, the United Nations. Palme's commitment was to the future. 'Politics', he said, 'is to a large extent to form ideas about the future. At the same time politics is a question of acting now. The essence is thus to have present actions taken in a manner which is consistent with and supportive of our image of the future.' This is indeed the central theme of the international work Palme was involved in, and which we must carry forward. As a member of the Independent Commission on International Development, chaired by Willy Brandt, Olof Palme could muster his skills and indignation against the vast inefficiency and lopsidedness which characterized and still characterizes international economic relations. In his own commission, the ICDSI, Olof Palme could take the analysis further and concentrate on the questions which perhaps more than anything else were of the deepest concern to him. These questions concern a world which spends close to a trillion dollars per year on arms and military equipment, while at the same time more than 800 million people live in absolute poverty. They concern a world which employs the brightest brains and the sharpest skills to develop ever more sophisticated weapons and nuclear devices, while children die every minute because they do not have enough to eat. The report of the Palme Commission, *Common Security*, points out how the weapons' burden is a strain on all economies, and how increased armaments do not create security, but greater insecurity. In the Third World, as elsewhere, military expenditures are requiring more and more resources at the expense of peaceful economic development. But without economic and social development there will be no lasting security.

In the World Commission on Environment and Development, which I have the honour to chair, we are keenly aware of these and other linkages and feedbacks. Indeed, the basic challenge to our work is to address the increasing interdependence between issues and between nations, and to demonstrate ways and means to achieve sustainable development. In the spirit of Olof Palme we must learn to think and act globally and in a long-term perspective. All of us share a responsibility for a common future.

In this article I will endeavour to put the Scandinavian views on the North–South dialogue into a brief historical context, before turning to the agenda of the pressing issues which are facing us. It is important to understand that Scandinavia's policies and perspectives on the North–South dialogue are deeply rooted in tradition and based on the common experience of the Nordic countries. Olof Palme once said: 'It may seem that we in Scandinavia live in a peaceful corner of the world. It is not true. We are basically facing the same type of problems and dangers as any other industrialized country in the world.'

It goes without saying that Palme's influence on Swedish North–South policy was deep and fundamental, serving as he did in the Swedish government for 13 continuous years, from 1963 to 1976, during seven of which he was prime minister, and then serving as prime minister again from 1982 to 1986. It was during these years that his policy was shaped and refined. Through close collaboration with Norway and the other Nordic neighbours it emerged as a distinct and well-defined Scandinavian approach to the North–South issues.

Scandinavian Traditions

To better appreciate the Scandinavian approach it is necessary to take a glance backwards in time and identify certain basic features of Scandinavia's own development. It is, for example, a sobering thought to remember that no more than some 80 years ago relations between Norway and Sweden were extremely strained, and the outbreak of war was avoided only through sensible statesmanship combined with strong pressure from public opinion. Eighty years is a brief time span in the history of nations, but during that period our relations have evolved to a point where a confrontational atmosphere of a similar nature between Norway and Sweden has become the remotest of possibilities. The climate created by a background of common traditions and views has pushed all the Nordic countries towards ever closer co-operation through most of this century.

The Scandinavian countries are small and, economically speaking, were relatively poor until the twentieth century. Poverty, shortage of agricultural land, and under- and unemployment particularly plagued Norway and Sweden through much of the nineteenth century, and one visible consequence was large-scale emigration from both countries, to the USA in particular. Gradually, however, a strong grass-roots movement emerged, and a mobilization of human resources developed through education and health care. The mass mobilization of farmers and fishermen, and of workers in trade unions and social democratic parties, created very powerful forces in the development process. The ideology of equality and concern for social justice are closely linked to this process. In the formerly poor Scandinavian countries there was little opportunity for the individual to become economically and financially successful through his own energy and enterprise alone. But by joining forces through political or other organizational action, economic and social status could be improved.

As industrialization expanded and universal suffrage was introduced, the influence of the social democratic parties increased rapidly. In all of Scandinavia they became the strongest political movements and have remained so for the last half-century. It was during this period that we witnessed the build-up of the welfare societies which combined comprehensive and progressive legislation with increased emphasis on economic planning. Attempts were made to remedy the uncertainty and waste caused by the vicissitudes of economic cycles through longer-term planning and measures to manage the economy. Coupled with rapid economic growth these policies led to the elimination of dire poverty and glaring social injustices, and today the per capita GNPs of the Scandinavian countries are among the highest in the world.

In Scandinavian countries knowledge of peoples and conditions in the Third World was neither widespread nor profound until the full impact of the modern mass media started to be felt. One reason for this is that Scandinavia did not take part in the race for colonies in the nineteenth century. But the liberation of former colonies from European powers was followed with great interest and approval, and the provision of assistance to the newly independent nations was a logical consequence of the ideological support offered them during their fight for independence.

Another element should be stressed. The Scandinavians have long been interested in closer international co-operation and gave strong support to the League of Nations between the wars, and to the UN after the Second World War. There is a clear element of self-interest inherent in this attitude; small nations can have only very limited influence in a world dominated by great powers, but they can make themselves heard in international organizations where they can speak, vote, and act as full and equal members. To the extent that the UN took decisions on policies in favour of the Third World, the Scandinavians wanted to take these decisions in earnest, not merely to assist the developing countries, but also to build up the image, strength, and authority of the UN.

In the post-war period the Scandinavian governments also became more active in their foreign policies than they had been before the war. Their interest in making the UN successful as a peacekeeping organization was very strong. It quickly became accepted doctrine that unstable and unrepresentative governments in poor countries might represent a special threat to world peace. The need for economic and social development in the Third World was perceived as an international concern.

The above-mentioned factors are vital elements of what may be called the Scandinavian heritage. They explain, at least partially, the background for Scandinavia's present-day attitudes and policies towards the North–South dialogue.

The core of these policies was actually shaped during the 1970s when a series of UN resolutions were passed and a number of conferences held on various fundamental issues. The basic support in Scandinavia for the ideas behind an NIEO was rooted not only in the need for international solidarity and social justice, but also in the conviction that joint efforts and close collaboration are a must in a rapidly shrinking world. The old international order that was formed at the end of the Second World War was made for 'the world of 1945'. That was a 'world' of about 50 nations. The South and the East were not part of that order. The old economic order is losing its relevance for obvious reasons.

Today the world consists of more than 150 nations. For our present world there is not a new order. Small countries like the Scandinavian ones and Third World countries are directly interested in strengthening international order and organizations. Our alternative is to be recipients of decisions over which we have no, or only minor, influence. The efforts of the Scandinavian governments to achieve an NIEO are therefore not only an act of charity but also one of self-interest.

Olof Palme came to be the living symbol of these attitudes. In his passionate manner he could articulate the necessity for peaceful co-operation like no one else and his will for change never tired. The challenge to us is thus to continue, in his spirit, the struggle for a more prosperous, more just, and more secure world, and this we must do with an eye to the urgency of the situation.

Interdependence

After many years of work, negotiations, and discussions, have we made any real progress? Is the world a better place in which to live now than it was 20 years ago? For many it is, but for many others it certainly is not. Let us not forget the facts: more than 500 million children and adults suffer from chronic malnutrition and more than 800 million live in conditions of 'absolute poverty'. Over the last decade many countries in Asia and Africa have made little or no progress. At the same time serious imbalances have developed in the industrialized countries, with millions out of work in societies of increasing affluence.

We are thus facing the maddening paradox of a situation where we have vast unmet needs combined with huge resources lying idle, and where the possible remedy to such an illogical problem seems to defy all imagination.

There is no basic disagreement about our goals. What we want for everybody is that they have food for every day, sufficient clothing, shelter, drinkable water, basic health care, fundamental education, etc; in short, that what we often think of as basic needs and rights are satisfied. This reminds us of the fundamental concern of development; that is, human beings and their needs. These are indeed very concrete and specific. At the same time we must admit that the work towards meeting these fundamental development objectives presents us with enormous complications in our search for the right framework for international co-operation. On the one hand we have the detailed basic needs of individual human beings. These are fundamentally domestic issues in each and every country, and it is ultimately the responsibility of national governments to find the right solutions. On the other hand we are preoccupied in the North–South dialogue with creating relations between nations which will better regulate the creation and movement of goods, services, and financial resources, i.e. aggregate economic variables. On closer examination, however, we see that there is no basic conflict between the two approaches. They must be advanced simultaneously because they illustrate the real core of the challenge facing us, how to improve productivity and create conditions for sustainable economic development. On the one hand major new efforts must be made with regard to international co-operation between the North and the South on the overall issues of global concern, while, on the other, self-reliant and efficient policies which can mutually reinforce international co-operation must be applied within the developing countries themselves.

In today's global economy there is little use in restructuring the international economic framework if the resulting improvements are wasted because of poor and inefficient domestic policies. But at the same time there is equally little use in shaping dynamic and efficient domestic policies if their effects are lost in an unresponsive international framework. If a government were determined to undertake structural adjustment with the aim of improving its export capacity, for example, and first met almost unsurmountable difficulties in obtaining the necessary external financial assistance, and then perhaps protectionist barriers which hindered the sale of the goods in question, it is obvious that the said government would be facing a dead end. The fact is that the North–South dialogue is essentially a plus-sum game. There is increasing recognition of the concept of interdependence. Ironically this recognition is very much a function of the present debt crisis, where typically the stage has been reached where the problems are rapidly becoming just as big for the creditors as for the debtors, if not bigger in certain cases. Interdependence has become the dominant characteristic of the whole range of issues relating to development. It encompasses broad security concerns, environmental and ecological issues, economic and cultural relations, etc. There is also the geographic dimension of interdependence, regionally and globally, and there is virtually no end to the examples we can point to in order to illustrate this. Earlier I touched upon how resources allocated to security and military purposes are draining away resources for development. We have recently experienced the awesome problems we face across borders when a nuclear disaster occurs, even in a remote geographical area. We see how the population problem is creating migration patterns which strain both national and cross-national systems. On the financial front we see a vital link between a non-protectionist trade regime and the ability of debtor countries to meet their debt obligations and generate the resources necessary for their own development.

Indeed, these and other examples illustrate some rather obvious links with which we are already familiar. There also exist much more complex linkages and feedbacks between issues and nations which we must find ways to tackle. The web of interdependence stretches across even the most apparently remote of our economic and social activities. The IMF, for example, as it lays down its conditions for a new line of credit, may be the cause of environmentally destructive practices. A decision taken in GATT that restricts the market for goods in which developing countries have an advantage, may slow down their development generally, thus extending poverty, increasing pressure on the environment, and leading to something as apparently remote as, for example, the increased cutting of wood for fuel as kerosene imports are restricted. Even more remote, but still connected by that chain of interdependence, is a decision in GATT that might lead to the production of alternative goods resulting in the non-sustainable use of land or other resources.

The important point to bear in mind about interdependence is therefore the web of connections between and among the components. The factor which limits us in our efforts to work out policies that will permit us to live and develop in a sustainable way is not the capacity to analyse the elements of our interdependence with each other and with nature; the limiting factor is our incapacity to put it all together to form a guide to future action.

An Urgent Agenda for North–South Dialogue:
the Scandinavian Perspective

To overcome this incapacity we must apply a certain degree of flexibility. We will get nowhere unless we recognize the need for a global approach. Many of our problems are of a global nature, they transcend systems, and their number is growing. We must therefore work towards the adoption of global rules far beyond the traditional ones, and this will call for mechanisms which guarantee the observation of such rules. At the same time it is vital that we do not become paralysed by the need for global solutions. A global approach does not mean that everything has to be negotiated and solved simultaneously; nor does it mean that everybody must participate in the same manner at all times. What it means is that the global perspective must permeate all the processes and work we are engaged in, and that this work is becoming more and more urgent.

And because forward movement is more important than fruitless confrontations, we must put more emphasis on flexibility in our future work. Where there are issues on which differences between developing countries and industrialized countries are relatively small, they should be negotiated and solved separately. Where it is possible to reach regional or subregional solutions to issues, we should go ahead and do it. The heterogeneous character of developing countries and the complexity of the problems involved necessitate this, and we must never let the global perspectives become an excuse for inaction.

Economic policy

A number of the pressing problems we are facing should first and foremost be tackled through adjustments in general economic policies, both in industrialized and in developing countries. A sound macro-economic environment, characterized by sustainable and balanced growth, is vital. When it comes to economic policy, industrialized countries have a special responsibility. A number of adjustments are called for in the policies of major countries and they must be undertaken within the framework of closer policy co-ordination between their governments. The policies must be more compatible and mutually reinforcing. Experience tells us that structural adjustment can best be achieved in an environment of strong growth and rising employment. Economic and trade policies in industrialized countries are vitally important in determining world economic conditions. The prospects of the developing countries crucially depend on the industrialized world. But the economic policies pursued by developing countries themselves must also form part of a comprehensive strategy to deal with the current problems in the world economy.

Trade policy

Part of such a strategy must include determined action to resist protectionism and to improve market access. In the first half of the 1980s the developing countries were severely affected by an increase in protectionist measures, particularly in textiles and clothing, steel, and agricultural products. The trend we have witnessed, that of moving away from multilateral free trade towards the bilateral, controlled exchange of goods, constitutes one of the gravest threats to sustainable economic development. The exchange of goods based on barter-type arrangements will only make the already skewed relationship between developing and developed countries even more skewed, because bilateralism favours the strong against the weak. And in the long run everybody will lose. Analyses indicate, for example, that the potential loss of jobs in industrial countries, because of newly industrializing countries' inability to buy capital goods, is much greater than the jobs lost because of imports from the South. Indeed, the protection of industries in the North is often a major obstacle in the work towards their own structural adjustment. It increases cost levels and hinders new and emerging industries.

A new round of trade negotiations is therefore of the utmost importance and must be conducted in the spirit of global inter-dependence. Its primary goal should be to strengthen the multilateral trading system and to further open the world markets, with particular emphasis on the interests of the developing countries. While actual negotiations should take place in GATT, the issues form such an integral part of overall development prospects that they cannot be left to GATT alone. High-level discussions of trade policy should be undertaken in the context of major economic meetings, such as the Western 'summits', those of the IMF Interim and Bank-Fund Development Committee, the OECD Ministerial Council, the UN Conference on Trade and Development (UNCTAD), and the UN itself.

We must recognize the fundamental fact that economic dynamics have definitely shifted from the national economy to the world economy. This is not least demonstrated by the role of transnational corporations. Indeed, many contend that these corporations are perhaps the best example of how politics and intergovernmental co-operation lag behind the times and fail to provide for the new situation. Transnational corporations have for quite some time grown and adjusted through global planning and co-operation, and they have profited from the competition between governments, basing their activities wherever they found conditions most favourable, often to the detriment of the research base and at the risk of doing long-term harm to the environment.

Let there be no mistake; the point here is not necessarily to criticize the transnational corporations as such. The point is that the increasing concentration of economic power entails a danger of dominant market positions. Government intervention and intergovernmental co-operation in this context are precisely to *further* the concept of free trade, within reasonable environmental and social standards, and not to restrict it. True competition has always been achieved by way of certain rules and regulations, and never by excessive *laissez-faire*. The future of the global research base and the global environment illustrate this fact more clearly than ever before.

Commodities

In the field of commodities in particular there are also signs that we are facing fundamental shifts in development. First, there has been a tremendous increase in world food production. The old Malthusian prophecy seems ready to be buried for good, because on a worldwide basis the supply of food has steadily outrun population growth, parallel with increasing signs of environmental degradation. This is not least due to the active subsidization of food production in the industrialized countries; the vast production increases in countries such as India, China, and the rice-growing countries of South-East Asia also contribute substantially. At the same time we know that in many developing countries there is a crucial need to increase local food production. The deplorable fact is that although large surpluses of food accumulate in certain areas of the world, there are hundreds of millions of people in other areas who are suffering from malnutrition and hunger. Emergency aid is necessary, but it will solve no problems in the long term. What is required is technical assistance, above all to indigenous agriculture, and tools and expertise, particularly to help co-operative institutions. Action must be taken against the disregard and neglect exhibited by the agricultural sector in many developing countries, while at the same time adjustments must be made in industrialized countries to achieve a more sustainable pattern of production.

Second, both agricultural and non-farm commodities have suffered from a considerable drop in prices, and many believe that raw material prices will never again rise substantially as compared to the prices of manufactured goods. One major reason for this is the steady drop in the raw material intensity of manufacturing processes and manufacturing products. In the new high-technology industries, for example, this represents such a dramatic shift in production patterns that we may not yet grasp its full impact. The raw materials in a semi-conductor microchip account for 1–3 per cent of the production cost; less than 50 kg of fibreglass cable transmit as many telephone messages as 1 ton of copper wire. One implication of this sharp shift in the terms of trade of primary products is the need for greater participation by the developing countries in the processing, marketing, and distribution of these new primary products.

In the shorter term, however, we are faced with the fact that many developing countries are essentially dependent upon commodity exports, and we must find ways to alleviate their problems. The establishment of commodity agreements will continue to be important. And despite the signs of some of the fundamental shifts as indicated, there will be an advantage in commodity price and market stability, to the benefit of both producers and consumers. And precisely because of these shifts, the need for clarity in production and consumption will be greater than ever.

Finance

The international debt situation offers a curious mix of grave problems and hope. Problems, because for many countries it represents the most severe economic crisis in this century; hope, because the debt situation is making it clear that we are mutually dependent on each other. The initiative of the US Secretary of the Treasury, which called for a comprehensive approach and a framework of a coherent, long-term strategy, was thus a positive signal. The responsibility for addressing the debt problems must be shared between debtor countries, creditor governments, commercial banks, and multilateral financial institutions. It is becoming rapidly clear, however, that sharing the responsibility of alleviating the debt crisis will also entail a sharing of burdens.

To incur debt in the process of development is quite normal, but when the servicing of that debt takes on such drastic proportions as to literally drain capital away from development, we are not involved in a manageable situation. Let us be frank about one thing: much of the outstanding debt of developing countries will not be paid back in any real sense. To maintain such a demand would entail political and environmental disturbances in many countries of a magnitude that would be completely unacceptable from everybody's point of view. The issue is thus to shape a strategy that in reality means a managed write-down of the mountain of debt. A flexible approach is called for. It is necessary to extend new credits on longer terms. The rescheduling of old loans by way of introducing extended grace periods and 'capping' interest should be considered. In certain cases, however, outright debt relief will be necessary. This will be especially true in poorer countries where the unsustainability of the debt burden presents a major obstacle to adjustment and growth. In such cases this will be the only solution.

Concerning the need for more growth-oriented policies and continued adjustment in debtor countries, it is important to make a clear distinction between the middle-income countries and the poorest countries. Their problems are fundamentally different and call for different remedies. It is particularly important that governments in industrialized countries contribute to strengthening the multilateral financial institutions, and to increasing the number of bilateral financial institutions, and to increasing bilateral development assistance to deal with the special problems of the least developed countries. For these countries neither improved export performance nor effective import substitution will be feasible without the substantial inflow of external resources.

The multilateral institutions must continue to play central roles in solving the debt problems. To this end they will need increased resources. If the World Bank is to make any important contribution to support growth-oriented structural adjustment policies, firm commitments are needed to increase its capital. The same is necessary if we are to avoid the absurdity of the Bank receiving more in debt service than what it is disbursing to certain countries which are in need of financial assistance. A closer World Bank–IMF collaboration is also necessary, and the focus must be on assistance which enhances the room for internal adaptations needed for sustainable growth in borrowing countries.

Security

The North–South dialogue has traditionally centred around economic issues. As the Palme Commission showed, however, there is no alternative to common security. The right to life is the most basic human right of all, and although there does not seem to be much difference between starving to death and dying in war, there is increasing awareness that there is a link between these two dramatic factors. The Palme report observed:

> The major proportion of military budgets may be allocated to the payment of soldiers and civilian employees, and governments also obtain goods, services and buildings for defence purpose from the civil area. But since the beginning of the 1980's, expenditure on military equipment and defence research has shown the biggest rise. More and more developing countries are importing technically sophisticated weapon systems, which must often be financed as normal purchases and not with military aid.

Armaments thus represent a drain on resources which could be used for development purposes. In fact, cuts in spending on armaments could stimulate new growth in the world economy, and thus contribute towards international economic security.

In this connection it is obvious that superpower relations are paramount. A senseless competition in acquiring ever more abhorrent means of destruction only leads to greater insecurity. International security must rest on co-operation for common survival, not on the threat of mutual destruction.

Environment and ecology

There is now a growing concern, not so much that the management of our small planet is proving unexpectedly difficult, but that there is some deeper malaise; that the machinery we created after Stockholm, 15 years ago, is not working; that perhaps it cannot work and that we need to rethink the issues of environment and development from new perspectives. It was this feeling on the part of a growing number of governments over the past few years that led directly to the establishment of the World Commission on Environment and Development in 1983.

It is important to bear in mind that some parts of the world have registered successes in improving environmental quality over the past 15 years. Those who remember the environmental destruction that accompanied the rapid growth of the 1950s and 1960s can confirm that. Public opinion demanded action against pollution, and governments responded with new legislation, institutions, policies, and programmes. Developing countries, however, have quite simply not been able to afford the costs of the react-and-retrofit approaches that have dominated the environmental policies of the industrialized nations. Most have seen a massive deterioration of their environment. In many countries the natural resource basis for future development is deteriorating rapidly and, in some cases, such as in Africa, large regions are in jeopardy. We have learned that some of the most threatening environmental and developmental problems of today are caused to a considerable extent by the widespread poverty and the inequitable distribution of resources within individual nations and among nations and regions. Many of the most serious effects in the Third World are rooted in economic and social injustice and in a worsening imbalance in the relationship between man and his capacity to manage natural resources. We are beginning to learn that there are better ways to manage our small planet than to react and cure: we must anticipate and prevent. This may sound simple and obvious, but it requires that we recognize environment and development at the earliest possible stage. Otherwise it will not be economically sustainable. The world—and especially the Third World—North Africa, for example—is littered with cases of 'development without environment', often aid-supported, that have literally consumed their own bases—in soil, in water, and other resources—and thus ended up reducing rather than increasing the future economic potential of their countries.

Finally, improvement requires that we begin to take a much broader view of environmental policy, seeing it not just as air, water, waste, and noise policy, but also, and more importantly, as resource, energy, agricultural, and transportation policy, and as development assistance, trade, and economic policy. And, of course, vice versa. These views are gaining ground, but we have to admit that they run counter to the political and institutional realities of almost all governments and large industries where, whatever the rhetoric, environmental policy is in fact treated as a limited policy field, essentially as an add-on to other policy fields, whose mission it is to react to damage done and cure it after the fact. We must change those realities, not only in industry and national governments but also in international organizations.

Conclusion

The essence of the North–South dialogue is gaining ground; the fact that we on planet earth are mutually dependent upon each other is becoming increasingly recognized. This confirms the need for close international co-operation, and indeed a type of co-operation that breaks the existing patterns and influences policies and events in the direction of need changes. All actors must shoulder their responsibilities and 'lift their sights to the far horizons', as Willy Brandt said in *North–South: A Programme for Survival & Common Crisis*? All too often we have a tendency to throw up our arms in frustration as we are overwhelmed by the quagmire of daily issues. In the words of Harry Dexter White, the leading US delegate to the Bretton Woods Conference: 'We must substitute, before it is too late, imagination for tradition, generosity for shrewdness, understanding for bargaining, thoroughness for caution and wisdom for prejudice.' The delegates took 17 days to draw up the terms for the creation of the IMF, and five days for those of the World Bank.

The tasks of the various actors are all important. Governments must constantly bear in mind their international obligations and strive towards an internal working which never loses the overall perspectives. Industry and business can influence policy-makers to focus more on global issues. International organizations must never lose sight of their objectives and the need for efficiency and close collaboration among themselves. Non-government organizations should influence policy-makers and public opinion, as should the media.

As I stated at the beginning, the vision is there, but it is the striving for its fulfilment which counts. As Olof Palme once said: 'Politics is practical work in inertial environments, it is a never-ending dialogue with people, and it presupposes the constant testing of arguments against cool rationality. But it must always be driven by a protest against injustice, and the longing for a better society and larger community.'

SECTION TWO

The Politics of Power

5

North–South: The Task Ahead

WILLY BRANDT

Olof Palme's international reputation was based on his openness and his sincere political convictions. In his opposition to world armament; his fight against world hunger; his condemnation of dictatorship, invasion, and oppression—whether in Chile or in Eastern Europe, in Vietnam or Afghanistan, South Africa, the Middle East, or Korea, his position was always clear and straightforward. And he would say what he meant. He was convinced that democracy was a precondition for socialism. He believed that democratic ideas would always remain alive in some minds. Above all Olof Palme was convinced that those who believe they possess the whole truth and intend to create paradise here and now are always very much in danger of destroying the very conditions of an acceptable human order.

Evil forces are threatening in many parts. They took the life of Olof Palme, our beloved brother. But we must understand that there are situations in which defending oneself cannot be restricted to words. And there is no doubt in my mind that constructive ideas—and resolute action—are the only valid instruments to defeat destructive illusions. The great deception of the neo-conservative offensive lies in the complete lack of moderation with which a majority is being deceived by promises of what only a minority will ever get. But this is a serious weakness of that offensive, and it is there that we must apply the lever.

We Social Democrats and democratic socialists stand for the expansion of individual freedoms of which others only love to talk. We are the ones who recognize each individual's right to a dignified life and to personal happiness. What else is it that history shows? The history of the labour movement, of liberation movements, of democratic socialism? But history also reminds us that social decline and degradation of a majority was too high a price for the good life of minority elites. History has demonstrated the creative talents of large groups of society and that these must be released if progress is to have its chance. History tells us that widening personal freedom remains just a slogan as long as only a minority enjoys the benefits, while the so-called free play of capitalism produces a rather skewed distribution of opportunities in favour of that minority.

Contrary to what the neo-conservative philosophy of the right tries to pretend, the democratic social or welfare state is not a brake on the wheel of progress but rather provides the wheel on which progress rides. Let me put it this way: we must create a situation in which a majority understands us when we say that we want a future based on co-operation more than on excessive competition. We expect nothing from competitive greed as the basic philosophy of government. Without solidarity there is no peace—neither within nor between states and nations. It has always been our principle that peace—domestically and internationally—must be secured through freedom and justice. Now, nobody would argue that in these last few years the world has become a safer place or that it has gained in hope—quite the contrary. For many years there have been talks about disarmament. If the arms build-up cannot be stopped there is but little hope for the future of the human race.

The fate of our globe may well depend on whether a new mode of coexistence can be achieved between the two nuclear superpowers, something which recently one might have thought possible. We must address all states with a certain military potential of their own: by now all people should understand how foolish it would be if they did not listen to what the other side has to say. And this also means that all serious proposals must be taken seriously, and must be appreciated and analysed, even if they happen to originate in Moscow. Testing all relevant proposals for arms limitation is to me much more important than tests of ever more advanced weapon systems.

Everybody knows about the fundamental differences between democratic socialism and authoritarian Communism. Yet we also know that the overriding obligation towards preserving peace takes priority over opposing ideologies.

Above all we need a new way of thinking in conformity with the rules of the atomic age. It is necessary for both superpowers—and all of us together with them—to accept the fact that for all of us and even for them there is no alternative to common security.

In October 1985 at a special conference in Vienna we summarized and tried to project our own thinking on security and disarmament policy. At that meeting both superpowers as well as the People's Republic of China, India, and Yugoslavia—on behalf of the Non-Aligned Movement (NAM)—and the UN were represented. We shall have to reinforce and broaden our appeal:

—— that a test stop—in fact a comprehensive test ban treaty—would make sense and therefore should be agreed; the Five-Continent summit to take place in the summer of 1986 could be of considerable importance in this connection;

—— that new and serious talks are needed for the withdrawal on both sides of missiles which were deployed without any real need (i.e. talks must be held about the limitation of troops and of nuclear as well as conventional arms);

—— that we really do not need any more development of binary chemical means of mass destruction.

And we need bread for the hungry rather than weapons in space.

The state of the world economy continues to be a matter of considerable concern. Some objective conditions have improved to a certain extent but mass unemployment and underemployment continue to exist even in the so-called North. For the so-called South a solution to the debt crisis is not in sight, and the danger of new trade wars is very real indeed. We are all very pleased with the important progress of democratization in Latin America. We were able to make a small contribution, and we will certainly not remain silent until Chile and Paraguay are free from dictatorship; and until Central America, free from military interventions, is allowed to seek its own way. It deserves to be recognized that the USA did help to promote democratization in a number of Latin American countries—as well as to end the Marcos regime in the Philippines. But one should also see the links between debt and democracy, between development and peace; and one should draw appropriate conclusions.

On several occasions during the past few years we had to concentrate on the crisis in Central America. That was not our choice. Our partners in Central America, but also some in Washington, informed us of their views of this problem; and I am very much aware of the fact that, from a Third World point of view, North–South issues take on a dimension considerably different from that for many European observers. Nevertheless, I think we agree when I say that revanchism has always turned out to be detrimental. And international law must of course be observed by all; it is not only binding for small states but even for the biggest. It is not some kind of two-class law.

Our world has no need for interventions such as in the case of Nicaragua and it cannot accept occupations as in Afghanistan. In this context it appears to me that in the strongest possible terms we must encourage the peace initiative of the Contadora process, including the South American support group. What has been tried in this regard deserves encouragement and support.

Incidentally, I believe the areas of our activity in the coming years are pretty much predetermined. They are partly determined by problems in old and new crisis regions. Thus, repeatedly, even if without real success, we tried to assist in overcoming the conflicts in the Middle East. Without overextending ourselves it should be evident, and there should be no doubt, that our good offices will be available when they might be of use.

Not least this holds for Africa. I believe our African friends realize that in recent years the Socialist International has made great efforts—for us as a matter of course—to support their justified aims. With our meetings in Arusha and Gabarone we sent out signals: above all we support the struggle against apartheid. And in my view the new report by the Commonwealth Eminent Persons Group on Southern Africa is of considerable importance in this connection.

I myself visited South Africa in April, and I was rather depressed when I left. The picture I saw was much bleaker than I had anticipated from earlier descriptions. What is at stake in South Africa is more than just a verbal reaction to a pre-revolutionary situation. What is really at stake is the fate of a large number of people who are threatened with being crushed. We cannot remain silent on this situation. We will have to prove our solidarity by action.

We have been in the forefront against terrorism and for the implementation of human rights everywhere. We remain adamant on this—not just where certain conservatives prefer to raise these issues. For us this is a matter of concern in Chile *and* in Cambodia; in the Middle East and in South Africa; in the case of illegal interventions and of misdeeds in the name of state security.

The struggle for human dignity and human rights, against hunger and poverty, is a task that must continue to determine our day-to-day activities. And nothing can be more important than the fate of endangered people and how best they can find relief.

That was the principle followed by Olof Palme whom we miss so much:

—— Time and again he told us and others that apartheid could not be reformed; that it could be abolished.

—— He was concerned about the crisis in the Middle East, and on behalf of the UN he tried to find a solution to the Gulf War.

—— Two years ago at a meeting of the Socialist International in Denmark he told us that whoever had a kind heart could not fail anti-Somozist Nicaragua.

—— The Commission that carries his name established new standards in the moral-oriented as well as pragmatic fight for disarmament.

—— His very last signature he put to a document of the Five-Continent Peace Initiative.

—— All this—in addition to his great contribution to achievements in his home country—had been inspired and informed by the strong tradition of Scandinavian Social Democracy.

I really cannot see any reasonable alternative: I see no alternative to peace and development. I see no alternative to human rights and solidarity—there is no other hope. And we will not get anything for free. We must make even greater efforts.

6

The Art of the Possible, or the Politics of Radical Transformation

IMMANUEL WALLERSTEIN

Politics, we have long been told, is the art of the possible. But what is possible? Was it possible for the Bolsheviks to come to power in November 1917? Was it possible for Mao Zedong to lead a cultural revolution that would transform China? Was it possible for the USA to invade Cuba in 1961? Was it possible for the Vietnamese NLF to defeat the USA? Was it possible to create a United States of Africa in 1963? Some of these historically concrete attempts to change things by political and military means were obviously possible, since they occurred. Others were not. Any such list, however, leaves us a bit mystified as to what criteria we can use to determine what is/was indeed possible, even retrospectively, not to speak of prospectively.

Yet, in the real world, we are always making decisions about political priorities in terms of what we think to be possible. Since 1945 at the very least, a large number of people—ordinary people, political movements, governmental leaders—have been concerned with the fundamental and growing economic disparity between the North and South, and have sought in various ways to change this. They have tended to call such change 'development'. They have sought to pursue 'development', persuading governments of the North that it was somehow in their self-interest to pursue policies that would result in the 'development' of the South.

One cannot say that these attempts have been very successful on the whole. No doubt there have been changes in the 40 or so years since the end of the Second World War, but the net result of all such changes has not yet been any significant reduction in the so-called gap between North and South. Given the fact that a great deal of political effort has gone into seeking to effectuate such changes, it is worth taking some time to reflect upon why our efforts have been so unsuccessful.

There seem to me to be four major explanations of why the fundamental changes that so many have sought have not yet occurred. All four are probably true.

1. *The states of the North and the principal economic enterprises of the world economy have not really been interested in such a change—quite the contrary—and have on the whole exerted their very considerable power to prevent it.*

I have little doubt that this is a fair summary of the real situation. Of course, there has been a good deal of 'aid' in one form or another. Much of it, however, has not in fact helped to transform the situation, and quite often it has made the situation worse. Some of the 'aid' may be seen as primarily serving the cause of political co-operation rather than the cause of economic transformation. Only a small part of the aid may actually have aided the South.

The governments of the North have engaged in military actions—ranging from full-scale wars to small-scale covert interventions—to oppose, slow down, or eliminate from power such political groups in the South as were determined to pursue significant middle-run transformations of the structure of the world system. Not all such attempts were successful, but many were. And even when they were not fully successful, they forced massive expenditures of energy on what may be thought of as the 'preliminary' steps of transformation, thus making it harder to get to the real business at hand.

2. *There have been politically important groups in the South whose self-interest was tied into the maintenance of the present world order.*
I do not speak here merely of the group some call the 'comprador bourgeoisie'—that is, those groups in the South who have concrete and immediate business interests in existing arrangements because of their participation in certain economic networks controlled by transnational corporations. Such groups exist and often play an important role, but they represent only a small part of the problem.

A much larger consideration is the fact that for large sectors of the more skilled, better educated portions of the population, the major channel for significant personal accumulation of capital, as well as for access to the modes of transmitting economic status to their offspring, is via government service, whether as political appointee or as civil servant. The government in power is not necessarily served by fundamental economic transformation. And even if it could be argued that government employees' self-interest could be served by economic transformation in the long run, they might be called upon to make significant sacrifices in the shorter run. When the prospect of the period of sacrifices runs over one's lifetime and beyond, the ability to sustain ideological renunciation of private material advantage is severely strained. Thus it is not surprising that there is often a considerable difference between officially proclaimed policies of movements and governments in the South and actual practices.

3. *The fact that the North has been preoccupied by the East–West conflict has meant that any consideration of North–South issues has been subordinated—by both East and West—to the issues which primarily concern them.*

This is a factor additional to explanation 1. above. It means that not only is the North dominated by forces who have no interest in fundamental transformation, but that even those few forces who are really interested in it are diverted—self-diverted, or diverted by others—from expending the necessary political energy on North–South issues.

The mere fact that the budgets of the states of the North are so massively geared to military expenditures locks out significant alternative uses of the same capital. Furthermore, it leads the governments of the North to press similar uses upon the governments of the South, for both geo-political and narrowly economic reasons.

4. *The real existing weaknesses of the state structures in the South—both in terms of state power and control of production processes—has meant that control of such state machinery represents, objectively, very limited power, and that therefore the abilities of the governments of the South to effectuate real change has been correspondingly limited.*

This could be thought of as the consequence of the previous considerations, but it is a reality in its own light. To be sure, the power positions of some states in the South, because of their size, strategic location, or previous economic development, is considerably greater than others. None the less, the realities of the interstate system and the economic constraints of the capitalist world economy are enormous. Not even states of the North can ignore them, and states of the South discover, if ever they doubted it, that their ability to undertake lasting fundamental transformation is quite limited.

Thus we have had the regular phenomenon that governments which have come to power in one way or another on the basis of their commitment to bring about such change have had to back-pedal in some fashion after initial attempts at radical change. Some have called such back-pedalling 'revisionism', but such language is far too voluntaristic. The sources of 'revisionist' behaviour are structural, not volitional.

What, then, is to be done? To answer this, one has to start by asking: Who are the doers of whom one is speaking? In the case of North–South relations, I see four possible politically significant doers whom one might think would be interested in transforming North–South relations in a more egalitarian direction: the people of the South; the revolutionary movements of the South; the post-revolutionary governments of the South; a stratum of self-interested but far-sighted persons in the North. I propose to deal with each as actors for change, and to assess both past performance and future potential.

The 'people' of the South would be the clearest beneficiaries of fundamental change. Collectively they have no conflict of interest, although subgroups might believe they might profit more from individual or subgroup upward mobility within the system than from collective struggle. The question is how much of a role the 'people' have played in the process. They have of course been the loudly acclaimed protagonists on whose behalf others have claimed to have laboured. But to what degree have the 'people' acted, and how could we measure this? Obviously, the 'people' or rather the 'peoples' of the South have erupted suddenly into angry demonstrations and have done so with some frequency. As has always been true, such so-called spontaneous eruptions have a certain efficacy. They frighten the holders of power, and they often force immediate concessions. But, as has often been noted, it is commonplace for spontaneous eruptions to decline as suddenly as they emerge. Unless channelled, it has been argued, such spontaneity is at best unimportant and at worst self-destructive. No fundamental transformation can occur in the absence of an organized movement leading the struggle.

There is much to be said for this assertion that the key element is the social movement, but it can be overstated. Movements cannot organize successfully except in a milieu in which there is a latent willingness to make short-run sacrifices for middle-run gains. Political action has real costs for real people, and it is simply not true that people are always ready to move vigorously against the oppressors under whose ill deeds they suffer.

However, in situations in which the power of oppressive groups has been already weakened for whatever reason, and in which some organizational base for resistance has been created, the readiness of the people to act can come forward as a very strong independent variable, one far more radical and far more disinterested than even the leadership of revolutionary movements. Indeed, the moment of greatest concession to revolutionary movements is usually that precise moment when popular sentiment comes nearest to being out of the control of the movements themselves. This 'out-of-control' element is exactly what the partisans of the status quo seek to eliminate by making concessions to revolutionary movements, hoping that the latter will be able thereby to rein in this popular fury and recreate a semblance of conventional order.

If you reflect upon it, this leads to a most curious conclusion about the art of the possible. If people make quite impossible demands, and if they seem to hold to these demands in an irrational fashion, it is frequently the case that it becomes possible to achieve significant sudden political change in a conflictive situation. Indeed, it is often more possible to do so in the presence of such 'irrationality' than in its absence. Of course, the key is how much short-run sacrifice people are ready 'irrationally' to make, and how seriously others take them. The second, and more obvious, agent of change is a revolutionary movement. These have been widespread because they have been efficacious.

It is never easy to shake established structures. It usually requires the patient acquisition of combative strength, the maturing of political strategy, the amassing of appropriate support, the slow undermining of the enemy's defence structures, coherence, and self-confidence. All of this requires social organization, which is what the revolutionary movement has to offer. We now have almost a century of concrete experience behind us to observe just how crucial such an organizational framework has been to the achievement of the intermediary revolutionary objective, the obtaining of state power.

Yet there have been two problems with the revolutionary movement as revolutionary actor. One, which has been discussed for most of this same century of concrete experience, has been the fact that the socioeconomic interests of the leadership of movements operate. The second is that the leaders of the movements cannot survive without significant support beyond their own ranks. Before achieving state power, movements need popular support or they die on the vine. There is, however, no point in coming to power unless one stays there for a while to carry out the radically new policies. The source of support now changes. What determines whether or not such revolutionary movements actually stay in power becomes less their popular base (as in the past) than the degree of support (or at least non-opposition) from the governments of other states in the interstate system.

This leads us to the paradox that while movements are more likely to achieve state power than the 'people' organized quasi-spontaneously, they are less likely to use such power in a fundamentally radical way. This is precisely why conservative forces of the world system are so frequently ready to welcome the accession to state power of well-organized and quite popular revolutionary movements. Nothing, think the conservatives, is so likely to tame a movement than a dose of 'responsibility'—that is, a dose of the constraints imposed by operating 'within the rules' of the interstate system. None the less, it may be argued that it is only where there has been a powerful social movement, well-tempered in struggle and efficient in its mode of organizing the arenas in which it operates, that real alterations in the politico–economic arena have become for the first time really possible.

In the South, all such revolutionary movements have sought to achieve state power, and not a few of them have succeeded, sometimes as the result of armed struggle, sometimes in less dramatic and more 'constitutional' ways. In almost all cases, such movements have been able to mobilize significant amounts of popular support as part of their struggle. It has largely been such post-revolutionary governments which have initiated and participated in the so-called North–South interstate dialogue of which this volume speaks. The states have means at their disposal which movements lack. They have armed forces, police, and frontiers. They have the right to tax. They have the legitimation of jurisdiction which derives from the doctrine of sovereign independence, a centrepiece of the interstate system. In short, they have legal power and theoretical autonomy. And this is not a small thing. They can decide on a policy concerning matters that are internal to their boundaries, and they can carry it out. In theory, their power is absolute, limited only by the constitutional structure they themselves have put into place and which they themselves can amend.

But, as we know, this is the theory and not in fact the practice. First of all the sovereign states are bound together in an interstate system, and this system also has rules, many, but certainly not all of which are written and formal. The states must function within these rules or be subject to the sanctions which other states will bring to bear upon them. Furthermore, states are very unequal in real strength, as we have noted already, and almost by definition the weaker states of the South are more constrained in the exercise of their sovereign rights than the states of the North.

Even more, however, states have interests, and the interests of any given state are not at all necessarily consonant with the objective of evening-out world distribution of goods or power. Even small and weak states may find themselves in proximity to smaller and weaker ones, and find the temptation to increase their own relative wealth and power at the expense of their neighbour's wealth and power very difficult to resist. This is all the more the case if some other state, even more powerful and further away, is eyeing the neighbour as prey. Dominating the neighbour may seem an alternative to having some third power dominate the neighbour and you.

On the other hand, since states have interests, they negotiate. And they may find that the condition of negotiating a successful and advantageous arrangement with some stronger, richer state may be not to interfere with this stronger state's role in the even weaker neighbour's domain. The solidarity of the South may find itself sacrificed on the altar of the advantage of one of its members, or several. It is therefore no surprise that the international solidarity of post-revolutionary states has often suffered from an overdose of rhetoric and an absence of substance, of substantial short-term sacrifices. There have been, to be sure, notable and noble exceptions, but the fact that these acts of solidarity stand out in our minds should make us suspect that they have not been as frequent, or as extensive, as claimed.

As these states come to operate more and more exclusively in the diplomatic arena, they tend to look increasingly for valid inter-mediaries (or *interlocuteurs valables*) in the North. They become ever more dependent on the role of the far-sighted, albeit self-interested, statesmen of the North, the comprehenders of the mutual dilemmas of North and South, the constructors of a New International Economic Order. Thus we come to our fourth actor. And once again we search for disinterestedness in a group with very strong interests. For such valid intermediaries have the identical problem of the leaders of post-revolutionary states in the South. Without acquiring and retaining state power, there is little they can do.

The political base of the valid intermediary—whether it be statesman, or political party, or even whole state—is in the North, not the South. If a government of the North wishes to promote, or even to agree to, some change in the international economic order that will reduce the gap between North and South, it must thereby be surrendering some advantage that has hitherto been available. Politically this is justifiable to the peoples of the North on only one of two grounds. One is the argument of long-term advantage, achieved by short-term sacrifice. The second is the same but in a very different guise, a less appealing guise. It is the argument of short-term disadvantage to ward off even greater long-term disadvantage.

The valid intermediary of the North must therefore hold up either the prospect of rational long-term world planning or the spectre of imminent disaster as his internal political justification for sacrifice. Neither is easy to sustain. Long-term world planning strikes those who are currently well-off as woolly, and the spectre of imminent disaster seems to call for more dramatic (and violent) responses than short-term sacrifice. It is no wonder if the statesman or parties of the North refrain from pressing too hard this programme of structured bene-volence.

Where then are we? None of the actors are perfect. All of the actors have their limits as proponents of fundamental change. But it is very clear that some have been more efficacious than others. Actors three and four, the post-revolutionary states of the South and the valid intermediaries of the North, have not between them accomplished very much, which is why the gap has grown wider rather than narrower. And what they have accomplished has been largely by virtue of their acting out the last stages of a process initiated by actors one and two, the peoples of the South and the revolutionary movements of the South. It is then to these two groups—the peoples and the movements—that we must turn for hope. I will not review again their limitations, only their merits. Movements are organizations, hence have claim to a certain efficiency and efficacy. But efficiency and efficacy are less important in some ways than reckless determination. Only peoples have that, and only sometimes, never continuously. Still, what has been accomplished thus far is largely attributable to the coming together of popular determination and movement organization.

It is perhaps time to underline how much more has been possible through this combination than through the combination of post-revolutionary states and their valid intermediaries. It is perhaps time to think together how we can sustain the former and not let them be swallowed up by the leaden ways of the latter. Since politics is the art of the possible, we should reject political paths which manifestly have not worked, or at least worked only very badly, in favour of those political methods which have worked better.

7

Issues in North–South Dialogue

KOFI BUENOR HADJOR

On 18 March 1987 Chris Patten, Minister for Overseas Development, informed the British House of Commons that his government was planning to devote a larger share of its aid to 'policy reform' in Africa. Just what kind of policy reform he had in mind became clear in the course of his speech. Patten enthused: 'It is interesting to observe how many aid-recipient countries have turned their backs on fake socialist solutions and chosen to take a more balanced course with greater emphasis on market forces.'[1] Modestly Patten remarked: 'I do not, of course, pretend that Adam Smith and Milton Friedman are now bestriding the African continent', but he assured the House that the virtues of the market were proving irresistible to African governments.

For Patten the path ahead was clear:

> We must therefore do all we can to help aid recipients make the painful adjustments which are sometimes necessary. Aid should be used to assist the passage along the path of virtue. For our part, we will devote a greater share of our aid budget in the coming year to policy reform in Africa.[2]

Like the benevolent parent handing out pocket-money to a difficult child, Patten is not above dictating terms on how it ought to be spent. Assisting Africa along the 'path of virtue' is Patten's euphemism for forcing aid recipients to accept his government's policies. Patten's patronizing lectures about the relevance of Adam Smith and Milton Friedman for Africa just about sum up the state of play with North–South dialogue.

Looking back over the last three decades it is clear that North–South dialogue never became anything more than a good idea. It is difficult not to draw cynical conclusions about the whole experience. International initiatives as regards the Third World have seldom been motivated by anything other than geo–political considerations. Even the very creation of 'development studies' and the 'development industry' was the product of superpower rivalries. It was the obsession with the Red Menace looming on the horizon that informed the literature on the development of the Third World in the 1950s and 1960s. Rostow's influential *The Stages of Economic Growth* is appropriately subtitled *A Non-Communist Manifesto.*[3] Two or three decades ago there was no pretence of dialogue or even of consultation. It was simply a question of imparting the wisdom of Western civilization to the impatient pupils of Africa, Asia, Latin America, and the Middle East.

But the pupils turned out to be ungrateful. Something within the Third World began to stir which showed that people had their own ideas about their future. The Cuban revolution proved to be an important milestone. It became evident to foreign policy experts in Washington, London, and Paris that what could happen in Cuba could be repeated elsewhere. Suddenly Latin America looked very vulnerable and strangely immune to the philosophy of Adam Smith. The response of the Kennedy administration was the comprehensive aid package for Latin America, the *Alliance for Progress*. The *Alliance for Progress* proved singularly unsuccessful in its implementation. But what the *Alliance* showed was that international aid initiatives are the consequence of geo–political and not humanitarian considerations. Kennedy was forced into something of a dialogue by the exigencies of US foreign interests.

Throughout the 1960s there was little in the way of North–South dialogue. The Third World lobby in the UN General Assembly made several attempts to put forward its point of view, but the powerful industrial nations had little time for the views of the ex-colonies. It was ironic that the 1960s were designated by the UN as the *First Development Decade*. But the countries of the South were forced to discuss amongst themselves to work out their own strategy.

It was not until 1964 that the first forum for the consideration of North–South issues was established. Under the aegis of the UN, the first Conference on Trade and Development (UNCTAD) was held in Geneva. This conference set the pattern for the future. Representatives of the South put forward demands for ameliorating the position of their countries in the world order. The Western powers responded by rejecting any specific reforms and argued for the adaptation of meaningless general platitudes. And yet a decade later North–South dialogue was all the rage. Western leaders who had hitherto dismissed Third World aspirations as unreasonable now preached the importance of the dialogue. So what had changed?

The emergence of OPEC as a global force at a time when the industrialized nations were heading into an economic recession had a traumatic impact on the thinking of Western leaders. Suddenly the Third World had become a major issue, even a threat to the existing international order. There were fears that other developing countries would unite and follow the OPEC bloc, flexing their muscles. There were uncertainties about future economic trends and about the power of the Third World to disrupt the existing world order. Under such pressures the North was now prepared to treat the South more seriously. The new mood was clearly evident at the *Sixth Special Session of the UN General Assembly* in April 1974. At this session decisions were taken which expressed the need for a new international order to reduce the gap between developing and industrialized countries. Many of the demands of Third World nations which had hitherto been rejected by the industrialized countries were now incorporated in a Declaration and Action Programme for a New International Economic Order (NIEO). Although the Declaration was of a non-bonding nature it was a sign of the times that it was adopted without being put to the vote. During the next few months it became clear that the industrialized nations were prepared to make significant concessions. In February 1975 a trade and aid agreement (the Lome Convention) was concluded between the EEC and 48 states in Africa, the Caribbean, and the Pacific region. Whilst far from radical, the agreement made significant concessions and guaranteed the 48 states free access to EEC markets. The Lome Convention represents a turning point. By the summer of 1975 the industrialized countries felt less threatened by the potential power of the South. The shift of power towards the Third World was not as significant as they first feared. In this new climate the North adopted a new strategy. In contrast to the past the leaders of the industrial powers did not rule out negotiations. Negotiations were seen as an insurance against any unpredictable turn of events, such as unilateral Third World initiatives. At the same time negotiations were not to be taken too seriously. The aim was to drag out the discussion until the old order could be restored. Discussions, yes, but on the condition that they were general, inconclusive, and without practical consequences. This was the immediate background to the North–South dialogue.

The North–South dialogue (Conference on International Economic Co-operation) was brought about by an initiative of the French government. It began in Paris in 1975 and involved consideration of such issues as energy, raw material prices, development, and finance. This dialogue was eventually concluded in June 1977 without achieving any practical results. The call for more dialogue and more negotiations was the main legacy of the Conference.

At least, it could be claimed, the general acceptance of the need for a North–South dialogue constituted a recognition of the Third World's claim for an NIEO. And for a while some optimists believed that something would emerge from such discussions. In 1978 the Brandt Commission was launched and the North–South dialogue appeared to have become a permanent feature of international diplomacy. However, by the end of the decade the dialogue had all but collapsed. The major Western powers regained their confidence and reverted to the old habit of dictating terms rather than engaging in negotiations. The 1980 Special Session of the UN General Assembly, which was meant to provide a focus for this dialogue, turned into a fiasco. Subsequent international forums only revealed that the powers of the North were not interested in anything but a public relations exercise. The Brandt Commission could publish a report so long as its recommendations remained just that. The North–South dialogue was shelved until the day when the Third World is perceived again as a threat to the existing international order.

The politics of power dominated North–South relations. In the nineteenth century the colonial armies came accompanied by the missionary with a bible in hand. Today the rapid deployment force is complemented by Mr Patten with copies of the work of Adam Smith and Milton Friedman ready for distribution. It is now customary for Western powers and international agencies like the IMF to work out the economic policies that the nations of the South should pursue. Even the UN has joined in the act. At the 1986 UN Special Session on Africa a new programme for recovery was explicitly linked to the acceptance of market-orientated economic policies. To add insult to injury the 22 African nations that have adopted such policies have seen very little of the promised assistance.

Lurking behind the new economic colonization of Adam Smith and Milton Friedman is the threat of more overt forms of domination. We are living in the era of the Reagan doctrine, and radical Third World regimes had better beware. It is worth recalling that since 1945 more wars have occurred and more people have been killed than in any other period in history with the exception of the two world wars.[4] Most of these wars have been fought in the South. With wars of intervention raging in many parts of the world, from Nicaragua to Mozambique, the question that is posed is 'Where next?' The militarization of the Third World has acquired astounding proportions. Between the years 1979 and 1983 almost 84000 million dollars' worth of arms was sold to countries in the Middle East.[5] The transfer of military technology appears to be the most significant contribution of the North to the South. The danger of balkanization in regions of the South cannot be ignored by any intelligent observer. It is through the barrel of a gun that the North–South issues are most sharply posed.

Joint Responsibility

At least intellectually the interdependent character of the international order is widely recognized. The events of the post-war decades have shown that developments in one part of the world can have far-reaching consequences in the rest. The future of the human race can be secured only through global solutions. This point is so obvious that publicly everyone seems to be in agreement. It provides both the pragmatic and the intellectual foundation for a North–South dialogue. Unfortunately the recognition of global interdependence becomes empty rhetoric unless it is acted upon. It is not enough to mouth phrases about global interdependence. The starting point for any real North–South dialogue must be the recognition that the solution to the problems of the South are the joint responsibility of both the industrialized and the developing countries. It is necessary to insist on this point. The South is not asking the North for favours. We are not asking for charity and kindness. It is high time that the responsibility of the North for the present state of affairs in the South was clearly recognized as the point of departure for any serious dialogue. Without such recognition the existing international economic order will be taken as the natural state of affairs which requires only minor modification.

Yet there is nothing natural about the existing international economic order. The world market is not the product of nature. Nor did God decree that the price of commodities should fall in relation to the price of manufactured goods. The existing terms of trade, the system of world finance, and even that holiest of holy institutions, the IMF, are all the creation of human beings. It is a creation that benefits some and discriminates against others. Without fundamental changes to the international economic order the South can have no real future, and, if the South has no future, in the long run neither will the rest of the globe. The present world economy tends to reproduce inequalities and benefits only those who are already powerful. Take just one example—the terms of trade. With the commodity prices falling, it appears that the more the Third World produces the less it gets back in return. Consequently, the terms of trade of non-oil-producing developing countries have declined by 10 per cent below their level at the beginning of the decade.[6] Some would tend to blame this decline on the invisible hand of the market. But why is it the South that tends to get penalized by the invisible hand? It would appear that attached to the invisible hand is the all-too-visible power of the nations that actually run the world economy.

The terms of trade are not some arbitrary event. It is one of the many mechanisms through which resources from one part of the world continue to flow to another. Just because prices fall does not mean that it takes any less resources and labour to produce a ton of coffee or a ton of tea. It only means that more resources are transferred abroad never to return to the South. That resources continue to flow in a one-way direction cannot be denied. No one is spared. Even Africa, the poorest and least-developed region in the world, continues to subsidize the North. Between 1980 and 1985, the ratio of debt service to export earnings in Africa tripled to 35 per cent.[7] That means that more than a third of Africa's exports are already earmarked for the purpose of interest payments to Western banks. Even the World Bank has been forced to concede that in Africa 'the burden of debt and debt service has generated a very substantial reflow of capital to the developed world.'[8] And Africa is paying the price, not just in terms of capital flows but also in terms of human lives. It is estimated that 50 million children will die of malnutrition-related illness by the year 2000.

At present the major powers of the North do not recognize the need to transform the existing international order. On the contrary. In recent years, under the leadership of Washington, many influential Western powers have insisted on celebrating the virtues of the world market. Rather than seeking changes in the structures of the international economy the North now insists that the countries of the South adjust to the realities of the world market. This is the meaning of all the 'adjustment programmes' and 'reform packages' which the international agencies like the IMF are forcing on the Third World. Poor nations starved of funds and foreign exchange are being pressurized to accept structural adjustment policies even before they get a penny from the IMF or the World Bank.

The market is not as free as its apologists pretend. Indeed, the international economy has become a battlefield where everything is decided by power and force. Western nations who preach the virtues of Adam Smith to Burkina Faso or Brazil are not at all inhibited from imposing severe tariffs on imports from the newly industrializing countries. It appears that protectionism makes sense for the powerful but is to be condemned when practised by the poor. Economic warfare is particularly aggressive against those nations whose political outlook is not to the liking of the North. Thus the Reagan administration has taken steps to prevent Nicaragua from acquiring new loans from the World Bank. The only adjustment programme that Washington has in mind for Nicaragua is the overthrow of the Sandinistas.

Economic warfare is not conducive to dialogue. Nor is it a rational way of managing international affairs and securing stability and peace. Just in passing it ought to be noticed that it is a war that cannot be won. The crisis of Third World debt has shown everyone that cares to look that it is only a matter of time before the international economic order explodes. Mexico in 1985, Brazil in 1987. Where will the debt crisis strike next? The South has had enough lectures and decrees. We need negotiations that recognize that affairs cannot continue in the old way. Let me repeat, the South does not want charity. It wants an NIEO that is not run on the principles of discrimination and exploitation.

An Agenda for Change

At present the future of North–South relations appears grim. Given the failure of past initiatives it could be argued that the construction of an agenda for North–South dialogue is a pointless exercise. We can neither predict nor control the future. What we can offer is an agenda for the establishment of an NIEO. If change is to occur, the initial impetus must come from within the South. It is the countries of the South that are confronted with the historic problems of development, of poverty, and of endemic crisis. And yet the South lacks a collective voice. The Non-Aligned Movement (NAM) has launched many interesting initiatives and has attempted to influence the course of international relations in a positive direction. Unfortunately this movement has had no real existence inbetween conferences and has not been able to promote practical action.

From time to time Third World nations have come together to co-ordinate their positions in the various international forums. The Group of 77 which emerged during the UNCTAD negotiations represented an attempt to forge a united bloc for the purposes of negotiations with the North. Unhappily such efforts have not been sustained for any length of time. Despite various initiatives the nations of the South have made little progress in establishing a unified bloc. If anything there has been an intensification of tension and rivalry within the South during the past two decades. At most international forums the South is not able to speak with one voice. Thus at the UN Special Session on Africa in 1986, Latin American countries were too preoccupied with their own problems to support Africa's demands for more funds.

Disunity and fragmentation within the South has meant that there has been no progress in the sphere of economic co-operation. Various attempts to extend co-operation through the establishment of common markets in Africa and Latin America have failed. As a result trade between the nations of the South is falling. It is not surprising that conflicts within the South provide rich pickings for the North. Such conflicts as the Iran–Iraq war and tension in the Horn of Africa, the Western Sahara, the Indian subcontinent, and elsewhere show the dimensions of the problem.

It is unlikely that harmony within the South can be established for some considerable time. With the escalation of externally induced conflicts one can only draw pessimistic conclusions. With billions of dollars at stake the world arms merchants do not want either Iran or Iraq to win—they merely want the war to continue into the next century. Foreign interference will continue to exacerbate conflict. Southern leadership has to recognize the implications of this problem and apply its creative energies to finding solutions.

The South has no choice but to develop its own institutions for confronting the issues raised by the existing international economic order. Without such institutions it is not possible to work out a consensus on a programme for action. The North has functioning international institutions such as the OECD, NATO, the IMF, and the EEC through which its common interests can be expressed. The South has no comparable framework for policy-making and action. Institutions such as the Organization of American States or the Commonwealth, which involve certain nations of the South, are in fact instruments of powers such as the USA or Britain. As long as the present situation continues the well-organized North will be faced with a fragmented and conflict-ridden South. And the demands of the South will continue to be ignored. The first priority then is the establishment of a basic consensus for the South. The existing NAM could provide the initiative for bringing the Third World countries together. It would be utopian to imagine that the serious differences which separate the Third World nations can be resolved through goodwill. But all Third World nations have a common interest in the establishment of an NIEO—and a way has to be found to give an institutional expression to this common interest. Once the South is able to speak with one voice, the North will find it difficult to ignore international dialogue and negotiations. This is one of the key lessons in the experience of the past three decades. It is necessary to recall that one united action by OPEC did more to get the leaders of the North to the negotiating table than decades of pleading.

The next stage is the establishment of international institutions that are genuinely international and cater for the interests of all sections of the world community. At present the rich nations of the world actually own the important international institutions. From one day to the next a US president can decide to change the funding and policy of the World Bank. Even the UN is not immune to the interference of the powerful. Take the campaign of slander orchestrated against UNESCO. Washington and London decided that the leadership was too independent. Unilaterally they withdrew their funds from the organization and made it clear that until UNESCO accepted the Anglo–American recommendations these two countries would stay outside the framework of this institution. This philosophy of 'take it or leave it' permeates the discussion in most of the existing international institutions. Serious discussions require an international framework which is based on the recognition of the equal rights of its participants. These are principles which the USA recognizes on paper—now it is time to act on it in practice. The recognition of equality is a precondition for negotiations and dialogue.

The structure of capital flows requires major modifications. At present the relation between the North and the South resembles that of a usurer and a debt-slave. Most Third World nations reel from one financial crisis to another. The banking system operates in such a way that capital flows tend to go in one direction. The system of aid devised under the careful supervision of the IMF and the World Bank is designed to assist the large banks and the donor countries. Thus the IMF will soon become a net recipient rather than a supplier of funds to the Third World borrowers.[9]

Aid has of course little to do with humanitarian gestures. If it were not so most of the resources earmarked for aid would have gone to the least-developed countries. But the need has nothing to do with the principles of aid allocations. The main recipients are countries which are most strategically placed to benefit imperial interests. Moreover, if donor countries were so highly motivated by humanitarian considerations then arms shipments would not constitute such a significant proportion of aid. As is well known the whole system of aid, like that of finance, is linked to the purchase of goods and services. Before the recipient nation receives its allocated funds, it has already been decided how it ought to spend it. What occurs is a paper transaction whereby resources remain in the North to be redistributed to the relevant banks and multinationals.

It would be useful to begin by breaking down the artificial distinction between aid and other forms of loans. Any discussion of financial relations should begin by examining what funds the South needs to survive and for essential developmental investment. Anything left over could be allocated to a global investment fund. At the same time the North ought to make available a proportion (to be negotiated) of the resources which it has obtained from the South in recent decades. This too should be allocated for a global investment fund. Such a fund, jointly administered, would be used to reverse the existing flow of resources from North to South.

The existing system of finance is in need of a major overhaul. The South cannot be expected to carry its burden of debt. The responsibility for these enormous debts lies with the international economic order. Countries in the Third World have been forced to borrow in order to compensate for the revenues they have lost through the worsening of their terms of trade. It is now widely recognized that in real terms commodity prices are at their lowest levels since the 1930s. This enormous loss of purchasing power represents a real gain for the North. Those who have made a killing from lending capital to the South have also enjoyed the benefits of lower commodity prices. More precisely the economic crisis of the South is in no small measure the responsibility of those who have profited from it in the North. The cancellation of interest payments is a reform that is long overdue. Such payments represent only a portion of the resources that have been transferred from the South to the North.

Future financial transactions between the North and the South could be regulated through the global investment fund in a way that ensures that it is not the laws of usury that influence the way capital flows. Such an institution would seek to harmonize trade, finance, and investment. It could link the allocation of resources to the objective of development. Thus one of its aims would be to establish a stable system of prices for commodities and help reverse the trend of falling commodity prices.

At first sight the proposals outlined may appear unrealistic, even utopian. There are no doubt real difficulties that stand in the way. However, it needs to be emphasized that there are no technical obstacles to the working of an international investment fund. Take the stabilization of commodity prices. The OECD countries have a long record of subsidizing agriculture so as to maintain stable prices for farmers. The EEC Common Agricultural Policy shows that the maintenance of stable food prices is technically a feasible proposition. If this is good enough for European farmers why not for Third World producers? There is no reason why commodity prices have to be regulated through the anarchy of the market whilst the prices of other goods are artificially maintained.

Nor are there any technical difficulties in cancelling interest payments. There is a long and honourable tradition of writing off debts in the banking system. Western governments have intervened on more than one occasion to demand that banks ease up on certain borrowers in the 'national interest'. Banks already have what they categorize as 'non-performing loans'. All that is required is to extend that category and make the necessary adjustments. If this is carefully planned then the inevitable explosion of the world banking system could be avoided. More to the point, relieved of this usurious burden, countries in the South could get on with the job of developing their wealth and resources. It is easy to get preoccupied with the need to reform the international economic order. And for obvious reasons most public concern about North–South relations has tended to concentrate within the sphere of economics. Such an emphasis can easily obscure other

vital issues which influence North–South relations. It is difficult to
avoid the conclusion that many of the economic problems facing
certain nations of the South are the consequence of external political
interference. It is a matter of public record that time and again
economic warfare has been used against Third World governments
who have displeased Western interests. The governments of Allende,
Castro, Nkrumah, and Manley, to name but a few, have faced trade
sanctions and the abrupt withdrawal of aid. During the 1980s there
has been an escalation of outside pressure. Thus Nicaragua is not only
denied loans. The USA spends hundreds of millions of dollars on
attempting to overthrow the Sandinista government. In the course of
this intervention the economy of Nicaragua has been shattered. The
economic problems have hardly been caused by economic factors.

Mozambique has become an economic disaster area. In Mozambique
the South African backed rebels are expressly devoted to destroying the
economic infrastructure of the country. The consequence of this
intervention is that four million people in Mozambique are now facing
starvation. After Mozambique comes Angola. Which Third World
country is next in the firing line? Under the Reagan administration the
Third World has become a legitimate hunting ground for 'international
terrorists'. The new term invented by Washington, that of 'state-
sponsored terrorism', has provided justification for foreign intervention. Predictably all nations accused of sponsoring terrorism are in the
Third World. A climate conducive to gun-boat diplomacy is not one
where negotiations about economic matters are likely to yield positive
results. Ideally one would like to see the demilitarization of the South.
That objective is not one that can be realized in the short and medium
term. For now it is necessary to assert the principle of national
sovereignty and demand that the North ceases its political and military
adventures in the South.

With contemporary Western diplomacy every major policy statement
contains a threat. Reagan's message to the Middle East is illustrative of
this point:

> There is no way, as long as Saudi Arabia and the OPEC nations there
> in the East—and Saudi Arabia is the most important—provide
> industry the bulk of energy that is needed to turn the wheels of
> industry in the Western world. There is no way that we can stand by
> and see that taken over by anyone that would shut that oil.[10]

This language of ultimatums has become all too real in the realm of
North–South relations. Carried to its conclusion it would deny the
right of the South to determine its future in the way it sees fit. With the
question of self-determination we reach the most fundamental issue of

all as far as North–South relations are concerned. North–South relations are fundamentally predatory. How would our friends in Belgium or Britain react if a group of experts in Bandung or Nairobe worked out some economic adjustment policies for them to implement? The reaction would be one of outrage and scorn. And yet scores of Third World governments have been relieved by the IMF of the responsibility for the working out of economic policy. The very terms of North–South relations represent an encroachment on the right of the South as a whole to determine its future. It is necessary to insist time and time again that without the recognition of these fundamental rights there can be no dialogue.

Until this principle of self-determination is recognized by the North, the South will have to look for solutions from within its ranks. This is not a matter of choice but of necessity. It is the only way that the South can avoid becoming the battlefield for the rapid deployment forces of the world. The scope for co-operation within the South is tremendous and it takes only an act of political will to begin to realize its potential. The common threat posed by the military machine of Pretoria and of the Contras in Central America should serve as a reminder that only a united diplomatic focus can preserve the integrity of the nations of the South. Much work and much thinking is needed so as to maximize the strength and the resources of the South.

We have no wish to promote a unilateralist all-South strategy. Such a strategy has inherent limitations in a world that has become truly international. It is also the case that the South is not without friends and allies in the North. Many in the North have been disgusted by the obscene menace represented by the apartheid regime in South Africa. Others have been shocked by the consequences of imperialist intervention in Nicaragua, Angola, and Mozambique. The Anglo–American air-strike on Libya deeply disturbed those in the North who uphold the cause of world peace.

Culture, Media, and Information

Power, both nationally and internationally, is also about who controls systems of communication and information. It is for this reason that the nations of the South have for some time sought to establish a New International Information and Communications Order. The recent battles over the future of UNESCO show that the North is still determined to retain its control of the instruments of communication and information. Cultural domination is one of the most insidious expressions of international power relations—it prevents the creation of a climate of dialogue in the North.

The offensive orchestrated in Washington and London against UNESCO was directed against the assertion of the cultural values and interests of the South. For some time now the North has attempted to play the role of cultural guardian of the world. During the colonial era the metropolitan powers pursued a policy which denied the validity of the historical and cultural experiences of the South. Cultural artifacts were plundered from their locations and placed in the museums of Europe and the USA. This plunder of history and culture is no longer the norm, but still continues. Thus the US invasion of Grenada was followed by the removal of the internal documents of the New Jewel Movement. The archives were promptly put on display in US libraries as a crucial period of Grenadian history was expropriated by the North. Not surprisingly it is Washington's version of the invasion that influences the discussion in the media.

Today the main threat to the South is not cultural plunder. Rather it is the new communications systems, controlled by the North, which can penetrate the nations of the South and threaten existing cultural values. It is well known that the North has encouraged the South to purchase its information and communications technology. Television systems have been sold to the South on the grounds that they will help consolidate its national cultures. Unfortunately the technology has had the opposite effect. As one study observes:

> Smaller governmental television associations soon found that they were incapable of competing with the massive, well organised and well packaged programmes coming from the West. Having acquired the technology, developing countries now find themselves limited to importing certain types of programmes, largely cheap semi-commercial ones produced in the Western world, which can be shown only by a particular instrument.[11]

Through this system of information the North seeks to influence the mind, the heart, and the purchasing patterns of the people of the South. Through this process it is often Western values that become the point of reference. This form of ideological domination is just as real as political and economic coercion. This explains why in so many parts of the Middle East the reaction to foreign domination has been just as much against Western dress and Coca Cola as against anything else. Almost instinctively it is recognized that the imported ideology of consumerism it in itself a threat to national sovereignty.

The media and other systems of information have been at the centre of power politics. During the past decade the media have played a key role in preparing the way for political and even military intervention. The manipulation of information and disinformation has been extensive. Thus the invasion of Grenada was preceded by a spate of horror stories about the dangers facing US medical students on the island. Nicaragua has had more than its fair share of Washington-produced disinformation. At one time or another it has been accused of harbouring aggressive designs against the neighbouring countries of Central America, of acting as a conduit for guerrillas from Cuba, and of preparing acts of subversion in Mexico. This bombardment of anti-Nicaraguan propaganda has served to legitimize foreign intervention in its domestic affairs.

It is the international media that decides what is right and what is wrong. Hence the Contras in Nicaragua, UNITA in Angola, and the MNR in Mozambique are 'freedom fighters'. Those who are not in the good books of the North are *ipso facto* terrorists. The concerted campaign to equate Arabs with terrorism in the USA shows how powerful the media can be in shaping attitudes and perceptions. Whatever the rights and wrongs of the matter, the conversion of Colonel Gaddafi into the supreme evil of the world system is more symptomatic of the supreme influence of the media than anything else. In an age of mass destruction the continued portrayal of the Arab 'terrorist' as the main threat to world peace is a testimony to the effectiveness of the Western-dominated media. Incidentally, it also demonstrates that racist stereotyping still remains the norm within the existing international information order.

We can now understand the significance of the attempt to destroy UNESCO. UNESCO was one of the four international institutions that fought to challenge the dominant systems of information and communication. Its efforts to combat racist and ethnocentric cultural values are well known. It is ironic that UNESCO's attempts to present matters from the point of view of the South were dismissed by the Western media as the 'politicization' of cultural issues. Information, culture, and the media are considered neutral as long as they are expressive of the views that dominate the international order. Any attempt to promote alternative views is discredited as political.

In fact, information and culture are not and never were above politics. The control of information is no less important than the control of world trade or the system of finance. Influencing the mind is no less important than the control of world trade or the system of finance. Influencing the mind is no less important than influencing the stomach. As matters stand at present, the international information order simply excludes the South from having its views and values expressed in an adequate form.

A New International Information and Communications Order represents a demand for an end to ideological enslavement. The South must have the right to communicate its views and to develop its own forms of culture in the way it sees fit. Without the recognition of the right to spiritual freedom there can be no dialogue. The South is tired of its own views being represented and interpreted by others. It knows what it wants to say. It now needs equal access to the international information order to say it. An end to a one-way ideological invasion is one of the central demands to be taken up in any North–South dialogue. Many of the contributors to this volume who come from the North have profound reservations about the existing state of affairs. And all the contributors have come together to honour the memory of Olof Palme. Olof Palme represents the best in Western statesmanship. He fought to change the existing international economic order—not just in words but through his deeds. More than any practising Western statesman Palme fought to make the North–South dialogue a reality. Through his example he demonstrated that such a dialogue can be achieved if there is the will.

The best way of honouring Olof Palme is to act on his ideals. This is particularly the responsibility of those from the North who are concerned with contemporary developments. It needs two to have a dialogue. The South is ready and prepared to enter into meaningful discussions about the future of this world. What we lack are those with power and influence in the North who are also prepared to take up this challenge. We believe that the contributions contained in this volume provide irrefutable arguments for such a dialogue. That such a wide spectrum of contributors representing the North and the South and a variety of political convictions could all point in roughly the same direction is in itself a powerful argument for a rethink on North–South relations.

Notes

1. *The Guardian*, 19 March 1987.

2. Ibid.

3. W. W. Rostow, *The Stages of Economic Growth: A Non-Communist Manifesto* (Cambridge, 1962).

4. R. Luckham, 'Operation El Dorado Canyon: Globalising the Cold War' in M. Kaldor and P. Anderson, eds., *Mad Dogs: the US raid on Libya* (London, 1986), p. 67.

5. H. Maull, 'The arms trade with the Middle East and North Africa' in *The Middle East and North Africa 1987* (London, 1986), p. 166. See also *Jane's Defence Weekly*, 5 October 1986.

6. See *Barclays Review*, February 1987, p. 23.

7. *The Economist*, 7 June 1986.

8. *Finance and Development*, March 1986, p. 22.

9. See C. Payer, 'The World Bank: a new role in the debt crisis?', *Third World Quarterly*, December 1986, p. 659.

10. Cited in L. Meo, ed., *U.S. Strategy in the Gulf* (Belmont, Mass., 1981), p. 128.

11. A. W. Singham and S. Hune, *Non-Alignment in the Age of Alignments* (London, 1986), p. 26.

SECTION THREE

The Global Economic/Information Order: Calls for Change

8

The Social Democratic Parties and the New International Economic Order

NEIL KINNOCK

Olof Palme was a beloved comrade to those who knew him and a good friend to millions across the planet who had never heard of him. He was a man of brilliant intelligence and enthralling vision. But his greatest quality was not simply to possess those attributes. It was that he put intellect to its finest use—the effort of solving the practical problems of humanity in the most peaceful and productive way. He said that he had the double advantage of having socialist commitment and of coming from a neutral country. In that assessment he quite typically undervalued his own instincts. Others are socialists; others come from neutral countries. But there are few from anywhere whose confidence comes so plainly from openness and breadth of understanding rather than from dogmatic insensitivity. And his country's neutrality, meanwhile, was for him an opportunity to organize against poverty and exploitation without vested interest, and not a refuge from involvement or a pulpit for sermonizing.

In his membership of the Brandt Commission, in his chairmanship of his own commission, in his work in the Socialist International, in his efforts to mediate on behalf of the UN in the war between Iran and Iraq, and in countless other actions, both public and private, he showed himself to be a citizen *of* the world and *for* the world. That role he believed, in a very matter of fact way, was one of realistic necessity. Insularity and isolationism, he thought, were stupid as well as selfish, when the migration of ideas and beliefs and technology and trade and the means of peace and war were daily making the lives and interests of people everywhere more intermingled. He was right. In a world where terrorism, warfare, pollution, desertification, drug-running, and a multitude of other plagues are all diseases of the human condition that are more easily communicated and more awful in effect than ever before, the old separations are redundant and deluded.

Yet it is precisely in those countries and amongst those governments where that sense of international interdependence should be most obvious and should be most positive that the perception is least acute. Instead of responding to the fragility and enforced intimacy of our planet in the 1980s with internationalism, the world's most powerful nations are elevating narrow national interests, supplemented, when financial instability threatens, by public and private accords that usually strengthen the strong insiders and weaken the weak outsiders. That selfishness of the powerful threatens the security and vitality of the rest of the world. But it also undermines the safety and prosperity of their own societies.

The limited vision of the rich has reduced many of the great global institutions of the world—particularly the international financial and trading institutions specifically established to prevent such economic introversion—to a state of near paralysis which is beginning to show all the signs of turning into rigor mortis. They have made the IMF into little more than a global debt-collector acting in the interests of the Northern banks and governments.

Similarly, the post-war intention to provide, through the UN, a framework which would allow governments of different persuasions to work out solutions to international problems without resorting to armed conflict, and to co-operate in initiatives which would not just avert war but positively promote peace and plenty, is increasingly looked upon as worthy but 'unrealistic'.

Such a view is nothing more than a surrender to helplessness—a refusal to believe that the problems which have been created by humans can be resolved by humans, an assumption that to invest too wholeheartedly in support of the international institutions is utopian, or naïve, or even dangerous.

Nowhere has that process been more clearly demonstrated than in the actions and attitudes of Mrs Thatcher's Conservative government in Britain, which has pursued a systematic policy of what can only be described as 'de-internationalization'. Instead of using its membership of the Summit Seven—the world's leading economies—to promote policies of debt relief for the Third World and expansion to beat trade stagnation and unemployment in the industrialized countries, the British government has upheld the regime of contraction, cuts, closures, and high interest rates. It has ignored some of the most important General Assembly resolutions on South Africa on the grounds that they are not mandatory, and then used its veto in the Security Council to prevent them from becoming mandatory. It has renounced ILO Conventions, withheld support from the Law of the Sea Convention, and, as the USA's sole companion in withdrawing from UNESCO, shown itself unwilling to work for reform of that reorganization or, still less, to support its creditable practical work in education, science, culture, and development—especially in the poor countries. In other acts of de-internationalization the British government has cut its aid to the poorest countries of the world while its own citizens have made it clear by their voluntary action that they recognize a compelling obligation to assist them; it has imposed full-cost fees on higher education students from the Third World, including the Commonwealth, thereby increasing the cost of a typical science degree course fivefold and reducing the number of overseas students by more than one-third since 1979; it has treated the Commonwealth itself as a collection of the insolent, the indolent and—to use Mrs Thatcher's phrase—'the immoral' when they seek strong sanctions against apartheid.

All of those actions obviously offend the sensitivities of the altruistic and the internationally minded. So they should. They are the product of bigotry and cynicism. But they also go against the commercial and political interests of Britain. And as citizens of that country we have an immediate and material interest in rejecting such a myopic view of the world.

That is particularly true of those of us who, like Olof Palme, are democratic socialists. The very core of our creed is the conviction that co-operation is essential in the best use of resources to meet human needs. It was conceived in large part by people who were revolted by the inefficiency and injustice of the purely market system—'the system of the sharp elbows' as Palme described capitalism. Their idea that planned organization of resources could replace the chaos of economic chance, and that economic decisions should be responsive to democratic disciplines, was scorned for many years. As ever, the rulers of opinion insisted that freedom for people confounded 'freedom of the market' and would produce disasters of prodigality and inefficiency.

But as our century has progressed the elements of those ideas of economic coherence have been operated nationally and internationally in peace, in war, and in the wake of war by the greatest critics of socialism. They changed in order to mitigate the damage that comes from market anarchy. And whilst their actions were not intended to do more than blunt the most jagged edges of capitalism, the danger of breakdown produced concessions to planning, to co-ordination, and to the establishment of international institutions for funding, for credit, and for co-operation.

The shift was reluctant and it proved to be transitory. But the existence of the system for more than 20 years proved its feasibility, and the needs of the world now, with so many destitute economies in the South and stagnating economies in the North, prove the necessity of a new era and new institutions of planet-wide partnership. For years democratic socialists have been putting the case for concerted action by the governments of the developed countries to ensure a co-ordinated planned investment which will stimulate world demand in industrial and Third World economies alike. High hopes have been raised for the birth of a New International Economic Order, not least by the publication in 1980 of the first report from the Brandt Commission on the mutual interests of the North and South in global development and survival.

Yet despite the generosity of individuals throughout Europe and the world in response to famine in Africa and disaster on other continents, the prospects for concerted action have diminished rather than improved during the last seven years. The report of the Brandt Commission has been filed and forgotten by governments in Europe and the USA. The opportunity to enact its recommendations in the wake of the Cancun Conference was ignored.

Recently, therefore, the case has been reformulated and presented more emphatically in *Global Challenge*, the report published in 1985 which reflected the thinking of socialist parties in the North and in the South. Under the leadership of Michael Manley of Jamaica they came together to present ways in which the world economy could be moved from a state of crisis and conflict to a state of co-operation with policies that systematically promoted recovery, redistribution, development, and democracy.

That rational approach becomes more urgent by the month, for instead of international and intergovernmental co-operation we have had words of 'free trade' side by side with the deeds of restriction and preference. Indeed, the strongest advocates of 'free trade' have been those who, not content with using their strength to gain self-seeking control of trade in manufactured goods, now want to extend that control to trade in services, intellectual property rights, and investment.

The truth is that 'free' trade begets creeping protection, as individuals, companies, institutions, and governments seek to mitigate its damaging deflationary pressures, with the result that, in place of formal and public international agreement and the cohesiveness it brings, the relatively strong use arbitrary and sporadic measures to safeguard their interests, and the relatively weak—who can find no shield—are made relatively weaker still. What we are seeing is not common action for the common good, which common sense and common justice require, but a scramble for self-protection and self-interest by the powerful which threatens the vitality of their own economies as well as the rest of the world.

In the 20 years from 1953–73 real output in the OECD countries—the world's 16 richest nations—grew at 5 per cent a year, exports at 8.6 per cent a year, productivity at 3.7 per cent. Inflation was running at an average of 4.1 per cent and only 2.6 per cent of the work-force was unemployed. Since 1973 output in the OECD countries has grown at less than its previous rate and unemployment has soared by 300 per cent so that there are now 18 million men and women out of work in Western Europe alone—6½ million of them young people under the age of 25. Exports have grown by only 4 per cent a year, productivity by 1.5 per cent, inflation has averaged 9 per cent. Roughly speaking, all the good things have been halved and all the bad things have been doubled, while poor countries have suffered a collapse in commodity prices and a crippling fivefold increase in debt.

Of course, the international trading system by itself is not entirely to blame for this catastrophic record—but its inefficiency and injustice have been major contributory factors. When the world has no efficient method by which countries which find themselves in persistent trade deficit can rid themselves of that deficit other than by deflation, that deflation is bound to be contagious. As one country deflates, cutting imports in an attempt to restore trade balance, then another country loses sales and in turn feels pressure to deflate. All are fearful of expansion since it risks the penalty of financial crisis. And without that impetus for growth, stability then sinks into stagnation.

We need a new international financial and trading system, one which facilitates sustained and resilient growth of material prosperity and secures expanding employment through the world. For that to work, we need an internationally agreed framework in which trade is planned in the interests of growth and employment, in which nations co-operate in trade in their mutual interest, and in which the poor have a chance of lifting themselves out of poverty. It must involve preferences for developing countries, and particularly for the poorest countries; measures to improve and stabilize the price of commodities; steps to help developing countries diversify production and develop local processing of their primary products; and negotiated agreements which encourage the adjustment of production patterns in the interests of both developed and developing countries. Those purposes can only be fulfilled through international co-operation. The same is true of action to tackle the most pressing of all development issues, the problem of international debt. Today the Third World countries owe some $1000 billion to Western banks, governments and international financial institutions. Indeed, they are paying out more in debt service than they get in new investment, so that money is actually flowing from the poor countries to the rich. The World Bank estimates that between 1986 and 1990 there will be a net outflow of well over a billion dollars from Africa alone.

For many countries that is an intolerable burden. High interest rates impose a crippling burden on Africa and Latin America. Deflationary solutions, imposed by the IMF and international creditors, shift that burden directly onto those least able to support it—the poorest social groups.

From any point of view, that is a terrible injustice. It is also a colossal waste of human resources and a threat to creditor governments and institutions. Unless change comes Third World governments will sooner or later be unable or unwilling to pay. If they are forced to default, the prospects for better economic relations and recovery throughout the world could, very obviously, be destroyed in the chaos. Yet, to quote the Socialist International's *Global Challenge* report:

> The global debt problem is played down by most of the governments and institutions in the North, including the OECD, the IMF and the World Bank. They admit it in their analysis, but omit it in their prescriptions, claiming by and large that the problem is manageable.

On their present approach it is not manageable. All they have done so far is to paper over the cracks, giving developing countries longer to pay in return for accepting economic management conditions that are often so stringent as to be strangling. Nothing meanwhile is done to reduce interest rates or increase trade and investment. On the contrary, performance is depressed and poverty is increased. By demanding the same economic reforms of every developing country—the same cuts in imports and public spending—the world's financial institutions are imposing deflation on a global scale. Developing countries are desperately competing to sell the same products to rich countries which, in the resulting buyer's market, can further reduce prices and returns to the poor.

Global Challenge offers an alternative strategy for the management of debt, one which shares the burden between the debtor and creditor countries. Its essential proposals are:

1. Conversion into grants of the debts of the poorest nations of Sub-Saharan Africa, combined with grant conversion of part of the debt of other developing countries.
2. Rescheduling of the remaining debt of Third World countries through extension of the time period for repayment of principal.
3. A ceiling on interest rates for developing countries at concessionary levels.
4. Fixing the ratio of debt repayment to a reasonable proportion of a developing country's export earnings, preferably as low as 20 per cent.
5. Increasing official development aid to meet the UN target of 0.7 per cent of GNP.
6. Increased resources through the IMF to support the process of debt

readjustment, recovery, and development, and allocated on a preferential basis to Third World countries.

Implemented by agreement, such proposals could free the developing countries from the shackles that currently impede their ability to tackle their urgent domestic economic problems. Co-ordinated pressure by like-minded governments is essential if they are to be implemented soon enough to avert catastrophe.

These steps to tackle the debt crisis must be accompanied by action to replace and renew the international financial system created at the UN Conference held in Bretton Woods, New Hampshire, in 1944. The key elements in that system, the IMF and the World Bank, together with GATT, were not perfect institutions but they provided practical solutions to the problems of their day: reconstruction in Europe and the re-establishment of peacetime economic relations. They served the needs of the nations that designed them well enough to see those countries build out of the ruins of war and through three decades of prosperity.

But in many respects the world for which those institutions were designed no longer exists. The bankers, economists and politicians who gathered at Bretton Woods could not have foreseen the new nations that would emerge with new expectations and new economic programmes of their own and they could not anticipate the scale and pace of technological change. They could not have foreseen the monetarist policies, the stagnation, the oil-price shocks which would threaten the world's economy in the 1970s and 1980s.

Nor could they have foreseen how the market system would change. In all their experience and all of their reasonable foresight that system made money mainly by making things. Today we have a system that increasingly makes money by moving money and which has developed what Alan Garcia of Peru has described as a 'logic of non-production'. The same financial and economic system which ensures that economic development in the Third World is inhibited or forbidden by debt and repayment disciplines also ensures that in the ageing industrial economies capital for investment is expensive, short term, and subject to speculative movement.

The mountain of money which the Western banks were so eager to make available to finance development and raise living standards in the Third World throughout the 1970s has become the mountain of debt, crushing the economies of those same countries in the 1980s. Among the casualties of this debt domination is the IMF's own declared purpose of:

... facilitating the expansion and balanced growth of international trade, and contributing thereby to the promotion and maintenance of high levels of employment and real income and to the development of the productive resources of all members as primary objectives of economic policy.

That principle needs to be firmly re-established for now, as in all previous times, debt and depression are contagious. It was the awful lessons of the epidemic failure in the period before the Second World War and the ruinous conflict that came in part from that slump which gave rise to the conference at Bretton Woods. With a similar experience of slump in our times our generation needs to make a co-operative and co-ordinated initiative that compares in scale and purpose with that taken 43 years ago.

Of course no one is suggesting that the Bretton Woods system as such should be exhumed and reinstated. It was far from perfect in many respects and, in any case, the world has changed too much in the past 14 years to go back to the system which, even in the 1960s, was showing signs of severe distress. Rather, the rallying cry 'Back to Bretton Woods' embodies a practical desire to return to the vision and common sense shown by those who gathered at Bretton Woods in 1944.

That call has been heard from many quarters in recent years. Only by re-ordering the financial institutions and by making them more accountable to all of their members, including the developing countries, can we create the climate for future decades of recovery and prosperity. Such a climate, however, cannot be conjured up in isolation from other aspects of international relations. Willy Brandt expressed this most sharply when in a speech in New York in 1985 he said:

There is no point in worrying about co-operation and mutual interests if we fail to avoid a nuclear holocost; or if we fail to master the consequences of famine on continental scales. . . . And it shows a considerable degree of stubbornness if people still refuse to admit that immensely rising worldwide military expenditure is not only politically damaging but does a lot of harm economically.

The $1000 billion which the world spends each year on military purposes amounts, said Brandt, 'to a death sentence for millions of human beings'.

Olof Palme's own international commission reinforced that truth. It called for confidence-building measures between East and West and for the strengthening of the UN system. It represented proposals designed to defuse the nuclear confrontation between the superpowers: to limit strategic nuclear forces, to uphold the Anti-ballistic Missile Treaty, to maintain and progressively reduce the balance of conventional weapons, to establish a zone free of battlefield nuclear weapons in Central Europe. The members of that commission echoed the feelings of millions in their recognition that there could be victors in a nuclear war and that any military strategy based on the assumption that a nuclear war could be fought and won was inherently dangerous.

The principles of the Palme Commission are principles which the British Labour Party shares. We recognize that the provision of secure defence is a first priority for any government and that for Britain in the 1980s such an objective can only be achieved by removing nuclear weapons from our country and achieving the conventional military capacity required for our own defence and the collective defence of Western Europe through NATO.

NATO was formed 40 years ago, when Britain had a Labour government, and it was the Labour Foreign Secretary, Ernest Bevin, whose energy and drive were instrumental in creating the system of collective security based on it. Successive governments had dedicated British troops to the defence of Germany and British ships to the defence of the Eastern Atlantic. Successive Labour Party conferences have voted, by overwhelming majorities, to continue Britain's full membership of participation in NATO.

So NATO is naturally the basis for Britain's defence and security within the framework of Western Europe. We welcome its contribution to our security and we welcome our responsibility to contribute to it. To be effective, however, we believe that NATO's strategy must change in line with changes in the international political and strategic environment. That has happened before, in the early 1960s, and there is widespread understanding now that it must happen again.

I share the belief that NATO strategy today rests on increasingly untenable assumptions. Chief among these is the strategy of 'flexible response', which includes the readiness to make first use of nuclear weapons in response to a conventional attack from Eastern Europe. For all of the clever verbal footwork with which it has been defended, that is a strategy for limited nuclear war.

It arose in the 1960s from a genuine desire to prevent massive early use of nuclear weapons by introducing the possibility of a gradual escalation that could be stopped by a cry of 'enough' from an enemy. That possibility is no longer credible on either moral or military grounds. Its military capability has been erased by subsequent awareness that the electro magnetic effects of nuclear explosions would completely disrupt command control communications, and by the recognition that the deployment of sub strategic nuclear weapons in the front line is inherently unstable because of the 'use them or lose them' pressure—the requirement to fire such weapons before they become threatened by a conventional attack.

We in Western Europe have also become increasingly aware that, for us in this small and crowded continent, proximity and population make the idea of limited nuclear war a fantasy. Many have long recognized that fact. Others were awakened to it by the explosion at Chernobyl in April 1986. Its results—a miniscule fraction of the warhead power of one Polaris missile—taught all Europeans that, even if a nuclear exchange could be confined to Europe, it would be an irreversible cataclysm for the continent.

That knowledge, growing over many years, has conclusively undermined the credibility not just of flexible response but of the whole theory of nuclear deterrence. It does so for a very straightforward reason, one put as plainly as anyone by Henry Kissinger, the former US Secretary of State who said, in 1979: 'It is absurd to base the strategy of the West on the credibility of the threat of nuclear suicide.' More recently, in Septmber 1986, he asked: 'How can one go on, decade after decade, telling a democratic public that its extermination is the best guarantee of its security? It is a nonsensical proposition.'

If it is accepted that the threat of nuclear suicide is not a credible deterrent, what are the consequences in practical terms for the collective defence of Western Europe? Until now NATO's answer has been to seek ways of making nuclear weapons usable by offering further variations on the theme of limitation. Yet while their purpose has been to make nuclear deterrence more credible, the result has been to make nuclear war more likely.

These considerations have led us, in the British Labour Party, to adopt a policy of effective non-nuclear pretence with real defence. We will remove nuclear weapons from Britain and make quantitative and qualitative improvements in our conventional forces in order to fulfil our contribution to the land, sea, and air defence of Europe. That contribution to our collective security is now being undermined by the Conservative government's determination to buy the trident missile system from the USA at a cost of some $10 billion.

That is not the right choice for Britain. At a time when, as is universally acknowledged, both NATO and the Warsaw Pact have far more nuclear weapons of all kinds than anyone considers to be necessary to deter attack, it is clearly the case that any shift of weaponry from nuclear capability to conventional capability increases stability. In addition, we will work with like-minded governments within NATO for a strategy of 'no first use' of nuclear weapons and to implement measures to increase stability in Central Europe. Already we have been engaged in successful work to prepare initiatives of this kind within the Socialist International's Disarmament Advisory Council, and in discussions with other socialist parties in the NATO member countries. For example, for both NATO and the Warsaw Pact, there is an obvious logic in ensuring that the nuclear weapon arsenal that does exist is removed as far as possible from the immediate potential battle line. That is a reason for supporting the recommendations of the Palme Commission and for welcoming the agreement between the West German Social Democratic Party and the ruling party in East Germany, which would have the effect of removing nuclear weapons from a 150 km corridor either side of the border between the two Germanies. That is the kind of practical step towards disarmament that could both increase security immediately and promote further progress in general arms reduction talks.

Ultimately, of course, we would like to see the mutual dissolution of both European military alliances, a process which we recognize can only be achieved by a lengthy process of *détente* and negotiations between the Alliances to ensure against any destabilizing of the relationship between East and West in the process. In the meantime, we should take advantage of every opportunity for dialogue.

A number of opportunities already exist. Some, like the Conference on Security and Co-operation in Europe (the 'Helsinki Process'), date from the earlier period of *détente* in the 1970s. Others, like the arms control talks in Geneva, are concerned purely with military matters. A Labour government in Britain would seek to push them forward to take advantage of the new openness in the Soviet leadership under General Secretary Gorbachev, and to break through the failure to reach agreement which has bedevilled superpower negotiations in recent years.

Apart from the obvious mutual merit of such an attitude, it is also necessary to take into account the fact that, if the impetus established by Mikhail Gorbachev is to be maintained and not diverted or impeded by those elements in the Soviet Union that are not similarly motivated, it is necessary to accomplish agreements that can secure the advantages of arms reductions for the West and simultaneously demonstrate the validity of Gorbachev's approach to the Soviet Union's foreign and domestic policies. In 1986 and 1987, General Secretary Gorbachev offered, at various times, a prolonged nuclear testing moratorium, the complete withdrawal and dismantling of medium- and short-range nuclear weapons, and substantial reductions in strategic nuclear forces. His motivation may—as many reports indicate—be directly related to an awareness of the immense dangers of nuclear weapons. Or it may—as more clinical reasoning suggests—be a product of his desire to transfer the gigantic resources of technology and skill now taken by armaments into the underperforming civil Russian economy where they are desperately needed. The motivation could be a mixture of both.

The nuclear arms reduction initiatives are, in any event, audacious and, without doubt, serious. And in a system brought up on conformity and still controlled in large part by people with a vested interest in the *status quo ante*, Gorbachev's audacity carries risks even for the highest in that system. He needs therefore to have tangible evidence that his approach works. It may not be a precondition of political survival for him—the relative strengths of the forces for and against radicalism within the Soviet system can only be guessed. But there can be no real doubt that such tangible evidence of success is a precondition of the survival of his reforms and changes in internal and external policies. That consideration would not by itself justify a significant shift in Western attitudes of course—'prop up Gorbachev with some agreement' is too crude to form a basis of international strategy.

But when the realistic chance exists of clearing Europe, East and West, of medium- and short-range nuclear weapons by accepting that 'zero is the best equality' then it is not a matter of the 'swiftness of the Soviet hand deceiving the Western eye'. It is a matter of the ability of the Western Alliance to recognize the opportunity of gaining a thorough, verifiable clearance of weapons that could and, if used, would exterminate life and the means of life throughout the continent. That opportunity exists as never before. If it is not pursued it will face and not return for some time simply because such offers can only stand for so long before those making them conclude that they will be interpreted as a lack of will to maintain the 'balance' of threat. When that occurs the arms rivalry shifts up a notch and the prospect of reduction ebbs for another generation.

Increasingly as Gorbachev makes fresh offers and President Reagan and his more purposeful representatives show interest, the opinion of those who speak of their hostility to 'de-nuclearization' on the grounds that it would shatter the Alliance and send the US forces scampering home must be set against the fact that the USA acknowledges that our continent is its forward defence and the intelligence and communication facilities in Britain and elsewhere are vital to US domestic security. Such claims also deliberately understate the scale and nature of the US attachment to democratic Europe. And whilst that attitude must not breed complacency about the relationship or the degree of US commitment to Europe it should not breed cynicism about the reasons for US engagement either.

Against that background of opportunity for nuclear arms reduction and of coherence in NATO a Labour government will work with other members of the Alliance to ensure that the chances for constructive change created at Reykjavik and elsewhere are taken, and to press for progress in arms control negotiations in Vienna and Geneva.

Arms control, however, is not the only area in which dialogue and co-operation are an urgent necessity. The nuclear accident at Chernobyl demonstrated with terrible clarity the need to share research and information between nations.

The limited nature of our trade, and the lack of integration in our transport and communication networks, holds us back. The lack of understanding between our societies fuels fears and suspicions which we should not allow to go unchallenged. Even though the Soviet Union has a long way to travel before it nears the standards of plural democracy which democratic socialists consider to be fundamental, it is still essential to take the opportunities for building confidence and understanding. If we do not take the small steps along that course we will certainly never take the big ones.

In his great essay, 'We Mean Freedom', R.H. Tawney wrote:

> There is no such thing as freedom in the abstract, divorced from the realities of a specific time and place. Whatever else it may or may not imply, it involves a power of choice between alternatives—a choice which is real, not merely nominal, between alternatives which exist in fact, not only on paper. In short it means the ability to do—or refrain from doing—definite things, at a definite moment in definite circumstances, or it means nothing at all.

For millions of people and scores of nations a choice between alternatives is an unaffordable luxury. The parameters of their existence have been set by others, consciously or unconsciously. That is not true for a nation like Britain. Although our scope for choice is obviously not limitless, it is extensive. We have the right, and therefore the responsibility, of being able to choose between alternatives— whether to work for the regeneration of the international trading economy, or to turn our back on it; whether to use our financial power to help build the economies of the developing world, or to squeeze them dry; whether to lead in the improvement of the natural environment and the conservation of the earth's assets, or to abuse our and our neighbour's habitat; whether to co-operate in bringing about the speedy end of apartheid, or connive at its continued existence; whether to end dependence on nuclear weapons, or to retain the illusion of major power while denying the reality of far-reaching influence.

We have the power to choose whether to work with our global neighbours or to work against them, whether to serve only the narrow interests of one generation or to use current assets to build for the future. In the British Labour movement we choose change and co-operation. We 'confide'—as Olof Palme put it—'in the magic of human solidarity and compassion'. We do so partly from the moral obligation that goes with being socialists who believe that the privilege of strength is the power which it gives to help those who are not strong. We commit ourselves to solidarity and compassion too, because it makes material sense to combine the nations of the world in common cause against slump, insecurity, poverty, and the instability and waste that they bring.

That mixture of ethical commitment and economic sense inspired the work of Olof Palme. It survives as a source of vitality for those who follow him in all lands.

9

East–West–South Relations in the World Economy

ANDRE GUNDER FRANK

The policies and accomplishments of Olof Palme in promoting East–West relations and especially a denuclearized zone in Europe, as well as those involving North–South relations such as his participation in the Five-Continent Peace Initiative, should be examined in the context of the real world political economy, which shaped his initiatives. The post-war political economic development of the world first gave shape to the East–West and North–South *problematiques* that Olof Palme addressed along with his friend Willy Brandt, who eulogized him at his funeral. The same contradictory development, particularly of the world economy, however, also posed the real alternatives and possibilities, which Palme sought to promote through his initiatives. In particular, the development of the world economy and the new place of Europe, both West and East, within it now render Palme's European initiatives at once visionary and realistic. Economic, political, and strategic developments now make the Europeanization of Europe into the new European challenge. These same developments also demand new initiatives in European relations with the Third World South.

Unexpected post-war world economic developments and the development of the even more unexpected world economic crisis since the mid-1960s have surprisingly transformed transatlantic and trans-pacific West–West relations. Germany and Japan, first defeated in war and then allied to the USA in peace, have risen to pose formidable economic challenges to the USA. European and Eurasian East–East relations have also changed in surprising ways, first through the Sino–Soviet split and post-Mao political economic developments in China, and also through increasing Soviet economic/technological dependence on its East European allies—and their economic/techno-logical dependence on Western Europe in turn. Under these circum-stances, US and Soviet hegemony are in decline, apparent East–West differences increasingly mask real West–West and East–East conflicts,

77

and the new US Star Wars dream becomes a European nightmare. The
dreams of decolonialized North–South relations, based on the results
that were expected from political independence in some countries,
from socialism in Asia and Africa, and from industrial development in
Latin America, have also proved largely illusory. The economic/
technological dependence of these three continents' Third World
countries has been maintained, and in many cases increased, during the
course of post-war world economic development, as the present
economic and Third World debt crisis has so dramatically revealed.
Thus real world economic development has confounded the plans and
illusions of Western capitalism, Eastern socialism, and Southern
independence alike. But, at the same time, this development of the
world economy has also created the conditions which have generated
pressing need, political relevance, and hopeful realism of the initiatives
of Olof Palme and others like him.

Indeed, developments driven by world economic forces, which are
largely beyond anybody's control, lead to unexpected political ironies.
After worsening economic conditions had prompted the USA again to
put *détente* on ice and replace it with a new cold war, the *International
Herald Tribune* wrote under the title 'Reagan Sending New Signals to
Moscow':

> . . . it was ironical that President Carter, who came to office without
> any anti-Soviet bias, ran for re-election in 1980 after having virtually
> cut off all high level contacts with Moscow. Mr Reagan, known for
> his strong anti-Soviet views, will now be campaigning for re-election
> offering to put new life into most of the accords worked out by
> President Nixon during the period of *détente*.[1]

President Reagan, however, surprised even this commentator with
unexpected ironies. He went even further and on to Reykjavik to meet
Secretary Gorbachev, who was himself driven there by the economic
necessity to reduce arms expenditures and tensions. And there, the two
leaders 'nearly' agreed to eliminate both intercontinental and European
nuclear missiles. While critics at home charged that the President had
nearly given the whole shop, his Secretary of State rushed across the
Atlantic to assure Europeans that their defence does not require US
missiles in Europe anyway—and some Europeans complained that the
unreliable North Americans had nearly abandoned them to their
European fate.

Introduction to the World Economy

The world economy is a fact of life. Its influence on international relations, domestic policy and individual behaviour is inescapable. The socialist economies of the East, including that of the Soviet Union, have failed to escape from the exigencies of world economic development through planning, as they sought. The Third World South, all its nationalism notwithstanding, is more dependent than ever on its participation in the world economy. The industrial economies of the West, including the strongest, those of the USA and Japan, have lost whatever autonomy they had in the face of the forces unleashed by the operation of the world economy, whose long-term development and short-term cyclical fluctuations are beyond anyone's control. Most economic and political policy, and many cultural attitudes and ideological positions are but ineffectual responses to world economic events. What is more, most policy-makers delude themselves and others into thinking that their actions are the causes of events, when in reality they are but the effects, whose consequences in turn are largely unintended. Like Frankenstein's monster, the world economy may have been created by man; but it is no longer subject to his, let alone woman's, control.

The world economy is composed of its constituent producer, consumer, trader, financial, national, regional, local, sectoral, enterprise, and individual parts; but like the proverbial whole, it is more than the sum of its parts. Any of its parts may be affected by others and by what is going on in the whole. To understand what is going on—and to be able to intervene intelligently—it is essential not to lose sight of the forest for looking at the trees. For the forest has a life of its own—growth, evolution, decay—beyond that of its constituent trees. Moreover, the development of the forest—through the interaction of the individual trees with each other and with the forest as well as with their physical environment—determines more in the life of each tree than its life cycle affects the whole forest.

In the world economy, even more than in a forest, what happens in one part can affect many others, even on the other side of the globe, through multifarious connections of market offer and production supply, consumption and investment demand, price-making and -taking, increased outputs in and outputs from, or improved productivity by the world sausage machine, as well as financial speculation, political intervention, military force, psychological reactions, etc. The interaction of all of these put together seems to generate a life/development of the world economy, which manifests itself through apparently autonomous economic and political fluctuations—including cycles of expansion and contraction, crisis and recovery. Also manifest are apparently persistent inequalities—regional, sectoral, class—despite, or perhaps because of, the particular life and product cycles of its constituent parts.

The development of this world market economy has worked both wonders of riches and horrors of deprivation. Policy intervention more often than not has reinforced already existing market tendencies instead of—as sometimes supposedly intended—counteracting them (Reagan and Thatcher increased budget deficits and the share of government expenditures in GNP instead of reducing them as they intended). Moreover, this development of the world economy produces sometimes ironic anomalies in or among some of its constituent parts.

The following pages will review how the underlying historical development of the world economy has influenced international political relations and domestic economic policy since the end of the Second World War. In particular, we will examine how East–West and North–South relations have changed, often contrary to political intentions, largely in response to unintended and unanticipated developments in the world economy.

East–West vs, West–West and East–East Relations

World economic development over the past four decades has substantially unsettled post-war institutional arrangements, policy expectations, and international relations. East–West relations have become much closer in Europe, as they have between the USA and China. West–West relations have become much more competitive and tense, such as between the USA and Europe and Japan; and East–East relations have been substantially transformed between the Soviet Union, Eastern Europe, and China. North–South relations have also undergone important changes in the course of world economic development.

The Second World War started in Central Europe, as did the First World War and several wars before that. It seems unlikely, however, that another war will start there, despite post-war political blocs and the military build-up in Europe. France and Germany were traditional enemies in Europe through three major wars in the last century, but have become secure, if not entirely trusting, allies. Ex-Chancellor Helmut Schmidt of West Germany has proposed the unification of their conventional armed forces, and President Mitterand of France has broached the subject of a French nuclear defence of West Germany. However, the thought of any reunification of West and East Germany still generates fears in France and in quite a few other places in Europe.

Yet another war might start in Europe about European issues. More plausibly, such a war might start somewhere in the Third World and escalate into another European and world war. The main reason for this scenario is the development of economic relations within Western Europe and between Western and Eastern Europe as parts of the process of world economic development since the last war.

At the end of the Second World War, Central Europe was intentionally transformed by the Soviet Union into a political buffer zone under its control. This zone was to keep Western influences out of the Soviet Union and to protect it from another military threat. What used to be called Central Europe came to be called Eastern Europe, east of the Elbe, which already was the traditional dividing line between Western and Central Europe in the fifteenth and sixteenth centuries.

Many Soviet intentions in Europe were negated by economic events. World economic developments and East European economic needs have converted this ex-buffer zone into a transmission belt of economic, political, social, ideological, and other relations between the West and the East. Eastern Europe increasingly has a position or role of intermediary between West and East, especially between Western Europe and the Soviet Union. For instance, Eastern Europe and especially East Germany imports advanced technology from the West and uses it to produce industrial products, some of which it exports in turn to the Soviet Union to meet its increasing needs for the same. That is just the opposite of what Eastern Europe was designed to do.

The Soviet Union intended to be dominant in Eastern Europe for a long time. It is still often thought that the Soviet Union is hostile to any change in Eastern Europe that initiates economic, political, ideological, and social changes—Poland is a recent example observed by all. Increasingly, however, circumstances beyond its control, especially economic developments, oblige the Soviet Union to accept these changes; and eventually they will oblige the Soviet Union itself to change as a result, if the examination below of the limitations of socialist planning and the reintegration of the socialist countries into the world economy are any indication.

The Soviet Union's Warsaw Pact military and COMECON economic allies are supposedly under the Soviet thumb on the one hand and supposedly surrounded by friendly allies on the other. Yet the Soviet Union is increasingly using its military power to blackmail its Eastern European allies to extend political and in some cases economic concessions to the Soviet Union, on pain of losing Soviet military protection; or else being invaded by Soviet military forces as in Hungary and Czechoslovakia or as threatened in Poland. The two statements are not contradictory: change is initiated in the economically richer and socially more open Eastern Europe, and the Soviet Union tries to limit that change through blackmail; but its power to blackmail is increasingly limited by world, East European, and Soviet economic developments and especially by Eastern European economic progress and Soviet economic needs.

The Eastern European socialist countries increased their economic integration into the world capitalist market during the 1970s. This was intended as a way out of their internal economic difficulties and to take advantage of the changes in the international division of labour, such as world-wide sourcing and relocation of manufacturing to lower cost producers in the 1970s. But this economic integration and this increasing reliance on the market—first and foremost in Hungary, now also increasingly in Poland and elsewhere in Eastern Europe, recently most spectacularly in China, but also in Vietnam and Cuba, and forseeably in the Soviet Union—far from being a simple solution of their old problems, becomes itself a major source of their new problems, for instance in Poland, as we will observe below.

In the Second World War, the Soviet Union and the USA were allies, perhaps allies of convenience, against Nazi Germany. The allies have become major enemies, perhaps also enemies of convenience. The USA claims with considerable correctness that the Soviet Union is economically very weak relative to the USA so does not pose an economic threat or constitute economic competition. The Soviet Union also is not, or is increasingly less, an ideological threat and offers little ideological competition. Even its political challenge is relatively limited. So the Soviet Union requires military might, not only for its defence but because it provides its only basis for any political influence in the world.

The USA formed an alliance with the Europeans after the war, and its enemy, Germany, became the main ally in Europe. On the other side of the world, the same happened with Japan. But also increasingly, the relationship between the USA and its allies in Western Europe is analogous to that of the Soviet Union and its allies in Eastern Europe: although the USA remains economically and politically more powerful than the Europeans, its relative economic and political power has been declining. So the USA, not so unlike the Soviet Union, relies increasingly on its military power, and particularly on its so-called nuclear umbrella, to blackmail its Western European allies to extract economic and political concessions from them as the Europeans become increasingly independent. World and European economic development, however, is increasing the conflict of interest between each nuclear superpower and its respective European allies, whose commonality of interests is growing in turn. The world economic crisis has furthered Western European needs for Eastern European markets and the latter's need for Western European technology and capital. USA–Japan–West European rivalries and competition are exerting further pressure for the Europeanization of Europe, and the loss of Western European markets to its competitors and the net recession are likely to drive Western and Eastern Europeans towards greater economic and political co-operation.[2]

To a significant degree, the Soviet–US conflict or the East–West conflict, of which the Soviet–US conflict is the main one, is also a conflict of convenience for both superpowers in that it provides each with a cover: a cover for intrasocialist East–East conflicts for the Soviet Union, and for the West–West conflicts across the Atlantic Alliance for the USA. It also helps them—indeed they need it—to exert pressure on and to blackmail their respective allies. In that sense, to put it in extreme form, the best enemies are in a sense each other's best friends. They need each other's enmity to deal with their own friendly allies. The Soviet bogeyman is also used in the USA and inside the West for internal political purposes. In the same way, the imperialist bogeyman is used in the East for a whole series of political, economic, and other domestic purposes.

The USA became dominant or hegemonic after the Second World War, and its German and Japanese enemies have become the main pillars of the Atlantic and Pacific Alliances. At the same time they have also become the principal economic competitors of the USA. It was some years ago already that West Germany displaced the USA as the principal exporter in the world, and the growing Japanese challenge to the USA is well known. In 1960 the USA accounted for 18 per cent of world exports and 12 per cent of world imports. By 1970–75 both had become roughly balanced at 13–14 per cent. But by 1985 the 1960 proportions had become reversed, with the USA accounting for 18 per cent of the world's imports but only 11 per cent of the world's exports. The USA share of world manufacturing had declined significantly, and it had been outpaced as a manufactures' exporter by Germany and Japan, who had much higher growth rates of manufacturing output and productivity than the USA.

This is a reflection of the fact that the so-called US century, *pax Americana*, lasted only a quarter of a century. A century ago Britannia ruled the waves under *pax Britannia*. How long she did so is subject to interpretation, but the really top-dog position of Britain was during the long economic expansion between 1850 and 1873. Britain's power began to decline relatively during the 1873–95 economic crisis: and during the crisis of half a century ago, the 1930s, Britain's power declined absolutely and was replaced by the USA. This was to be the beginning of the US century, but the US century also lasted less than a quarter of a century. The decline of US hegemony had already started by 1967. Politically, it was manifested by the Tet Offensive in 1968 in Vietnam and ultimately the loss of the Vietnam war. Economically, the relative US decline was expressed by the rise of Western Europe and Japan as economic competitors and challengers.

Moreover, there is an important connection between these two. The war in Vietnam and the expenditures that it involved benefited the US economy in some ways in the short run, but eventually they became prejudicial to the US economy and its place in the world economy. First the deficit expenditure of so many new dollars undercut their value and forced the USA to devalue the dollar after cutting it loose from gold in 1971. In 1973 the dollar was also de-pegged from the European and Japanese currencies, so that the post-war Bretton Woods monetary and US financial dominance unravelled.

Another way that US military expenditures have been partly beneficial but substantially prejudicial to the USA is that while the USA spent a high proportion of its GNP on military hardware the Europeans and the Japanese did not, investing instead in civilian technology and thereby beginning to out-compete the USA. All through the 1960s the rate of growth of productivity in Europe was nearly twice that of the USA, and in Japan nearly twice that of Europe, that is to say, nearly four times that of the USA. Then rates of productivity growth declined everywhere from average annual rates of 3 per cent in the decade before 1973 to 1 per cent in the decade after. But the growth of productivity declined faster in the USA than in Japan and Europe (and even turned negative for some years), so that the overall gap in productivity growth rates continued or increased. However, in the last few years Europe has lagged far behind the USA and Japan in some high-technology fields. Moreover, productivity has grown at the expense of jobs, and Europe's inability to match the USA in creating jobs, even though many are in MacDonald-and 7-Eleven-type low-wage services, has been termed 'Eurosclerosis'. It remains to be seen whether the US Strategic Defence Initiative (Star Wars) programme or its European Eureka and possible European Defense Initiative rivals can significantly intervene in this race of productivity, technology, and competition on the world market. None the less, it seems unlikely that competitiveness in civilian technology and productivity can be furthered better and cheaper through spin-offs from military R & D than promoting it directly as MITI does in Japan and Eureka might in Europe.

The USA is now pressing both the Europeans and particularly the Japanese to spend more on armaments—i.e. US armaments. The US NATO commander General Bernard Rogers' air–land battle plan of relying more on conventional weapons and less on nuclear ones in Europe is first and foremost a proposition that the Europeans buy US conventional weapons which are much more expensive than nuclear ones. The USA wants the Japanese to spend more money on arms and less on technology, with which they are increasingly out-competing the USA. Ironically the USA is attempting to persuade Japan to change its US-imposed constitution, which prohibits nuclear arms and an army with offensive capabilities. If the USA succeeds then the Japanese will also spend more money on their own arms development, enabling them to compete on the world and US arms markets. In this the Japanese will be able to escape the blackmail of US nuclear supremacy. So here too the USA is damned if it does and damned if it doesn't. At the same time West Germany is able to use the US threat to the Soviet Union in Europe to improve its bargaining position on East–West trade and in turn use the Soviet Union to negotiate with the USA from a position of greater strength.

With regard to China, while on the one hand there is something of a political Washington–Tokyo–Beijing axis, on the other hand, economically, the Japanese and the USA are competing with each other for the Chinese market. It is not accidental that even Taiwan lobbyist Reagan went to Beijing and signed a major deal for the sale of nuclear reactors. While not a single nuclear reactor has been sold in the USA and hardly any elsewhere in the West in the last ten years, China, Eastern Europe, and to some extent the Third World, have become an attractive market in this regard.

What seemed unthinkable a generation ago has become the norm: the two major socialist states in the world are each other's principal enemies and one of them is an effective ally of the USA. Not so many years ago, the principal danger of war came not from intra capitalist hostilities but from intra socialist war between the Soviet Union and China. Then intra socialist war took place, in the form of the Chinese invasion of Vietnam and the Vietnamese invasion of Cambodia.

The real place and role of the socialist economies of the East in these developments has turned out rather differently from their spokesmen's theoretical hopes and ideological claims. Just before he died Stalin claimed in *The Economic Problems of Socialism* that by then there were two separate and different economic and social systems in the world, one capitalist and the other socialist. His successor, Khrushchev, belied part of this claim by inciting the Sino–Soviet split in the socialist 'system', and he introduced 'goulash Communism' in the Soviet Union with the promise to 'overtake and bury the USA' economically by 1980. The Soviet Union introduced timid economic reforms in the mid-1960s, and some of its Eastern European allies, especially Hungary, introduced bold reforms in economic organization and policy. But the hallmark of the latter was the increased role of market prices and increasing integration in the world market, including the progressive introduction of world market prices in the domestic economies of Eastern Europe, especially for trade among each other. The afore-mentioned massive import of Western technology followed in the 1970s. None of these industrial policies or central economic planning in the 'command' economies of Eastern Europe and the Soviet Union have produced all of the intended results, and some have had quite a few unintended ones.

Since the mid-1960s the rate of economic growth has declined from each five-year-plan period to the next (except for the forward jump in Poland from 1971 to 1975, which had the severest negative consequences a few years later). Plans have been underfulfilled in practice year after year, especially in the Soviet Union, and planned growth targets have been lowered for the subsequent year and missed again, until the 1982 target was the lowest since Stalin started planning in 1928. In the early 1980s, economic growth slowed down to zero in the Soviet Union, and became negative in 1981 and/or 1982 in Czechoslovakia, Hungary, and Poland. Poland's national income declined by one-quarter through negative 'growth' rates of 2 per cent in 1979, 4 per cent in 1980, 14 per cent in 1981, and 12 per cent in 1982. In the face of this experience, it can hardly be claimed that central planning is a sure-fire method to formulate and implement economic policy, and still less so in the face of the world economic crisis.

It turned out that 'independent' polices of 'planned' goulash Communism required the import of Western technology to ease the transition from extensive growth (stuffing more raw meat into the goulash sausage machine) to intensive growth (improving the productivity of the machine) in order to be able to produce and afford more goulash. Moreover, the import of this technology—and the imported technology itself—made the socialist East increasingly dependent—not only technologically, but financially, economically, politically, socially, ideologically, and culturally—on the capitalist West. The world capitalist economic crisis then exacerbated this dependence or its manifestations in the East. Western inflation and other manifestations of the crisis were imported wholesale. The socialist economist Koves ironically points out in italic emphasis that 'the share of trade with the West grew in general also in the total trade of CMEA [COMECON] countries. . . . The objective process of development demands that economic policy should give preference to export orientation at the expense of import substitution' and 'in other words, opening towards the world economy was put on each CMEA country's agenda by the requirements of domestic social and economic development.'[3]

The requirement of this increased international participation is the strongest and has the most far-reaching domestic consequences precisely in the field in which the socialist economies were supposed to offer the most independent alternative and the strongest development policy, that is, in technology. But, as it turns out, technological development is a sub product of world economic development and the long cyclical process of capital accumulation on a world scale. Far from having escaped from this process through socialist planning, the socialist economies of the East ironically turn out to be integral parts of this world economic development. Moreover, although they have pulled ahead of many Third World countries, the advanced socialist economies ·still remain dependent on and increasingly behind the most technologically advanced sectors of the capitalist world economy. Far from burying the USA in 1980, the Soviet Union has lagged further behind and is being bested by Japan.

Certainly the socialist countries no longer pursue any active policies to help or even applaud the erstwhile prospect of capitalism burying itself in the ashes of its own crisis and then being succeeded by socialism. Soviet Premier Chernenko, addressing a commission charged with drafting the Communist programme to be presented to the next Party congress, proposed that Krushchev's 1961 prediction of the impending triumph of Communism over capitalism should be eliminated from the programme, since capitalism 'still possesses quite substantial and far from exhausted reserves for development'.[4] Although Chernenko maintained his faith in the ultimate victory of Communism over capitalism, his and his predecessors' and colleagues' practice in other socialist countries in the meantime was to pray for and advocate the recuperation of capitalism from its present crisis. In the words of Chernenko's predecessor, Leonid Brezhnev, 'because of the broad economic links between capitalist and socialist countries, the ill effects of the current crisis in the West have also had an impact on the socialist world', and, in the words of his colleague 'Todor Zhivko the president of Bulgaria, 'It may be hoped that the crisis which is raging in the West may come to a rapid end, since it affects and creates uncertainties for the Bulgarian economy.'

Thus the leaders of the socialist 'alternative' to capitalism are waiting for the crisis of capitalism to end as soon as possible, so they can get back to business as usual.

This business involves not only far-reaching economic reforms in Eastern Europe and in the Soviet Union, as the new Soviet leader Gorbachev appreciates and promotes. The desire, indeed need, for business as usual in the socialist East also requires the expansion of the East–West (European) trade and productive collaboration as well as progressive Soviet integration in the world market both directly and through Eastern Europe. The Deputy Director of the Institute of World

Economy in Moscow, Ivan Ivanov, observes that exports already contribute about 10 per cent of the Soviet product (which he notes is about the same as the USA), but they are concentrated in primary commodities, especially oil and gas. Soviet plans call for replacing or supplementing these by machinery exports. But these in turn require increased imports of industrial equipment and technology from the West and from Eastern Europe, or from the former via the latter. The Soviet Union is increasingly dependent on its East European allies as a transmission belt (rather the opposite of a *cordon sanitaire*) for Western technology. The need for peaceful *détente*, especially in Europe, is evident.

The World Economic Crisis

The preponderant role of uncontrolled and unintended world economic development has become spectacularly manifest by the onset of another world economic crisis since the mid-1960s, which has influenced if not determined all economic events and policies since then. The crowning irony is the world economic crisis itself. Not only was it unintended and unpredicted, but it has been declared impossible.

Keynesian gurus in the West, led by Economics Nobel Prize laureate Paul Samuelson (who is also author of the world's most widely adopted introductory economics text, with a dozen reprints of several million copies and numerous translations) declared in the early 1970s that another depression was impossible. He was echoed by political leaders such as US President Gerald Ford, who said in 1970, 'there'll never be another depression.' We now know that the present world economic crisis had already started with the long cyclical decline in the rate of profit, which began in 1967, and the recession of that year. But hardly anybody recognized and still less understood what was going on. Especially ironical is that the Marxists in the socialist countries of the East were also caught unawares by the development of this capitalist world economic crisis. All of these countries, from Eastern Europe and the Soviet Union to China and North Korea, decided in 1971–72 substantially to increase their imports of Western technology (perhaps, also ironically, because its price had declined with the crisis-occasioned devaluation of the dollar by President Nixon in August 1971). These socialist countries made two important miscalculations, both of which are related to the development of the world economic crisis: they thought they could use the imported technology to produce industrial goods for export in order to pay for it, and they thought they could sell enough on the Western markets to pay off their debts. As it turned out the crisis in the West prohibited the second, and its repercussions in the East prevented the first. The irony is that the Marxists in the socialist countries were banking on the continued prosperity of the capitalist economies just as much as the capitalists themselves and just at the time that the continuation of this prosperity was about to end in 1973. Moreover, neither in the West nor in the East did any establishment economists or economic policy-makers seem to see that the 1973–75 recession was one in a series of world economic crises that would structurally transform the world economy. Instead they wrongly—as we will observe below—attributed this recession to the 'external' oil-shock increase in the price of petroleum, which the socialists in the East then copied from OPEC. If anybody in a policy-making position understood, or at least sensed, the ongoing transformation of the world economy, it was those businesses and the governments in the newly industrializing countries (NICs) of the Third World who sought to take economic advantage of this transformation to relocate some industry and to promote non-traditional manufacturing and other exports from some NICs in the South and socialist countries in the East to the world market. The most successful and best known of these is the export-led growth of the so-called four tigers of South Korea, Taiwan, Hong Kong, and Singapore. Among the socialist countries, Hungary more successfully, and Poland and Rumania less successfully, have also adopted similar policies, albeit under the label import-led growth, which comes to much the same thing, since the latter must export to import while the former must import to export.

Thus the NICs and OPEC countries in the Third World, and the socialist countries in the East, substantially increased their manufacturing imports from the Western industrial economies, for whom they provided a sort of safety net to lessen the decline of their economies during the economic crisis. These economies in the South and East became increasingly important markets for Western exports (the South's share increased from 30 to 40 per cent in the 1970s) that could not be sold at home. This was particularly the case for the export of capital goods, for which there was a reduced market in the West, while investment declined there because of the economic crisis, which was first manifested in the decline of the rate of profit and the increase in unutilized productive capacity.

The continued development of the world economic crisis in the West, East and South, then, poses three alternative scenarios, especially for Europe and its relations with other parts of the world. These are muddling-through business as usual, Star Wars militarization of the economy, and political economic bloc formation. The first scenario of continuing business as usual by muddling through the near future is made highly unlikely by the development of the world economic crisis itself. This crisis, which began in the mid-1960s, has already gone through four recessions: 1967, 1969–70, 1973–75, and 1979–82. Each of these recessions was longer, deeper, and more completely worldwide than the preceding one; and, following each of these recessions, each cyclical recovery has been weaker than the last. The recovery since 1983, moreover, has already required excessive reliance on the ordinary monetary and fiscal policies, such as growing debt finance and budget deficits normally used to muddle through a recession, so that they will scarcely be available adequately to muddle through the next recession. This coming recession (which may have already begun with the declines of growth rates in 1986) therefore threatens to be far more severe again and may well turn into a fully fledged depression of the 1930s-type in the West and possibly in the East, as it already has in much of the debt-crisis South. (The recent and prospective development of the world economic crisis is detailed in Frank 1986.[5]

The second alternative scenario would be the renewed reinforcement of already weakened NATO and Warsaw Pact alliances based on the sharply increased militarization of their economies along Star Wars lines. The USA and the Soviet Union would seek to maintain their waning positions of bipolar hegemony and to respond to the accentuated economic and political crisis by trying to oblige their respective alliance partners to follow their respective dictates. But these policies would have to rest on a Star Wars militarization of the economy, which would sacrifice the civilian economies of their alliance partners as well as their own to their own accelerated military programme. Therefore the economic and political costs of the Star Wars alternative, including increased political repression at home and abroad, would be enormous. Indeed the costs would be so high as to make it realistic to hope that this Star Wars alternative will be rejected, especially through the intervention of Social Democratic parties in Western Europe.

The third alternative scenario is some kind of European policy, including one that might lead towards the formation of an East–West European bloc with privileged ties with the Middle East and Africa. Such a European neo-mercantilist policy and possible bloc formation would be in the context of analogous economic crisis-driven tendencies in the Americas (Kissinger speaks of a possible hemispheric bloc) and in the Far East, under US and Japanese leadership respectively. Moreover, Europe would be disadvantaged by US and Japanese pursuit of their Pacific Rim or Basin strategy. Such seemingly unthinkable scenarios are not as far-fetched as they might seem if we consider the already existing and ever growing economic and political conflicts between the USA and its European and Japanese allies.[6]

The USA has been pressuring Germany and Japan to adopt more

expansive monetary and fiscal policies and to increase their defence expenditures. So far they have resisted. They argue that the effects would be domestically inflationary. They would lose markets to others at home and abroad (as French reflation did at the beginning of the Mitterand Presidency). They also point out that their economies are too small to serve as locomotives for the world economy, as the USA does and is asking them to do. But Europe and Japan might reconsider this option in the face of another recession and the loss of significant sales in the USA, reduced market demand, a probable decline in the dollar and a rise in their own currencies, possible US protectionism, and other US economic policies in the deflation and inflation scenarios. Upgrading their currencies would be of interest if it increases their relative autonomy in a more neo-mercantilist world. Would Europe and Japan be willing and able to co-ordinate their economic policies with those of the USA for the common good, which the USA has always interpreted from a US point of view? Would the Europeans and the Japanese be willing and able to reflate to save the world economy? Or would they prefer to or have to reflate and try to use their upgraded currencies nationally or regionally, where the costs and benefits are more subject to the accountability of those who have the responsibility for any economic and political decisions? If the Europeans and Japanese withdrew some of their capital from the USA or even ceased to supply any more, where would they put it and how? It might be desirable for the Japanese to withdraw their capital from the rich USA and to use it instead to relieve the debt crisis, not to mention the poverty in the Third World. But is that likely and if so, would they not require in return greater export markets there in competition with the USA and Europe, and the socialist countries? It would be at least as plausible to suppose that Europe and Japan would try to reflate and invest domestically or regionally.

Indeed, Japan may be obliged to do so to the extent to which it is excluded from the export markets on which it now depends. Such exclusion of Japan could be the result of recession elsewhere and especially in the USA; a rise in the value of the yen as the dollar and perhaps other currencies decline; the flight of Japanese capital from overseas and especially from US markets; and the growth of protectionism and anti-Japanese measures elsewhere as the USA and Europe try to redirect Japanese exports to or against each other. Moreover, a combination of all of the above is a real possibility in the next recession. Japan, especially, could devote its large savings and capital surplus no longer to finance consumption and speculation in the USA but instead to update its own lagging social and residential infrastructure through a New Deal type domestic construction programme: and/or it could substantially increase its capital export to China, perhaps Siberia. If the immediate political obstacles could be overcome, a triangular arrangement to develop Siberian natural resources with Japanese capital/technology and Chinese labour would offer many economic advantages to all three national partners (and would open up new strategic options in Asia). European reflation would have to address the major and still growing European problem of unemployment, which would be immediately exacerbated by recession and either the deflationary or the inflationary scenarios and accompanying policy in the USA. Since the world market export option would no longer be immediately available, national and/or regional options could become the order of the day. All strictly national options in the (by world standards) now relatively small and highly integrated West European economies would entail additional large sacrifices of income in the short run and of competitiveness in the long run.

A West European reflationary strategy has already been proposed by Europeans themselves. The more right-wing proposal envisages a fortress Europe, which would use the existing EEC as a base and seek to include other West European countries in a common expansionary economic programme. A related military–industrial complex and strategic component of the fortress Europe strategy could be a European arms and military strategy centred on a Franco–German axis. A more left-wing alternative to 'reflate, restructure, and redistribute' was proposed by parliamentarians and economists from a dozen West European social democratic parties under the leadership of the British Labour MP Stuart Holland and published under the title *Out of Crisis*. A third alternative would extend a European economic programme to include both Western and Eastern Europe (with some possible extensions to the Middle East and Africa). Such East–West European economic co-operation and confidence building could also increase the basis for a denuclearized Europe, or at least for the nuclear-free zone in Europe, which the Palme Commission proposed. A policy to extend *détente* into a Pan-European *détente* has also been proposed by the present author in *The European Challenge*.[7] It seeks to take advantage of West Europe's interests in exporting capital and technology and East Europe's interest in importing the same. Any Western European loss of markets in the USA and Japan, which would accompany a recessionary decline of domestic markets, could substantially increase Western European interests in markets elsewhere in Europe. (A conceivable partial solution to the Eastern European's foreign exchange problem could be an extension of the already incipient triangular trade arrangement under which Western Europe would export technology to Eastern Europe, which the latter use to produce cheaper manufactures for export to the Soviet Union, which could in turn pay for both by exports of oil and gas to Western Europe.) Progress in this direction towards greater East–West European economic co-operation and political *détente* could also be encouraged by the widespread popular objections to the new US missiles in Western Europe—their rejection by the British Labour Party, the West German Social Democratic Party, and the European political parties—as well as by Gorbachev's attempt to delink European-based nuclear arsenals from US-based ones by offering to remove Soviet nuclear missiles from Europe in return for a French and British agreement not to increase theirs. To summarize the European-ization of Europe: European economic/ecological co-operation is preferable to military competition and should lead towards the Yugo–Finlandization of Eastern Europe and the Austro–Swedishization of Western Europe.

East–West vs. North–South relations

The course of world economic development and the development of the world economic crisis not surprisingly have also been far more determinant of economic—and political—events in the Third World than any wilful domestic economic policies, including even the repressive political policies of right-wing regimes such as that of Pinochet in Chile or of Marcos in the Philippines. The world economic crisis has also undercut most of the economic and social advances of progressive regimes such as Nyerere's in Tanzania, which sought to be more self-reliant. The crisis has also completely undermined the demand for a New International Economic Order (NIEO), which the Third World countries and the Non-Aligned Movement (NAM) launched for themselves at the UN and elsewhere in 1974.

Before the world economic crisis of the 1970s, the Third World version of Keynesianism was import substitution to produce at home for the internal market what used to be imported from the West. This policy was replaced by monetarism—Milton Friedman became the high priest of economic policy in Chile, Argentina, Uruguay, Peru, Israel, and other countries. This monetarist policy, plus supply-side economics in the form of export promotion, or export-led growth by reducing production costs and working for the world market, was supposed to solve all problems. The so-called economic miracles, this policy, the theory behind it, all fell through in the early 1980s. Economic and political crises shook Israel, Chile, Argentina and others.

This policy of trying to ride the stream and to integrate in the world

economy as much as possible through export promotion has now
brought the full weight of the world economic crisis to bear on one
Third World country after another. National income declined in 16 out
of 20 Latin American countries between 1981 and 1983. These
declines varied from 5 per cent in some countries to 10–15 per cent in
others and 20 per cent and more in some, to make an average of a
10 per cent decline for the continent as a whole. Some form of new
industrial policy combined with nationalist populist political stances is
the likely next step there as well.[8,9]

The apparent success of the gang of four tigers (South Korea,
Taiwan, Hong Kong, and Singapore) through export-led growth is not
readily extendible to the rest of the Third World, as the highly touted
'model' contends. Singapore has already faced a crisis during the
present world economic recovery, and others may face difficulties in
the next recession. China is attempting to emulate them; if it succeeds
in penetrating the world market—the linkages to the domestic one—it
would offer formidable competition for everyone else. Imagine all or
even much of China attempting to promote exports in the same way as
Hong Kong. Other competitors could be driven out of business before
the world market is economically able and politically willing to absorb
an avalanche of cheap Chinese exports.

On the other hand, it may be noted (as observed by the Soviet
Union's director of UNCTAD's division on East–West/South trade
among others) that the capitalist East Asian NICs have been out-
competing the socialist East European NICs on the world market for
industrial exports. Whether the new economic reforms in China will
permit it to do the same remains to be seen. The major foreign
exchange and domestic development problems of the Third World will
also be immediately affected by the next recession: the chronic foreign
exchange problems are likely to reach new crisis proportions as Third
World exports, export prices, and terms of trade decline further, and
interest rates and debt-service charges possibly increase. Further drastic
declines in imports, investment, production, income, and consumption
are likely to ensue. The Third World debt bomb may explode.[10,11]
More economically nationalist and politically populist stances are
likely. As import capacity declines further, and particularly if the world
financial system and international trade relations experience greater
difficulties, many parts of the Third World are likely to opt for greater
reliance on the internal market and import substitution, as well as on
more producer/consumer-oriented agriculture on a regional or national
basis. So-called countertrade barter arrangements are likely to flourish
as emergency measures to maintain international trade. All of these
trends are already in evidence in many parts of the Third World, and
especially in Latin America, as a response to the economic and debt

crisis of the first-half of the 1980s. What national and regional arrangements will emerge in various parts of the Third World in the second-half of the 1980s will also depend on the trade and bloc policies of the industrial countries.

These observations raise further serious questions about North–South and East–West relations and about the apparent and real relationships between these two groups. In particular, it seems necessary to re-examine more objectively how real the options are: either to build an NIEO, and especially one based on alternative 'socialist' North–South relations with the help of COMECON: or, failing that, to delink from the old international economic order and establish socialist relations on national or regional levels, or at least to pursue socialist-oriented development (which is the new Soviet terminology for what they used to call non-capitalist development).

Any objective analysis soon reveals that North–South relations and Third World development have turned out to be far more the consequences of the cyclical course of world economic development, and subject to its limitations, than of intentional political choice. Even the 14 supposed Third World revolutions in the decade after 1974 have in reality done far less than their protagonists proposed, their supporters claimed, and their opponents feared. Despite the entrenchment of ideology in some capitals of the North and the South, in reality ideology in the Third World has made far-reaching concessions to economic expediency.

The European and Japanese colonialism of the pre-war era was largely displaced by what some call US neo-colonialism or (neo-) imperialism. The USA held that colonialism was detrimental and that everybody should open their markets to anybody. Free trade was a particularly attractive proposition for the USA at the time, when they were industrially dominant and could thereby penetrate the Third World markets of the old colonial powers. Britain had also been a free trader in the mid-nineteenth century when it was the industrial topdog. But now the Europeans and the Japanese have become the principal challengers to the USA in the previously US-dominated neo-colonial Third World.

The last depression and the last war set the stage for substantial decolonization in the world. However, decolonization did not everywhere lead to the liberation that was anticipated, but led instead to neo-colonialism in many parts of the Third World. National liberation became an important movement against colonialism in the colonial regions, and it continued, and in some cases grew, in neo-colonial regions like Latin America, where national liberation continues to be an important political policy and movement. This is because bitter experience has taught that accession to formal political

independence is not the same as achieving real economic independence
from the world economy. But does the capture of state power by
another class or coalition open the way to real political independence
and economic development through national liberation and socialism
or, at least, through socialist orientation?

Both Washington and Moscow can count 14 different countries in
the Third World that in the 10 years after 1974 have become either
socialist or what the Soviet Union calls 'socialist-orientated', or, as the
USA claims, have fallen 'under Soviet domination'. The Soviet Union
thinks this process must be supported and promoted; the USA wants to
contain it and, under Reagan, roll it back. The Kissinger Commission
report on Central America makes it clear that the issue in Central
America in the eyes of the Reagan administration is not North–South,
nor internal responses to internal problems, but an East–West
problem. There are very few who agree with that point of view, which
seems at odds with all the evidence. Both the Soviet Union and the USA
believe that national liberation movements (in the eyes of the USA,
'totalitarianism') are advancing. This is belied by facts. The 14 cases
are well known: socialist Vietnam, Laos, and Kampuchea in Indochina; the ex-Portuguese colonies, Angola, Mozambique, Guinea-
Bissau, Cape Verde, and Sao Tome; Zimbabwe and Ethiopia; in West
Asia, South Yemen, Iran, and Afghanistan; and in the Caribbean and
Central America, Nicaragua and, formerly, Grenada. But, first of all,
the ones that have become socialist are not very many and their
socialism has been, all things considered, a bit disappointing, both to
the people and their leadership there and to many elsewhere who
supported the national liberation struggles, especially the very heroic
struggle in Vietnam. Second, the countries the Soviets call socialist-
oriented, those that are not yet socialist but supposedly on the road to
it, are not travelling very far or very fast along that road. None of them
have severed their economic and political relations with the West or
even tried to do so, and those that went a little way along that road in
the mid-1970s backtracked in the early 1980s. A supreme example is
Mozambique, which under very severe pressures—economic, political,
military, and drought-related—signed a pact with South Africa. Most
of Angola's oil, its main export, and its diamonds and coffee, etc., are
exported to the West, and there has been no real attempt to cut these
ties.

In Zimbabwe, which was also decolonized through protracted
guerrilla struggle, progress toward socialism or even away from
dependence on the West, or indeed on South Africa, has not been any
greater. So all of these regimes are well on the road to neo-colonialism
on the Kenyan or Ivory Coast models, though probably without the
relative successes of these countries prior to their present crises. In each

case, world economic realities have frustrated national political illusions. So, to begin with, these 14 revolutions are not all that they are claimed to be either by Moscow or by Washington. Nor is there mention of what has happened on the other side of the balance: first and foremost the Sino–Soviet split, and then the de-Maoization of China. Second, Egypt, third, Somalia, changed sides.

Particularly revealing in this regard is the experience of Cuba and Fidel Castro's recent observations about revolutionary social change. He noted that the widely acclaimed Cuban welfare state, and especially the maintenace of its social services during periods of world economic recession, were only possible with the generosity of Soviet aid. Henceforth the same level of social services could not be maintained, and Cuban economic policy had to be changed radically. From then on the first order of priority would have to be export promotion to hard currency (capitalist) areas. The next priority would be export promotion to socialist countries. The third priority would have to be import-substituting production to save both hard and soft foreign exchange. The last priority would be to save the minimum necessary welfare state services. Everything else, including many other welfare services, would henceforth have to be sacrificed.

As a realist, in view of the dominance of the world economy and the present effects of the world economic crisis on the Third World, Castro said in 1985:

> I sincerely believe that the cancellation of that [Third World] debt and the establishment of the New International Economic Order is much more important than two, three, or four isolated revolutions. . . . It is preferable to achieve the new order immediately, so we shall all have the right to make social changes, then to have three or four revolutions.[12]

The position of Cuba and the revelations of Fidel Castro highlight a major additional problem for Third World development, socialism, and North–South and East–West relations. As titular head of the NAM of Third World states from 1979 to 1982, Fidel Castro had already experienced the failure of the NIEO at first hand. The ideological roots of NIEO had been planted at the founding of NAM in Bandung in 1955. The economic philosophy was developed at the Afro–Asian Economic Seminar in Algiers and the founding of the Group of 77 (now 125) countries and UNCTAD in Geneva in 1964. The political imperative of NIEO was supplied by the apparent success of OPEC and expressed at the NAM head-of-state meeting in Algiers and the UN General Assembly resolutions in New York in 1974. Countless negotiations followed for a decade without avail. Finally, in

1983, all practical hopes for NIEO were buried in the sands of Cancun in Mexico by the failure of the North–South face-to-face dialogue of presidents at the instance of the Brandt Commission (to which symbolically Fidel Castro was not invited at President Reagan's insistence). The NIEO to which Fidel Castro seems to refer has already proved to be a non-starter and a pipe dream.

So is Fidel Castro calling for a new and different NIEO? In the above cited interview and speech he says that 'as a Third World developing socialist country, Cuba has already established a form of new international economic order with the rest of the socialist community. Without these foundations, our great economic and social successes . . . wouldn't have been possible.'[13] Yet in the speech on the Cuban economy Fidel Castro already recognized that this new order could no longer be maintained without reversion to more trade with the capitalist countries and more domestic economic and social sacrifices, even by Cuba. Still less is any such new order an option for Nicaragua, Angola, Mozambique, or other 'socialist-oriented' countries, as Fidel Castro himself recognizes when he names their revolutions and examines 'what happens when they occur: since we are totally dependent, they immediately blockade us; they grab the pygmies one by one when they rebel.'[14]

But the real problem of this dependence is not so much that capitalists take advantage of it to blockade or invade, as in Nicaragua and Grenada, but that economically the Third World countries even China, apparently, have no where else to go—and especially not to escape into a socialist NIEO. There is no alternative 'third way non-capitalist' NIEO, and the socialist countries, led by the Soviet Union, have failed to create a second alternative socialist NIEO. We will examine some of the limitations of COMECON for the Soviet Union and Eastern Europe below. For the Third World it offers few options beyond some trade expansion, and certainly no alternative socialist world market or NIEO with significantly different rules of the game. In fact, as we will observe below, the socialist countries themselves are increasingly reintegrating into the same old international economic order of the world capitalist economy. This reintegration may or may not be due to the limitations or failures of economic planning in the Soviet Union and Eastern Europe (or China). However, even more and better economic planning in the Soviet Union COMECON would not offer wider and better opportunities for the Third World to participate in an alternative socialist world economy, as Rumanians have found to their cost. Instead, the better the intra-COMECON planning, the more it excludes integration of additional outsiders who have only recently made political revolutions; more COMECON market integration offers the Third World wider trade options, but with a division of labour and on price terms that are not significantly different from those in the remainder of the world capitalist economy. The irony is that, as Fidel Castro is forced to recognize, political revolutions alone, not to mention political rhetoric, offer little chance of escaping from the world capitalistic economy. In other words, much Third Worldist socialist rhetoric is just that and no more. This also means that the anti-Communist rhetoric and anti-socialist or anti-Third Worldist political and military policies of some capitalists—and especially of the Reagan administration—are also little more than a quixotic illusionary right-wing response to left-wing political illusions. For without a viable economic alternative, which does not now exist even on the horizon, the political alternative of a socialist new order for the Third World has no real foundation. For the same reason the conservative political opposition to this non-existent radical alternative has no sense—or at least not the one that is claimed for it by both right and left ideologues alike.

These observations among others suggest that much of the East–West conflict, especially between Washington and Moscow, is a smoke-screen cover for North–South conflicts. We have already observed that the East–West conflict is used both by Moscow and Washington to press harder bargains and even to blackmail their respective allies. One of the areas in which Moscow and especially Washington does so is on North–South issues. There are many examples of US pressure on its European allies to back up or at least condone US policy, such as Vietnam previously and now in Central America, as well as continuously in the Middle East, on the supposed grounds of the need to combat a Soviet Communist threat. The successful pressure exerted by conservative US President Reagan on Socialist President Mitterrand of France again to intervene militarily in Chad is another recent example.

However, the East–West conflict also provides a welcome if not actually necessary pretext for US and Soviet direct intervention in the Third World to further their own interests in the North–South conflict. The intervention of the USA in Central America under the Reagan administration is only the most recent example of a long list that stretches back through Grenada in 1983, Lebanon in 1983 (and in 1958), Vietnam, Laos, and Cambodia; Chile from 1970 to 1973; Santo Domingo in 1965; and many other cases too numerous to mention. The argument is always the same, to combat or prevent Soviet Communist intervention or take-over; and without this pretext US intervention would lack the necessary 'legitimacy'. Perhaps the most revealing aspect is that the Soviet Communist bogeyman is used in Washington to drum up congressional and public support for ever larger military expenditures, the vast bulk of which are not for nuclear and other arms directed at the Soviet Union but for conventional arms specifically designed for use in and against the Third World. The US rapid deployment force is only the most conspicuous tip of the iceberg of this military strength to be used for direct intervention and other shows of force in the Third World.

Without the convenient availability of the Soviet Communist enemy, neither US military expenditure nor this policy of intervention to keep the neo-colonial Third World in line, and especially to keep the US backyard in Latin America subservient, could be politically justified. Moreover, the maintenance of US capitalist economic neo-colonialism does not usually require political intervention; for the dependent Third World countries have few real alternatives. Just about the only alternative is closer economic and political relations with US rivals in Western Europe and Japan, as long as the Soviet Union and Eastern Europe remain unable to offer adequate trade and industrial alternatives. This means the continued use of East–West conflicts in West–West rivalries. The same East–West conflict also plays a significant role in the domestic class struggle within each of the countries of the West and South, where the supposed Communist threat and the Soviet bogeyman are used to legitimate virtually any policies of the ruling classes and to strengthen their bargaining power against the interests of the majority of the people. The usefulness of the Communist scare at home then exposes US allies to its use against them by the US abroad.

Is it any different in the East? Perhaps. But there can be no denying that the allies of the Soviet Union are also under pressure to accept its foreign policies in the Third World in the name of combating the common US-led imperialist enemy. Moreover, the Soviet intervention in Afghanistan was a clear case of defence or promotion of the interests of the Soviet Union or of its Russian ruling class against the threat of a Muslim movement that might spread into Muslim areas of the Soviet Union itself. But this threat was backed up by the USA and its CIA against which Soviet intervention is supposedly necessary. Soviet aid and trade in the Third World, much of which is often on terms that are no better and sometimes even worse that those of the West, is also justified by reference to the imperialist enemy. Soviet and allied social control at home and abroad, as recently occurred in Poland, is also fortified by reference to defence against imperialist subversion. So the East–West conflict is also used to promote Northeastern interests in the South and to defend the status quo in the East. The East–West conflict is useful for other purposes on both sides.

At the same time, the North–South economic realities, which we have examined above through the smoke screen of East–West political conflicts, offer fertile ground for the combination of Olof Palme's

East–West European initiatives with his participation in the North–South Five–Continents proposals.

Notes

1. 29 June 1984.
2. A.G. Frank, ed., *The European Challenge* (Nottingham, 1983).
3. A. Koves, *Acta Oeconomica*, 19878, 21(4), pp. 301–2, 306.
4. Tass report, *International Herald Tribune* (27 April 1984).
5. A.G. Frank, 'Is Reagan Recovery Real or the Calm Before the Storm?', *Economic and Political Weekly*, Bombay (24 and 31 May 1986).
6. Ibid.
7. Frank, 1983, op.cit.
8. A.G. Frank, *Crisis in the Third World* (New York, 1981).
9. A.G. Frank, *Critique and Anti-critique* (New York, 1984).
10. A.G. Frank, 'Defuse the Bomb? Can the Bomb be Defused?' *Economic and Political Weekly*, Bombay (7 July 1984).
11. Frank, 1986, op.cit.
12. 'Battle for Latin America's Real Independence'; address given at the Fourth Congress of the Latin American Federation of Journalists, Havana, 6 July 1985 (official Cuban translation).
13. Ibid.
14. Ibid.

10

Latin American Debt:
The Choices Ahead

ROBERT POLLIN AND EDUARDO ZEPEDA

The Latin American debt crisis is halfway into its fifth year with no end in sight. Since August 1982, when Mexico announced its inability to make interest payments on its outstanding debt of $90 billion, tremendous hardship has been imposed on the indebted countries through austerity programmes devised by the IMF and, more recently, the Latin governments themselves. Amidst an almost constant swirl of activity—new pronouncements, policy twists, and even news of occasional economic upturns—the burden of the debt drags on. While the manifestations of the crisis have been most dramatic in Mexico, Argentina, and Brazil—Latin America's three largest and most heavily indebted countries—the suffering in fact has been widespread, in Latin America and beyond. Even the US economy has been harmed, most seriously through the shrinkage of what had been a huge Latin market for US exports.

One major change has occurred over these five years. It has become apparent that Latin America's creditors—the international bankers and their allies in governments and international lending institutions—have become willing to make small concessions in exchange for basic restructuring of the Latin American economies. More specifically, they are calling for Latin American countries to become bastions of free-market capitalism, with minimal government, open borders for multinationals, and free trade serving as guiding precepts. In other words, while previously the debate over the debt was shrouded in a pretence of technical neutrality, it has now become an openly politicized struggle over the nature of Latin America's economic development path.

Within this context, we wish to consider here three basic questions: first, how the dynamics of the debt crisis have led to the present conjuncture; second, what consequences would result if unbridled free-market restructuring were allowed to occur; and third, what alternatives should be advanced now by progressive forces, both for resolving the crisis and for achieving sustainable and equitable development in the region.

IMF Austerity and the Creditors' Cartel: Phase One of the Crisis

As has been widely documented, many factors contributed to the onset of the crisis in 1982. The immediate cause was a combination of shocks: the unprecedented rise of real interest rates in the US financial markets, the declining prices for Latin American exports, and the increasing protectionism in industrialized countries—all of these factors being themselves linked in some way to the deep international recession of 1982. The final shock of 1982 was the refusal by international banks to provide new loans throughout Latin America after Mexico's difficulties became known.

Prior to this immediate period, the origins of the crisis can be traced to the 1970s, when the Latin American economies' financial structures became overextended and thus vulnerable to shocks. This was the result both of zealous loan pushing by the international banks and equally of the ardent pursuit of funds obtained, which were then not spent on productive development projects, but were used to finance military hardware purchases, wasteful construction projects, and capital flight. And finally, at a more basic level, we cannot forget that Latin American economies have experienced chronic financial instability since the nineteenth century. Historically, this occurred primarily because a major portion of the surplus generated in the Latin economies was shipped back in the form of profits and interest to the home offices of the Western enterprises operating in Latin America. Such practices have continued to the present, producing persistent balance-of-payments deficits for the Latin American economies.[1]

Given this array of causes, what was remarkable in 1982 was that, thanks to the IMF austerity programme, the costs of adjusting to the crisis were foisted entirely on to the Latin countries, and specifically on to the working classes and poor of these countries. The reason for this is self-evident: the IMF has always represented the interests of the international banks and the developed countries' governments, particularly those of the USA, and has taken the initiative in organizing this group into what is in effect a coherent creditors' cartel. The Latin governments, by contrast, have been unable to recognize sufficient common interest to pursue joint action. Partially this is because the crisis did not begin in each country at precisely the same time or with the same degree of severity. More importantly, though, the class interests represented by the various Latin American governments are not generally hostile to the interests of the creditors' cartel. Indeed, a significant proportion of the capitalist classes in Latin America initially supported IMF austerity and still at present are primarily concerned with re-establishing their countries' good standing in international financial markets.[2]

The aim of IMF austerity programmes is therefore in full accord with the primary goal of the creditors' cartel-full and prompt interest payments on the $360 billion of loans outstanding to Latin American countries (nearly 70 per cent of which is dues from Mexico, Argentina, and Brazil alone). In pursuing this aim, the IMF is motivated, as it has always been, by a simple idea: excessive government intervention in Third World economies is the fundamental cause of their financial difficulties. Such intervention, in the IMF view, suppresses free-market forces and thereby renders these economies inefficient and uncompetitive on the world market. The austerity programmes therefore involve eliminating public enterprises, sharply reducing government subsidies and deficit spending, weakening cost-of-living allowances, and decontrolling prices and exchange rates. The IMF view is that these policies force down the purchasing power of all sectors of the economy. When general purchasing power falls, the demand for imports declines as well. These policies aim also at generating falling prices for domestic products, making them more competitive as exports on the world market. With exports rising and imports falling, the IMF programme is thus a strategy for improving a country's trade balance through replacing big government with a heavy dose of private enterprise and allowing mass living standards to fall.

Measured even by these criteria, however, IMF interventions have achieved only limited success in the first phase of the debt crisis. The Latin American economies did become increasingly privatized and living standards did indeed fall. Most dramatically, in the period 1981–84 real wages fell by 28 per cent in Mexico and by 43 per cent in Brazil. Government deficits and consumption per capita declined substantially as well. And, as anticipated, these changes produced a massive drop in imports, a fall of 53 per cent in Mexico, of 43 per cent in Brazil, and of 51 per cent in Argentina between 1981 and 1984. Exports, however, were much less responsive to the austerity treatment. In Argentina, exports actually declined by 11 per cent; Mexico and Brazil did increase exports over these years by 21 per cent and 16 per cent respectively. But these gains must be considered modest at best, given that both countries undertook huge currency devaluations, and that 1984 was a cylical boom year for the US economy, a major market for both countries.[3]

Overall then, by 1984 all three major debtors did manage to run significant trade surpluses, but these were achieved for the most part through the import side of the equation, by forcing down aggregate purchasing power and hence the demand for imports. More importantly, the costs incurred in achieving the trade surpluses were so great that the overall impact of austerity was to actually weaken these countries' basic capacity to service their debt.

Why did IMF policy fail here? From the vantage point of the IMF and bankers, the problem was not that costs were involved in implementing austerity—they fully anticipated many of the costs. It was rather that substantially *unanticipated* costs emerged which prevented the establishment of a stable financial environment. What the IMF did not adequately calculate was the extent to which the attacks on living standards would arouse widespread (if unorganized) discontent, and that this in turn would weaken the credibility of the Latin American governments and worsen the climate for private investment.

Similarly, the IMF was never ambiguous in its intention to cut back sharply on public enterprise, government subsidies, price control, and deficit spending. But it did not recognize that these public-sector activities provide the primary basis for effective demand in all Latin economies. Severe reductions in such programmes inevitably raise havoc with domestic markets. The IMF argues that domestic firms should shift to an export orientation after the public sector contracts. But this ignores what almost all economists recognize, that capturing export markets requires time and sustained promotional effort, even after a country's products have become more competitive through devaluation. This situation especially holds for most products of Latin America, which for a generation have been geared to domestic markets and protected from international competition. Latin American firms therefore face moribund markets as an avoidable consequence of severe government cut-backs. Investment in the region plummeted as a result, falling by 44 per cent in Mexico, 37 per cent in Argentina, and 17 per cent in Brazil between 1981 and 1984. At the same time, acute inflationary pressures were also generated through the devaluations and slashing of price controls and subsidies. In 1981–84, average annual inflation rates were 667 per cent in Mexico, 362 per cent in Argentina, and 141 per cent in Brazil.

Finally, by breeding social unrest and destroying investment opportunities, the IMF policies opened the floodgates to the speculative financial activities that Latin capitalists had already been pursuing intensively, particularly in Mexico and Argentina. As a rough estimate, capital flight from Mexico, Brazil, and Argentina between 1981 and 1984 totalled around $60 billion, amounting to some 60 per cent of the increase in these countries' foreign debt over these years.[4]

The IMF programmes thus failed to achieve the financial stabilization and enhanced debt-serving capacity they aimed at. What occurred instead was a tragicomic cycle in which debtor countries would first accept the IMF programme, then fall out of compliance, then, amidst solemn pronouncements, return again to the fold, only to fail yet again to fulfil the IMF's demands. The full cycle, from agreement to rejection to agreement, took roughly one year, with debtor countries' reputations with the IMF ranging all the way from 'model debtor' to 'irresponsible backslider.'

Opposition to IMF Policies

Because of the failure of austerity, even on its own terms, widespread opposition to the IMF began to emerge by the end of 1984. Included among the dissenters have been major US established figures such as Henry Kissinger, the investment banker Felix Rohatyn, Senator Bill Bradley, and former Federal Reserve Vice-Chairman Preston Martin. In some form each has called for an increasing flow of public and/or private loans for the indebted countries, and an easing of the terms of the loans. The US Roman Catholic bishops have advanced a stronger position, arguing in their recent pastoral letter on the economy that a substantial moratorium or even outright cancellation of the debt may be the only viable way to relieve suffering and restore sustained development in Latin America.

Even more important has been the activity of Latin Americans themselves. The most vigorous initial intervention of course, was that of Fidel Castro. Like the US bishops but more strongly, Castro advocates an indefinite moratorium on debt payments. During 1984–85 he argued his position in travels throughout Latin America and in the several 'debt conferences' in Havana. What Castro accomplished through these efforts was to articulate a persuasive leftist position on the question and thereby to shift the entire debate in Latin America to the left. This had the effect of establishing increased bargaining space for the more conservative and cautious Latin American politicians in power.

Two major Latin American initiatives followed Castro's. The first was that of Peruvian President Alan Garcia who announced at his inaugural speech in July 1985 that Peru would limit its debt-service payments to 10 per cent of Peru's export earnings; since then he has also refused to negotiate with the IMF. The other initiative was the formation in June 1984 of the Cartagena group. In addition to Mexico, Argentina, and Brazil, the group included Columbia, Peru, Ecuador, Uruguay, Bolivia, the Dominican Republic, and Chile (the latter's participation suggesting that even the normally devout free-marketer Pinochet had temporarily strayed into agnosticism). The group met several times during 1984–85 to consider the possibility of united action on the debt, proposing increased loads, lower real interest rates, a softening of IMF austerity, and ceilings on debt-servicing payments linked either to their countries' growth rates or export levels. Nothing more concrete has resulted since the 1985 meeting, however, evoking charges that the Cartagena group was simply a talking shop for bourgeois politicians seeking to placate their constituencies while remaining in the IMF's good graces. While there is truth in this view, it is also the case that after the 1985 meeting most Latin American governments began increasing their demands for easier debt-servicing terms and the substitution of growth-oriented policies for IMF austerity.

The Baker Plan and its Progeny: Phase Two of the Crisis

The growing opposition in Latin America has aroused deep concern within the creditors' cartel and its governmental supporters. The Reagan administration was the first to respond aggressively to this development with its 'Baker plan', named after US Treasury Secretary James Baker who first presented it in October 1985 at a joint annual meeting of the IMF and World Bank. In unveiling the plan, Reagan administration officials made no secret that their primary motive was to thwart the growing Latin American opposition. As David Mulford, Baker's Assistant Treasury Secretary for International Affairs explained, it is 'far better for us to take the initiative rather than be taken on the defensive'.

Two points were emphasized in Baker's strategy. The first was that the Reagan administration would pressure private banks to extend $20 billion in new credit to 14 heavily indebted Third World countries through 1988, and the World Bank would contribute an additional $9 billion (Yugoslavia was the one non-Third World country included among the 15 targeted for Baker plan loans). The full $29 billion in new credits was hardly commensurate with the roughly $130 billion these 15 countries are obligated to pay in interest alone in the 1986–88 period, but Western bankers were reluctant to endorse even this minor concession. The second point was that in order for these countries to be eligible for the new credit, they must agree to carry out comprehensive structural adjustments to promote free-market capitalism in their economies. Such structural adjustments would include lowering taxes, especially for businesses and the wealthy; eliminating subsidies for consumer goods and export-oriented industries; opening domestic markets to free trade; encouraging foreign investment through tax incentives and other inducements; and allowing market forces to determine exchange rates, interest rates, and wage levels.

By introducing the Baker Plan, the Reagan administration was implicitly conceding that the IMF austerity approach had failed. The US officials contended that, by contrast, the Baker Plan would work because it is not an austerity policy, but rather a strategy for promoting economic growth in the indebted countries. The contention is that growth will accelerate in the indebted countries when the proposed market-oriented reforms are implemented, and this in turn will enhance their debt-servicing capacity. Indeed, in official discussions of the Plan and in the mainstream press, an interesting linguistic innovation has occurred: a 'pro-growth' economic policy has become *by definition* one which dismantles state intervention and delivers the economy, via the 'free market', to private capital.

As yet, the Baker Plan has not been embraced officially by a single Latin American government. A variety of programmes have instead been pushed, all broadly with the priorities of the Baker Plan. The most dramatic initiatives have been in the anti-inflationary programmes undertaken by the governments of Argentina and Brazil, in June 1985 and February 1986 respectively. Announced after gaining endorsements from major economists and banking figures such as Federal Reserve Chairman Paul Volcker, these programmes involved the imposition of strict wage and price controls, devaluation, and the creation of a new currency, the austral in Argentina and the cruzado in Brazil. Through devaluation and wage/price controls, proponents of these plans contend that inflation and capital flight could be stifled without requiring further cuts in public spending. An improved business climate would then be established, encouraging more investment both from domestic capitalists and from multinationals. With inflation and capital flight down and investment growing, the countries' ability to service their debt should then strengthen.

The programmes did succeed in dramatically lowering inflation. In Brazil's case, moreover, sharp increases in consumer spending and output did follow. But this was largely because consumers began purchasing heavily in anticipation of a revival of inflation after the lifting of price controls. Neither programme, however, managed to encourage investment growth, since the controls restricted potential profit opportunities. Moreover, neither country has succeeded through these programmes in reducing its debt burden: debt servicing relative to exports, at 51 per cent in Argentina and 35 per cent in Brazil in 1986, represents no improvement from previous years. In addition, the controls themselves began to unravel by the fall of 1986, with no significant gains to show for their anti-inflationary programmes. In Brazil's case, the government is now demanding major concessions on debt payments and is threatening a partial or full debt moratorium if the concessions are not granted.

A programme that was more directly modelled on the Baker Plan was agreed to in October 1986 by Mexico and its creditors. This package, put together to prevent yet another incipient Mexican default, provides $12 billion in new loans during 1987 and early 1988, with an additional $1.7 billion committed as contingency credit should the Mexican economy weaken over this period. In addition, the interest rate on these new loans as well as on some outstanding debt was set at 0.3 per cent below what Mexico had been paying. The timetable for repayment was also lengthened. Consistent with the Baker approach, these loans and concessions are clearly of modest magnitude, given that in 1986 alone Mexico paid $9 billion in interest. The creditors' strategy here is simply to give Mexico an 18-month respite, during which time the Mexicans have agreed to implement Baker-type structural reforms. Proponents of the programme claim that such reforms will then dramatically increase Mexico's capacity to generate balance-of-payments surpluses and thus service debt. 'Privatization, trade liberalization and a further relaxing of foreign investment rules are the three central themes', according to *Business Latin America*.

A final well-publicized initiative has been the promotion of 'debt/equity swap' agreements. Under these arrangements an investment bank or private corporation purchases outstanding Latin debt at a discount from a creditor bank, then sells the debt to the Latin government which originally issued it. The Latin Government thus retires the debt. Meanwhile, the foreign firm uses the funds obtained, which are issued in local currency, to purchase equity in local enterprises. Depending on the country in which the transaction occurs, either public, private, or both types of industries are up for sale under these arrangements. Mexico, Argentina, and Brazil all have adopted such programmes. Conceived originally by the prominent monetarist economist Allan Meltzer, these arrangements are clearly consonant with the main thrust of the Baker plan. They represent a mechanism of directly reducing Latin American debt by opening the borders to foreign investors and also—when state enterprises are being swapped—privatizing the domestic economy. While such programmes have had minimal practical impact thus far, proponents are nevertheless enthusiastic, predicting, for example, that as much as 10 per cent of Mexico's debt could be converted to foreign-owned equity over the next decade.

Overall, then, the situation has been clarified substantially since the Baker plan was first presented. It is now apparent that the Latin economies cannot reasonably function without concessions on the debt, regardless of what other policy initiatives are pursued. This has been the lesson of the anti-inflationary programmes in Brazil and Argentina, which are disintegrating under the burden of the debt. From the Mexican agreement, it is clear also that the creditor's cartel will insist on free-market restructuring before even minor concessions are granted. The creditors' demand for free-market policies is further underscored by the increasing prominence they attach to debt/equity swap arrangements. In short, it is now clear that, unless the Latin American governments are willing to dismantle their public sectors, welcome free trade, and actively encourage multinational investors, the Reagan administration and the creditors' cartel are prepared to allow their economies to smother under the debt burden.

Free-Market Policies in the Third World

Given these intentions of the Reagan administration and the creditors' cartel, the major question then becomes: What do such free-market policies portend for the debtor countries? Administration officials point to alleged 'economic miracles' in South Asian countries, such as South Korea, as evidence that the future under free-market capitalism would be bright indeed. But this comparison is groundless. However one may assess the experience of the South Asian economies, it is certain in any case that their rapid growth was not achieved by practicing *laissez-faire*. Rather, the engine of accumulation has been the dominant position assumed by the state in both planning and financing economic activity. This important point has been demonstrated many times and, with respect to South Korea in particular, was clearly summarized by Aiden Foster-Carter in a recent issue of *Monthly Review*:

> The etatisme that pervades South Korea makes nonsense of any claims on behalf of the 'free market'. Seoul is emphatically not Milton Friedman territory... The state has persistently intervened in every way and at every level in the South Korean economy: by no means just 'fine tuning' or correcting market imperfections, but shaping and directing the entire process. Thus the state's command of investment funds (until recently it owned all major banks) has been reckoned to be comparable only with Communist countries. And the situation in agriculture, with the state setting prices, providing inputs and credit, and buying the crop has been described as virtually equivalent to a single gigantic state farm. Many other examples could be cited.[5]

To understand what actually occurs when a Third World country pursues Baker-type 'structural reforms', one should rather examine the experiences of Chile and Argentina after military governments came to power in these countries in 1973 and 1974 respectively. For almost a decade, vigorous free-market policies were actually practiced in both countries. To begin with, state spending and regulation of market activity were sharply reduced, and the economic and political position of the domestic capitalist class was strengthened. In addition, both countries opened up their economies by eliminating both protectionist barriers to imports and subsidies to domestic export industries, and by providing substantial incentives for foreign investors.

The results of these authentic free-market experiments are well known: they were both disastrous. Both countries, first of all, experienced sharp declines in living standards as real wages fell and unemployment rose. In addition, in both cases the distribution of income became significantly more unequal, output and investment fell sharply, and potential future output was lost due to the decimation of industry. Both countries did manage to increase exports over this period, as severe wage reductions and exchange rate devaluations lowered prices charged by the exporting firms. But imports increased even more. This was because of the decline in local production and the consequent need to purchase necessary goods from abroad at prices that were inflated because of the devalued currencies. Demand for luxury imports also increased because the wealthy were capturing an increasing share of the national income. The balance-of-payments deficits were thus exacerbated in both countries, and this in turn contributed to their crises of the 1980s.

Why did this occur? Clearly, in these countries, just as in South Korea, the state has been the centre of the economy. It was the largest employer and the primary source of effective demand. It was also responsible for planning and financing investment activity and support for export- and import-competing industries. When the state's dominant role is rapidly withdrawn from such economies, the market is simply not capable of taking its place. Power of this kind may be ascribed to the market in conservative economics textbooks, but there is no evidence that the textbook model accords with reality.

In short, what can be gleaned from the Chilean and Argentine experiences is that implementing the Baker plan or similar programmes will foreclose any possibility for decent economic development, just as did the IMF austerity policies. Indeed, rhetoric and minor concessions aside, Baker-type plans turn out to be virtually identical to that of the IMF; the bottom line in both cases is a simple insistence that Latin American governments, at whatever cost, swear allegiance to free-market capitalism.[6]

The Need for a Debt Moratorium

James Baker and others have argued that Latin governments will embrace free-market restructuring because, as Baker put it, 'there is no alternative'. In fact, however, a debt moratorium is an obvious alternative, though it is not surprising that Baker chooses to ignore it. As Castro, the US bishops, and increasingly the Brazilian government contend, a great deal can be gained from a moratorium now. It would bring immediate and deserved relief from the punishing austerity of the past four years; it would allow the domestic industries to recover some momentum; and it would also, ultimately, force more reasonable financial agreements from the creditors' cartel. Of course the cartel would initially react with tremendous hostility to a moratorium, but this reaction would not be universal in developed countries. US exporters, for example, would clearly welcome the revival of the huge Latin American market. It is now also clear that the banks themselves—whose profits have actually been rising since the onset of the debt crisis—could weather a moratorium without requiring a massive government bail-out.[7]

A moratorium is not a complete solution, of course. The Latin American economies must indeed be restructured. Among other things, they need to undertake more equitable and democratic development paths, and to pursue policies less tied to foreign loans and less vulnerable to shocks. A New International Economic Order would help in reaching these aims. But to get that far will first require the breathing space that a moratorium affords.

The theory and practice of debt moratoria hold a respected place in the history of economics. Keynes's 1920 classic *Economic Consequences of the Peace*, for example, was a passionate but unheeded brief in favour of cancelling the huge war reparations imposed on Germany after the First World War. Aside from the moral issue which Keynes raised, he also correctly recognized that this obligation would have a severe destabilizing effect on the post-war international economy. Because Keynes was ignored and the reparations were not cancelled, a fragile international financial structure was carried into the 1920s and became a major factor contributing to the collapse of the international economy after the 1929 stock market crash.

Nor is Latin American history irrelevant. Fourteen Latin countries actually suspended interest payments partially or in full during the depression of the 1930s. According to a recent study by Washington University economist David Felix:

... this allowed the largest among them ... to finance the imports needed to regain economic momentum via augmented public-works programs and import-substituting industrialization. Refunding agreements with creditors were eventually reached in the late 1940s or early 1950s, but these involved debt writedowns of up to 80 per cent, reduced interest rates, and extended maturities or refunded debt.[8]

And finally, more recently and closer to home, the USA itself effectively cancelled a foreign debt obligation of $68 billion in 1971 (equal to $180 billion in 1985 dollars) when it unilaterally renounced its commitment under the Bretton Woods agreements to convert foreign holdings of dollars into gold at $35 an ounce. The justification for this action is debatable. But given this experience, the US government can hardly claim to be opposed in principle to debt cancellations when circumstances appear to require them.

In the present circumstances, at least as much as in any of these historical cases, it is clear that progressive forces in Latin America and elsewhere need to fight for a moratorium as a first step toward halting free-market restructuring and capturing the initiative in the struggle for Latin America's future.

Acknowledgement

The authors, editor, and publisher are grateful for permission to reproduce this chapter which originally appeared in *Monthly Review*, February 1987, pp. 1–16.

Notes

1. A most lucid presentation of this historical relationship is presented in R. Triffin, *Our International Monetary System: Yesterday, Today and Tomorrow* (New York, 1968), vol. 1. Harry Magdoff discusses the issue well for the more contemporary period in 'Economic Distress and the Third World', Monthly Review, April 1982.

2. In this connection, see especially A. MacEwan, 'Latin America: Why Not Default?', *Monthly Review*, September 1986.

3. Data reported here and elsewhere are taken from four basic sources: the 1985 edition of the IMF's *International Financial Statistics*; the Inter-American Development Bank's *Economic and Social Progress in Latin America: 1985 Report:* the ILO's *1985 Yearbook of Labour Statistics*; and the Banco Central do Brasil's *Boletim Mensual.*

4. Capital flight, of course, is not normally reported to governments, and therefore no official statistics exist on it. The methodology utilized here in estimating capital flight is adapted from Carlos F. Diaz–Alejandro, 'Latin American Debt: I don't think we are in Kansas Anymore', Brookings *Papers on Economic Activity*, 2, 1984, pp. 362–3.

5. A. Foster-Carter, 'Korea and Dependency Theory', *Monthly Review*, October 1985, pp. 29–30. A useful study which provides more detail on this same issue is L. Harris, 'Financial Reform and Economic Growth: An Interpretation of South Korea's experience', unpublished typescript, The Open University, Milton Keynes, UK, February 1985.

6. Four studies which evaluate the Chilean and Argentine experiences well are V.E. Tokman, 'Global Monetarism and Destruction of Industry', *Cepal Review*, August 1984, pp. 107–1221; H. Alvaro Garcia and John Wells, 'Chile: A Laboratory for Failed Experiments in Capitalist Political Economy', *Cambridge Journal of Economics*, September/-December 1983, pp. 287–304; V. Parkin, 'Economic Liberalism in Chile, 1973–1982: A Model for Growth and Development or a Recipe for Stagnation and Impoverishment?', *Cambridge Journal of Economics*, June 1983, pp. 101–24; and M. Teubal, 'Argentina: the Crisis of Ultramonetarism', *Monthly Review*, February 1983, pp. 18–26. See also the brief useful discussion in Inter-American Development Bank (Cf. note 3), pp. 133–7.

7. Data on US banks with loans outstanding in Latin America and an assessment of the impact on their profits of a partial payment suspension is presented in the Joint Economic Committee of Congress staff study, 'The Impact of the Latin American Debt Crisis on the US Economy', reprinted in *Business Mexico*, August 1986, pp. 71–83.

8. D. Felix, 'How to Resolve Latin America's Debt Crisis', *Challenge*, November/-December 1984, p. 47.

The Global Political Order: National Powers and Superpowers

11

The Arms Race as an Impediment to Third World Development

LUIS ECHEVERRIA

Let me start by putting the problem into perspective and outlining a basic working hypothesis. In the Cento de Estudios Economicos y Sociales del Tercer Mundo in Mexico this issue has been the subject of constant research. The term Third World is used because the First and Second worlds exist: the industrially advanced capitalist countries and the industrialized socialist countries.

It is no simple matter.

The stance adopted by the countries of the Non-Aligned Movement (NAM) is equidistant between the two. In practice, however, it is tinged in some countries by their struggle to survive; in others by their need to request aid from countries powerful enough to grant it; and in a significant number by efforts to obtain new loans or a certain flexibility in interest payments on existing ones. So to the initial, oft-repeated doctrine of non-alignment implying a centripetal force there is all too frequently added an understandably centrifugal tendency. At the same time, in international meetings and negotiations the term 'developing countries' is used to preserve the dignity of the poorer nations. The term conjures up faith in their creative potential, in the certainty of a prosperous future on a par with the industrialized nations. The representatives of these countries, many of whom have been educated at British, French, or US universities, are thus able to take the floor with all the dignity and noble intent befitting a representative of a sovereign state. And rightly so in the case of those who have acquired formal political independence in recent times. But the plain truth of the matter is that most of these countries are not 'developing', much as they might wish they were. In most cases they are heading towards even greater underdevelopment.

And within the family of the United Nations, although the Group of 77 now has 125 members, it continues to use its original name. Could this be a case of exaggerated deference to tradition? Or does it perhaps stem from a concern not given away by the fact, by its very name, that the group will always obtain 80 per cent of the votes, not counting those of the socialist countries which are often inclined to vote with it? If 'Third World' means not yet achieving the success of the industrialized countries in both camps; if the non-aligned countries include those who sincerely wish they were, or say that they are, although only a few can afford to be; if the 'developing countries' are now, disquietingly, on a distinctly downhill path, and the 77 are taking liberties with arithmetic, we need to find a new basis around which to co-ordinate our reflection on certain vital problems that are often a matter of sheer survival.

This is no mere geometric pattern. The above-mentioned confusion in terminology is symptomatic of a very serious situation related to world economic disorder, the arms race, and the very real possibility of war. It concerns the effective existence of the balance of terror and the possibility of nuclear war, against the multiple threat of which the 125 Third World countries, with their belief in non-alignment and their eagerness to do away with underdevelopment, could provide a useful counterbalance.

This does not mean channelling arms expenditure to more peaceful ends, a now impossible hypothesis which has only been put forward in association with over-simplified schemes that have no bearing on reality. Indeed, the multifaceted reality of the Third World, the diverse origins of its problems stemming from financial and technological dependence on the industrialized nations, both capitalist and socialist, have led us to a new form of colonialism aggravated by the expense of the arms race which appears to be paving the way for nuclear war.

It is as if this state of affairs were the fruit of a death wish, a will to kill and be killed, directing us down a road of madness towards a universal holocaust.

The clearsightedness of Olof Palme's vision, which determined his approach to domestic and international politics ever since his earliest 11 years and which eventually led to his carefully planned assassination, could go a long way to alleviating some of the effects of the constant deterioration in the economic situation of the world's peripheral areas.

If the new barbarianism would only restrain its colonialistic bent, which precludes any chance of its being considered by the Third World as a political example to follow; and if, on the other hand, those who still cling to the long-outmoded mystic appeal of revolution as a universal solution would only face up to reality, the dependent, indebted countries would in their distress have more stimulating social ideals to look up to and follow.

Of course we agreed with the efforts of the group led by Palme, the Swede, the European, the international thinker, and pacifist who died for the cause. *Common Security. A Programme for Disarmament*, was studied with the keenest interest. Some distinguished personalities took part in the Commission that Palme set up and headed. Not only in Latin America, but all over the world, the presence of the Mexican Nobel Prize-winner Alfonso Garcia Robles, who has devoted his whole life to the struggle for law, disarmament, and peace, kindled a new awareness. The pursuit of common security; the proposal for winding down the spiral, gradually reducing weaponry to the point of general disarmament; the certainty that the power of dissuasion was, in fact, counterproductive, constant stimulus; the conviction that there would be no limited nuclear war, but total conflagration; the prediction that the civilian population would be the first and hardest hit; and above all the knowledge that no side could ever win and that the whole world would lose; all these arguments provided a basis for a better understanding of the dangers involved in a war in which neutrals and belligerents, North and South, would all meet their doom.

In December 1941, Roosevelt coined the name United Nations to designate the countries fighting against the Axis and for democracy. Two years later, in Teheran, Churchill, Roosevelt, and Stalin declared: 'We are certain that through mutual understanding we shall achieve lasting peace. We realize that it is our supreme responsibility and that of all the United Nations to create a peace which will thrive on the goodwill of the overwhelming majority of the peoples of the world and banish the scourge and the terror of war for generations to come.'

In February 1945 the same leaders on the brink of victory ratified the idea of holding a conference in San Francisco, California. On 24 October that same year the Charter was signed setting up the organization for international peace and security, to resolve economic, social, and cultural questions, to defend human rights and basic freedoms, and to prevent the use of force and the interference of some states in the affairs of others.

Throughout this period, however, nuclear war was being prepared. In mid-July 1945, after many years of research, the first successful nuclear explosion was carried out in New Mexico, USA, and days later the order was given to drop bombs on Hiroshima, and Nagasaki, Kokura, or Niigata as soon as there was sufficient visibility. On 6 August the first nuclear bombs were dropped on Hiroshima and Nagasaki respectively. The first killed or wounded some 200,000 people. The second only 100,000. They were the small, first-generation bombs equivalent to only 13,000 ton of TNT.

Thus began a new era for mankind. Our era.

By the time the Palme Commission had finished its work, there had been no mention yet of Star Wars, but the Commission had had the foresight to recommend that the superpowers should discuss the use of outer space for military purposes in order to forestall the dangers involved. The present confrontation over the Strategic Defence Initiative (SDI) has direct antecedents in the numerous violations of the Treaty on Principles Governing the Activities of States in the Exploration and Use of Outer Space including the Moon and Other Celestial Bodies. The treaty was passed by the UN General Assembly in December 1966 and signed on 27 January 1967 in London, Moscow, and Washington for the benefit of all nations, whatever their level of development. It declared outer space to be open to all, provided for freedom of access to every region of the celestial bodies, and proscribed the deployment of arms in outer space.

The world wonders what the real aim of the SDI is and whether it is really feasible. It would need to be built to absolute perfection. It would have to provide for every conceivable form of attack. And there is no way of pre-testing it, other than by simulation. To date, nobody believes the system would be capable of detecting and destroying every enemy missile. Arms so new that they only exist in theory would need to be directed by sensors of an accuracy as yet unknown to ballistic science. The computer programs would have to be drawn up on the basis of battle conjectures which scientists estimate would need approximately 100 lines of instructions with no margin for error whatsoever. They are not even sure that they can build a computer facility sufficiently powerful to handle such a task. It is also quite rightly argued that any defensive system is potentially offensive and always embodies a latent capacity for initiating an attack.

In view of the huge cost of the project, the Third World would be contributing—through the interest payments on its debt—to an initiative which, far from guaranteeing peace, would only serve to increase the colonial dependency of many countries. Furthermore, the project will inevitably bring about a new geo–political balance, affecting not only the underdeveloped countries but also those industrialized ones which, by alliance or subjection, would find themselves in a situation comparable to that of the Third World.

NASA has developed and presented to the White House a plan to set up a colony of some 100 persons on the moon. It would take 20 years to accomplish and would require the construction of a special transport network for the trifling sum of $80,000 million (which would be financed, I assume, out of the Third World's interest payments).

The first 'US lunar town' would be powered by four nuclear generators. It would be set up in stages, rather in the same way that the early pioneers conquered the Wild West, forming their wagons into circles to protect themselves (obviously, one would think). It would certainly open up whole new horizons for the adventures of Secret

Agent 007. By contrast, the rural areas of the underdeveloped countries are sadly lacking in internal communications facilities. The use of outer space for communication satellites, which are one solution to regional communication problems, has been practically monopolized by the more prosperous countries.

New remote detection technologies in reconnaissance satellites have increased our knowledge of the whereabouts of natural resources in different regions of the globe. But here again these sophisticated detection systems are in the hands of the technologically advanced countries. The poorer ones, which are becoming increasingly poorer, have to rely on the major capitalist or socialist countries for information about their own resources. If the world were better organized in the interest of all its peoples, such technological progress in radio transmission, telecommunications, and remote detection in general could be used to foster a more efficient exchange of useful information such as the existence of available resources.

Perhaps the presence, in addition to those of Mexico, of eminent Third World personalities and advocates has brought us slightly nearer to the crux of the problem, even though the move was over cautious to my way of thinking.

In the introduction to his programme, the Chairman says:

> . . . we share the view of the Brandt Commission that the North and the South have a mutual interest in the recovery of the world economy. Government revenues now spent on the military—and the scientists and technicians and other skilled workers who work to perfect the gigantic military machine—are one of the few resources available to meet social needs and to finance development.

To a certain extent, but still with caution, the group chaired by the great German democrat came closest to the heart of the problem afflicting the Third World countries. At its summit in Algiers in 1973 it protested that the industrialized countries had shown a lack of political drive in fulfilling their pledges for the second decade of development.

The Palme Commission rightly suggested that the money which the poorer countries spend on arms could just as well be spent on developing their own economies. The programme states, quite correctly, that imported equipment is paid for in foreign currency and that this type of spending has been rising constantly: from 1975 to 1979 it rose to $316 billion measured in constant 1978 prices, i.e. $147 billion for the OPEC countries and $169 billion for the other, 'developing' countries. In the 1970s this expenditure rose by 6 per cent a year. It increased from 19 per cent in 1971 to 25 per cent in 1980. Some of the foreign currency used in these transactions actually belonged to the countries concerned, whereas some was borrowed. Be that as it may, this money could still have been spent on capital equipment to promote economic growth.

At their Algiers meeting in 1973 the NAM denounced the lack of effort by the industrialized countries to fulfil their promises for the second decade of development. This lack of international co-operation, the behaviour of the transnational companies, the inflationary growth of the developing countries' imports, the pressure on their balances-of-payments transfers by foreign investors, the repayment of loans, the cost of servicing their debts, and the general monetary crisis, all emphasize the need to bring urgent reforms before the international community.

The NAM called a special UN meeting which took place during the three historic weeks from April to May 1974 and which adopted, by a vast majority, the Declaration and Action Programme for the New International Economic Order, invoking the highest principles that had inspired the creation of the UN itself: equal sovereignty, interdependence, common interests, co-operation, redressing inequalities, eliminating differences between the industrialized world and the developing countries, peace, and justice.

I believe that behind the economic arguments there lies the old experience of the countries of Asia, Africa, and Latin America, which, for the last 30 years, more so than many industrialized nations, have not only had to face their understandably unpleasant situation of poverty, but have also glimpsed the modern traumas that they defined in 1973.

The very real danger facing us could be a motive for changes in ideologies and interests which might narrow the gap between the socialist bloc and the capitalist world. The fundamental differences between the two systems have always seemed irreconcilable; but the risk both sides are evidently willing to run goes beyond political backwardness and smacks more of a death cult than of any faith in life. The Third World tends to produce involute social forms, with autocratic regimes with foreign backing taking over from incipient democratic experiences. It falls prey to the attractions of certain aspects of the industrialized countries' subculture that end up by undermining traditional moral and aesthetic values. The very existence of formerly great civilizations is now in jeopardy.

Since the models offered by the industrialized countries—which are not necessarily as successful or as advanced as they may appear—are not always suited to the needs of the Third World, the latter must develop a deep, self-critical insight into its real interests, a brave mature outlook, rather than simple self-pity and denunciation. Nevertheless, faced with the threat of total annihilation, and as a primary form of a natural instinct to survive, there still exists an ability in many communities to stand up and defend the values without which society loses all that is best in it; in other words, the human vocation for freedom.

This must not be destroyed, not even surreptitiously, in the pursuit of material gain or of apparent political freedom which, in fact, merely serves the interests of the monopolies and oligopolies. Rhetoric aside, to be quite realistic, it is evident that mankind in every latitude has an essential inclination toward and an inalienable vocation for security, dignity, and liberty. In this respect, *Common Security* and the personal convictions and activities of Olof Palme, constitute a worthy contribution to a new awareness.

We in Latin America were deeply shocked by the assassination of Olof Palme, as we were by the crime against Salvador Allende, for similar reasons. But the legacy of both men is indestructible, an essential part of the heritage of two peoples so distant and yet so close.

My wife, Maria Estber, has asked me to hand a red rose to two ladies, Hortensia Allende and Lisbeth Palme, who courageously shared in their husbands' struggle to the bitter end. To them I dedicate the preceding thoughts.

12

Superpower Rivalries in the Third World

FRANK FUREDI

Introduction

Ever since the breakdown of the grand alliance of the Second World War in the late-1940s the conflict between the USA and the Soviet Union has dominated international affairs. The rivalry between the two superpowers has not only shaped the pattern of events in post-war Europe, it has also had an overwhelming significance in the Third World. In recent years the renewed intensity of East–West animosities has had a disruptive effect on attempts to promote a North–South dialogue. The climate created by the new cold war waged under the Reagan presidency has paralysed wider developments in international relations.

It is important to emphasize at the outset that, given the balance of power in the post-war world, relations between North and South cannot be equalized through dialogue or diplomacy. The Third World remains a battle ground for the superpowers. The best that Third World nations can expect is to be treated as favoured clients; they can never be accepted as equal partners in negotiations. Observers of international affairs generally agree that, whereas Europe and North America are relatively stable, the Third World is where the trouble spots of the 1980s are to be found. Shulman sums up the prevailing view in a recently published collection of essays on East–West tensions in the Third World:

> The importance of the subject stems from the fact that although the regulation of nuclear weapons may have the most immediacy and urgency on the US–Soviet agenda, the conflicts that arise in the Third World, sometimes unpredictably and explosively, may be more likely to engage the superpowers in a confrontation than the intersection of their interests in Europe, which they have learned over the decades to handle with great caution.[1]

Shulman's outlook has long been the conventional wisdom in the USA. Back in the 1960s President Kennedy told Paul-Henri Spaak candidly that in his view the real struggles were not in Europe, 'but in Asia, Latin American and Africa.'[2]

Since the Second World War the Third World has emerged as the main focus of international conflict. Virtually all the wars fought since 1945 have taken place outside Europe and North America. According to our calculation, in this period the USA has intervened militarily in the Third World on more than 110 occasions.[3] The countries in which significant numbers of US or Soviet military personnel have died over the past 40 years—Korea, Vietnam, Afghanistan—are all in the Third World. The global flashpoints of the 1980s are in the Middle East, Southern Africa, Central America—the same regions which have experienced military strife intermittently throughout recent decades.

Before exploring the differences between the USA and the Soviet Union in relation to the Third World, it is worth noting what they have in common. Despite much rhetoric on either side, from the point of view of the international order, both the USA and the Soviet Union are *status quo* powers. Not surprisingly neither power has much sympathy for the demands associated with the New International Economic Order (NIEO). Through various international institutions such as the IMF and the World Bank, the USA in particular has sought to preserve the *status quo*. Since Reagan came to power in 1980, the US administration has dropped even the pretence of being interested in promoting a North–South dialogue.

It is widely known that Washington is hostile to any attempt to change the existing international economic order. It is less widely recognised that in recent years the Soviet Union too has become an ardent champion of the post-war balance of economic and political power.

The Soviet leadership rejects the term 'Third World' and criticizes commentators who analyse international relations in terms of a North–South conflict.[4] Yet, whereas in the past Soviet leaders advised Third World nations to make a fundamental break with the world economy, since the mid-1970s they have been recommending a more moderate course of action. Over the past decade the Soviet authorities have been critical of Third World leaders who have put forward proposals for forging stronger economic links among the countries of the South. Soviet leaders have also become much more reluctant to guarantee economic support to Third World nations seeking to strike out from the grip of Western domination.

There has been a striking convergence between the views of Soviet and Western experts on Third World development matters. Both are increasingly united in opposition to radical economic critiques of imperialist domination. Valkenir cites a recently published collection of essays by the Soviet Institute of Africa which challenges Samir Amin's recommendation that Third World nations raise the prices of their raw materials.[5] Soviet scholars take issue with writers of the dependency school, accusing them of 'exaggerating' the harmful impact of the world economy on the Third World.

Soviet contributors to debates about the NIEO have become more conciliatory towards the existing international order. At the fifth UNCTAD summit in 1979 Soviet delegates insisted that it was possible to 'democratize' the prevailing world economic system. The conservatism of the Soviet approach is apparent in the recommendations issued from Moscow to Third World regimes. Zaslavsky has commented on the pro-Western drift of Soviet perspectives:

> Soviet authors now advise Third World countries to remain attached to the capitalist world market, to attract Western capital for the development of the national economy, to make maximum use of their own resources instead of relying on foreign aid.[6]

The latest version of the programme of the Communist Party of the Soviet Union, drawn up and approved in 1980, endorses the *status quo* orientation of Soviet foreign policy. Previous references to the Soviet Union's 'international duty to assist' the peoples of the Third World in fighting for their independence from the capitalist world order have now been dropped.

The tensions between the superpowers in the Third World are not a matter of ideology or principles. Let's first look at the aspect of international relations that commands the greatest media attention: the military role of the superpowers in the countries of the South.

The Militarization of the Third World

Great power intervention in the Third World has become an enduring theme in international relations. Military interference and the threat of force are habitual features of great power diplomacy towards the South. The diplomacy of force is complemented by the militarization of the region. In recent years the major contribution made by foreign 'aid' to the Third World has become the supply of arms. For example, since 1980 US spending on developmental aid has fallen in nominal as well as real terms. At the same time spending on military and security aid has shot up. In 1980, security assistance accounted for 46 per cent of the US aid budget—by 1980 it had risen to 66 per cent.[7] In 1980 Washington provided military and security aid to 43 countries. Today

102 countries, including Fiji and Botswana, are recipients of US military assistance. The Soviet Union has also stepped up its role as a peddler of arms. For example, between 1980 and 1984 the Soviet Union provided nearly $2.1 billion in economic assistance to Sub-Saharan Africa, while its arms deliveries were worth more than $5.9 billion. For North Africa the comparable figures are even more dramatic: $650 million in economic aid and $7.9 billion in arms transfers.[8]

The damaging consequences of the militarization of the Third World are evident in the economic and social breakdown that has reduced substantial areas of Africa to famine and destitution. The prevalence of military conflict in the Third World is no passing phenomenon. Warfare has not only become a way of life in parts of Africa, Central America, and the Middle East; the conflicts in the Third World are fuelled by the tensions in international superpower relations. The trends towards deeper world recession, and towards the continuing stagnation of the Soviet system, in the late-1980s suggest that the situation for the South is likely to deteriorate still further.

US strategy in the Third World

The past involvement of the two major superpowers in the Third World has been of a quite different order. Whereas the USA has been continually involved in the Third World since the mid-1950s, it was a decade later before the Soviet Union took its first steps into the countries of the South. It is also important to differentiate between superpower *involvement* and superpower *rivalry*. Thus when US diplomacy directed its attention to the Third World in the 1940s it faced no Soviet rivals.

Under Presidents Truman and Eisenhower in the late-1940s and early-1950s, the USA tried to drag the Third World into the cold war. Washington strategists sought to draw up a series of military pacts with Third World countries around the borders of the Soviet Union. They devoted special attention to the Middle East's so-called 'northern tier'—Turkey, Iraq, Iran, and Pakistan. The USA established military bases in these countries as a way of putting pressure on the Soviet Union. As Francis Fukuyama of the Rand Corporation observes, the 1955 Baghdad Pact involving the northern tier nations had a 'clear cut (if not openly admitted) military objective'.[9]

Truman's policy of containing the Soviet Union itself provided a justification for the USA to assume the role of the policeman of the Third World. As early as 1947 Truman had outlined the philosophy of containment that was to guide US policy well into the post-war years: 'At the present moment in world history nearly every nation must choose between alternative ways of life. The choice is too often not a free one. . . I believe it must be the policy of the USA to support free peoples who are resisting attempted subjugation by armed minorities or by outside pressures.[10]

After the end of the Second World War, Truman insisted that the Third World must take sides in the cold war. As far as he was concerned, since no nation would voluntarily opt for the Soviet side, US intervention was justified as a legitimate policy to uphold freedom. The implications of the Truman doctrine were far-reaching. Any Third World nation acting against US interests was now labelled as part of a Soviet plot targeted for retaliation.

Although the containment of the Soviet Union was of central concern to Truman, for the US administration there were other, arguably more important, considerations at stake. By 1947 the lines of demarcation were clearly drawn across Europe. However, the situation was still fluid and potentially unstable in the Third World. After the victory of the Chinese revolution in 1949 the threat of nationalist regimes and national liberation movements to Western interests became something of an obsession in Washington. The containment of radical Third World nationalism now emerged as the overriding concern of US foreign policy. A former official of the State Department in the Kennedy era observes that 'from the Truman doctrine on, the suppression of insurgent movements has remained a principal goal of US foreign policy'.[11]

It is well known that successful insurgent or national liberation movements rely on their strong roots among the people in the countries in which they are fighting. After emerging covered in glory from a war against Germany and Japan waged under the banners of democracy and freedom, intervening against such popular movements presented the USA with a considerable propaganda problem. To justify intervention the USA was obliged to link national liberation struggles to a mythical Soviet threat. In countries like Guatemala, Lebanon, and the Dominican Republic, the US propaganda machine was obliged to invent Soviet connections and communist subversives where neither existed to provide a pretext for sending in the Marines.

Virtually every US president in the post-war period has proclaimed a new doctrine which justifies intervention in the Third World on the grounds of halting Soviet subversion. In January 1957 Eisenhower outlined his doctrine of preventing communism from gaining a foothold in the Middle East. In his speech Eisenhower gave a blanket endorsement for 'the employment of armed forces of the USA to secure and protect the territorial integrity and political independence of such nations, requesting such aid, against overt armed aggression from any nation controlled by international communism'.[12] The following year the marines landed in Lebanon and US gunboats subsequently became a central instrument of Washington's Middle East diplomacy.

President Johnson's justification for the US invasion of the Dominican Republic in 1964 followed the pattern set by Truman. According to Johnson, revolution 'in any country is a matter for that country to deal with', but it 'becomes a matter for hemispheric action only when the object is the establishment of a communist dictatorship'.[13] Fifteen years later President Carter reiterated the same position in relation to the Middle East:

> Let us be absolutely clear. An attempt by any outside force to gain control of the Persian Gulf region will be regarded as an assault on the vital interests of the USA, and such an assault will be repelled by any means necessary, including military force.[14]

It has been left to President Reagan to implement the Carter doctrine in the Gulf. Reagan has also felt the need to proclaim his own doctrine. In his 1985 'State of the Union' address, he targeted radical Third World regimes along the lines of his predecessors.

There has been a remarkable consistency in Washington's foreign policy objectives towards the Third World over the past four decades. What has changed are the means used to realize these objectives. The USA has succeeded in creating a network of alliances through which it can influence developments in the Third World. Nevertheless the USA has not been able to hold back the tide of Third World revolt. In Cuba and Vietnam, Angola and Nicaragua. Libya and Iran, radical regimes have come to power, challenging the whole framework of US global authority.

The traditional approach of US diplomacy was to deploy military force and *force majeure*. The pacts and alliances which supported the network of US bases in the Third World from the 1950s onwards were rapidly abandoned if it became apparent that local allies were less than fully reliable. The problem was that the very existence of US military bases fostered a powerful nationalistic and anti-US reaction. The overthrow of the monarch in Iran in 1958 by a radical nationalist movement led to the collapse of the Baghdad Pact. In a number of other countries such as Libya, Pakistan, and Thailand, popular pressure forced the regimes to demand that US forces evacuate their military bases.

US gunboat diplomacy reached its high point in the 1960s. US forces were directly involved in the overthrow of radical Third World regimes in the Dominican Republic, Indonesia, Brazil, Ghana, and Zaire. However, the high cost of this policy soon became clear in the Vietnam War. It became evident that US military might could not guarantee victory against a popular national liberation movement. It also became apparent that the price of maintaining the *pax Americana* through force of arms could be high. Vietnam taught the USA that it could not expect to interfere in every Third World trouble spot and win. The humiliation of Vietnam led to a shift in US strategy under President Nixon away from direct intervention.

The Nixon doctrine was proclaimed in Guam in 1969. It stated that from now on the USA would rely on its Third World allies to bear the brunt of military intervention. Stability in the Third World would now be secured through pro-USA regimes such as Brazil, Israel, and South Africa. The Shah of Iran was the model regional policeman under the Nixon doctrine.

In the late 1970s the US policy of using regional proxies to uphold Western interests sustained a series of blows. Halliday provides a list of 14 countries across the Third World where revolutions took place between 1974 and 1980.[15] This dramatic upsurge of anti-Western sentiment removed a number of key US allies—most notably the Shah of Iran who was forced to flee in 1979. The overthrow of the Shah was a catastrophe for the USA, marking the definitive end of the Nixon doctrine. For a time US foreign policy was thrown into disarray. But soon a perceptible swing back in favour of direct military intervention was apparent.

Since the late-1970s the USA has steadily built up its capacity for military intervention in the Third World. Carter's 'rapid deployment force', later renamed CENTCOM, aimed to provide the USA with the capacity to control events in one of the most unstable and most strategically important areas of the world—the Gulf. Under the Reagan Presidency it has become the norm to despatch the Marines, the Air Force, or the Navy to teach Third World countries a sharp lesson—Grenada, Lebanon, Libya, and Iran have all received Reagan's rough justice. One major innovation of the Reagan Presidency is the deployment of local 'freedom fighters' such as the Contras in Nicaragua, UNITA in Angola, and the MNR in Mozambique in an attempt to overthrow radical Third World regimes. In the 1980s the USA has been obliged to develop a greater variety of responses to cope with the simultaneous eruption of foreign policy crises in different regional theatres.

The Soviet response

The Soviet Union has only become directly involved in the Third World relatively recently. It was under Khrushchev in the mid–1950s that the Soviet Union first began to adopt an active orientation towards the Third World. This shift was influenced by a number of considerations. China was fast emerging as a competitor for radical allegiance in the Third World. The instability which followed the departure of Britain and France from their former colonies in Africa and South-East Asia created openings for the extension of Soviet influence. Probably the most pressing concern in Moscow was to prevent the USA from transforming Third World regimes into anti-Soviet bases.

Khrushchev's diplomacy was focused on the Middle East. As Fukuyama notes, it was in this region that the Western presence constituted the greatest military threat to the Soviet Union:

> Moscow's chief concern was to undermine the series of US-sponsored pacts being erected around its borders, the most important of which was the Baghdad pact with the SAC bases in the northern tier.[16]

To counter Washington, the Soviet Union cultivated diplomatic relations with Egypt under Gamal Abdul Nasser.

The evolution of the links between the Soviet Union and Egypt set a pattern which was to be repeated again and again in relations between Moscow and Third World countries over the next 30 years. Egypt first turned to the Soviet Union because it had previously been rebuffed by the West. Under pressure from Israel and pro-Western Iraq, Nasser looked to the Eastern bloc for weapons. An arms deal between Egypt and Czechoslovakia led to a further deterioration in relations between Nasser and the West, which in turn strengthened his ties with the Eastern bloc. An unstoppable chain of events was set in motion. In mid-1956 Washington told Nasser that the USA was no longer prepared to help finance the construction of the Aswan high dam, a major prestige project for the Nasser regime. Nasser reacted by moving closer to Moscow and he hit back decisively at the West by nationalizing the Suez canal. After the invasion of Egypt by a joint task force made up of British, French and Israeli troops in October 1956, Nasser became entirely dependent on Soviet arms.

The Soviet Union took advantage of the tensions between Egypt and the West to establish a foothold in the Middle East. It stepped in promptly and offered to finance the completion of the Aswan dam. (It is worth noting in passing that the other major Third World prestige project which received Soviet finance, the Bihalai steel plant in India, was also previously boycotted by the USA. In both cases the Soviet Union was able to exploit the conflicts in the relations between the West and a Third World country.) In the medium term Soviet links with Nasser paid handsome dividends. Anti-Western sentiment in the Middle East provided a fertile terrain for Soviet diplomacy. In 1958 the pro-Western regime in Iraq was overthrown by a group of military officers influenced by Nasser. The demise of the Baghdad pact which followed this coup was a set-back from which US policy in the Middle East never fully recovered.

Triumph in the Middle East was combined with modest Soviet gains in other parts of the Third World. Two sorts of situation were favourable to Moscow. First, the Soviet Union could step in where demands for economic or military assistance had been rejected or ignored by the USA—India and Somalia are examples. Second, the Soviet Union could make important gains by establishing relations with radical regimes which were at loggerheads with the West. The classic example is Cuba, where US hostility towards Castro played a key role in radicalizing the regime. In the end Cuba could only survive the US embargo by establishing closer relations with the Soviet Union.

Most radical Third World regimes under Western pressure did not go as far as Cuba. However, the Soviet Union was able to create strong links with these regimes and hence threaten Western interests. In the late-1950s and early-1960s Moscow forged important ties with the regimes of Ben Bella in Algeria, Keita of Mali, Nkrumah in Ghana, and Sukarno of Indonesia.

Although the upsurge of Soviet diplomacy in the Third World was a major departure from the norm, it was still of modest proportions compared to that of the USA. Moscow's success was due, not so much to the effectiveness of its policy, as to the mistakes of its superpower rival and the upsurge of radicalism in the Third World. At this time Soviet involvement was based primarily on selling arms and establishing economic links. It lacked the capacity and perhaps the inclination for military intervention in the Third World until the 1970s. As an alternative focus for Third World allegiance the Soviet Union created problems for Washington. The USA's inability to destroy the Castro regime in Cuba was largely the result of Soviet involvement. However, Cuba was the exception. The Soviet Union lacked the resources to sustain an extensive presence in the Third World.

Soviet policy was guided above all by the geo–political consideration of protecting its borders. This central policy objective was supplemented by a stratagem of opportunistically taking advantage of the difficulties which the West encountered in the Third World. In specific situations Soviet economic assistance could play an important role. However, in general the Soviet Union lacked the economic weight to compete effectively with the USA. The most important resource available to the Soviet Union for strengthening its influence in the Third World was military hardware. Soviet supplies of arms were the key to its diplomatic successes in Algeria, Egypt, Ghana, Indonesia, and India.

The Soviet Union soon discovered that its role as a superarms dealer did not guarantee lasting influence in the Third World. Many of the pro-Soviet Third World regimes soon succumbed to Western pressures.[17]

The overthrow of such Soviet allies as Ben Bella in Algeria, Lumumba in Zaire, Nkrumah in Ghana, and Sukarno in Indonesia underlined the insecurity of the Soviet presence in the Third World. These setbacks provided the background to the most significant defeat for Soviet Third World diplomacy—its expulsion from Egypt.

The growing conflict between Egypt and Israel in the late-1960s and early-1970s forced Nasser and later Sadat to step up their demands for Soviet support. In 1970 Moscow despatched 20,000 combat troops to back up Egypt's air defence system. This was the first time that Soviet troops had ever been deployed in substantial numbers in a Third World country. Despite this commitment of troops, Egypt demanded still more military support. Fearful of the consequences of being drawn into a major military engagement in the Middle East that would inevitably involve the Western powers, the Soviet leadership called a halt to further backing for Egypt. In July 1972 Sadat decided that if the Soviet Union was not prepared to provide the level of support that Egypt needed to cope with the Zionist state, then it was not worth maintaining the alliance with Moscow. He expelled all Soviet technical and military personnel and within months Egypt was firmly back in the Western camp.

Today it is easy to forget that 1970 marked the high point of Soviet influence in the Third World. A number of dramatic events in subsequent years, such as the airlift of Cuban troops to Angola and Ethiopia, the expansion of the Soviet Navy, and the invasion of Afghanistan, are often cited as proof of the extension of Soviet power in the Third World. However, one former British diplomat sympathetic to the USA has openly admitted that 'the USA has persistently exaggerated' the Soviet threat.[18]

The decline of Western influence over the past decade often helps to create the impression that the Soviet Union is stronger than it really is in the Third World. In fact the Soviet Union has been obliged to play a more limited and defensive role in the Third World since the setbacks of the early-1970s.

Over the past decade Soviet diplomacy in the Third World had depended largely on its capacity to relate to Third World revolts against pro-Western regimes. The revolutions in Ethiopia, Angola, Nicaragua, and Iran between 1974 and 1979 owed nothing to local pro-Soviet Communist parties or to official Soviet backing. Yet they helped to boost Moscow's influence in the Third World.

In the 1970s the Soviet Union developed a military presence in the Third World for the first time. The most dramatic manifestation of this trend was the Soviet invasion of Afghanistan in 1979—the first occasion on which the Soviet Union had invaded a Third World country. The Eastern bloc now maintains around 35,000 troops, mostly Cubans, in Africa (21,000 in Angola, 7,000 in Ethiopia, 1,150 in Mozambique). It has also established two important naval bases in the Third World: Cam Ranh in Vietnam and Al Anad in South Yemen. These developments have made the Soviet Union a global military power on a very modest scale.

The major preoccupation of Soviet policy in the Third World is the security of its own borders. It was the fear of the instability caused by Islamic fundamentalism in Afghanistan spreading to the Islamic republics within the Soviet Union that precipitated the invasion and continuing occupation of the country. In other regions, Moscow seeks to establish alliances pragmatically to counter Western influence. While many in the West still believe that Moscow is concerned to spread the gospel of international revolution through its relations with Third World regimes and movements, there is little evidence of any such consideration affecting Soviet foreign policy in the Third World. Moscow was prepared to support the corrupt pro-Western dictator Ferdinand Marcos in the Philippines, even after he had been abandoned by the USA in the face of popular revolt. In the Iran–Iraq war, the Soviet Union supplies arms to both sides—its only concern is diplomatic advantage.

Although the Soviet Union is fully complicit in the militarization of the Third World, its role has been a strangely defensive one. There has been much controversy about the growth of Soviet naval power in the South, and it is true that the expansion of the Soviet fleet has helped to strengthen its diplomatic influence. However, it is important to note that the Soviet naval build-up is a response to US military strategy, as a leading Western specialist has observed:

> Most specialists in the field now accept that the critical shift to forward deployment was a response to the threat to Russia from sea-based nuclear delivery system . . . triggered by President Kennedy.[19]

A quick glance at the statistics of US and Soviet naval power and at the map showing their overseas bases reveals the unequal balance between the superpowers in the Third World. Cam Ranh in Vietnam is the only Soviet base worthy of the name. The base in South Yemen is far from secure: during the January 1986 coup there Soviet diplomats had to rely on Western boats to secure their evacuation. The Soviet Union has 15 foreign ports which provide facilities for its ships. By contrast the USA has 360 major bases and 1600 installations in 36 countries. The USA enjoys overwhelming naval superiority through massive bases such as the island of Diego Garcia in the Indian Ocean which is entirely self-sufficient and independent of any local control.[20]

Soviet policy in the Gulf War confirms its defensive posture and its limited domestic concerns. As long as its borders are safe, the Soviet Union has little interest in pursuing broader economic and political objectives during the Gulf War, as the *World Oil Report* observes:

> The Soviets appear to be far more concerned with political developments in the three border countries (Iran, Turkey, and Afghanistan) than with countries further to the south. Even in the Gulf War, where the two parties directly involved are major OPEC producers, the major Soviet concern appears to be related more to strategic issues than oil.[21]

In pursuit of strategic geo-political objectives the Soviet Union has made a significant contribution to the militarization of the Third World, but not on a scale that can effectively compete with its US rival.

A Balance Sheet

In drawing up a balance sheet of influence in the Third World, it is important to avoid drawing too close a parallel between the success of one superpower and the failure of another. The fortunes of the Soviet Union and the USA in the Third World are only in part a consequence of their rivalry. Many of the most significant events of the post-war period have taken place quite independently of superpower rivalry. Yet such wars, revolts, and revolutions have had a profound impact on the international balance of power. The fact that the fortunes of the superpowers in the Third World are not reducible to the interaction between them is illustrated by the fact that the influence of both the USA and the Soviet Union has declined in recent decades.

Vietnam strikingly confirmed the limits of US power. Washington's defeat and its humiliating withdrawal from Saigon unleashed a crisis in foreign policy from which it has not yet fully recovered. The establishment of a series of radical regimes in the Third World in the 1970s was a further challenge to the USA's self-appointed role as the world policeman. The overthrow of the Shah in Iran was the culmination of the wave of Third World revolutions and the most severe blow to US foreign policy. Throughout the 1980s Washington has been struggling to regain its former position of strength in the Middle East.

The Soviet Union too has suffered a series of reverses since the high point of its power in the Third World at the beginning of the 1970s. Since its expulsion from Egypt the Soviet Union has not succeeded in forging an alliance with a major Third World country. Moscow's closest relations have been established with small and impoverished countries like Ethiopia and South Yemen. The dangerous instability of these countries was revealed by the January 1986 coup in South Yemen. The Soviet Union's arms sales have grown enormously, but it has not managed to translate military muscle into wider political influence. A revealing survey conducted by the Washington-based Center for Defence Information in 1980 showed that in the 1970s the Soviet Union experienced a marked decline in its influence in the Third World. The authors concluded that setbacks in China, Indonesia, Egypt, and Iraq outweighed Soviet gains in the smaller countries of Ethiopia and South Yemen.[22]

The apparent decline of both major superpowers in the Third World prompts the question of why the failures of one do not necessarily benefit the other. Why in particular have the reverses suffered by the USA not always been to the advantage of the Soviet Union?

The non-military dimension of superpower rivalries

In one sense the growth of Soviet presence in the Third World has been proportional to Western decline. As we have seen, from the 1950s on Soviet gains have been made in countries whose claims have been ignored by the USA or whose aspirations have been scorned by Western interests. However, the pattern which was established as a result of rivalries between the superpowers in the 1950s has been modified in recent decades. The shifting balance of power in the Horn of Africa illustrates the changing character of superpower rivalry in the Third World.

In the past neither the USA nor the Soviet Union had much interest in the Horn. The Soviet Union in particular had no direct links with the area. After achieving its independence from British and Italian rule in 1960, Somalia looked to the West for arms and aid. However, the Western powers were reluctant to respond positively since they had close ties with neighbouring Ethiopia and Kenya, both of which had less than friendly relations with Somalia.[23] As far as Washington was concerned Somalia had nothing to offer which it could not already obtain from Ethiopia and Kenya. Left on its own, Somalia turned to Moscow and it established military links in 1963. The creation of a Soviet foothold in the Horn was the result of the West's indifference to Somalia.

The downfall of Emperor Haile Selassie of Ethiopia in 1974 and the overthrow of the Shah of Iran in 1979 provoked greater US concern about the Horn. Under growing Western pressure, Somalia soon followed Egypt's earlier example and expelled all Soviet military personnel and re-established relations with the USA. The effects of this setback for the Soviet Union were mitigated by its success in forging a close relationship with Colonel Mengistu's newly established radical regime in neighbouring Ethiopia. However, the Soviet presence in Ethiopia is no more secure than its previous alliances with Egypt and Somalia.

Makinda argues that the decline in the US presence in Ethiopia in the early 1970s was the key factor in pushing Mengistu's Derg regime to look towards Moscow for support.[24] As Ethiopia's links with the Soviet Union are a mere relation of convenience it may well choose a different partner when the opportunity presents itself. A former official in the US Embassy in Addis Abbaba may have been overconfident in his anticipation of a rapid shift of alliances in 1981, but his perception of the general trend seems well founded:

> As one assesses the prospects of the future of the Ethiopian revolution, it is clear that the Soviet Union and its allies are of decreasing relevance to the solution of Mengistu's domestic and foreign problems.[25]

This assessment was simplistic and its prediction of a rapid restoration of Western influence in Ethiopia has yet to be born out by events. However, the continuing instability that prevails inside Ethiopia exposes the fragile foundations of the Soviet presence in the area.

The Soviet Union is better at establishing a presence in the Third World than it is at retaining it. This weakness is the consequence of the inability of the Soviet Union to compete with the USA in the economic sphere. The USA has an overwhelming economic impact on the Third World. Its two major clients in the Middle East alone receive $6.1 billion a year in military aid. By comparison the economic impact of the Soviet Union is minimal. The Soviet Union lacks the resources to make a decisive difference to the economic life of the Third World. Its share of overall trade in the Third World has remained stable in recent decades at a meagre 2–3 per cent.

The Soviet Union's lack of economic clout makes superpower rivalries a heavily unequal contest. As a result the Soviet Union has only a marginal role in the more developed Third World regions of Latin America and East and South-East Asia. The fact that the Soviet Union's closest allies are in the most impoverished Third World regions is a telling indication of its weakness.

The economic weakness of the Soviet Union prevents it from consolidating its gains in the Third World. Iraq provides a characteristic illustration of Soviet difficulties. In 1969 the Soviet Union helped Iraq to establish a national oil company. Moscow extended a loan of

$248 million which Iraq agreed to repay in oil shipments. But when the barter agreement ran out in 1974, Iraq took advantage of the high price of oil in the world market and redirected its sales towards the West.[27] Since the mid-1970s the Soviet Union has managed to retain a presence in Iraq only through arms sales.

The fundamental lack of economic dynamism in the Soviet system explains why Third World allies can so easily drift out of its orbit.[28] Apart from military occupation, the Soviet Union has no mechanism for dominating its Third World partners. By contrast, the Western powers can use their control over the world economy to sustain their influence in the Third World. One of the key features of imperialist domination is that it can be exercised indirectly, through the operation of economic forces. Thus the Western powers, unlike the Soviet Union, do not have to rely on direct political control. The domination of Third World countries by a small number of imperialist powers is automatically reproduced through the operation of the world market.

The ruling classes of Third World countries have been happy to accept military assistance from the Soviet Union. But they have treated military aid as a temporary expedient before moving on to establish closer economic links with Western powers. Apart from weapons, the Soviet Union has very little to offer Third World countries. Indeed the trade patterns of the Soviet Union resemble those of a developing nation: it exports raw materials and imports manufactured goods and food. There is little demand even in the Third World for the products of Soviet industry. Even a long-standing ally like India prefers to import its manufactured goods from the West.

The Soviet Union's Third World allies have derived little economic benefit from their close links with Moscow.[29] Cuba is one exception— but the US boycott has given Castro no choice but to maintain strong direct links and Moscow could not be seen to desert such an important ally. Soviet relations with Angola and Ethiopia are more revealing. Both countries rely on Soviet political and military support, yet their economies are heavily dependent on the West. According to Zeebroek, in 1986 only 9.8 per cent of all Angola's imports came from the Soviet Union, while 56.6 per cent came from Western Europe and a further 11.1 per cent from South Africa.[30] Ethiopia has been critical of the lack of Soviet assistance it has received in the form of famine aid between 1984 and 1986.[31]

Unlike the Soviet Union, the USA has the resources to reward its friends and the economic clout to punish its opponents. The ruthless imposition of economic sanctions against radical regimes, for example against Iran under Mossadegh in the early-1950s or against Chile under Allende in the 1970s, succeeded in restoring US control.

The Soviet Union's economic weakness also explains why it has not always sought to take advantage of the USA's problems. Since the mid-1970s the Soviet Union has carefully weighed up the dangers and potential costs before intervening. The economic constraints resulting from the stagnation of its domestic economy have forced Soviet strategists to adopt a more modest perspective towards the Third World. Moscow has discouraged Angola and Mozambique from becoming too economically dependent on the Eastern bloc. When presented with opportunities for expanding its influence in the 1980s the Soviet Union has adopted a policy of wait and see.

Take Grenada. The Soviet Union was reluctant to get too closely involved with the radical regime installed under Maurice Bishop and the New Jewell Movement in 1979. It clearly did not want to be in a position of having to subsidize another Cuba in the Caribbean, whatever the geo–political advantages. In July 1983, three months before the US invasion of the island, the Grenadian Ambassador in Moscow wrote to inform his superiors at home that the Soviet leaders were 'very careful and for us maddeningly slow in making up their minds about who to support'.[32] In 1983 Soviet leaders rejected Colonel Gadaffi's request for a friendship and co-operation treaty between Libya and the Soviet Union.

Over the past decade economic problems at home have forced the Soviet Union to play safe and refrain from responding to the sort of opportunities that it would have seized in the 1960s. Economic weakness constrains the advance of Soviet diplomacy in the Third World and continually undermines its influence on its existing allies. This is how one recent survey of the 'Soviet threat' summed up the reality of the situation:

> Soviet activism in the Third World has confirmed what was already known about the Soviet Union: a one dimensional dependence on military strength and a basic lack of economic, ideological and cultural appeal.[33]

In contrast to the USA, Soviet diplomacy is one-dimensional. Providing arms may win short-term friends, but it cannot secure long-term influence or secure strategic objectives. Bennett concludes from his study of Soviet arms transfers to the Middle East that a 'state's dependence on Soviet arms imports has not necessarily augmented the Soviet Union's influence in its domestic and foreign affairs'.[34]

Status quo politics

As the Soviet Union has become a global power, it has become more and more committed to maintaining the existing balance of forces in the Third World. With each succeeding decade, the Soviet Union has become more conservative in its dealings with the Third World. Moscow supported the Shah of Iran and President Marcos in the Philippines to the bitter end. As tension has mounted in the Gulf, the Soviet Union has scrupulously avoided any direct challenge to the US intervention in the region.

The *status quo* inclinations of the Soviet Union are readily apparent in Africa where it has consistently affirmed the legitimacy of the existing borders. In 1984 Moscow firmly supported Mozambique's rapprochement with South Africa. In Central America, the Soviet Union gives only the most cautious and qualified approval to the regime in Nicaragua. The conservative orientation of the Soviet Union has become so overwhelming that it has given rise to a degree of disenchantment among Third World countries which are dependent on Soviet military aid. In Libya Colonel Gadaffi clearly miscalculated the degree of support he could count on receiving from the Soviet Union to strengthen his position against US aggression. Not only is the Soviet Union less able to respond because of economic considerations, it is also less and less willing to upset the existing balance of power. Since its invasion of Afghanistan the Soviet Union has become cautious to the point of not taking any risks at all.

The rhetoric of superpower rivalry

At the very time when the Soviet Union was beginning to pull back from its involvement in the Third World, the USA launched a new era of Third World brinkmanship. Since the beginning of the Reagan Presidency, the US administration has adopted an increasingly interventionist posture, accompanied by military aggression overseas on a scale not seen since the 1960s. This approach, codified in the 1985 Reagan doctrine, has been justified on the grounds that it is the only way to meet the menace of Soviet expansionism.

The anti-Soviet shift in US foreign policy since the early 1980s cannot be explained by any change in Soviet policy in the Third World. The Soviet Union has lost its political impetus in the Third World and its army has become heavily bogged down in Afghanistan. The main motive behind Reagan's new cold war rhetoric has been to prevent the decline of the USA as the dominant global capitalist power. Within the Western world, the USA has begun to lose ground to Japan and West Germany. In the Third World, the *pax Americana* has had to face a number of challenges. Reagan hoped that by militarizing US diplomacy, he could reverse the trends towards decline.

The decline of US hegemony in the Third World was the result of internal stagnation and anti-imperialist revolt, not the rise of Soviet power. But it has been more convenient for Reagan to tackle the difficulties in the Western camp under the guise of countering Soviet subversion. In the early-1980s the myth of Soviet expansionism acquired ludicrous proportions. The first major foreign policy statement of the Reagan administration in 1980 was the claim that Cuban and Soviet 'aggression' were responsible for the revolts in El Salvador and the rest of Central America. Over the next two years the Reagan administration put considerable resources into fabricating evidence that would confirm Soviet aggression in the USA's 'backyard'.

In February 1981 the US State Department published *Communist Interference in El Salvador*, marshalling 'evidence' of Soviet and Cuban involvement. Within a month the evidence was exposed as a tissue of lies. The *Wall Street Journal* expressed the view that the authors of the report on insurgency in Central America 'probably were making a determined effort to create a "selling" document, no matter how slim the background material'.[35] Similar tales served as a pretext for the invasion of Grenada and for US backing for right-wing rebel forces in Nicaragua and Angola.

The dearth of evidence made the fiction of Soviet expansionism increasingly difficult to sustain, Reagan's top advisors were obliged to shift the grounds on which they justified military interference in the Third World. After 1985 US strategists supplemented rhetoric about the need to 'roll back communism' with propaganda directed against the bogey of 'international terrorism'.

The Reagan doctrine developed the previous doctrines of containment by widening the range of targets. The USA was still committed to 'rolling back' allegedly Marxist regimes through techniques of low-intensity warfare and covert action. By using rapid military strikes and promoting local right-wing resistance movements, Washington hoped to minimize direct US involvement. Through sponsoring guerrilla organizations such as the Contras in Nicaragua, UNITA in Angola, and the MNR in Mozambique, Reagan aimed to legitimize US intervention in key Third World trouble spots.

In situations where it was impossible to sustain the myth of Soviet expansionism, the USA has played the terrorist card. This is not a new technique: the need to rescue 'women and children' provided the pretext for military intervention in the Congo and the Dominican Republic in the 1960s. However, the prominence given to the problem of international terrorism in recent years is unprecedented. Washington insists that every summit of Western powers issues a vehement denunciation of international terrorism. The menace of terrorism has become the standard justification for US intervention in the Middle East—in Lebanon, Libya, and the Gulf. It has provided an argument for rearmament and for the escalation of the US military presence in the Third World.

Reagan's bark has been worse than his bite. He has picked on easy military targets such as Grenada and has avoided any major long-term military commitments. The CIA car bomb in Beirut in December 1984 and the air-strike in Tripoli in April 1986 are the sort of ignominious episodes in which US forces now specialize in the Third World.

Since 1979 the USA has been obliged to extend its operations in the Third World. Low-intensity war and covert action are only one dimension of US involvement. The USA has also worked behind the scenes to establish reliable local allies. The coup in Fiji in 1987 seems to have been encouraged from Washington. Washington has learnt from its mistakes in Iran and Nicaragua. It now attempts to remove its right-wing stooges from power before popular discontent blows up into a revolution. This strategy has paid dividends in El Salvador, Haiti, and the Philippines. In all these countries Washington has forced its friends out of office to pre-empt popular revolt. In South Korea US advisors forced the government to make major concessions in the face of mounting street protests against the regime.

The build-up of US interference in the Third World on several fronts has little to do with superpower rivalries. Washington faces little pressure from the Soviet Union since Moscow is even less inclined to raise its Third World profile today than it was in the past. The failure of the USA to impose its policies on Third World trouble spots is the product of local opposition rather than a result of Soviet diplomacy.

In recent years the Soviet Union has tended to modify its version of superpower rhetoric. In the past the Soviet Union tried to promote an image as the champion of the struggles of the oppressed against imperialist domination. Since the mid-1970s, there has been a perceptible shift in emphasis: in contrast to Washington, Moscow is now inclined to play down the rhetoric of superpower confrontation.

The Soviet Union has become unwilling to jeopardize its relations with Third World countries because of its links with radical forces. For example, in the Horn of Africa, Moscow has withdrawn its support from the Eritrean Liberation Movement in order to strengthen its ties with the Ethiopian government. The Soviet author Simonov attempts to justify this *volte-face* with a remarkable display of verbal acrobatics:

> Many researchers recognised the progressive character of the Eritrean movement in the years when it opposed the anti-popular regime of Haile Selassie. However, by identifying the revolutionary regime with monarchy, the Eritrean insurgents showed their political immaturity and acted as a tool in the hands of those hostile to the cause of national liberation.[36]

The pragmatic drift of Soviet policy means that its Third World allies cannot expect the kind of support that has been extended to Cuba in the past. It is significant that during his tour of Latin America in October 1987 the Soviet Foreign Minister Eduard Shevardnadze did not stop in Nicaragua. This is how one US journalist assessed the tour:

> Moscow does not recognise the latter day Monroe Doctrine of President Reagan, any more than it did the original version that the Tsar received a copy of. But, in practice, unlike during the heady days of the Cuban revolution and its aftermath, Moscow gives it due attention. Ever since the election in 1970 of Salvador Allende, the Marxist president of Chile, Moscow has been playing it cool in Latin America. And, since the Nicaraguan revolution, it has become even cooler, reaching the point a couple of months ago of briefly suspending its supplies to Nicaragua to express its disapproval of the Sandinistas' hard line.[37]

The reluctance of the Soviet Union to give firm support to Nicaragua stands in sharp contrast to the determination of the USA to destroy the Sandinista regime. The reality of Nicaragua—a tiny and impoverished country left by the Soviet Union to stand alone against the ravages of a guerrilla war and economic sanctions backed with all the might of the USA—exposes the rhetoric of the superpowers.

Conclusion

Superpower rivalries have a profound impact on the Third World. However, the militarization of the Third World is only in part a consequence of East–West tensions. The main actor remains the USA, with the Soviet Union in a secondary role. In recent years the former's diplomatic aspirations in the Third World have become more modest. US policy is inspired by the need to contain Third World revolt; its conflict with the Soviet Union is only a side-show.

Nevertheless the Soviet Union always poses a potential threat to US, and more broadly to Western, interests. The very existence of the Soviet Union means that it always provides a potential alternative in situations where anti-imperialist sentiments cannot be contained within the existing structures of Western domination. The Soviet Union can benefit from the USA's problem but it lacks a capacity to create its own opening. The build-up of Western militarism, notably in the Gulf, is likely to create new opportunities for the Soviet Union. Gorbachev has demonstrated his skills in projecting the Soviet Union as a worthwhile diplomatic partner in the contemporary unstable environment. Any significant escalation of US interventionism will inevitably throw up problems from which the Soviet Union may make gains. The Third World can only hope that the threat of Soviet gains will force Washington to think twice before its next intervention.

Notes

1. Shulman, 'Chapter One, Overview' in M.O. Shulman, ed., *East–West Tensions in the Third World*, (New York, 1986), p. 15.
2. Cited in A. Schlesinger jnr. *A Thousand Days, John F. Kennedy in the White House*, (Boston, 1965), p. 507.
3. For other estimates see S. Kaplan and B. Blechman, *Force Without War*, (Washington DC, 1978) and S. Kaplan, *Iron Fist, Velvet Glove*.
4. See D.S. Papp, *Soviet Perceptions of the Developing World in the 1980s*, (Lexington Mass, 1980), p. 2.
5. E.K. Valkenier, 'Revolutionary Change in the Third World: Recent Soviet assessments', *World Politics*, no. 38, 1986, p. 422.
6. V. Zaslavsky, 'The Soviet World System: Origins, Evolution, Prospects for Reform', *Telos*, 1986, p. 14.
7. See Table 1 in J.W. Sewell and C.E. Contee, 'Foreign Aid and Gramm-Rudman', *Foreign Affairs*, October 1987, p. 1022.
8. D.E. Albright, 'East–West Tensions in Africa' in Shulman, op. cit. p. 136.
9. F. Fukuyama, 'Military Aspects of US–Soviet Competition in the Third World' in Shulman, op. cit., p. 184.
10. H.S. Truman, 'Address before Joint Session of Congress', 12 March 1947.
11. R.J. Barnett, *Intervention and Revolution*, (London, 1968), p. 22.
12. *The New York Times*, 6 January 1957.
13. Cited in Barnett, op. cit., p. 23.
14. *The Guardian*, 24 January 1980.
15. F. Halliday, *Beyond Irangate: the Reagan Doctrine and the Third World*, (Amsterdam, 1987), p. 12.
16. Fukuyama, op. cit., p. 186.
17. See the discussion in F. Furedi, *The Soviet Union Demystified*, (London, 1986), p. 23.
18. R. Johnson, 'Exaggerating America's Stakes in Third World Conflicts', *International Security*, 10(3), Winter 1985–86, p. 67.
19. Cited in Furedi, op. cit., p. 242.
20. X. Zeebroek, 'Soviet Expansionism and Expansive Anti-Sovietism', *Socialist Register*, (London, 1984), p. 290.
21. *World Oil Report* April 1987. p. 1.
22. Cited in Furedi, op. cit., pp. 233–4.
23. See S.M. Mackinda, *Superpower Diplomacy in the Horn of Africa*, (London, 1987).
24. Ibid. p. 38.
25. P.B. Henze, 'Communism and Ethiopia', *Problems of Communism*, May–June 1981, p. 71.
26. Sewell and Contee, op. cit., p. 1030.
27. E.K. Valkenir, 'East–West Economic Competition in the Third World' in Shulman, op. cit., p. 162.
28. Ibid, p. 168.
29. For a more extensive discussion of the domestic constraints on Soviet foreign policy, see Furedi, op. cit., pp. 211–47.
30. Zeebroek, op. cit., p. 294.

31. Makinda, op. cit., p. 190.

32. Cited in J.I. Dominguez, 'United States, Soviet and Cuban Policies Towards Latin America', in Shulman, op. cit., p. 64.

33. M. Bentinck, 'Nato's Out-of-Area Problem', *Adelphi Papers*, no. 211, 1986, p. 47.

34. A.J. Bennett, 'Arms Transfer as an Instrument of Soviet Policy in the Middle East', *The Middle East Journal*, 39 (4), 1985, p. 773.

35. *Wall Street Journal*, 8 June 1981.

36. V. Simonov, *Seething Continent: the Soviet Viewpoint*, (Moscow, 1980), p. 35.

37. I. Power, 'In Latin America, the Soviets are Capitalists', *International Herald Tribune*, 10–11 October 1987.

The Non-Aligned Movement

13

The Role of the Non-Aligned Movement in Global Politics

ROBERT MUGABE

Introduction

This essay is taken from a speech given by Robert Mugabe at the Eighth Summit Conference of Heads of State of the Non-Aligned Movement in Harare on 1 September 1986.

Our world is faced with many challenges: the quest for economic development, for human rights, for justice, and for human dignity. But all these are predicated on the assumption of the continued existence of human life. The one question therefore that today precedes all others, in that without an answer to it answers to all other questions become pointless, is the question of disarmament. Preventing the annihilation of mankind consequent upon nuclear war is the precondition of all our endeavours.

This fundamental fact was recognized as early as 1978 when the international community, in adopting the Final Document of the Tenth Special Session of the General Assembly, the first devoted to disarmament, stated unequivocally that: 'We must halt the arms race and proceed to disarmament or face annihilation.' Yet in the eight years that have intervened since, we have seen more, not less, expenditure on nuclear weapons; more, not less, nuclear weapons and other weapons of mass destruction; greater, not less, insecurity. Global military expenditures are now in the order of $1 trillion per year.

Indeed the statistics are as gloomy as they are familiar: global military outlays currently run at $2 million dollars per minute. For every 100,000 people in the world there are 556 soldiers, but only 85 doctors. For every soldier the average world military expenditure is $20,000, while for every school-age child the average public education is a paltry $380. Developed countries spend 20–times as much on military expenditures as they do on economic aid. Only one-fifth of arms expenditure, in just one year, could wipe out the scourge of world hunger by the year 2000. All these facts illustrate the central theme of our time—the conspicuous misuse and abuse of scarce resources in the midst of poverty, hunger, and disease. Surely the time has come to call mankind back to sanity: to re-order his priorities in favour of life and development, as against death and destruction.

We welcome the joint statement by the two superpowers that a nuclear war cannot be won and therefore must never be fought. Consequently we urge them to follow through the logic of that reasoning by abolishing from the face of the earth the means for waging such a war. It is our conviction that an essential step in this direction would be the conclusion of a comprehensive test ban treaty; prohibiting all nuclear weapon tests by states in all environments, for all time.

Pending the conclusion of such a treaty, it is essential that there be a moratorium on all nuclear tests by all nuclear weapon powers. In this regard the world lauds the unilateral moratorium by the Soviet Union which ran for a year from August 1985 to August 1986 and was extended till January 1987. We urge the Soviet side to continue its self-imposed restraint and call on all other nuclear weapon states, in particular the USA, which, together with the Soviet Union, accounts for the bulk of such tests, to join in the moratorium. It is also essential that all nuclear weapon states enter into internationally binding agreements on a nuclear weapon freeze. In this connection we commend the efforts of the Six-Nation Five-Continent Initiative whose proposals on these and other disarmament issues are in line with the positions espoused by our Non-Aligned Movement (NAM). In particular we call upon the nuclear weapon powers to seriously consider the constructive proposals on verification presented by the Six.

Confidence-building measures in disarmament in themselves, however, will not lead to long-lasting peace and security unless they are accompanied by similar measures in international economic relations. The current state of the world economy, especially as it relates to prospects for development in non-aligned and other developing countries, is a cause for grave concern to us. The development crisis of the early 1980s is by all accounts far from over. If anything, it has escalated. Over a third of developing countries experienced zero or negative growth rates of real GNP per head in 1985 and in many cases the situation shows no sign of improvement this year. Commodity markets, particularly those of primary commodities, of which developing countries are major exporters, remained depressed and unstable in 1985 as they were throughout most of the 1980s.

Between 1980 and 1985 the price of primary commodities produced by developing countries declined by an average of 7.4 per cent per annum; that is, over double that of manufactured goods. This, coupled with a rise in protectionism in developed markets, a general worsening in the terms of trade of developing countries, high interest rates, and a decline in the flows of official development assistance in real terms to developing countries, has resulted in an unprecedented 'bleeding' of the developing countries.

The truth is that the economies of the developing South are subsidizing those of the developed North. As a result we have seen a deepening of the economic crisis. For example, the United Nations 1986 World Economic Survey estimates that the decline in commodity prices, including oil, has resulted in substantial gains for the developed countries of over $100 billion. At the same time, the net interest paid in external debt servicing by developing countries amounted to $54 billion in 1985 and the net income outflow of foreign direct investment amounted to $13 billion during the same year. Meanwhile the transfers of resources from developed to developing countries continue to decline and amounted to only $13 billion in loans and credit facilities, $14 billion in official development assistance, and $9 billion in direct investment. Such heavy financial haemorrhage coupled with severe economic undernourishment has robbed many developing countries of the capacity to service their external debts.

The debt crisis, in particular the debt-service burden it imposes on economies of the debtor countries concerned, has reached grotesque proportions. The World Bank estimates that the accumulated debt of the developing world has risen to $812.4 billion and that the debt-service payments alone account for 61.2 per cent of the overall payments of debt. This is a cause for serious concern, not only for the debtor countries concerned, but also for all of humanity interested in the survival of the world economy. The debt crisis evokes the imagery of a voracious primordial beast, of gargantuan appetite, gobbling up all the export earnings of the developing countries. The monster must be neutralized before it devours not only our earnings, but our very independence of action and sovereignty over our natural resources and economic activities. We must develop co-ordinated plans, initiatives, and schemes to tackle the problem. To do nothing is suicidal. To allow the monster to deal with us on a 'case by case basis' is a recipe for disaster.

The direct relationship existing between money, trade, debt, development, and stability in the international monetary and financial system cannot be overemphasized. The persistent instability in the financial markets, the prevailing high interest rates, and exchange rate misalignments militate against the expansion of the world economy. Sustained and equitable economic growth, beneficial to all, can only be possible in a world economic regime free from the imbalances, inequalities, and inadequacies of the present international economic system. In the light of the current situation, the establishment of the New International Economic order, based on justice, equity, and sovereign equality, remains an absolute necessity of our time. The forces ranged against us may be many, but we should not be deterred. We should continue vigorously to pursue all options available with the view to creating a new and better world.

The revival of growth in the world economy demands that dialogue between the developed and developing countries be resumed without further delay. The current stalemate in global negotiations does not augur well for the future. In this context the forthcoming meeting of UNCTAD, therefore, provides an opportune moment for both the developing and developed countries to take joint action with a view to launching a programme for world economic recovery and the reaction of balanced and sustained growth and development.

Increased South–South co-operation and collective self-reliance, particularly in view of the present adverse world economic environment and the continuing deadlock in the negotiations for the restructuring of international economic relations, is an indispensible and integral part of our efforts to restructure the current unjust and inequitable world economic system.

Besides reducing the vulnerability of the developing countries' economies, such co-operation further enhances our collective bargaining strength in global negotiations. It is high time that we face up to the fact that so long as the impressively long list of areas of mutual assistance and co-operation in our Action Programme for Economic Co-operation remains largely a series of blueprints, so long will our partners in the developed North remain sceptical of our resolve to bring about changes in the present world economy. Let our solidarity and mutual assistance be truly action-oriented. We should resolve, here and now, to reaffirm our commitment to action-oriented solidarity, mutual co-operation, and assistance among non-aligned and other developing nations. There is much we can do to help each other. We must do it. And the time is now.

It is only through the promotion of co-operative relations, not only among the developing countries, but also between the North and South, that we can arrest and reverse the present retreat from multilateralism to unilateralism and bilateralism. In the world of today, interdependence is a fact of life and, hence, the promotion of international co-operation and multilateralism should be the concern of every nation.

Forces opposed to the freedom of peoples continue to frustrate the realization of the rights of peoples still under colonial domination to self-determination and independence and violate the sovereignty and territorial integrity of non-aligned countries. One such evil force is the system of apartheid in South Africa; a system that denies our common humanity; assails our sense of decency, violates all norms of morality, and dehumanizes both its victims and its perpetrators. It is a system which the United Nations has rightly declared to be a crime against humanity.

The apartheid regime kills defenceless demonstrators as a matter of routine; violently uproots and relegates millions of its black citizens to wretched dustbowls, and tortures and murders those whom it holds in detention. It has incarcerated Nelson Mandela, that heroic and legendary symbol of the struggling masses of South Africa, for nearly a quarter of a century just because he dared to demand the freedom of his people. In addition it holds thousands of its opponents in jail without trial.

The defence of apartheid requires not only internal repression and genocide at home but constant aggression against neighbouring states. Pretoria follows a policy of state terrorism directed at the neighbouring independent states. Against these states South Africa has devised an integrated and comprehensive regional policy of hegemony that combines the use of economic sanctions with the fomenting of political unrest in neighbouring countries though the agency of armed bandits, recruited, armed, financed, and directed by it. Through these activities of state-sponsored terrorism the regime has truly become a threat, both to regional and international peace and sovereignty. It is common knowledge that the regime has also extended its abhorrent system to Namibia, which it has continued to subject to colonial bondage two decades after the UN had terminated its mandate over that territory. The plight of the people of illegally occupied Namibia differs little from that of the majority of the people of South Africa. They too are oppressed, brutalized, and denied the most elementary human and other rights. Furthermore, the racist regime presides over the plunder of Namibia's natural resources by transnational corporations, and uses the territory of Namibia as a springboard to commit aggression against its neighbours.

Much of this analysis of the nature and character of the apartheid regime is well known. What is needed now is action: action to eradicate the evil system of apartheid; action to resist Pretoria's aggression against the neighbouring independent states; and action to stop South Africa's illegal colonial occupation of Namibia. In this context I welcome and commend for your consideration, adoption, and implementation the recommendations of the World Conference on Sanctions Against South Africa held in Paris from 16–20 June 1986 and those of the International Conference for the Immediate Independence of Namibia held in Vienna from 7–11 July 1987. Both conferences endorsed the position long held by our NAM that comprehensive mandatory sanctions are the only effective peaceful means left to force South Africa to dismantle apartheid; stop its naked acts of aggression; and terminate its illegal occupation of Namibia. I earnestly urge that, pending the adoption of comprehensive mandatory sanctions under chapter VII of the UN Charter by the Security Council, members of the NAM should agree to adopt and implement for a start the voluntary selective sanctions against South Africa outlined in the declarations adopted in Paris and Vienna.

We should continue to press the key industrial countries, in particular the governments of the United Kingdom, the Federal Republic of Germany, Japan, and the present US administration, to agree to the imposition of comprehensive mandatory sanctions against South Africa. Our actions must be co-ordinated and concerted. In this context we may wish to consider the sending of a team of foreign ministers from our NAM to visit capitals of key industrial countries to canvass for the adoption and implementation of mandatory sanctions. Also, we should endeavour to increase the nature and amount of concrete material assistance we render to the liberation movements of South Africa and Namibia. In this regard support for the Front Line and other independent states in the region is critical so that they may become dependable bulwarks against apartheid. Our NAM's commitment to justice, freedom, and equality obliges us to support fully all struggles for these cherished values, not only in Africa but also in the Middle East, Central America, Asia, and the Mediterranean, where people are struggling to free themselves from imperialism, external interference, intervention, hegemonism, destabilization, and other forms of domination.

In relation to Africa, we are appalled that in Angola naked interference with the sovereignty of that country has proceeded, beginning with the demand for the withdrawal of the Cuban forces as a condition for Namibia's independence, to assume a more dangerous dimension, that of affording military assistance to the counter-revolutionary and reactionary forces of UNITA bent on overthrowing a legitimate government; so that UNITA now enjoys the full support of both apartheid South Africa and the Reagan administration. Perhaps an even more shocking event was the recent undiscriminating bomb attack upon Tripoli. Surely such international 'bullyism' serves only to exacerbate rather than ameliorate tense bilateral relations and constitutes a grave threat not only to regional but also to international peace and security.

In the Middle East, Israel's continued bellicose conduct poses a serious threat to international peace and security. We support the call for an urgent international conference on the Middle East at which all the parties involved in the dispute, including the PLO, would participate. There can be no lasting solution to the Middle East problem until the Palestinian question, which is a part of the problem, is resolved and the occupied Palestinian and other Arab lands are returned to their rightful owners.

It is most disturbing that the largest number of international hotbeds of tensions today exist mainly on the soil of non-aligned countries. This sad state of affairs is primarily due to the intensification of bloc power politics and general interference in the internal affairs of small states. We are deeply saddened by the initiation and continuation of the war between the two sister non-aligned countries, Iran and Iraq. Use or threat of use of force in the settlement of international disputes is contrary to the Charter of the United Nations and the principles of the Non-Aligned Movement. We earnestly appeal to our brothers of Iran and Iraq to put an end to the carnage and to respect international humanitarian law. We urge them to see their way clear to a peaceful resolution of this cruel and tragic conflict.

The situation in Cyprus continues to threaten the sovereignty of that country and peace in the entire Mediterranean region. We call upon all external powers to cease forthwith all interference in the internal affairs of Cyprus and withdraw their troops from the island state so as to facilitate negotiations between the two Cypriot communities.

There will neither be peace nor security on the Korean Peninsula for as long as foreign intervention continues to perpetuate the idea of 'two Koreas'. Foreign interference must stop and enable both the North and the South to engage in the intercommunal talks aimed at the peaceful reunification of that country. It is important that all foreign troops are withdrawn from the Peninsula immediately in order to set the stage for the process of peaceful reunification.

Tension in the Central American, the Caribbean, and South Atlantic regions has persisted largely because of foreign intervention aimed at destabilizing and undermining progressive governments there. In Nicaragua we are witnessing the use of military force against the territorial integrity and political independence of that country, all because it has dared to choose a political and socio–economic system which is at variance with that of the dominant power in the region. The US government openly finances, trains, equips, deploys, and directs Contras against Nicaragua. The Contras have inflicted indescribable human and material damage against the peace-loving people of that country. We call on the USA to promote international law by respecting and abiding by the recent decision of the International Court of Justice. We ask that Nicaragua be allowed to pursue its chosen course of socio–economic development. We are convinced that the Contadora peace process is a rational route to a comprehensive regional peace plan that will satisfy the concerns of all parties in the Central American conflict.

We would similarly urge that foreign intervention, especially as expressed through the presence of foreign forces, in such countries as Afghanistan and Kampuchea, should be speedily terminated and the peoples of these lands left to determine their own destiny.

Our NAM stands for very little if it does not stand for the freedom and self-determination of colonized and oppressed peoples. In New Caledonia, Saharawi, Mayotte, and other territories, the peoples yearn for their freedom and they must be allowed to enjoy it. Colonialism is thoroughly discredited in our day and age. It should thus be rooted out of these lands so that their peoples may shape their own destinies in the same manner and to the same degree as other people.

14

Olof Palme and the Legacy of Bandung: A Balance Sheet

FRED HALLIDAY AND MAXINE MOLYNEUX

In April 1955 the leaders of 29 Asian and African states, including China, met at Bandung in Indonesia for the First Conference of Afro–Asian Solidarity. A generation of new Third World leaders had come to power and gained international prominence. The old colonial empires, mortally weakened by the Second World War, were retreating. A new force, which by the early 1960s came to be known as the 'Third World', was coming into existence. Today, over 30 years after that historic event, the number of independent states in Asia, Africa, and Latin America has greatly increased, to around 120. In 1955 only six African states were represented at Bandung: today over 50 are independent.

The issues posed at Bandung remain vital and, in some cases, are even more pressing. They are the ones to which Olof Palme dedicated enormous energy and concern in his work on the effects of the arms race and in his attempts to encourage dialogue between Iran and Iraq. A balance sheet of the intervening three decades, schematic and provisional as it may be, can therefore serve not only as a retrospective on what has passed, but as a guide to the agenda for the future. It may also serve, in part, to suggest just how pressing was this internationalist work of Palme and how much remains to be achieved if the goals for which he campaigned, and which were enunciated at the first Bandung Conference, are to be reached.

The Achievements

The ensuing years have certainly produced some major changes in world politics, one called for and symbolized by that initial gathering at Bandung.

The process of decolonization, begun immediately after the Second World War, has been virtually completed. The empires of Britain,

157

France, Belgium, Holland, and, belatedly, Portugal have disappeared. The value system associated with colonialism, the belief held for over a century that some European states had the right to rule other parts of the world, has been swept away: metropolitan colonialism, which even in the 1950s many expected to last for decades, has gone for ever. Over two-dozen European colonies remain in existence, but the great majority of these are insignificant enclaves where, for anomalous local reasons, the populations prefer to remain attached to metropolitan states. Puerto Rico, Montserrat, and the Virgin Islands, Guadeloupe and Martinique, Ceuta and Melilla, New Caledonia and Guam, Hong Kong and Macao are the crumbs of a now bygone system.

In the Non-Aligned Movement (NAM) only two of the 101 members represent liberation movements—the PLO and SWAPO—while a third, the ANC of South Africa, is an observer. All the other former colonies, most recently Zimbabwe, have acceded to statehood. Beyond their individual accession to statehood, the countries of the Third World have come together in a variety of alliances and coalitions to represent, jointly, their shared political and economic interests. The Afro–Asian People's Solidarity Organization, founded at Bandung, lost its vitality after 10 years, following the Boumedienne coup in Algeria and China's loss of influence in the Third World. But the NAM, founded in 1961, has gathered over 100 members and represents a clear persistent voice in international affairs, in support of decolonialization, non-interference in the Third World, and a reform of the international economic system: this latter goal, first raised collectively at UNCTAD in 1964, was to find its clearest codification in the proclamation of the programme for a New International Economic Order (NIEO) in 1973 at the Fourth NAM Summit in Algiers. Parallel to the NAM, the Group of 77, now with 126 members, has lobbied for international economic reforms. Other more specific coalitions and successes can be registered: OPEC, established in 1960, has since 1971 been able to substantially multiply the oil revenues of its members; the 64 African, Caribbean, and Pacific (ACP) states who have negotiated the three Lome Conventions have achieved a significant new bargaining position with the EEC; and, although not formally united in one organization, the dozen or so new industrializing countries (NICs) have, in the 1970s, broken what was previously seen as an absolute block on industrialization in the Third World.

The growth of OPEC, and of the ACP states and NICs, points to a further major dimension of change over the past 30 years, namely that of economic and social transformation.

The idea commonly held in the 1960s, that the newly independent countries were condemned to a condition of neo-colonial stagnation without agrarian change, industrial growth, or expansion of welfare services, is clearly inadequate in the face of the record of recent decades. The rise not only of NICs, like South Korea, Singapore, and Mexico, but of countries like India, the Philippines, and Brazil, demonstrates that there is great industrial potential in the Third World. Agricultural change, whether through land reforms, as in Taiwan, or through green revolutions, as in Punjab, point to a variety of possible new paths in the countryside. The great expansion of education and health services in many Third World states is not compatible with a view of these countries as all destined to constant misery.

The achievement of independence and the pace of socio–economic change have done more than just alter the political institutions and governing bodies of these states. For attendant upon and following independence, a considerable number of Third World countries have undergone social revolutions of a wide range of character and depth. The overthrow of colonialism has in many cases been accompanied or paralleled by the overthrow of established ruling systems, be these of local or metropolitan origin. The history of the post-war world has been that of a series of Third World earthquakes, which have come in three major waves. The first, immediately after the Second World War, included those of China, Vietnam, Korea, Egypt, and Bolivia. The second, in the late-1950s and early-1960s, included Cuba, Iraq, North Yemen, and Algeria. The third, and by far the greatest, came in the period from 1974 to 1980 when 14 Third World states underwent social revolution—some as part of the decolonization process (Zimbabwe, and the Portuguese colonies in Africa), others as a result of indigenous struggles against foreign occupation (Vietnam, Laos, and Cambodia) and others still against local, formally independent, ruling classes (Iran, Afghanistan, Ethiopia, Grenada, Nicaragua). Since 1980, events in many parts of the world—Central America, Haiti, Sudan, the Philippines—indicate that the social order in the Third World has not found a new stability in the mid-1980s.

In both the independence struggles and the Third World revolutions a major redefinition of power in the contemporary world was achieved through the defeat of metropolitan armies in a series of wars. At the very beginning of the century the first wave of colonial resistance had been impelled by the Japanese defeat of Russia in 1905. Of the 150 or more wars since 1945, in which over 20 million people have died, virtually all have been in the Third World: the only significant exception was the Greek Civil war of 1944–49. The greatest number of victims have also been people from the Third World: the gruesome arithmetic of Vietnam—57,000 US personnel, two million Vietnamese killed—tells its own tale, as do the more than one million dead in the Algerian War. Yet, at terrible cost, the countries of the Third World have inflicted many defeats on states who vaunt military power as the supreme dimension of national greatness and who have tried over decades to maintain their controls—colonial and post-colonial—on the Third World. In Vietnam and Algeria, Cyprus and South Yemen, at Suez, Playa Giron in Cuba and on the Yalu River, and in Angola and Mozambique, the Third World armies have faced and defeated the colonial states. In 1983, by a combination of military and political resistance, President Reagan may have had a walkover in Grenada, but he was unable to keep the Marines in the far more significant contest of Lebanon.

Beyond these specific changes and achievements, there lies a further dimension, imprecise yet of great importance, namely a shift in perceptions of international politics. The old system of a world dominated by the great powers of Europe and the USA, and subservient to them, had, despite the rise of Japan and China, survived the Second World War. The early UN was under undisputed Western control. But as the number and activity of the Third World states increased, this changed, and the countries of the Third World won new status and influence. They gradually formed a more independent bloc in the UN and wrested it from Western manipulation. They continued to lobby against colonialism and for universal independence. A generation of Third World leaders stepped on to the world stage. It was Bandung which, more than any other event, ushered in this new era, and the new world which these leaders represented. Nehru and Nasser, Sukarno and Nkrumah, Castro and Guevara, Mao and Zhou En-lai, Cabral and Neto, Giap and Ho Chi Minh, even such despots as Haile Selassie and the Shah of Iran, were leaders of international reputation in a rapidly changing configuration of power.

The Failures

Yet the 30 years since Bandung have not been ones of unqualified or continuous success. For all that the Third World has achieved, it has endured terrible sufferings, calamities, disappointments, wastages, and deceits. Few in 1955 could have envisaged the many setbacks that the original proponents of independence, coexistence, and economic prosperity were to undergo.

Despite substantial socio–economic change and the growth of incomes and output in many Third World countries, the majority of these states have experienced a worsening of the economic conditions inherited from colonialism. By mid-1982 between 700 million and 1000 million people in the Third World are at or below the poverty line, faced with malnutrition or starvation. One over-arching reason for this has been the explosion in Third World rates of population growth, such that the strain on resources, habits, and social structures has grown immensely over the past few decades. The massive migration of people to cities, such that it is now reckoned that half the world's population live in urban areas and the peasantry may for the first time be a minority on this earth, has led to the growth of vast new domains of misery and squalor, underemployment, and despair. The substantial industrialization of the Third World has not kept pace with the growth in urban population. In the countryside, vast areas have been hit by famine, ecological disaster, and chronic underemployment. Provision to Third World states has been meagre measured against the requirements of these countries and the donor capabilities of the rich. A considerable amount of this aid has been misdirected and stolen. Third World states have also misused their new resources: the record of the OPEC states, where corruption, inefficiency, agricultural decay, and new forms of social parasitism have mushroomed in the past decade, is the most striking index of this missed opportunity. Some Arabs now see oil as a curse.

The record on the political front is hardly more encouraging. Of the 100 or more Third World states, few have established and maintained politically democratic systems. All too often the weakness of post-colonial state structures, the acute tensions in Third World societies, and pressure from imperialist states, have led to the emergence of dictatorships, in which the military have played the leading role. The oppression visited upon post-colonial Third World peoples has been different in character from that of imperial rule; but it has involved ferocious repression, cruelty, and violation of human rights. Much of the responsibility for this lies with imperialism.

But the nationalism of Third World states, which served to mobilize people against colonialism, has all too often been used in demagogic form to justify the crushing of opponents, the denial of rights to ethnic and religious minorities, and the silencing of individual critics. In some countries, too, religious nationalism, sanctified with all the fanaticism of the divinely inspired, has been used to re-introduce some of the forms of oppression that capitalist modernization under colonialism had undermined—the fate of women in Khomeini's Iran and the Hindu promotion of caste being cases in point. The hopes of the 1950s, that independence would lead to greater democracy and social justice, have proven as unfounded as those concerning economic development.

On the external front the record is little better. The countries of the Third World have won formal independence, and the new state structures have established themselves. But in numerous ways the metropolitan states retain and exert predominant influence over the South: the world, albeit one of independent states, remains a hierarchical one, not just in terms of the distribution of wealth, but in terms of power relationships. The dependence of the Third World on the richer economies, the political and cultural influence exerted in the Third World, the increasing predominance of a mythified 'modern' lifestyle, all point to these enduring dependencies. The collective instruments of the Third World have fared little better. The NAM's ability to negotiate an NIEO with the North has proven illusory; the last attempt at global negotiations, held at Cancun, Mexico, in October 1981, led to no significant change. With Reagan's ideology in power in the USA there is no prospect of a change of heart in the North. The numerical domination of the Third World in the UN General Assembly has led to the evacuation of the great powers from significant activity in that arena. OPEC's ability to raise oil prices for a decade was real enough: but its intention to convert this economic power over one commodity into an instrument for broader pressure on the North, over the Palestine issue or the NIEO, has proven illusory. The most dramatic change in North–South economic relations over the past decade has been the enormous increases in Third World debt.

This pattern of weakness and disarray *vis-à-vis* the North is also evident in relations between Third World countries. The most dramatic index of this is the rising incidence of armed conflict between Third World states: the Arab–Israeli and Indo–Pakistani Wars have now been succeeded by many others—Somalia and Ethiopia, Uganda and Tanzania, Iran and Iraq—and in a gruesome appendix to the solidarity of the 1960s, Vietnam and China. Third World states are spending increasing amounts of their scarce resources on arms. In 1982 Third World states purchased over $20 billion worth of arms, equivalent to nearly two-thirds of the total world arms trade. The incidence of nuclear proliferation in the Third World demonstrates the dangers that may lie ahead: over 20 Third World states could have the bomb by the year 2000. The disarray is equally evident in the economic sphere: despite much talk of greater economic co-operation between developing countries the record is dismal indeed. Over 70 per cent of Third World economic relations is carried out between individual Third World states and developed countries. There has been no real increase in economic co-operation since the proclamation of the NIEO in 1973. Where there has been a change is in the character of intra-Third World economic relations towards greater differentiation and exploitation of the poorer by the richer: the OPEC extortion of higher oil prices from the poorer Third World states and the exploitation of Third World labour through migration are the signs of what has in effect become the new economic order, one of greater inequality between Third World states. Attempts by regional groupings of Third World states to forge more effective forms of political collaboration between themselves have proven equally exclusive. The more coherent regional alliances have in effect been trojan horses of the West—the Organization of American States and the Association of South-East Asian Nations, with, in earlier epochs, the Baghdad Pact and the South-East Asian Treaty Organization. The dreams of African unity propounded by Nkrumah and of Arab unity by Nasser have found no greater realization than the idea of Latin American unity espoused one-and three-quarter centries ago by Simon Bolivar.

These general North–South and intra-South failures are underlined by the difficulties of Third World countries in resolving the two deepest, most entrenched, and challenging legacies of colonialism, namely the issues of Israel and South Africa. Despite decades of fighting, rhetoric, and diplomatic activity these two states remain powerful, and their recent attacks against their neighbours are, if anything, signs of an even greater ability to defy their opponents. The Arab and African states have evolved neither the military power nor the political strength to impose solutions to the problems posed by these two issues, and their periodic regression into disunity in the face of supposedly common enemies underlines their failures in this regard. The two lines of policy apparently available to opponents of Israel and South Africa—intransigent but impotent rejectionism on the one hand, docile acceptance on the other—reveal the weakness of Third World countries in this domain. The continued resilience of Palestinian nationalism, despite its many divisions and setbacks, and the resurgence of opposition in South Africa, indicate very clearly the depth of hostility to these states, but the supporters of the Palestinians and the black South African population still lack the wherewithal materially to weaken the oppressor regimes. At the same time, the protracted persistence of these problems makes more remote the prospect of a solution that would guarantee the rights of all ethnic groups, including those currently in the dominant position.

The lack of progress *vis-à-vis* Israel and South Africa itself draws attention to one of the most enduring and worrying features of Third World politics in recent years, namely the retreat of some of today's Third World leaders from reality and from responsible assessment, into various forms of rhetoric, evasion, and self-delusion. The myriad conferences and seminars, anniversary celebrations, official communiques, and telegrams of congratulation in which these leaders have indulged have not moved their opponents or improved the lot of their own peoples one jot. The depreciation of truth in such rhetoric, a pursuit now embodied in the campaign for a New, that is, censored and repressive, International Information Order not only weakens the Third World *vis-à-vis* the developed world but also weakens the ability of Third World leaders to confront and resolve their own pressing problems.

Conclusions and prospects

These achievements and failures, presented in schematic fashion as they have been, present a balance sheet that is both substantial and alarming of a Third World still in the midst of upheaval, conflict, suffering, and change, and of a hierarchical international system that has adapted to change, without abandoning its fundamental structures of inequality. Amidst this diversity and evolution, it is none the less possible to indicate certain general results of the three decades since Bandung.

The pattern of Third World states as it now exists is the more or less permanent legacy of colonialism. Amidst all the talk of weak and 'penetrated' states, and of arbitrary frontiers, it is striking how far the administrative and interstate boundaries inherited from colonialism have survived, and how the new state structures have consolidated themselves. Despite calls for fusions or unity none has occurred, except at the moment of independence itself, as in Somalia and Cameroun, or to overcome very recent divisions, as in Vietnam. On the other hand, there has been only one clear case of post-colonial secession in the Third World, that of Bangladesh in 1971, and this was in an atypical case of a state that was already split into two. Tshombe, Ojukwu, and Zarzani are no more. The Eritreans and Polisario, and now the Sikhs, fight on, but few believe they will succeed. Even Chad, for all its division, remains one state.

The record of economic development in the South indicates that it no longer makes sense to talk of a unified or homogeneous Third World. The process of development and change has been so uneven that in socio–economic terms there is more that divides an Argentina from a Haiti, a Singapore from a Bangladesh, a Kuwait from a Sudan, than unites them. Talk of a common 'Southern' interest, of a shared interest in a new economic order, and of global renegotiation is illusory, both because of the refusal of the North to accept such changes and because of the disaggregated, competing, and increasingly exploitative relations of Southern countries with each other.

Similarly, talk of common political interests is illusory. Non-alignment is a necessary ideal, and the NAM serves important and necessary functions. But a Third World that includes Afghanistan, Vietnam, and Cuba, on one side, and Singapore, Zaire, and Jamaica, on the other, can hardly be seen as generically non-aligned. The politics of the Third World are permeated by those of East–West rivalry: while some states can stand relatively outside either camp, a considerable number neither want to nor can. Many states that are formally part of the 'Third' World can, in political terms, be redistributed to the 'First' (pro-US) and 'Second'(pro-Soviet) camps.

In the longer run the independence celebrated and demanded at Bandung, and implemented in the years since then, will appear not as the end of a process, the attainment of something ideal, but as a punctuation mark on a much longer road of political, social, and economic transformation. The ability of states to rule themselves is certainly enhanced by attaining formal independence; but this juridical transfer acquires deeper significance only when it is accompanied by other changes within the society in question. A ruling group that ties itself to the West is not capable of ensuring independence, equity, or the proper use of natural resources. Those that seek to break away are faced with an awesome set of alternative problems—the terrible human costs of social revolution in the Third World, the horrendous price which imperialism visits upon those who try to evade its controls, and the exiguous economic aid which the Soviet Union offers to those who seek assistance. To see independence as such a punctuation mark is also, however, to recognize that not all the legacies of colonialism need to be rejected: centralized states, a measure of economic development, a commitment to secularism, and a confrontation with traditional obstacles to change may all, properly used, be positive aspects of the colonial experience. The truth of this is nowhere clearer than in those cases, where in the name of a benighted and retrospective 'authenticity', Third World countries have plunged back into the darknesses from which even colonialism sought to extract them. The idea that a political or ideological system is necessarily valid because it can be presented as 'anti-imperialist' is as much a nationalist illusion as the claim that with independence an ideal era must open.

We are left with a Third World of over 120 states in which, even omitting China's one billion, close to three billion people will soon live. For all the disappointments of the past decades, a new state system of independent Third World nations has come into existence and has begun, in some limited domains, to exert its power and initiative. If the old generation of independence leaders is virtually gone, and many of their successors are corrupt and inept by comparison, there are also many others in the Third World who have learned from these experiences and who remain committed to the goal enunciated three decades ago. The challenge facing them, in Asia, Africa, and Latin America, remains as great as it is unavoidable.

Yet it is a challenge which concerns not just the peoples and leaders of the Third World, but the whole of humanity, and not least the more developed countries who grew rich, in part, through the centuries-long domination of the South, and who today collectively show such low regard for the problems of the Third World. The role of Olof Palme in developing a more active, concerned, and effective North–South relationship was in several respects a unique one: coming from one of the few industrialized countries that had not had a colonial past, and whose population has shown a consistently higher concern for the plight of the Third World than most all others, he was a committed internationalist in his dedication to, and active working for, improved relations between North and South and within the South itself. His work on the arms race, on the one hand, and on the Iran–Iraq War, on the other, were two aspects of a broad commitment that finds too few parallels within the North and its politicians. The urgency that he recognized, and the need to transcend the limits of national and purely Northern concerns, are a central part of his great legacy.

The Mechanisms of Dialogue

15

The Non-Aligned Movement and the New International Division of Labour

TIMOTHY M. SHAW

The purpose of common security applies with great force to Third World countries . . .. They too must find political and economic security through a commitment to joint survival . . ..
In the Third World, as in all our countries, security requires economic progress as well as freedom from military fear.[1]

The Heads of State . . . expressed grave concern that since . . . 1983, the world economic crisis has continued to escalate, characterised *inter alia* by the accentuation of structural imbalances and inequities resulting from the inadequacy of the present international division of labour for the balanced and equitable development of the world economy as well as in the breakdown of the international payments system. The widening gap between the developed and developing countries and the persistence of the unjust and inequitable international economic system constitute a major impediment to the development process of non-aligned and other developing countries and poses a serious threat to international peace and security. In this regard, they reiterated the commitment of the Movement to continue to work for a restructuring of the international economic system with a view to establishing the New International Economic Order based on justice, equity, equality and mutual benefit.[2]

The 'new international order' is, at one and the same time, a programme and analysis. It is a programme of social transformation; it is an analysis of why such social transformation is possible or even probable.
The very discussion is part of the *kairos* (crisis/change) . . ..
It is an attempt to keep us all operating within the temporality of conjuncture, when an understanding of the temporality of the *longue durée* will make it clear that we are participating in the *kairos*. This attempt will not succeed.[3]

A sense of *kairos*—common crisis?—is apparent in the dialectic between the reality projected by the New International Division of Labour (NIDL) and the ideology expressed in demands for a New International Economic Order (NIEO). Ironically, the Non-Aligned Movement (NAM), which 25 years after its establishment calls for the latter, is increasingly divided and diverted by the imperatives of the former. Hence its political divergences as reflections of economic differentiation. Thus any analysis of the NAM in the contemporary global context a quarter century after its founding requires the adoption of a political economy perspective: how to explain the contradictions within and around the NAM? Will the NIDL forever remain essentially unaffected by claims for an NIEO? Will the imperative of interdependence continue to be undiminished by the incidence of dependence? Will conjuncture or contradiction prevail in international affairs until the end of the present century?

One indicator as well as factor in the continuing struggle to redefine the world political économy is the proliferation of reports and debates about the current crisis. Following in the tradition of the late-1960s Pearson Commission on International Development are the Brandt and Palme 'Independent Commissions' on Development and Disarmament, respectively.[4] Yet as consensual, reflective, and bourgeois these can at best describe and prescribe; they cannot really criticize or blame. Hence the articulation of new internationalist concepts: 'mutuality of interest' and 'common security', respectively. These formulations influence perspective and discourse but they can hardly be implemented as they are neither operational nor socially rooted. Nevertheless, they do point towards a more rational and sustainable, albeit idealistic, way to organize the global system. Yet unless they come to represent transnational constituencies their proposals are likely to remain still-born. Their long-term aspirations are compatible with those of the NAM yet their short-term goals are more immediate and explicit: an NIEO rather than mutuality; redistribution rather than commonality.

Olof Palme's vision of a new world as reflected in both the Brandt and Palme Commissions was essentially compatible with the claims of the NAM. And as an international Social Democrat, his missions to the Middle East and Southern Africa gave rise to hope that significant change could be combined with minimal violence. Yet his enlightened internationalism was based on an idealistic premise: that all countries and classes are essentially reasonable and rational. Unhappily, common security is likely to remain elusive while the bases for it in the global political economy are so elusive: 'common prosperity'.[5] Hence the imperative of an NIEO not only for Third World development but also for the South's security, as indicated in his opening quotation. Until most of the social correlates for war are removed or contained, common security will remain a dream. As Prime Minister Robert Mugabe indicated in an evocative phrase at the mid-1986 NAM summit in Harare: common 'mental liberation' is a prerequisite for both security and development.[6] And such liberation may be threatening to some established interests in Third as well as First and Second Worlds.

So although a sense of *kairos*, as conceived in the third opening quotation from Wallerstein, is apparent in the regular demand by the NAM for an NIEO, its members cannot easily escape from their collective inheritance of dependence and incorporation. For the contradictions and crisis into which the ruling classes of member states have been plunged cannot be resolved without fundamental structural transformation: transformation within both national and international political economies.

Non-Alignment as Ideology and Diplomacy

In the absence of such interrelated fundamental changes, the NIEO becomes an ideological construct, designed to salvage residual dignity and development for a few countries and classes in the Third World. If the NAM's call for an NIEO is not merely an exercise in frustration, it must constitute an attempt to devise an ideology to legitimize and protect the interests of the new indigenous ruling classes, as indicated in the second opening quotation.

To conceive of the NIEO demand and debate as an ideological construct is to deny neither their seriousness nor their prospects of success. Rather, it is to recognize the inherent futility of the NAM's calling for a fundamental and fast restructuring of the global capitalist system, which has evolved over several centuries and continues to evolve under pressures more salient than those generated by the NAM. Changes in the international division of labour, in the prices and supplies of essential factors of production, and in particular relations of production in different parts of the world system have more impact on prospects for development than endless resolutions at non-aligned and UN conferences.

Moreover, some elements among the NAM are themselves both ambivalent and nonchalant about the NAM's declarations, because various classes and countries within it have variable chances for growth. This is due to the fact that some factions within Third World bourgeoisies and some economies within the less developed countries are better able than others to take advantage of the continuing evolution of the world system. In addition to this, the apparent cohesion of the NAM coalition remains intact, because occasional efforts by major forces within the advanced industrialized states of the OECD—for example, the Trilateral Commission—to 'peel off' particular leaders and countries from the ranks of the NAM are less important than continuing historical trends within the international division of labour. To be sure, such efforts do yield some results; but the essential cause both of tensions within the NAM and of collaboration between First and Third Worlds towards an NIEO is the structural position of major classes and countries in the world system of the late-twentieth century. In short, substructural relations determine outcomes rather than superstructural manifestations, appearances and assertions to the contrary notwithstanding.

The NAM will continue to change as dominant interests within it rise and fall; hence the relevance of the relationship between its past characteristics and likely trends in its further evolution over the next 15 years. To this extent, the Eighth Summit in Harare constituted a symbolic turning point: the first NAM meeting since the demise of OPEC and the appearance of major development difficulties in Africa. The last time the NAM met in Sub-Saharan Africa—neighbouring Lusaka in 1970–it was preoccupied politically by Rhodesia; 15 years later it focused on the liberation of South Africa and Namibia—special appeals on both, a package of proposals for the Front Line states, and a solidarity fund for the region. But its Africa Declaration also included the contemporary legacies of drought and debt: the unfavourable 'Fourth World' position of the continent in the new global division of labour.

The NIEO, as a complete package of reforms, is therefore likely to remain elusive, but some issues on its agenda will be recognized and resolved whenever they are of salience to major interests in the North and/or South. This chapter thus proceeds from an overview of central changes (and contradictions) in the contemporary world system—the NIDL—to a history of the evolution of the NAM as its perceptions of and location in the system have developed.

The major theme presented here is that, because of the continual interaction between the NAM and the system (and, of course, interaction among and between central forces within both the NAM and the system), neither can be understood out of historical context.[7] In short, the non-aligned states are both products of, now actors within, the global capitalist economy; so their design of and demand for an NIEO are historically conditioned. Hence the initial focus on an NIEO as ideology: and idealist, mystifying, and ambivalent responses by the ruling classes of the global periphery to their unsatisfactory inheritance and uncomfortable dependent situation. The elements of idealism and ambivalence increase as changes in the world system become more apparent: the uneven incidence of recession, inflation, and protectionism between both countries and classes.

As we approach the last decade of the twentieth century, we are, then, as Wallerstein indicates, 'at the beginning of one of those periodic downturns, or contradictions, or crises that the capitalist world economy has known with regularity since its origins in Europe in the sixteenth century.[8] This contemporary crisis, which commenced in the mid-1970s with the ending of the post-war Bretton Woods system and the beginning of an era of unstable oil prices, has three major features:

1. US hegemony is over and a period of inter-Western rivalries—involving both countries and corporations—has begun.
2. The unity of the socialist Commonwealth is also over and a period of intense Sino–Soviet rivalry, as well as fragmentation in Eastern Europe, is in process.
3. Although most Third World countries continue to be very marginal in the world system, a few—those newly industrializing countries (NICs) at the semi-periphery—are increasingly important to international production and exchange.

These three factors are of course interrelated; major states, capitalist and socialist alike, are engaged in competition for the scarce resources and markets of the minority of Third World countries with expanding economies. Together they could constitute a historic conjuncture—a turning point in the world system.[9] And it is with such a situation that the NAM has now to deal in its quest for order and justice for the majority of countries and peoples.

If the NAM was declared pregnant in 1955 at Bandung, it was born in the era of the early 1960s, at Belgrade in 1961. The 1970s were a difficult decade for it as development became ever more elusive. And by the mid-1980s it had begun to appear quite middle-aged, established, pragmatic, even defensive. Its first decade has been characterized by optimism—decolonization, development, and *détente* were both possible and probable—but its second decade was characterized by greater pessimism (realism?); decolonization, development, and *détente* were problematic and generated ironies rather than irreversible advances. The NAM recorded continued progress towards political decolonization in the 1960s—in many ways its golden age—but by the early 1970s it had begun to appreciate its lack of power to force economic decolonization or strategic *détente*. Indeed, the prospects for its second 20 years are, if anything, gloomier in this regard than for the previous 10 or 20: Southern Africa may come under majority rule by the year 2000, but dependence and under-development are likely to be not only perpetuated but also intensified. Hence the growing concern of non-aligned leaders in New Delhi as the 1980s opened:

Reviewing developments in the international economic situation
since the Havana summit, the Ministers noted with grave concern
that while, on the one hand, the acute problems facing the
developing countries had been aggravated and increased as a result of
the pursuance of policies contrary or unfavourable to their interests
by the developed countries; on the other hand, there had been no substantial progress in resolving the stalemate in international negotiations
for the restructuring of international economic relations.[10]

Nevertheless, the NAM is caught in the web of its own contradictions
and can hardly opt out of the halting process of so-called 'global
negotiations' as advanced by Brandt and Palme.

Indeed, the heady optimism of the 1960s and the new cautiousness
of the 1970s were reflective not only of shifts in the world system but
also of a growing self-consciousness among non-aligned leaders: their
position as the ruling class at the periphery remains tenuous; hence the
imperative of external association and support. Unless this leadership is
willing and able to opt out of such global networks—even though its
place in them is marginal—it has few options other than to hang in
there and hope that an NIEO will somehow, someday materialize.[11]
Meanwhile, the NAM itself has little choice but to revise its ideological
position to incorporate contemporary demands and concepts from
both external associates and internal constituents: on to common crisis
and security.

In short, non-alignment can be seen increasingly as an ideological
construct—a form of collective 'defensive radicalism'.[12] This chapter
provides a critical overview of the intellectual history of the NAM in
terms of the current conjuncture and the contradictions surrounding
non-aligned leaders especially following the new inequalities apparent
since the mid-1970s.[13]

Non-Alignment as a Collective Response to Decolonization

The charter members of the NAM in the early-1960s were the first
independent states of the post-war period, eager to maintain the
momentum towards global decolonization. Given that the central
issues of the time were considered to be essentially political, the NAM
concentrated also on the decentralization of the world power structure.
However, a combination of successful *political* decolonization and
decentralization (i.e. *détente*) plus the elusiveness of economic
decolonization and decentralization (i.e. development) fostered a shift
away from the political towards the economic in the second decade of

the NAM's history. The perpetuation of some elements of colonialism and centralization of world power along with the continued elusiveness of development generated a return to some of the original concerns of the 1960s as the 1980s opened: dominance, interference, and exclusion. These retrieved concerns are now expressed as *self-reliance rather than decolonization, as an NIEO rather than development.*

If non-alignment was a response at first to bipolarity, it is now a reaction to underdevelopment. The shift away from cold war issues along an East–West axis towards rich–poor issues along a North–South axis is symbolic both of changes in the world system including the increase in Third World influence. This has resulted in a tendency towards South–South preferences: from global to South commissions. Continuing trends in international affairs are reflective of these interrelated transitions away from strategic and political questions and towards a new concentration on economic and social issues. These are representative of the impact of the processes of decolonization and underdevelopment in the world system—the dialectical relationship between formal independence and actual dependence–and the continuation of inequalities.

Global politics have evolved in important ways for the non-aligned, away from a Eurocentric system and towards a complex hierarchy of myriad actors, both state and non-state. The rise, first of non-European superpowers (presently the USA and the Soviet Union and, for the future, China and Japan); second, the multiplication of states (particularly in the Third World); third, the explosion of non-state actors (especially transnational, transgovernmental, and intergovernmental ones at both regional and global levels); fourth, the appearance of new coalitions as well as axes amongst these; and fifth, the recognition of a range of new issues, from gender to environment, together constitute a major change in the superstructure, if not substructure, of the world system. Students of global superstructure may argue that these several shifts represent a trend towards decentralization and democratization as the number of small states and non-state actors grows. However, a more radical approach would tend to examine continuing international inequalities and hierarchies despite the proliferation of actors, institutions, and issues.[14] This latter approach sees a perpetuation of the trend towards concentration rather than to diffusion, looking in particular at modes and relations of production rather than at diplomacy or resolutions at the UN. To be sure, substructure and superstructure are related in both analysis and practice. Yet the different levels and modes of analysis and prescription associated with the two major approaches lead to divergent explanations and expectations. These affect different perceptions of the place of the non-aligned states in the world system as well as ideological definitions and defences of their place.

The alternative forms of analysis and advocacy represented by the orthodox and radical approaches respectively are reflected in the resolutions of the NAM summit. As suggested below, these two approaches are espoused by different factions in the NAM, leading to a growing debate and division. For the present, however, I merely note that the former, orthodox, perspective welcomes *détente* but continues to emphasize politico–diplomatic issues of a superstructural variety, whereas the latter, radical perspective concentrates on (under) development as an aspect of political economy; i.e. on substructure. These two, differing emphases are reflected very clearly in the political and economic resolutions of the Eighth Summit Conference of the NAM in Harare.

A.W. Singham has captured the common thread of these two approaches to (political and economic) decolonization by arguing that 'the Non-Aligned Movement has indeed come of age in the contemporary era. It is slowly transforming itself from being a social movement into a much more highly organized pressure group.'[15] This new concern with 'economics' and its impact on 'politics' have implications for strategy and ideology. It also has implications, as shall be seen later, for unity. Nevertheless, for now note is just taken of Singham's succinct summary of the NAM's transition:

> ... the major thrust of the Non-Aligned Movement has been its demand for a new economic order which is broadly defined at the United Nations and gradually translated into a programme of action through UNCTAD and other international gatherings. The Non-Aligned Movement had developed into what can be broadly described as a trade union strategy in dealing with capitalist nations of the world. It has essentially advanced a trade union bargaining process on to a global level.[16]

This trade-union-type activism on an NIEO is a considerable step from its earlier role as an advocate of decolonization and is reflective of its collective espousal of *dependencia* assumptions.

In the first decade (from Belgrade, 1961 to Lusaka, 1970) the NAM was mainly preoccupied by issues of political independence and East–West tension. It largely defined its international position in terms of 'positive' support for nationalist movements throughout the Third World and 'neutral' abstention from (any overt and long-term) association with either of the cold war blocs. It was 'positively neutral'. It designated an activist role for itself in terms of:

1. Mediation and arbitration in specific interstate disputes.
2. 'Bridge-building' between the blocs.

3. Presenting an alternative, a third force, for those bloc states opposing bloc membership.
4. Active support for liberation movements and acting as their spokesmen in international bodies.
5. Criticism of countries violating peace, i.e. acting as the conscience of the world, putting blame on those who deserve it.[17]

This concern for independence and impartiality, both as status and spirit, continues, although it is harder to define and maintain in a consensual manner in a more complex multipolar system. Moreover, it has come to be conceived in terms of political economy rather than legality alone, in an era when economic pressure is being increasingly seen to be as effective as the political or the strategic. Hence the growing focus on South–South connections as a counterbalance to any South–North negotiations: from the Brandt to the Nyerere Commissions.

It must be recognized that resistance to 'external' forces requires more than declarations and solidarity: economic autonomy and resilience are prerequisites to enhanced 'independence'. But in the case of the NAM this is always a function of the degree of ideological cohesion and challenge displayed by it.

Not only has the international environment changed over the last two decades but the composition of the NAM has also evolved. Because of the history and incidence of formal decolonization, the almost balanced 'Afro–Asian' complexion of Belgrade shifted dramatically by the time of the Lusaka Conference when Africa had double the number of representatives compared with Asia. Moreover, given the large number of highly dependent and very poor, largely francophone African states that were eligible for membership by 1970, the balance shifted away from a more radical and towards a more conservative or orthodox orientation. As Hveem and Willetts note in their empirical analysis of 'new' and 'old' members at Lusaka:

> ... the Movement increasingly has been taking aligned countries into its ranks ... there is a decreasing degree of Non-Alignment from the 'veterans' through the 'once before' to the 'newcomers'. Moreover, there is a considerable change of balance between East and West. Formerly those that were aligned were split between an Eastern and Western alignment. Now the West predominates completely. The explanation seems to be that the Movement really ... has remained an 'open club'. It recruits new members willingly if they meet at least two criteria: that they are underdeveloped or developing countries, and that they are relatively small. The Movement has maximised membership at the expense of non-alignment.[18]

Using their four indicators—diplomatic association, military alignment, UN voting, trade with the Communist bloc—Hveem and Willetts conclude that at Lusaka 'only four nations, Ghana, India, Nepal and Kuwait, are Non-Aligned on every one of the four indices'.[19] And even given a liberal interpretation of their data, less than half of the 64 invited states were 'objectively non-aligned'.

However, with the changed nature of the decolonization process in the 1970s compared to that of the 1960s, the pro-Western composition of the NAM shifted once again at Colombo (1976) when up to 30 of the 86 members claimed to be 'socialist'. This shift to the left continued with the Sixth Summit in Havana, although the ideological complexion of the NAM is considerably more 'progressive' than members' actual political economies. By the Harare Conference, however, under pressure of political and economic 'privatization' as well as strategic and ideological differentiation, the NAM had returned somewhat to its first principles of democracy, *détente* and development, seen most clearly in the Harare appeal to Presidents Reagan and Gorbachev.

The NAM constitutes, then, both a continuing response to and an influence on the world system. In its first decade it was a reaction to, but also a constraint on, international bipolarity; in its second decade, it has been a critical reaction to international inequality. As shall be seen in the concluding section, in its current, third, decade, the NAM is reacting to a combination of inequality and intervention and is seeking to advance both the development as well as the integrity and democracy of its members against bloc politics; at least this appears to be the direction in which its ideological predispositions are pointed.

The NAM has moved, then, from being as impartial and objective as possible during the cold war era to being partial and insistent during the North–South debate. In the 1980s, given the prospects of multipolarity and bloc politics on the one hand, and uneven development and resource scarcities on the other hand, the NAM has become preoccupied with a combination of issues, particularly those to do with intervention, of both structural (economic) and crisis (political) varieties as reflected in both the Brandt and Palme Commissions. Moreover, as differentiation increases within the NAM because of unequal exchange and uneven development, so will questions about development strategy and foreign policy come to affect its dynamics and diplomacy. And it is on these central issues that the tension between orthodox and radical states and analysis will continue to be acute, even after the passing of the crisis-ridden 1970s. Hence the welcome unity of purpose over apartheid in South Africa.

So ideological ambiguity and argument are unlikely to decline in the 1990s despite the growing threat to the NAM from revived forms of neo-colonialism—political pressure and economic exertion—characteristic of the trend towards neo-mercantilism. However, in the 1970s, especially the first-half of the decade, it was assumed that economics were the panacea; hence the ideology of development in response to the reality of independence.

Non-Alignment as a Collective Response to Dependence

Faith in development among the non-aligned was short-lived as a collective ideology because insufficient resources were released by dominant classes, corporations, and countries in the world system to effect significant change in the Third World before the mid-1970s; and shocks to the system from the mid-1970s onwards provided dramatic opportunities for a few Third World forces but retarded prospects for the majority. However, the pervasive sense of crisis that has characterized the world system for much of the last 10 years has both affected and, in part, been caused by the non-aligned states.[20] Political nationalism and decolonization have begun to threaten the continuation of capitalism, at least in its characteristic Keynesian post-war variety. In turn, the age of *détente* and (under)development has necessitated changes amongst the non-aligned. As Singham notes, 'the growing global economic crisis, especially the disparity between the rich and the poor nations, has dramatically changed the whole course of the Non-Aligned Movement'.[21]

According to the radical mode of analysis, partly reflected in the Harare Political Declaration, the series of interrelated crises which have disrupted the global economy since the second-half of the 1970s is reflective of a set of contradictions in the world system:

> The heads of State or Government noted with grave concern that the world continues to be confronted with increasingly difficult problems stemming from deep-rooted and interrelated contradictions in international economic relations. This deepening crisis is manifested in the drastic widening of the gap between developed and developing countries, many of which are unable to meet even the most basic needs of their people or realize their development priorities. Prospects for the establishment of the New International Economic Order based on justice and sovereign equality continue to diminish. The North–South dialogue is in a state of paralysis and international co-operation for economic and social development through the multilateral process embodied in the United Nations system is threatened.[22]

This crisis can be seen to exist at two rather distinctive levels—the superstructural and substructural. The former consists of the diplomatic debates and political posturing that occur in a variety of fora and media. The latter consists of the economic relations and social structure that underlie the former. A fundamental question about both the NAM and the NIEO debates is whether they seek change at the level of super and/or substructure. Before the 1970s, the NAM was largely concerned with superstructural issues—decolonization, diplomacy and *détente*. It only became concerned with substructure as it became clear that dependence affected development and that incorporation in the global economy largely determined place in the world system as a whole. In other words the contradictions and debate at the level of substructure affected diplomacy and debate at the level of superstructure. There was not only a 'gap' between economic dependence and political independence: there was a tension or a contradiction between the two.

Given the growing awareness of this relationship between sub and superstructure a central question arises about the NIEO issue: is it going to be treated and (possibly) resolved at the level of superstructure only—ideological and diplomatic agreement—or will it also lead to change in the global economy, the substructure? The non-aligned states (particularly the radical faction amongst them) increasingly demand change in substructure, recognizing that this will inevitably affect superstructure. By contrast, the industrialized states advocate change at this level of superstructure only, hoping that they can prevent diplomatic agreement from affecting economic exchange and meanwhile re-establishing their dominance throughout the global economy. There are constraints on the class-type struggle between 'bourgeois' and 'proletarian' states because of the simultaneous class conflict occurring with each of them and the continuing connections between bourgeois interests in North and South. In short, there are limits to the ideology of confrontation articulated by the NAM given the place of its countries and classes in the world system.[23]

If the 1960s was a relatively optimistic decade of effective decolonization, then the 1970s was a rather pessimistic decade of disillusion. The crisis which started in the 1970s has been characterized by several interrelated features, the rank-ordering of which varies between 'worlds' and over time. Moreover, these aspects are related to changes in the world system as identified above and listed below:

1. Continued underdevelopment in most of the Third World so that basic human needs are increasingly not being met.
2. Growing incidence of resource shortages and depletion affecting level and price of production in the First World.
3. Impact of the mid-1970s' 'oil crisis' leading to financial disarray, especially debt.

4. Threat of protectionism and unilateralism in the North.
5. Increasing environmental vulnerability in the South, especially Africa, as underdevelopment and overpopulation erode ecological reserves.[24]
6. Impending changes in the international division of labour with the emergence of a group of NICs and of a Europe of the Twelve (EEC).[25]

Recognition, ranking, and treatment of these several components of the current crisis are a function of theoretical perspective as well as of national status; of mood as well as ideological orientation; and of region as well as race.[26] The orthodox, superstructural approach tends to deal with them as temporary, local difficulties, whereas the radical, structural approach treats them as inherent, long-term contradictions. The former believes that they are susceptible still to incremental decisions whereas the latter asserts that they are merely features of a structural condition that requires fundamental change. From a radical world-system perspective, the crisis may represent a historic conjuncture, not a passing problem.

The orthodox prescription to overcome the crisis consists of a routine response—negotiation and co-operation—whereas the radical reaction is the opposite—confrontation and conflict. The former represents the traditional reply from the old majority within the NAM while the latter reflects the reaction of the new minority. Tradition is still contained in some of the resolutions from the Colombo and subsequent conferences:

> The international trend is . . . favourable to peaceful coexistence, . . . it is furthermore a fact of great importance that the world is becoming increasingly interdependent, a factor of crucial significance in shaping the world of the future. In an interdependent world, the only alternative to international cooperation is international rivalry, tension and conflict, and the human aspiration towards a better world has inevitably to manifest itself through international co-operation. Consequently the trend is favourable to international co-operation in accordance with the Non-Aligned principle of peaceful coexistence.[27]

By contrast, a growing number of new states recognize the inevitability of conflict between rich and poor if the latter are to be free to develop. Their more radical perspective represents a more critical historical mode of analysis; one that sees incorporation and co-operation as the problem, not the solution; hence the emphasis on South–South as both insurance and preference lest South–North dialogue becomes pointless.[28] The ambiguities of the NIEO debates are, then, an aspect of the tensions within the NAM over how to respond to the current crisis.

Heightened awareness of the elusiveness of development and the pervasiveness of dependence generated something of a metamorphosis in the NAM in the 1970s. As consciousness grew of the gap between political independence and economic dependence, so determination increased to bridge it by realizing a greater degree of economic control and autonomy. The demand for international development and democratization—instead of dependence and domination—labouring with the parallel dependency discourse produced the NIEO debate. The 1970 Lusaka Summit (of Heads of State) and the 1972 Algiers Summit (of Foreign Ministers) led to the Sixth and Seventh Special UN General Assemblies. The international agenda for the decade after the second-half of the 1970s was dominated by this debate,[29] for, as Ervin Laszlo suggests,

> . . . the historical process which gave the majority of the world's population sovereign and equal status, but left them at the same time in a position of economic dependence, triggered a set of factors configuring the context for the emergence of the NIEO.[30]

But definitions, interpretations, and expectations of an NIEO vary within the NAM: hence the ambiguities of its ideology. And, although some states still retain faith in incrementalism, many have come to recognize the imperative of structural change. New structures in the global economy are essential if co-operation is to replace conflict once again and if development is to reduce dependence:

> The heads of state . . . consider that collective self-reliance within the NIEO is an important and necessary step in the wider process arriving at the establishment of international cooperation which would be a concrete and genuine expression of interdependence within the global economy. International cooperation is nowadays an imperative necessity. It requires the effective participation of all in decision-making and demands that those processes and relationships which lead to increasing inequality and greater imbalance are put to an end. In their strategy of international economic co-operation, concurrently with the intensification of the relations between themselves, it is desirable that the Non-Aligned countries diversify their economic relations with the other countries, developed capitalist as well as socialist, on the basis of the principles of respect for national sovereignty, of equality and of mutual benefit.[31]

If mutual and stable forms of political and economic co-operation are to be established then new values and structures have to be agreed upon and constructed, otherwise interdependence will continue to be a cover for dependence. It is for this reason that the Ministers of the NAM declared in 1981 that they categorically rejected any attempt:

> ... to impose, under the pretext of interdependence, a world economy which would once again leave no place for the developing countries as full partners in their own right. [They] were of the view that interdependence could only result from the establishment of the NIEO. . . .[32]

A persistent theme in the orthodox school of both states and scholars in both Third and First Worlds is that international conflict over the maldistribution of income and opportunity can be overcome not by continuing tension but rather by writing a new global contract: 'mutuality of interest' or 'common prosperity'. The possibility of resolving differences in this manner is reminiscent of earlier attempts by international lawyers to design world governments or federations. It also reflects the awareness that some degree of change in the global economy may be essential for the advanced industrialized states too, as resource shortages and environmental pollution increase. And it is a characteristic response of the rich to challenges of the poor—a superstructural rather than a substructural remedy. As Laszlo himself recognizes, 'The establishment of the NIEO is not only historically appropriate; it is also universally expedient.'[33] The NAM adopted aspects of this notion of a new international contract or order for two reasons. First, they saw it as a goal that would enhance their own unity and hence effectiveness. And second, they saw it as a means to put pressure on, and to blame, the rich. Moreover, if simultaneously they advanced their own national and collective self-reliance, then should the contract prove elusive they could always retreat into their own 'world'.[34]

The advantages—both developmental and tactical—of adopting self-reliance were reflected in the Economic Declaration from Colombo:

> The principle of self-reliance, thus seen in its individual and collective aspects, is not only compatible with the aims of the NIEO but is a highly important factor in the strengthening of the solidarity of Non-Aligned and other developing countries in their struggle to achieve economic emancipation.[35]

Finally, as already indicated, self-reliance may also be a response to the *Limits of Growth* debates and decisions in the North, as well as to a history of dependence. It consists of intellectual and political reactions which are mutually reinforcing: the dependence approach advocates disengagement because in the past integration has only produced underdevelopment, whilst the 'overdevelopment' approach advocates disengagement because in the future integration might well be impossible given ecological preoccupations in the North: the growing acceptance of national and collective self-reliance as a development strategy represents a victory for scholars who, during the 1960s and 1970s, have championed what is termed 'dependency' theory.[36] The intellectual as well as political ascendency of dependency was most delayed and subsequently realized in Africa: Samir Amin and the *Lagos Plan of Action*, respectively.[37]

Although dependence and overdevelopment perspectives disagree profoundly on the causes of self-reliance—no development and no growth, respectively—they have been able to reinforce Third World perceptions of the imperative of disengagement and restructuring. This solidarity has been achieved at a time when some elements in the North—corporations and commissions, even if not nationalistic regimes—have begun to reconsider and to advocate interdependence based on Southern growth, rather than isolation based on ignoring Southern demands. But it may be rather late to revive such classical economic doctrines. So the convergence of limited growth and self-reliance—the ideology of an NIEO and global contract—is problematic now that the dominant interests in the world economy seek economic revival through Southern markets and activities. The pressure on the Third World to abandon self-reliance even before it is really tried is likely to grow, especially within the semi-periphery, as discussed below: the familiar package of liberalization, devaluation, and privatization rather than regulation.

Non-Alignment as a Collective Response to Divergencies

The non-aligned states, for reasons of faction (class elements within national and transnational bourgeoisies) and function (divergent national elements within the less developed countries), have attempted to render compatible contract and confrontation, interdependence and self-reliance. This continuing quest for ideological as well as institutional order is reflected in the re-interpretation of notions of co-existence and *détente*. So economic as well as political co-existence is supported and *détente* is advocated by the NAM as well as the Palme Commission for conflicts and areas outside the original narrow and East–West nexus. And the NAM agenda continues to grow from the colonialism and independence, race and conflict, disarmament and interference to Southern Africa, Palestine, the Indian ocean, and the media.[38] A particularly problematic question underlying many of these items and issues is how the NAM copes with a growing diversity of interest and ideology, endowments and expectations.

The elusiveness of economic decolonization and development, let alone indigenous forms of democracy, has led not only to increasing concern amongst the NAM members for a change in the global economy; it has also produced a profound re-evaluation of development policy in a growing number of members. The majority continue to demand an NIEO as proposed at the Lusaka and Algiers meetings, compatible with an essentially orthodox approach to development. By contrast, a new minority rejects any notion of externally oriented growth, preferring instead to overcome underdevelopment by escaping from dependence. This radical approach and faction advocates self-reliance rather than incorporation, autonomy rather than integration. And this division has important implications for the cohesion and influence of the NAM and reflects the emergence of a group of new states following a non-capitalist path.[39] By contrast, a subsequent minority has in the 1980s espoused structural adjustment and policy reform with encouragement from the IBRD and the IMF: peripheral capitalism for the late-twentieth century.

The established consensus (and optimism) favouring a new global economic structure is expressed in the Colombo Political Declaration:

> The Conference noted with satisfaction that the principles of peaceful coexistence advocated by the Non-Aligned Movement as the basis for international relations had won widespread recognition from the world community. The timely initiative taken by the Non-Aligned countries has led to the decision of the world community to create a New International Economic Order based on equity and justice.[40]

And the Economic Declaration related the call for the NIEO to the whole issue of development, a central focus—both ideological and instrumental—of the Movement:

> The Heads of State . . . are firmly convinced that nothing short of a complete restructuring of international economic relations through the establishment of the New International Economic Order will place developing countries in a position to achieve an acceptable level of development.[41]

However, whilst the majority, reinforced by Bank and Fund conditionalities, still favour an outward-looking strategy, a growing and influential minority prefers an inward-looking direction. Approximately 25 (i.e. over a quarter) now favour self-reliance and some form of non-capitalist path because of the inadequate results—in both

aggregate and distributional terms—of the established growth policy.
And within this more radical grouping there is something of a
distinction between those who favour collective self-reliance (as a
revised form of regionalism) and those who seek national (or
'individual') self-reliance (as an aspect of non-capitalism or socialism).
The former collective variety is considered to be an important part of
the demand for an NIEO:

> The Heads of State . . . are of the firm belief that only a confident
> spirit of collective self-reliance on the part of the developing
> countries can guarantee the emergence of the New International
> Economic Order. Self-reliance implies a firm determination on the
> part of developing nations to secure their legitimate economic rights
> in international dealings through the use of their collective bargaining
> strength. . . .[42]

But, as Singham cautions, self-reliance is not an easy strategy. And it is
one that poses difficulties for the NAM itself between the old majority
and the new minority; between more and less benign definitions of the
ideology of development:

> In developing a trade-union strategy, the Non-Aligned Movement
> has no doubt recognized the fact that within its union there are a
> number of contradictions . . . there are indeed divisions between the
> nations who attempt to negotiate collectively with the capitalist
> nations, just as there were contradictions within the working class
> when they negotiated with capital.[43]

This tension at the level of substructure is most acute between those
states in the semi-periphery and those following a non-capitalist path,
as noted below. The somewhat hopeless, and possibly misguided,
attempt to forge a new consensus bridging the orthodox–radical,
NIEO–self-reliance 'gap' is reflected in Singham's own idealistic yet
representative (as well as historic and non-empirical) juxtaposition:

> The present era of economic reconstruction is a transitional one
> when a variety of nations will choose between the old capitalist order
> and a new world economic order. The Non-Aligned Movement has
> entered a dramatic era in its history. It is calling for a new economic
> system.
> The Non-Aligned Movement which began as a broad anti-colonialist
> movement seeking world peace by exhorting the powers to avoid a
> nuclear holocaust, has become the advocate for a new political and
> economic order on a global level . . . . Most of the Non-Aligned

countries are experimenting with non-capitalist paths of development. The search for a NIEO, then, is simply a demand by the Non-Aligned nations to rectify the present imbalance that exists among states.[44]

The issue of appropriate development strategy and ideology is a central one confronting the NAM. It has become more acute since the mid-1970s, initially because of inequalities among members and more recently because of 'inter-imperial' rivalries among OECD states, as well as 'policy' rather than North–South dialogue between NAM members and the IBRD–IMF. Historically, non-aligned states have been differentiated according to whether their leaders were influential in the NAM; now they can be ranked according to economic position, potential, and orientation.[45]

Changes in the world system at the level of both super and substructure have generated an intermediate stratum of states between the centre and the periphery—the semi-periphery. This group of 'middle powers' has been variously characterized as the Newly Influential Countries (superstructural role) or the Newly Industrializing Countries (substructural position). The NICs are semi-perhipheral in the sense that they are larger, more powerful, more industrialized, and have more 'developmental' potential than most countries in the Third World. They have also generated a lively intellectual and political debate over their role in the world system.[46]

Orthodox scholars take confidence from the 'success' stories afforded by the NICs to defend the claims of established development theory that outward-looking growth is still possible. Their renewed faith in 'trickle-down' approaches has been joined by the growing interest taken in such states by global strategic planners who seek close ties with regionally influential actors. The 'Nixon–Brezhnev' doctrine has in turn been reinforced by the proposal of the Trilateral Commission to bring at least more OPEC or NIC states into the charmed circle of the OECD.

The new attention accorded the new affluence of the NICs has raised questions about their role in the Third World. The orthodox position is that the semi-periphery can lead the Group of 77 and apply classical growth strategies without generating divisiveness, The radical response, given the close association between centre and semi-periphery and given the different experience of orthodox development policies in most of the periphery, is that the NICs are becoming sub-imperial and will thus split the NAM and upset its unity. Ali Mazrui is a defender of the former position, arguing that through 'counter-penetration' the NICs can advance common Third World interests.[47] He sees the semi-periphery as serving a positive, integrative function of benevolent leadership rather than one of sub-imperial domination. Mazrui's optimism in seeing counter-penetration by the NICs as advancing both development and the advent of 'mature interdependence' was not shared by more radical analysts, even before the demise of OPEC. Instead, they saw the rise of the semi-periphery as a stage in the evolution of the world system brought about by emerging contradictions both within and between countries. For them, the emergence of NICs is not a vindication of established development strategy but rather an indication of the continuing power of corporate and state interests in the centre.

For the semi-periphery has not emerged on its own but rather by invitation and by design: the rich need regional branches and bases in the more complex contemporary system. And because of the semi-periphery's structural position, it can hardly avoid the charges of sub-imperialism.[48] It may attempt to be beneficient regionally and to practise counter-penetration globally but its intermediary status prevents it from contributing unequivocally to the cohesion of the NAM. This is particularly so in the two salient areas of the contemporary period—bloc politics and political democracy—which are the focus of the concluding paragraphs.

The non-aligned states have sought independence and autonomy through political and economic decolonization and development. But inequalities, both structural and behavioural, in the world system tend to perpetuate dependence and domination, especially in the periphery but also, albeit in modified form, in the semi-periphery. The ubiquity of underdevelopment has led the NAM as a group to oppose bloc politics; in practice, some members have been prepared to take advantage of them whilst a few seek to avoid them altogether by implementing a comprehensive self-reliant strategy. Nevertheless, the official ideology of the NAM remains that it has 'contributed significantly to the relaxation of tensions and the solution of international problems through peaceful means. It noted the contribution that the NAM had made towards preventing the division of the world into antagonistic blocs and spheres of influence'.[49]

As with the issue of 'interference', the NAM sees bloc politics as an 'external' rather than as a structural or transnational phenomenon, so avoiding any notion of apparently 'national' ruling class being dependent or comprador. On the one hand, therefore, the real significance of, or constraints on, self-reliance are ignored. On the other hand, recognition of continued foreign threats is a healthy antidote to the naïve assumption that the world system is becoming more benign or equal. Bloc politics becomes a convenient motif for the variety of challenges and forms of domination in the contemporary international system for the NAM as a whole, the removal of which all can agree to as the *sine qua non* of development and independence:

Although colonialism as traditionally understood is coming to an end, the problem of imperialism continues and can be expected to continue for the foreseeable future under the guises of neo-colonialism and hegemonic relations. The Non-Aligned have to be alert against all forms of unequal relations and domination that constitute imperialism.

The Conference noted also that the international trend is against power blocs and notions of international order based on balance of power and spheres of influence, all of which imply unequal relations between nations which could amount to domination. The Non-Aligned will continue to oppose the principle of polarization around power centres as it is inconsistent with true independence and the democratization of international relations, without which a satisfactory international order cannot be realized.[50]

NAM's rejection of international and national inequalities is a crucial antidote at the level of ideology to its membership's growing differentiation at the level of reality. As Fred Halliday has noted in his critical analysis of the NAM after Delhi, it is now plagued by regional and political differences as well as by personality and economy distinctions. If the NAM is maturing it is also diversifying and dissipating as the world political economy evolves. Halliday argues that its advocacy of an NIEO is bound to be problematic:

> ... an appeal to the richer states of the capitalist world, whose self-interest and power to pursue it do not lead them to accept any radical restructuring of the world market. The failure to launch an NIEO ... reflects a structural reality of the world economy, not a failure of negotiating skill or a lack of diplomatic energy.
> ... the countries of the South are themselves, in the main, part of the capitalist market, and so both disposed to compete with each other and to seek closer integration with the richer economies of the developed world. This again is a matter of the working of the market, rather than of lack of political will. The 1970s have seen substantial economic change in the Third World, most vividly represented by OPEC and the NICs: but these changes have been brought about by breaking ranks with the rest of the world, not by collective efforts of the NAM states. A new international economic order has been created since 1973, but it is a new, more viciously competitive capitalist economic order, in which differentiation between Third World states has increased.[51]

Thus the rejection of blocs and dominance at the level of ideology is essential not only for national development but also for collective cohesion. As noted already, the emergence of a semi-periphery may pose problems for the NAM. However, some radical scholars reject any notion of differentiation *within* the Third World as being of consequence compared to that *between* First and Third Worlds, thus saving the NAM from further fragmentation.

Such scholars see the Third World as an historical and ideological rather than contemporary category. Ismail-Sabri Abdalla, for instance, rejects any idea that differentiation within the NAM is either important or increasing. Instead, he asserts that the members still share a common experience of exploitation and subordination:

> The Third World is a historical phenomenon that is part and parcel of the process of emergence of the present world order . . . the differentiation process did not produce during the last fifteen years effects of such a magnitude that any group of 'developing nations' can stand outside the Third World . . . the 'gap' between the higher income group and the industrialized nations was still growing.

Abdalla is critical of any notion of Third World differentiation and fragmentation, arguing instead that a shared historical and existential experience will serve to reinforce cohesion and so support confrontation against the rich:

> . . . dependence is with all its corollaries the basic common denominator of Third World countries and comprehensive decolon-ization is the only path out of it. Features and specifications that distinguish countries or groups of countries in the Third World fall short of destroying the fundamental community of condition and goal.[52]

Abdalla rejects superstructural approaches in favour of a more critical substructural and historical analysis. But while the former's focus on some aspects of differentiation may be dismissed as threats to the NAM's cohesion, the latter's orientation towards self-reliance poses a new and more profound challenge to the NAM.

National self-reliance is, in many ways, a logical extension of the ideology of decolonization, a strategy that reduces external association and domination. Yet precisely because of the history of Third World incorporation in the world system, and the dependence of much of its leadership on links with countries and corporations in the North, it has not been widely espoused. And its adoption by a growing faction within the NAM not only undermines solidarity at the level of tactics but also at the levels of ideology and political economy. So even if sub-imperialism can be regarded as a superficial problem, self-reliance cannot be so readily dismissed: it poses fundamental questions and dilemmas for the NAM.

The challenge of self-reliance as an effective response to dependence and underdevelopment is exacerbated if the goal of development is seen to be a transformation in political economy, not just political and/or economic decolonization. In other words, if development is defined in terms not only of stability and growth but also in terms of satisfying the demands for autonomy, order, and equitable income distribution, then self-reliance is a powerful and persuasive response to an inheritance of non-participation and non-production. When broadly conceived, self-reliance is a strategy designed to secure development and autonomy and to overcome underdevelopment and dependence. The very salience of this strategy, especially its emphasis on democracy and participation, is a challenge to an NAM which includes not only the least-developed states but also some rather oppressive regimes.

The Future of Non-Alignment: From Dependence to Democracy

Ultimately, then, the interrelated concerns of the NAM for development and equality come together in the notion of a political economy of democracy at the interrelated national and international levels. National development and international redistribution not only improve the prospects of satisfying basic human needs; they also serve to enhance the resistance of a country to external domination. At Colombo, the NAM declared that:

> . . . as a result of recent developments, the importance of ensuring the genuine and complete independence of states as distinct from merely formal sovereignty had been enhanced. The problem of unequal relations between states, often amounting to domination, continues to be a disturbing phenomenon even negating the hard-won freedom of some states. Today, one of the principal tasks of the Non-Aligned remains the combating of unequal relations and domination. . . .[53]

The demand for greater levels of development and equality to resist domination also enhances the prospects for democracy in both national and international domination. Given the adoption of welfare measures in the colonial metropoles on the basis of external exploitation, it may be a prerequisite for the achievement of basic human needs in the periphery: self-reliance, like non-alignment, may be an expression of self-interest. Singham comments from his world-system perspective:

That liberty, democracy, enjoyed by those living in the capitalist centre has been earned at the expense of those living in the colonies. The Non-Aligned Movement is suggesting not only that colonization and capitalism brought economic benefits to the centre capitalist countries but also that colonization was largely responsible for the evolution of democratic institutions in the centre itself.[54]

Given the nature and results of the incorporation, disengagement and self-reliance may be prerequisites, therefore, not only for development but also for democracy in the periphery. And even if the North is jealous for its own growth and welfare, it can hardly be selfish about its democracy. Political as well as economic redistribution and democratization may be a central feature and result of any NIEO, a paradox of political economy:

> The demand for a NIEO is an equalitarian as well as a libertarian demand. Redistribution of the world's economic resources is likely to weaken oligarchic and repressive regimes. Increases in standards of living should result in greater demands of democratic rights by those enjoying newly won economic rights. The struggle against poverty is, indeed, the most significant democratic goal.[55]

In which case, proletarian peoples as well as proletarian countries may yet come to benefit from ambiguities in the ideology of non-alignment. And, as Wallerstein suggests, this struggle between democracy and underdevelopment will be most acute in the NICs in the NAM, with special relevance given to their symbolic and strategic positions:

> The semi-peripheral states in the coming decades will be a battleground of two major transnational forces. One will be the multinational corporations who will be fighting for the survival of the essentials of the capitalist system: the probability of continued surplus appropriation on a world scale. The other will be a transnational alignment of socialist forces who will be seeking to undermine the capitalist world economy, not by 'developing' singly, but by forcing relatively drastic redistributions of world surplus and cutting the long-term present and potential organizational links between multinationals and certain strata internal to each semi-peripheral country, including such strata in the socialist semi-peripheral states.[56]

Hence, the NAM Conferences' recognition and rejection of 'external' interference: a fine ideological position but a highly difficult, even

idealistic policy, given the contemporary conjuncture, or the para-
doxical nature of the *Kairos*:

> At twenty-five today, rich in wisdom and moral strength, our
> Movement is better armed to meet these challenges (of disarmament
> and development) and to carry out its historical mission of seeking
> the establishment of a new, just and democratic world order. . . . The
> Movement . . . remains the foremost movement of peace, under-
> standing and equitable cooperation in the world as it enters the
> twenty-first century.[57]

Reflective of the mutual interest of North and South in common
reconceptualized security, or the mutual reinforcement between the
Palme and South Commissions, the NAM in Harare 'emphasized the
direct relationship between peace, disarmament and development.'[58]

Acknowledgement

The original version of this chapter appeared as 'The Non-Aligned Movement and
the New International Economic Order', in Herb Addo, ed., *Transforming the
World Economy? Nine Critical Essays on the New International Economic Order*,
(London: Hodder and Stoughton, 1984), pp. 138–62. It is reprinted in a
substantially revised version by permission of the publishers, to whom I am most
grateful.

Notes

1. Olof Palme, 'Introduction' to *Common Security: A Programme for Disarmament*
(London, 1982), pp. xi and xii.
2. 'Final Document: Economic Declaration Harare, September 1986', *Review of
International Affairs*, 37(875), 20 September 1986, p. 166.
3. Immanuel Wallerstein, *The Capitalist World-Economy*, (Cambridge, 1979), pp. 269
and 282.
4. See *North–South; A Programme for Survival*, (Pan, 1980), and *Common Crisis,
North–South: Cooperation for World Recovery*, (London, 1983).
5. *Common Security*, op. cit., p. 175.
6. See 'Harare Statement: South–South Cooperation—Experiences and Prospects', in
Bernard Chidzero and Altaf Gauhar, eds, *Linking the South: The Route to Economic
Cooperation* (London: Third World Foundation, 1986), p. 304.
7. For an earlier attempt to situate the NAM in the context of the world economy using
contrasting orthodox and radical approaches to analysis, see Timothy M. Shaw, 'The
Political Economy of Non-Self Alignment: From Dependence to Self-Reliance', *International
Studies* 19 (3), July/September 1980, pp. 474–502. For a related attempt to advance the
sociology of knowledge about non-alignment in a more critical and historical direction, see

A.W. Singham, 'Non-Alignment—from Summit to Summit', *Man and Development* 1(3), October 1979, pp. 1–40.

8. Wallerstein, *The Capitalist World-Economy*, op. cit., p. 95.

9. On the notion of 'conjuncture' as related to the development of national political economies, see James H. Mittleman, *Underdevelopment and the Transition to Socialism: Mozambique and Tanzania*, (New York, 1981).

10. 'Declaration of the Conference of Foreign Ministers of Non-Aligned Countries, New Delhi', February 1981, p. 30. See also note 51 below.

11. Non-aligned leaders are caught in a difficult dialectic: they are dependent upon external associates for support, capital, technology, markets, and imports yet they also require more of these goods than they can ever hope to get. Hence the ambivalence generated by simultaneous conflict and co-operation as leaders at the periphery attempt to improve their position *vis-à-vis* those at the centre of the world system. Hence the gap between superstructure rhetoric and substructural reality, with the former increasingly diverging from the latter.

12. On the adoption of such rhetoric ploy by Third World leaders in their attempt to improve their position between external associates (who exploit as well as support) and internal demands, see Claude Ake, *Revolutionary Pressures in Africa*, (London, 1978), pp. 92–4.

13. For an overview of these, see *World Bank Development Report* 1981, (New York, 1981) and *Financing Adjustment with Growth in Sub-Sahara Africa 1986–1990*, (Washington, 1986).

14. On these two approaches, see Timothy M. Shaw, 'Non-Alignment Redefined: Africa's Quest for Development and Self-Reliance' in Timothy M. Shaw and Ralph I. Onwuka, eds, *Africa and World Politics: Independence, Dependence and Interdependence*, (London, forthcoming).

15. A.W. Singham, ed., Preface to his collection on *The Non-Aligned Movement in World Politics*, (Westport, Conn., 1977), p. iii.

16. Ibid., p. 227. See also Dinesh Singh, 'Non-Alignment and New International Economic Order', *Review of International Affairs* 32(755), 21 October 1981, pp. 14–19.

17. H. Hveem and P. Willetts, 'The Practice of Non-Alignment: On the Present and the Future of an International Movement' in Y.A. Tandon and D. Chandarana, eds, *Horizons of African Diplomacy*, (Nairobi, 1974) p. 2.

18. Ibid. p. 28.

19. Ibid., pp. 21–2.

20. On this, see Timothy M. Shaw, 'Dependence to (Inter)Dependence: Review of Debate on the (New) International Economic Order', *Alternatives* 4(4), March 1979, pp. 557–8.

21. Singham, 1977, op. cit., p. 227. For more on the evolution of the NAM from political to economic preoccupations, see Miguel Angel de la Flor Valle, 'The Movement of Non-Alignment and the New International Order', *Review of International Affairs* 32(756), 5 October 1981, pp. 15–18.

22. 'Final Document: Political Declaration, 1986', p. 39.

23. See Craig Murphy, *The Emergence of the NIEO Ideology*, (Boulder, Colorado, 1984).

24. See Timothy M. Shaw, 'Towards a Political Economy of the African Crisis: Diplomacy, Debates and Dialectics', in Michael H. Glantz, ed., *Drought and Hunger in Africa: Denying Famine a Future*, (Cambridge: Cambridge University Press, 1986), pp. 127–47.

25. See Ankie M.M. Hoogvelt, *The Third World in Global Development*, (London, 1982).

26. See Claude Ake, 'Non-Alignment in the Contemporary World: An African

Perspective', *African Association of Political Science Newsletter* July–September 1986, 5–10; and L. Adele Jinadu and Ibbo Mandaza, eds, *African Perspectives on Non-Alignment* (Harare: African Association of Political Science, 1986).

27. 'Political Declaration', 1976.

28. See Chidzero and Gauhar, *op. cit.*, especially pp. ix–18 and pp. 303–18.

29. See Hoogvelt, op. cit., pp. 73–102.

30. Ervin Laszlo, 'Introduction: The Objectives of the New International Economic Order in Historical and Global Perspective', in Ervin Laszlo *et al.*, eds, *The Objective of the New International Economic Order*, (New York, 1978), p. xviii.

31. 'Economic Declaration of the Fifth Summit Conference of the Non-Aligned Governments, Sri Lanka, August 1976', in Singham, 1977, op. cit., pp. 263–73.

32. 'Declaration of the Ministerial Conference, 1981: Economic Part', op. cit., pp. 31–2.

33. Laszlo, op. cit., 'Introduction', p. xxi.

34. Timothy M. Shaw, 'Conclusion: African Development and the New International Division of Labor', in Timothy M. Shaw, *et al.*, eds, *Economic Crisis in Africa*, (London, 1985), pp. 267–83.

35. 'Economic Declaration, 1976', op. cit., para. 38.

36. Jack N. Barkenbus, 'Slowed Economic Growth and Third World Welfare' in Dennis Clark Pirages, ed., *The Sustainable Society*, (New York, 1977), p. 317.

37. See Timothy M. Shaw, *Towards a Political Economy for Africa: The Dialectics of Dependence* (London, 1985).

38. On this range—from producer associations and nuclear energy to sports and women—see 'Review of Implementation of the Action Programme for Economic Cooperation', *Review of International Affairs* 32(641), 20 February 1981, pp. 40–6.

39. See Mai Palmberg, ed., *Problems of Socialist Orientation in Africa* (Stockholm, Almqvist and Wiksell).

40. 'Political Declaration, 1976', op. cit., para. 13.

41. 'Economic Declaration, 1976', op. cit., para. 19.

42. Ibid., paras 34 and 35.

43. Singham, 1977, op. cit., 'Conclusion', pp. 227–8. For further analysis of some of these contradictions, see Bojana Tadic, 'The Movement of the Non-Aligned and its Dilemmas Today', *Review of International Affairs* 32(756), 5 October 1981, pp. 19–24.

44. Singham, 1977, op. cit., 'Preface', pp. x–xi.

45. See Wallerstein, op. cit., pp. 66–118, and Timothy M. Shaw, 'Kenya and South Africa: "Sub-Imperialist" States', *Orbis* 21(2), Summer 1977, pp. 375–94, and 'International Stratification in Africa: Subimperialism in Eastern and Southern Africa', *Journal of Southern African Affairs* 2(2), April 1977, pp. 145–64. See also Baghat Korany, 'Hierarchy within the South: In Search of Theory', in *Third World Affairs 1986* (London: Third World Foundation, 1986), pp. 85–100.

46. See Jerker Carlsson and Timothy M. Shaw, eds., *Newly Industrialising Countries and the Political Economy of South–South Relations*, (London, 1987).

47. Ali A. Mazrui, 'Technology, International Stratification and the Politics of Growth', *International Political Science Association*, Moscow, August 1979, pp. 10–12. For more on inequality and interaction within the Third World, see his *The Barrel of the Gun and the Barrel of Oil in North–South Equation*, (New York: World Order Models Project, 1978), Working Paper 5.

48. On this debate in the case of Nigeria in West Africa, see Timothy M. Shaw and Olajide Aluko, eds., *Nigerian Foreign Policy: Alternative Perceptions and Projections*, (London: Macmillan, 1983). See also Timothy M. Shaw, 'Nigeria in the International System', in I. William Zartman, ed., *The Political Economy of Nigeria*, (New York, 1983), pp. 207–36.

49. 'Political Declaration, 1976', op. cit., para. 12.

50. Ibid., paras 32 and 33.

51. Fred Halliday, 'The maturing of the Non-Aligned: Perspectives from New Delhi', *Third World Affairs 1985*, (London: Third World Foundation, 1985), p. 52.

52. Ismail-Sabri Abdalla, 'Heterogeneity and Differentiation—the End for the Third World?', *Development Dialogue* 2, 1978, pp. 10–11.

53. 'Political Declaration, 1976', op. cit., para, 15.

54. Singham, 1977, op. cit., 'Preface', p. xi.

55. Ibid.

56. Wallerstein, op. cit., pp. 117–8.

57. 'Solemn Declaration to Mark the 25th Anniversary of the Non-Aligned Movement', *Review of International Affairs* 37(875), 20 September 1986, p. 27.

58. 'Economic Declaration, 1986', op. cit., p. 66.

16

At the Receiving End of the North–South Dialogue

JULIUS K. NYERERE

To speak of dialogue is to speak of two individuals, or two groups, who are talking and listening to each other, and who have the intentions and the hope of reaching an agreed conclusion to their discussions. To speak of a North–South dialogue is, in international parlance, to speak of two distinct groups of countries which are—or have been—having a dialogue on a set of economic problems and relationships. And the first reaction to any question about the North–South dialogue is therefore a question: What dialogue? For the last six years, very little—indeed almost nothing—which could be called a North–South dialogue has been taking place.

Some people believe that this is as it should be. They argue that countries should not be divided into economic groups which deal with each other as groups, but that all nations should deal with each other bilaterally or at international fora which involve the whole world. For they point out that all peoples of the world, and all countries, exist on one planet, and that all are interconnected through trade, through modern communications—and some would add, through the great threat of nuclear war.

To argue in this way is to ignore the world we live in. We do all live on one planet, and all are interconnected; all nations are in legal terms equal sovereign members of the UN with the same rights and duties. But this statement of mixed fact and legal theory combines to hide a vicious reality. The world's unity, and the sovereign equality of nations, is mocked and nullified by the economic inequalities which exist between the so-called equal nations of the world, and in particular between the economic North and South of the world. In 1967 the average annual per capita income in the rich countries was $2790. In that same year, the average per capita income of the low income countries was $120. In other words, the income of a person in the poorest countries of the world was on average one-twenty-third that of a person in the rich countries.

197

If that gap were getting narrower over the course of time one could indeed argue both the beneficient nature of the interconnectedness which modern technology has created, and the irrelevance—indeed the destructiveness—of classifying countries into economic groups. But the gap is getting wider. In 1982 the average per capita income in the rich countries was $11,070 and that in the low income countries was $280. Thus in 12 years the average per capita income in the very poor countries had changed from being one-twenty-third of that in the rich countries to becoming one-fortieth; by 1983 it had become one-forty-third.

The figures do look a little more respectable if you compare the average per capita income of what is usually called the economic South, with that of the industrial market economies; i.e. the predominant part of the economic North. For when you include such tiny oil-rich countries as Kuwait and the United Arab Emirates in the economic South, the average per capita income in 1983 works out at about $690 per annum, as against a figure of $11,060 in the economic North. The average per capita income in the economic South was thus in 1983 one-seventeenth of that in the North. But since then it will have become a smaller proportion; many countries in Africa and some in Latin America have had negative income growth in recent years—and are likely to continue to do so in the foreseeable future. This is especially true of the poorer countries of Africa, whose per capita income (concealed in the overall Third World average) was about $240 in 1983.

This can be put another way. Leaving aside what the World Bank calls 'the European non-market economies', for which income figures are not easily available, approximately 55 per cent of the total population of the economic North and economic South share roughly 5.8 per cent of the combined North–South incomes. Just over 17 per cent of that total population receive approximately 77 per cent of this combined income. Such figures show that there is a clear distinction between the economic North and the economic South. The South is very poor; it is therefore powerless. The North is rich; it has the power which wealth brings in a world dominated by the market place and what high-technology goods you can make or buy and then use.

And given this inequality between two groups, constant dialogue between them is necessary if even the minimum precaution is to be taken against injustice being committed—albeit perhaps inadvertently —by the strong against the weak. Indeed, constant vigilance through the mechanisms of dialogue is necessary to prevent a violation of the national sovereignty of the weak countries by the strong countries.

And if—as used to be stated—there is to be a war against world poverty, and thus a reversal of the present trend towards constantly increasing economic inequality, then more needs to be done that that. There needs to be a deliberate North–South dialogue with the purpose of first identifying the underlying causes of this increasing inequality, and second agreeing on how to eliminate those factors and replace them by mechanisms which stimulate movement towards greater wealth production by and for the poor countries.

The term 'North–South dialogue' was first used in connection with this larger purpose of fighting world poverty. But the question 'What dialogue?' could even be asked about the narrower concept. For we are brought back to the argument that the world cannot rationally be so divided between rich and poor, or economic North and economic South. Most certainly the world is one; neither economic North nor economic South are monolithic. The North is at one end of the range of wealth and power in the world, and the South is at the other end. At the margins the North and South shade into each other. For national power in the world comes from more than just wealth as measured by per capita incomes. It comes from a combination of wealth and size and technological capacity, together with a history of independence, stability, and peace.

Thus Kuwait and Saudi Arabia are wealthy; but they are too small, and still too technologically backward to have any real power. Despite their wealth they are part of the economic South. China and India, on the other hand, are very large; but both have suffered from the exploitations and distortions of colonialism and foreign occupation. At present they could only wield power within the context of the economic South. When they are operating on the larger world scene, they have potential power but not actual power. They too are therefore part of the economic South.

Similarly, Sweden has a per capita national income approaching that of the USA; it has great technological capacity, and a long history of stability and neutrality. But with a population of less than 9 million it is too small to be a power in the world even if it had ambition. Switzerland—which is even richer than the USA in per capita terms—is in the same position. And except that many of them did suffer severely during the two world wars, the same considerations apply to the other small states of Europe.

All these countries are, by virtue of their wealth and their technological capacity, part of the economic North; but separately they do not wield power on the world scene, and bilaterally they have power only in relation to the countries of the economic South. It is at least partly in the hope of strengthening themselves in relation to the real powers of the economic North—with the USA in particular—that so many of the small European nations have joined with the larger West European powers to form the EEC. All recognize that they are

part of the North, with interests similar to those of the USA; but they
believe that by working together in unity they will have more power in
determining the economic governance and policies of the North.

Nor is either the North or South monolithic as regards the political
and economic policies or ideologies espoused by countries within that
group. The economic North can be divided ideologically into
Communist and capitalist countries; by and large these are hostile
towards one another, and, although they trade together, economic co-
operation among them is greatly circumscribed. The Communist
subgroup of the North has in general refused to accept any
responsibility in relation to the struggle against world poverty, on the
grounds that the inequalities between North and South arose from a
structure of colonialism in which they played no part. At least until
recently they have not been impressed by the South's argument that, by
taking part in international trade and finance, they are now indirect
beneficiaries of the outcome of colonialism and imperialism.

Even among the capitalist countries, however, there are differences
of political ideology and approach to economic questions. And similar
differences exist within the economic South. One could really say that
there is an ideological division in the world which is different from the
economic division.

The ideological division is between those governments (or individuals) who believe that economies have to managed; and those who
believe that everything should be left to the market, and that over the
course of time everyone will be better off provided they work hard.
There are countries of the North, and of the South, on both sides of
that ideological divide as far as national policies are concerned—
although virtually no country consistently applies this free-market
approach within its own borders.

Internationally, there are almost no countries of the Third
World—that is, of the economic South—which in practice favour an
untrammelled free-market approach. The economic North is divided
on the issue. There are some national political leaders—especially in
the small countries—who acknowledge that the free-market doctrine is
at the root of an unjust economic division of the world's wealth. Such
leaders sometimes allow that knowledge to be reflected by practical
sympathy for the efforts of the South to secure change in the
international economic order.

The current reality, however, is that those countries of the North
which have real power internationally are ideologically and aggressively
committed to a free-market philosophy internationally as well as
nationally. Countries like the USA, together with the lesser economic
powers such as Britain, Germany, and Japan, actively support the idea
of untrammelled capitalism internationally, albeit at the same time

breaking its rules when this suits their own domestic interests. They are hostile to international arrangements (whether organized through UN specialized agencies or by other means) which seek to ameliorate the effects of an international free market on the poor of the world; when such arrangements have already been put in place they seek to undermine them, and they veto any new proposals of that type. Yet at the same time they protect their own industries against international competition, and they subsidize some of their agricultural exports, as well as managing their own currencies in their own interests—all things which are contrary to the doctrines they seek to impose on the rest of the world.

Thus the dominant powers in the North are ideologically hostile to the very idea of a dialogue between the North and the South. They do not accept that there is a problem with the facts of abysmal and increasing poverty in the Third World; they attribute it to the actions and the failures of the governments and peoples of the economic South. Not being evil people, they are willing, sometimes, to give charity to the 'deserving poor'; beyond that, they urge the benefits of what they call economic freedom within the poor countries. But they reject any suggestion of serious and concerted world action to deal with world poverty. And in recent years they have been going further; they use the pressure of their own economic power to try to prevent the government of a poor country from controlling its imports, subsidizing its exports, or in any way directing its international trade and economic relationships in what it believes to be its own long-term interests.

Olof Palme was in the North; but he was the epitomy of the opposite view. He believed that it was the responsibility of men and of leaders to work positively for the welfare of all human beings— between whom he accepted no distinctions of colour, race, creed, or nationality. And both domestically and internationally he accepted the necessity for a managed economy in order to do this.

Olof Palme therefore led a party and governments which aimed at managing the Swedish economy so as to reduce internal economic inequalities. Further, he recognized both the unity and interdependence of the world, and the disunity and the assymmetry of power in the world. He therefore worked for change in the world power structure, and within his capacity as a leader of Sweden he tried to ensure that adjustments to international or technological change gave the maximum benefit to the poor of the world and the minimum of disruption to the lives of Swedish workers. For gross economic inequalities—whether within Sweden or in the world as a whole—were anathema to him. He rightly regarded extreme poverty, such as exists in the economic South, as obscene. He recognized also that such poverty is a pollutant, destroying the world environment on which all human beings depend.

Olof Palme was perhaps the greatest of the North's exponents of international economic action to promote international economic justice. Being also a man of peace, he was consequently a great advocate of genuine dialogue between the North and the South. He wanted North–South discussions leading to action about how the world economy could be managed to reduce the poverty gap, and about how to provide to Third World countries the means to develop themselves in terms of national sovereignty and equality. He went further. When, and to the extent that, no North–South dialogue was taking place or was failing to make progress, he led his country and a few others in a positive action through partnership between sub-groupings of the North and South. In Olof Palme the poor of the world, and the peace of the world, had a friend and an ally.

Olof Palme did not initiate the idea of international action to deal with world problems. The groundwork for a possible future North–South dialogue was really laid in the aftermath of the Second World War—that is, even before the economic division of the world was a matter of wide consciousness. For it was at that time that the UN was formed, together with the Bretton Woods Institutions and many of the basic UN specialized agencies. And whereas the first principle of the UN as laid down in the Charter is: 'The Organization is based on the principle of the sovereign equality of all its members', the expressed purpose of many of the associated institutions was to promote prosperity, welfare, and peace among all the peoples of the world.

The increasing success of the anti-colonial movement in the post-war world has meant that more and more countries from what we now know as the economic South have become members of the UN and are represented at its General Assembly. As they themselves have become conscious of their poverty, and its connections with the international economic order which existed when they became independent, so they have begun to use the UN machinery to voice their protests, and even to make proposals for change. These ex-colonial countries have used the right to speak and vote in the General Assembly, to be represented in the Security Council, and to have representation on the Boards (albeit with very limited voting power) of the Bretton Woods Institutions. And not completely unconnected with those facts has been the setting up of the IDA in 1960, the creation of UNCTAD in 1964, of UNDP and UNIDO in 1965 and 1967, and of IFAD in 1977. All these later bodies were set up to concentrate on dealing with the economic problems and needs of the Third World countries.

The high point of the consideration of North–South issues by the UN was the adoption by the General Assembly in December 1974 of the Charter of Economic Rights and Duties of States. Only six nations voted against this proposal, with a further 10 abstaining. The

Charter put great emphasis on the need for action to accelerate the growth of the developing countries (the terminology has changed over the years!) and proclaimed that 'The sea bed and ocean floor and the subsoil thereof, beyond the limits of national jurisidiction, as well as the resources of the area, are the common heritage of mankind.'

Everything seemed to be set for a deliberate North–South dialogue aimed at dealing with the problems of world poverty in an orderly manner. The Law of the Sea Conference began its long drawn-out task. And the Brandt Commission was set up at the beginning of 1978 to 'study the grave global issues arising from the economic and social disparities of the world community' and to 'suggest ways of promoting adequate solutions to the problems involved in development and in attacking absolute poverty.' The principle of global negotiations about North–South relationships in a changing world was—apparently—accepted.

Thus, there was a North–South dialogue of a limited kind from the end of the 1950s. What had been achieved by the end of the 1970s was, first, that world poverty and inequality were high on the world agen'da; and, second, that some important institutions had been set up in which economic dialogue could (if the political will existed) take place on terms of equality between rich and poor countries—for example, in UNCTAD. Further, research and much discussion had been promoted, and much groundwork necessary for dealing with the problems seriously had been done.

Unfortunately, just as averages can conceal nearly as much as they reveal, so this apparent advance of internationalist economic attitudes was based on weak foundations. The major powers of the economic North—and some of the smaller ones—found it politically advantageous to acquiesce verbally in the demand for a world war on poverty, but had a fundamental reluctance to any tampering with an international economic order which seemed to suit their own interests—as it had been designed to do.

Thus, although there is now a tendency to look back at the 1970s as a period of progress towards a North–South dialogue, the six nations which voted against the Charter on Economic Rights and Duties of States included the 'big three' of the North—i.e. the USA, the UK, and the Federal Republic of Germany. Indeed, all too often the policy of the North was to resist even the most moderate demands, and, when political pressure (domestically and internationally) became too strong, to concede as little of substance as possible. This was particularly true of the major powers of the North; some of the smaller countries in that group did play a helpful part on particular proposals, when once convinced of their justice and advantages to the world as a whole as well as to the poor.

And the fragile nature of such advance as had been achieved became very clear when political changes in Britain, the USA, and Germany took place at the turn of the decade. By the time the Brandt Commission report was published in 1980, supposedly to begin the herculean task of North–South global negotiations, nothing had been achieved—not even agreement on procedures, a time-frame, or an agenda. The real powers of the North were simply not interested. They no longer had any desire even to appear willing to discuss fundamental change in the structure of international trade and finance.

Attempts continued to be made. On the initiative of the Chancellor of Austria and the President of Mexico, a meeting of some 22 representative national leaders from North and South was held in Cancun in 1981. The purpose was to have a preliminary discussion about how to begin to deal with the problems pointed out in the Brandt report, and how to prepare to implement some of its recommendations. The result of that meeting was—nothing at all. The new US administration was not prepared to do anything on these issues, or to take part in any global negotiations, however these were organized. Further, it became clear that the other governments of the economic North which were present were not prepared to do anything at all without the participation of the USA, even when they themselves could see the advantages of particular detailed proposals.

Thus by 1980 the qualified internationalism of the post-war years had given way to the urge for power, and the untrammelled use of that power, on the part of the economically strong states. This has become very clear indeed during the last six years.

We have seen a continuing attack on all those multilateral institutions where control is exercised on a democratic basis of one nation, one vote—such as UNESCO, UNCTAD, and UNIDO. And finance has been cut for multilateral institutions even when the strong powers have had greater control, as in IFAD and the IDA of the World Bank. In so far as official development assistance is still given—and its amount has fallen in real terms—it is increasingly allocated on a bilateral basis, with the donor's strategic interests being the real determinant of its allocation between needy states. Alternatively, such bilateral official assistance is conditional on certain military or economic 'facilities' being given in return, or on certain macro-economic policies being followed by recipient states.

Nor is this all; there have now been a number of instances where economic might has been to threaten or blackmail small and poor states into using their UN General Assembly votes in support of the potential donor nation. It is also used, quite deliberately and openly, to try to force Third World countries into adopting internal economic and political policies which serve the interests of the major powers of the economic North. The arrogant belief is flaunted that the leaders of the USA and of some other major capitalist economic powers know better than the leaders of poor nations what is in the interests of poor countries and their people. Instead of at least a qualified internationalism and a desire for international co-operation on the basis of mutual respect, we now have blatant new-colonialism and international authoritarianism.

This does not imply that there is no dialogue at all between countries of the economic North and the economic South, or that there are no formal discussions within international economic institutions. The forms are sometimes observed! Nor does it imply that there is no contact on an economic level. However, limited by increasing poverty among the poor, world trade continues and world credit arrangements creak along under the constant threat of default.

Commonwealth countries meet and discuss international economic as well as political issues. Common ground is often found between members from the South and most of those from the North—for example on South Africa and on the need for a new international conference on the world's financial institutions. But the British government under Mrs Thatcher's leadership often stands outside such agreements; the Commonwealth influence on the world (it has no power) is therefore greatly reduced. The Nordic Council holds discussions and co-operates with the Southern African Development Co-ordination Conference (SADCC); through this means as well as bilaterally the Scandinavian countries are giving real and positive support to the Front Line States confronting South Africa. Again, the EEC and the African, Caribbean, and Pacific countries regularly renegotiate the Lome Agreements as they reach expiry; but Lome 3 showed no advance on Lome 2 (in real resource allocation it is probably a regression) and figures show that the result of these negotiations has not helped to reduce the imbalance of trade between the two areas—which continues increasingly to favour the Northern states.

And all the international institutions continue to meet, and to discuss a long agenda. But at these meetings there is an ever decreasing dialogue. The USA and the UK have both withdrawn from UNESCO, allegedly and ridiculously because they do not like the Director General, but really because they did not approve of all its decisions, and were unable to control it. At UNCTAD and UNIDO meetings, the powerful countries of the economic North send quite junior officials with firm instructions not to compromise on pre-set positions hostile to change, or to agree to any new transfer of resources from North to South. At GATT meetings, the Northern powers come with agreed positions in their own interests, and try to bully the weak and less strongly organized Third World countries into accepting their ideas.

Even the IMF and the World Bank—institutions controlled by the weighted power of Northern votes—have suffered from the anti-internationalist approach and been starved of funds. Thus, for example, when it was set up, the IMF quotas were equal to about 16 per cent of world trade; by 1983 they were equal to about 4 per cent of it. And the seventh replenishment of the IDA at $9 billion is 25 per cent lower in nominal terms and 40 per cent lower in real terms than the sixth replenishment three years before, in 1981. Even for its non-concessional lending activities, the World Bank has inadequate funding; all proposals to expand its capital base have been met with the rejoinder that it must instead go into partnership with private foreign investors.

Yet despite this resource starvation, the World Bank and the IMF (especially the latter) are still used to put pressure on Third World countries to conform to political philosophies and economic strategies approved by the USA and the EEC. Indeed, whereas the Reagan administration of the USA was originally hostile to both these international financial institutions, it has become more supportive of the IMF as it has discovered that this institution can be used to control the economies of the Third World countries. It is even looking again at the World Bank, in the hope that an extra injection of money could enable that institution also to be used for this purpose and to safeguard Northern investments in Third World countries.

Yet among the stated purposes of the IMF is that of providing members 'with opportunity to correct maladjustments in their balance of payments without resorting to measures destructive of national or international prosperity'. This purpose is ignored when increasing foreign exchange deficits force a Third World country to go to the IMF for credit. They are met with a litany of demands: devalue the local currency by a very large percentage at once; increase exports and liberalize imports; cut government spending; raise interest rates; eliminate any subsidies either for production or consumption, as well as price controls; impose a wage freeze. Such a series of actions, taken by a number of countries, inevitably does damage both national and international trade and prosperity; they are a prescription for deflation. For example, it has been estimated that during the 1981–82 recession, contraction in the developing countries—often a direct result of an IMF agreement—cost the USA alone more than $18 000 million in lost export earnings, and about 1 million jobs in export industries. This is to say nothing of the effect of such deflationary policies on the lives of the poor within countries.

By long and hard negotiations a determined Third World country can sometimes get a little flexibility on some of these demands—and because they are already in economic difficulty before they have recourse to the IMF, some of the things may have to be done whether or not there is an IMF agreement. But the final decision on how much flexibility will be allowed (and therefore whether an agreement is possible on any terms except surrender) is a political one. There is, for example, no possibility of Nicaragua getting an IMF agreement unless it changes its government, just as it cannot get World Bank loans for viable development projects—in both cases because the USA is willing and able to block such a proposal.

But it is made very difficult indeed—or even impossible—for a Third World country with a big balance-of-payments deficit to avoid seeking an IMF agreement. If it tries to raise needed foreign capital without applying to the IMF, it eventually finds that both the World Bank and potential bilateral lenders or donors refuse any help until an IMF agreement is in place. If any of the smaller countries in the economic North are reluctant to participate in this bullying, they in turn come under pressure from the more powerful countries until they yield to the international cartel.

Yet the USA and the EEC countries do not themselves abide by the conditions they force upon the weak. In 1983 the USA spent over $21,000 million on domestic farm price support; it now also has an expensive system of payment in kind which releases government stocks to the farmers if they reduce their output. The dramatic and abrupt fall in the cotton price of July 1986 was not unrelated to such a release of US stocks of cotton. And the US proposal to sell subsidized wheat to the Soviet Union brought strong protests from Australia and other traditional wheat exporters among the countries of the economic North, as well as from some countries of the economic South. And the costs of the EEC Common Agricultural Policy—a system of agricultural subsidies—account for something like two-thirds of its total budget; to reduce the mountainous stocks, the EEC sells some of this agricultural produce externally at below cost prices, contrary to the rules of GATT and its own free-market philosophy.

At the same time both the USA and the countries of the EEC protect their domestic industries against foreign competition. They do this through enforced 'voluntary agreements', through higher tariffs on processed than unprocessed commodities, specially designed 'health regulations', and openly protectionist measures. And this trend is increasing, despite the Northern governments' expressed opposition to protectionism. OECD figures show that the proportion of manufactured goods imported (from all sources, not just the Third World) into the USA that are subject to special restrictions has risen from about 6 per cent in 1980 to over 13 per cent in 1986; comparable figures for the EEC show a rise from 11 per cent to 15 per cent.

Instead of a North–South dialogue we have a situation where the

North says to the South, 'Do as I say—and not as I do!' But why are the countries of the economic South getting poorer relative to the North—and sometimes in absolute terms? Is it possible that the South is itself responsible for its own economic disasters, as alleged by the leaders of the economic North?

Increasing output requires preceding increased investment in capital goods, in public infrastructure, and in education or health. But when you are poor you have less resources that you can devote to investment than if you are rich. Even if other things were equal, and one country with a per capita income of $300 per annum and another with a per capita income of $10,000 both devoted 20 per cent of their income to investment, one would be investing $60, and the other $2000 for every inhabitant; inevitably the gap between them will increase! There is no record in history of a nation which was able to develop its economy without the injection of outside capital.

And, of course, other things are not equal. First, it is much more difficult for a very poor country to invest the same proportion of its national income as a richer country can. A man on the breadline has to spend whatever money he gets; in contrast, it involves little hardship for a well-fed, well-dressed, and well-housed man to save one-fifth of his much larger income. It is not surprising, therefore, that during the past six or seven years many low-income African countries have had a negative gross investment rate; as their national income has fallen they have been forced to allow their past capital investments to deteriorate, simply in order to continue feeding their people.

More important than this unequal starting level of their investment capability, however, is the fact that resources are being regularly extracted from Third World countries and taken to the economic North. This happens through almost consistently adverse movements of the international terms of trade, and—during the past six to eight years especially—through high interest payments on past debts. From Africa without doubt, and almost certainly from the Third World as a whole, the net resource transfer throughout the post-war period has been from the poor countries of the economic South to the rich countries of the economic North.

The World Bank has estimated that from 1980–82 the prices of non-oil primary commodities fell by 27 per cent in current dollar terms. As one example of what this means, 2.4 per cent of the GDP of the low-income countries of Sub-Saharan Africa is extracted from them each year in favour of the purchasers of those primary commodities—almost entirely the rich countries.

But although this was a particularly bad period for every poor country, the transfer itself was nothing new. In 1974 I was complaining that whereas it had taken 17.25 tons of sisal to buy a tractor in 1965, by February 1974 it was taking 27.25 tons of sisal (and in 1972 took 42 tons!). And in 1971—long before Tanzania's economy entered a crisis—Amir Jamal (then finance minister) told the IMF/World Bank annual meeting:

> The loss to Tanzania from devaluation of our reserve assets, revaluation of our external debts and deterioration of our terms of trade integrally related to repeated crises in currency over the years 1967–71, will approximate US $100 million. Through the sheer operation of the monetary system, determined by the actions of the industrialized countries, Tanzania has paid out the equivalent of eleven years of contribution of 0.7 per cent of its GDP to somebody–I fear to the rich—in just five years.

Nor has the situation improved. In March 1985, tea prices were an average of 250 pence a kilo; by mid-May they had dropped to 130 pence a kilo. At the beginning of October 1986 they were 122 pence a kilo. Comparable figures—a little worse or a little less bad—could be given for almost all the primary commodities exported by Third World countries, and upon which they depend to earn foreign exchange for development and even for the maintenance of their small modern sectors. The prices of the capital goods, and the spares, which they want to import, have not fallen. They have continued to rise—albeit at a slower rate during the last few years.

And as Tanzania tries to reorganize, and works hard to overcome its severe economic difficulties—caused in large part by the operation of the international economic system—the country's efforts are again nullified by a drop in the price of a major export. Tanzania deliberately left other urgent needs unsatisfied in order to make the maximum possible investment in fertilizer and insecticide, as well as transportation facilities, so as to increase its export earnings from cotton. Helped by the good rains, the major cotton-growing regions of the country therefore succeeded in doubling their output in 1986 in comparison with the previous season. Then suddenly the price of that cotton on the world market dropped from 68 cents a pound to 34 cents a pound between one day and the next in July 1986.

On that basis we shall not earn a single cent more of foreign exchange this year than we did last, despite the hard labour of our peasants who grow this crop. Indeed, the nation will be worse off. For the fertilizer, and the insecticide and the lorries and fuel used to deliver those inputs to the farmers and to bring their output to the ports, all have to be paid for in foreign exchange. Something like $28 million—or about 9 per cent of the current value of our exports—has been extracted from us and pocketed by someone in the rich countries.

That loss will not appear in any statistics purporting to show how resources are transferred from the economic North to the economic South in order to help in the war against poverty. Nor will it be taken into account when Tanzania is told it should be grateful to the countries of the North for aid it receives.

Loans and interest payments do show up on some statistics; sometimes the loans are shown as aid even when not advanced on concessional terms! And there was a period (especially from about 1973 to 1979) when loans could be obtained very easily by certain of the less poor countries of the economic South. The nominal interest rates were often high, or were 'floating' at a level determined by some US or European official interest rate; because of the high inflation in the industrialized countries at that time, however, the real interest rate was not abnormally high for as long as the inflation continued.

Deflationary policies in the industrialized countries from the early-1980s therefore changed the situation. The debtors found themselves simultaneously paying high real interest payments at the same time as their export earnings on commodities were falling, and protectionism was making it increasingly difficult for them to export any manufactured goods they might be producing. Africa had the additional difficulty of years of widespread and devastating drought which forced countries greatly to increase their food imports.

Thus, for Africa as a whole, nominal interest rates, which had been about 4.2 per cent on average in 1971, had increased to an average of 10.1 per cent by 1981—and in real terms the rate was by then much higher still. This was despite the fact that many of the low income African countries were eligible for concessionary loans from the IDA or from particular aid donors. The Lever Report of the Commonwealth suggested that in 1981–82, the real interest rate for non-oil exporting developing countries rose to about 20 per cent. And these interest payments are made by the poor to the rich—the only ones who have money to lend. For the most part the debts were incurred either for purposes of economic development and investment, or to meet a catastrophic and sudden worsening of the terms of trade which it was hoped would be temporary—but which in any case required a period for economic readjustment.

The total amount of Africa's overseas debt is often overlooked because of the political fragmentation of the continent. Debt is therefore usually regarded as a problem relating to Latin America. Yet African countries taken together have a higher ratio than any region in the world of debt-servicing costs in relation to exports, and of debt in relation to GDP. Sub-Saharan Africa—which owes about $90 billion— is thus supposed to pay out $12 billion a year on its long-term interest repayments to the IMF. As these countries are also among the poorest in the world, and have been hit by drought as well as the collapse of commodity prices, the debt servicing gets constantly further into arrears. For they simply cannot pay.

So there is constant talk about the 'debt crisis', and the political leaders and financiers of the North are fearful that a default by a major debtor could cause the whole international financial system to collapse. Yet even so, this terrible burden on the countries of the economic South is not regarded by the powers of the North as a legitimate subject for North–South discussion, much less North–South dialogue. On the contrary, when any particular Third World country gets into difficulties in servicing its debts, it is first forced into the hands of the IMF with its deflationary policies and its priority on debt payments. After it has got an agreement on whatever terms it can secure, the debtor country is forced, alone, to sit down with all its creditors as a group to discuss rescheduling those debts. Until it has done these things, it is denied any access whatever to new foreign exchange injection for any purpose whatsoever.

Thus, when the Organization of African Unity called for a meeting of African debtors and Africa's creditors to discuss Africa's debt problems, the answer was silence. No such meeting has taken place, or is likely to take place. For any hint that countries of the economic South might get together and act together on such matters brings forward accusations of dishonesty, of forming a 'cartel', and other crimes against the principles of a world free market. More important, it also brings the threat of economic sanctions against the Third World countries concerned.

For the financial centres of the North do regularly act as a group on all serious matters relating to the debts of the Third World countries; and they use the IMF as the debt collector whenever this is deemed appropriate to them. By now they have intimidated almost all the countries of the economic South by such use of their economic might. So we now have the position where, if there is any meeting of Third World debtors to discuss common problems, the participants are usually at pains to announce beforehand that they have no intention of working out a common strategy of action on the subject, and least of all of forming a debtor's cartel!

So successful has been the North's post-1980 counterattack against the very limited and modest internationalism of the preceding three decades that many countries—and leaders—of the economic South are beginning to feel guilty about their poverty. Many seem to have accepted the doctrine which attributes their nations' slow pace of economic progress—and recent economic regression in many cases—to their domestic failures of policy or action, or even to the laziness of their own people. Indeed that doctrine is now the most usual basis on which any discussion about world poverty does take place; discussions with Olof Palme and the few Northern leaders of like-mindedness were a refreshing exception. Thus Tanzania's problems are attributed to its policies of Ujamaa, Ethiopia's to its Marxism, Sudan's to its instability, Egypt's to Nasser, Argentina's to the generals; the problems of Zaire and the Philippines are attributed to corruption, those of India and Bangladesh to overpopulation— and so on around the world. And while the discussion takes place on this basis, the net transfer of resources continues—from the poor to the rich.

No one is suggesting that Third World countries—and Africa in particular—have not made mistakes in their policies or their implementation of good policies. No one is denying that there is widespread inefficiency and corruption in many poor countries. Africa in particular has done a great deal of self-criticism in recent years, and is engaged in trying to make changes based on that self-examination. But this does not excuse this process of self-criticism being used as evidence to support allegations that Africa's poverty is Africa's fault. For the truth is that the mistakes committed, and even the corruption which exists like a tropical ulcer in a few countries, are of marginal importance in comparison to the effects on Third World countries of the international economic structure in which they have to work and do business.

Nor do any of the Third World's economic or political mistakes weigh in the scale in comparison to the political interventions in the South of the great powers of the economic North. The term North–South dialogue is used in connection with economic questions; but political actions can have very heavy economic costs when a great power intervenes in a Third World country, or in disputes between Third World countries. Vietnam's current economic problems are attributed solely to its involvement in the Kampuchean conflict. But before that—and indeed as a precursor to that—Vietnam was the victim of two vicious and devastating wars by Northern countries against its people, which continued for almost 25 years. Post-revolution Nicaragua, where the people had to fight to get rid of a vicious and corrupt puppet of the USA, has since the beginning had to fight for its existence; $100 million was voted by the US Congress in 1986 to continue the previously covert or unofficial effort to overthrow the elected Nicaraguan government. Angola, after centuries of Portuguese colonial exploitation, has been under constant attack by South Africa and by dissidents armed and financed by South Africa and the USA. One could continue; the list is almost endless.

All the states of Southern Africa have suffered, and are continuing to suffer, from the direct and indirect effects of the South African apartheid regime—which has been buttressed by the major economic and political powers of the North. It has been estimated that the

SADCC countries have suffered economic damage in excess of $10,000 million through South African attacks; this is more than the total official development assistance those countries have received during the same period.

As regards all the examples quoted, and many others, dialogue between the North and the South is either completely denied to the South or any conclusions arising from discussions are vetoed in the UN Security Council.

It is in the light of the kind of recent economic and political history outlined above that the question 'What dialogue' is posed. But it is in the light of that recent history also that we pay tribute to Olof Palme. In that international atmosphere, and while leading a small nation itself subject to external pressure, he remained a fighter for justice for the Third World, and for freedom of all peoples. He epitomized many individuals, and a few political leaders in the less powerful nations of the economic North, who helped the struggle of the South for freedom and justice. His life and work encouraged us to continue our struggle when it became almost unbearably difficult.

People like Olof Palme in leading positions enable us to go on hoping that the people of the democratic North will see the need for justice, and for the people of the Third World to unite for their own defence against exploitation, neo-colonialism, and international authoritarianism. By co-operating for mutual progress, the economic South can become stronger either for effective dialogue with the North or for continued confrontation with the economic North if that is what the North continues to choose.

We salute the memory of Olof Palme, and welcome the co-operation of all those in the North who follow his example of internationalist justice to all peoples in the world.

17

The Politics of Aid

JUDITH HART

In an ideal world, there would no be politics in aid. The industrialized countries of the North would be generous in transferring resources to the developing countries of the South. They would regard development assistance as an imperative, expressing a social ethic which paid no regard to spheres of influence, power struggles, and considerations of self-interest. They would see aid as one important element in the whole complex of interrelated international action, encompassing trade, commodity prices, public and private lending, environmental protection, and so much else, to achieve a world of social justice.

But it is such a sad sweet innocence to suppose that the real world, nasty and brutish as it is, will allow moral principle to dominate its behaviour. The experience of those who write here in tribute to Olof Palme encompasses some two decades of involvement and effort in the issues of development: and I do not know if they in any way share my own conclusions. For I am driven to the view that there is no area of policy which is more sharply and abrasively political than this. This being so, it follows that the agenda for action must be based on a correct political analysis. It follows that it will inevitably be highly debatable and controversial—for right and left can share little common ground. So be it. Good people with good intentions must begin to understand that aid, and its associated policies, is no soft and gentle issue. It brings into play the fundamentals of political philosophy.

The exciting period of reassessment of the relationship between North and South was the 1960s. That was the decade when newly independent countries all over the world considered their economic position in a post-colonial era, and discovered that the flying of their new flags in the proud celebration of Independence Day had not ended their dependency. It was the decade when they began to analyse the nature and restraints of neo-colonialism. It was the decade when they began to formulate their demands for a new and different relationship, meeting together in their regional organizations and as non-aligned

214

nations, sharing analysis and experience in a way which colonialism never permitted.

It was also the decade in which the imperialist countries, for their part, made their adjustment to the ending of colonialism. It was a modest, not to say niggardly, adjustment. The direct financial responsibilities of colonial administration were replaced by miniscule aid programmes, with new governmental departments or agencies to organize them, and to determine 'aid policies' towards the new independent states and the larger countries which had achieved independence much earlier. They had a model to follow: the USA, which, from the days of the post-war Marshall Plan to assist war-torn Western Europe, the later Truman Point Four Programme, and the 1960s' impetus given by President Kennedy, had evolved a political and economic approach to aid. The US political approach was both simple and overt, unembarrassed and self-righteous. The cold war set its own priorities. Aid was part of the power struggle: to sustain its hegemony in Latin America, to provide economic assistance to underpin military assistance for countries ready to accept its bases or to offer military co-operation (or to refuse co-operation with the Soviet Union), and to compete with the Soviet Union in offering aid projects to countries which were both important and neutral in their attitude.

This approach was specific to the USA. But its economists deeply influenced the theories of development which dominated the aid donors during the 1960s and into the 1970s, and inevitably influenced the planning priorities of the developing countries themselves. The Rostovian theory was that aid should be used to create a 'big push' of industrial development, producing wealth which would 'trickle down' to the poor. It was a theory which nicely and neatly suited the transnational corporations seeking opportunities to exploit the natural resources and cheap labour of the South; for a large part of the necessary investment in industry could only come from them. It strongly affected the sectoral lending policies of the World Bank. It meant that much of the available official development assistance of governments was absorbed by spending on the infrastructure needed to support industrial projects. It was a theory which blended benevolence with capitalism.

Strangely enough, it was remarkably similar to the economic approach to aid of the Soviet Union, which drew on its own post-revolution experience in believing that industrial development was the key to progress in Third World countries, and, moreover, that the creation of an industrial working class would be the basis of further economic advance. For the Soviet Union, therefore, taking a very different starting point from that of Rostow and his fellow economists, aid for industrial development blended benevolence with socialism.

Thus it was, for example, that India had three steel mills—one built by the USA, one built by the Soviet Union, and one built by Britain.

What was wrong with the theory was very simple. It didn't work. By the early-1970s it was becoming all too clear that there was little or no 'trickle down'. The poor of the countryside were becoming poorer. And because medical science had ended some of the killer diseases and infections, there were more of them. Death rates had fallen, but birth rates were still high. Looking back now from the perspective of African famines and an awareness of rural poverty which is now widely shared, it seems extraordinary that such a theory could have been so readily accepted and have run unchallenged for so long. But it did. As for amounts of aid, the 1960s saw only one international target; 1 per cent of 'total net flow', which, in the language of development, meant, and means, official development assistance plus private investment, portfolio investment, and private export credits.

It was not until 1970 that the UN Strategy for the Second Development Decade proposed a specific target for official development assistance alone: the familiar 0.7 per cent of GNP. Setting this modest target was one thing; meeting it was quite another. Reporting progress as late as 1976, the OECD Development Assistance Committee (DAC) said:

> This recommendation has been accepted by 13 DAC Members: Belgium, the Netherlands, Norway and Sweden committed themselves without reservations; Australia, Denmark, Finland, France and New Zealand by 1980, and Canada, Germany, Japan and the United Kingdom without setting a date. No commitment was made by four countries: Austria, Italy, Switzerland and the United States.

In 1965 the average percentage of GNP provided for official aid by the member countries of DAC (which included all industrialized countries except the Soviet Union) was 0.44. By 1970, when the Second Development Decade was launched, it had fallen to 0.34. Nor did aid distribution reflect any poverty criteria. Other considerations— how well a country was 'performing' according to orthodox free-market assessments, traditional and historical links, and political factors such as those influencing the USA—determined the allocation of aid: that is, which country got how much. Such aid as there was took the form of loans at varying rates of interest, eventually to be repaid with interest.

But the average concealed remarkably different aid achievements. Between 1965 and 1970, Sweden, Norway, the Netherlands, and Canada doubled theirs; British, French, German and Japanese aid declined somewhat; US aid fell, in the post-Kennedy era, from 0.49 to

0.31 per cent. Sadly, the massive efforts of small countries such as Olof Palme's Sweden do not compensate for the failures of the major industrialized countries. In 1971 Sweden provided some $158 million. The USA provided $3,092 million: if it had merely maintained its 1965 levels, an extra $1,800 million would have been transferred to the Third World—each year.

Staying with the 1960s just a little longer, we should note three trends of immense importance. First, while official development assistance (ODA) was declining, private bank lending was flowing out as if there was no tomorrow, particularly to the middle-income developing countries of Latin America and the Caribbean, which were borrowing long on the assumption of future economic growth. The day of reckoning was far ahead, both for them and for the banks. Second, those industrialized countries which were so mean with aid were at the same time increasing their expenditure on arms. Third, the developing countries were working together on the construction of a coherent and integrated strategy. It was to become their demand for the New International Economic Order (NIEO), which was to occupy for some years the centre stage at every UN conference concerned with economic and social issues.

If those were the 1960s, what of the 1970s? It was, for its part, a decade of drama, shock, hope, disappointment, and looming crisis. Those of us who were immersed in its day-to-day events find it difficult—at least I do—to review them in retrospect with a dispassionate eye. But why should we? The committed cannot pretend to objectivity. Nor should they. But the facts are objective, and speak for themselves. And these were the facts of the 1970s, very roughly in date order:

1. The abandonment by the USA of Bretton Woods, and the consequent chaos in foreign exchange markets, deeply affecting the world economy.
2. Inflation in the countries of the North, increasing the price of essential manufactured imports for the developing countries.
3. Depression in the North, reducing demand for Third World exports of minerals and other industry-related primary products.
4. Fluctuating and then declining prices for Third World primary agricultural products.
5. Two sharp rises in oil prices, affecting the whole of the world economy, but most seriously the foreign exchange and resource position of the oil-dependent developing countries.
6. Superpower surrogate wars, absorbing expenditure overseas and involving increased spending on arms by countries in the regions affected:

7. The frustration of Third World efforts to achieve any substantial or meaningful acceptance of the principles and programme set out in the NIEO.

8. The growing burden of debt and interest repayment, especially for middle-income developing countries.

9. Population increase, unmatched by corresponding growth in most developing countries.

10. Tribal and nationalist conflicts, some of them stemming from arbitrary boundaries imposed by colonialism and inherited independence.

11. Residual armed struggles for independence—in Zimbabwe and the Portuguese colonies of Africa.

12. Increases in ODA by a number of industrialized countries counterbalanced by the stagnation of US aid.

These were some of the adverse factors affecting the developing countries in the 1970s. But there were signs of hope too. Against this background of adversity, the climate of opinion about aid to assist development was changing. The changes were of the greatest importance: in today's context of the late 1980s, it is not only of historical interest to appreciate and understand them; such an understanding can offer guidelines for future action. They embraced public opinion and political pressures; economic theory; the criteria for aid distribution; and the beginnings of a positive approach towards debt relief.

There were three strands in the new thinking, interwoven in the gradual shift of aid policy. The first was the concept of interdependence between rich and poor countries in a global economy which was going completely beserk and benefiting only those few with the financial base to make speculative and socially irresponsible private profit. We observed with shocked fascination the obscene growth of the Eurodollar market, fed in part by OPEC funds looking for somewhere to go, in part by the profits of the transnational corporations in search of easy speculative gains before repatriation, and in part by banks and pension funds seeking gains in the money markets rather than by investment in industry. It is a chicken-and-egg question to ask which came first: the economic depression which provided a disincentive to industrial investment or the diversion of investment funds to the money market which deprived national economies of the capacity for growth. Be that as it may, it was a fact that $3 billion at any given time was buying and selling dollars, sterling, yen, Deutschmarks, and francs while unemployment grew in the North and poverty in the South.

Some of us, seeing not only the obscenity but also the absurdity of it all, began to point out the paradox. While more and more men and women in the industrialized countries were becoming unemployed, as their work places closed or cut down on staff because there was no market for the goods they produced, two-thirds of the world's population in the developing countries desperately needed manufactured goods, but had no purchasing power. The argument we put forward was that it was therefore in the self-interest of the North to assist the development of the South to promote a revival of the global economy. It could be advanced in 'free-market' terms, and was, although in my view it was helpful to urge that a modest degree of economic planning should ensure 'production for need': developing countries needed trucks and buses rather than top-end-of-the-market cars, for example.

Sonnie Ramphal, Secretary General of the Commonwealth, called it 'mutuality of interest'; I, for my part, called it 'enlightened self-interest' (a phrase which had held some appeal in Britain in times past); the Brandt Commission, developing the theme in depth and detail, produced a report which was a bestseller. The intention of everyone concerned was to seek to persuade reluctant governments that increases in aid, and international agreement to provide a fair deal for developing country commodities, were sensible from everyone's point of view. The issue was not only one of social morality. It was also plain common sense.

At the same time the moral argument was gaining ground. There were countries such as Sweden, Norway, and the Netherlands where it had long been accepted. I recall a Conservative minister from the Netherlands, where the influence of the Churches was strong, telling me that no government there could ever dare to do anything other than propose increases in aid. But also in the larger industrialized countries such as Germany and Britain, the 'aid lobby' grew in strength and importance. It would be misleading, however, to exaggerate its political influence. My own knowledge is largely limited to the British experience. Many of the British members of parliament gave a personal commitment to the aid increases (reaching the 0.7 per cent UN target) urged by the aid lobby, composed of pressure groups, the Churches, and overseas charities and voluntary aid agencies. They included most Labour members, and a number of Conservatives. But a strong 'charity begins at home' theme was stressed by the popular newspapers; the more serious press gave the issue only marginal attention and coverage; and television companies were not yet alive to it. So it never succeeded in approaching the centre of the stage of debate, within or between the political parties. Yet it was undoubtedly running strong along the sidelines.

A number of governments during this period steadily increased their aid programmes. One is bound to observe that, almost without exception, they were socialist, social democrat, or left-inclined liberal governments. They were responding to both the self-interest and the moral arguments, and to a new momentum for positive action produced by the strong pressure from Third World countries and recognition of the effects of the rises in oil prices. And, significantly, there were encouraging trends in the USA. There, the Peterson Report proposed a clear separation between military assistance and economic assistance (but its recommendations were to be short-lived in practice); Robert McNamara had become President of the World Bank; and the Carter administration was demonstrating a real concern about development questions, particularly as they affected Latin America. The aid lobby there was building up support, mainly through the efforts of the Overseas Development Council. Compared with its European counterparts, its influence was modest: but there were at least a few senators and congressmen who were committed to giving the Third World second or third priority in their agenda. The general political outlook, in international terms, was promising.

Within the closer confines of aid administration, there was a sea-change in the mid-1970s. After so many years of the predominance of Rostovian theory, and with the realization that its application failed utterly to resolve the problems of Third World poverty, a new approach was emerging. It contained two related elements. First, if the objective of aid was to contribute to the ending of poverty, it was obviously of some importance to direct aid primarily towards the poorer countries. That so evident a proposition could have escaped so many people and governments for so many years is a conundrum which I cannot explain. But the light had dawned at last. At the formal level, it meant that resolutions concerning the needs of the poorest countries, the poorer countries, the land-locked countries—there were varying categories—were accepted by the industrialized countries at a number of UN conferences (UNCTAD, ECOSOC, the General Assembly); at the level of implementation, most donor countries began to adjust their aid allocation policies to some degree.

Second, it was equally important to direct aid towards the poorest people. And that was much more difficult. It meant that a new emphasis must be given to the workers of the country areas, the rural peasants, the villages remote from the capital cities: for in the poorer countries of Africa and Asia, between 70 and 90 per cent of the people struggle for subsistence in the rural areas; and in the countries of Asia and Latin America, there is a desperately acute contrast between the middle class of the cities—the urban elites—and the poor of the suburban slums or the Calcutta streets or the remote country areas. So agriculture and rural development, and how to assist it, became the new focus of attention for the development economists, in the context of the new thrusts of policy.

The new approach was rarely explained in terms of economic theory; it was rather supported by the simple moral precept that aid should seek to end poverty. But it is, to me, the only rational economic approach; it need not be defined in Marxist or Keynesian terms to command acceptance; and can be expressed in the simplest terms. If the mass of the population are struggling for mere subsistence, and have no surplus production to use as purchasing power, there can be no stimulus for economic growth. It follows that income creation among the poor is the essential prerequisite for growth, initiating consumer demand and providing the opportunity for savings to be used for investment in industry to meet demand. In the circumstances of most developing countries, it is essentially income creation rather than income distribution which is the key to economic advance: for there is far too little wealth among the urban minority to have any marked effect even if redistributed. The political principles to govern the management of growth arising from income creation are a matter for Third World countries themselves. Whether they choose free-market or planned economy methods is for them to determine: that is not a matter which should properly be the concern of aid donors, provided only that their intention to promote the ending of poverty is not frustrated.

How to use aid to help rural development, however, was a new and surprisingly difficult question, fraught with new problems. Aid, as all who have been involved know only too well, is not a matter of throwing money to a poor country and saying: 'Use this to help rural areas.' Every donor country must be fully accountable, in absolute detail, to its own parliament and taxpayers for every penny, even though few will seek to examine the fine print of its accounts for its bilateral country-to-country programmes, or, for that matter, the fine print of the accounts of the World Bank, the United Nations Development Programme, or the FAO, the WHO, UNICEF, or the regional development banks to which its multilateral aid is directed. (The recent controversies about UNESCO are the exception to prove the point.) Most of it will probably be devoted to 'project aid', which means spending on specific enterprises—roads, dams, hospitals, schools, fertilizer plants, bridges—where, at the end of the day, something has physically been created which was not there before. Whether it is financed by a multilateral aid agency or an individual donor government, the essential procedure is the same—and immensely elaborate. The more accountability the donor seeks the more complex the process. The project must clearly be one which the developing country wants, and has included in its own national planning (although there has been the occasional time, no doubt, where it has been persuaded to want it). There must be feasibility studies, contracts put to tender, phased construction, with finance transferred at the completion of each stage—and so on.

Some part of a donor country aid programme will be spent on 'technical co-operation', which is easy to administer, and takes the form of either sending professional people out to advise and help—with, for example, administration, agriculture, or education—or financing education and training for Third World country nominees within its own colleges and universities. A third part, a comparatively small element in the past, but increasingly relevant now, is what is usually called 'programme aid': directly financing the supply of essential goods which a developing country cannot afford but needs—capital equipment and vehicles rather than consumer goods, of course. Spare parts, not luxury consumer goods: that is the general principle.

The change in emphasis presented new problems. What indeed was the best way to transfer resources to the rural sector to help the poorest people? Technical co-operation could easily be adjusted to involve expertise and training in agriculture, forestry, animal breeding, and related subjects. A shift in the direction of project aid, with its inevitable in-built delays between the idea and its implementation, was more difficult for bilateral and multilateral donors alike—and still is, particularly against the background of famine and food shortage in Africa, of which the FAO was already giving warnings as early as 1974. What has emerged is a two-pronged approach. On the one hand, there is the 'small is beautiful' approach, which with support for appropriate intermediate technology and for the voluntary aid agencies which can work close to the people in a way that governments cannot, is immensely valuable. On the other hand, it is big money which is needed for interrelated power and water schemes to provide irrigation for the dry areas in which the deepest poverty arises; and for the roads and bridges needed to give them access to markets; and for the development of mineral and fuel resources to increase foreign exchange earnings and reduce oil dependency. The 1970s saw the beginnings of the new approach.

Yet the overwhelming need for an 'aid to the poorest' policy ran counter to the established criteria for aid allocation of some major donors. It was awkward that some of the most urgent need arose in countries which were socialist, or were outside the US sphere of influence. It was awkward that the conventional cost–benefit analyses applied to the appraisal of project proposals raised complex issues: taking the electricity required for a controlled water supply to a country area could be financed by aid, but if the subsequent maintenance and supply costs were to be borne by the poor, the proposition was absurd. But to contemplate continued state subsidy as part of the scheme shocked many economists trained in the precepts of the free market. It was awkward that projects for rural development involved considerable 'local costs', that is to say, raw materials and labour costs on site, which meant that donor countries must use precious foreign currency.

It all moved very slowly. But at least a new purpose was abroad—for a time.

Not for long. The 1980s have been, and are, disastrous for the Third World. To examine the elements of disaster and crisis is to throw into sharp focus the pervasive role of political attitudes, and the total failure of the free-market philosophy to confront the dilemmas facing the global economy. It is also to ask: What should good people with good intentions now do? There are times when anger should not be contained, nor tolerance stretched beyond its limits, provided only that there is a positive agenda for action.

Let us begin with this proposition: that it is no part of the proper function of the taxpayers of industrialized countries (most of them of only moderate or even low incomes) to finance aid programmes which merely offer modest help to the victims of the economic policies promoted by their own governments without demanding that those policies are changed. To establish the merits of the proposition, we must sustain the premise on which it is based.

The only source of foreign exchange earnings and the major factor in generating income and employment for any developing country is its export commodities. To quote the Commonwealth Secretariat:

> Commodity prices in real (purchasing power) terms are now (December 1986) at their lowest levels since the 1930s; overall they ... failed to rise significantly with the sharp upturn in world economic activity during 1983–84 and fell steeply during the slower growth of 1985–86. By mid-1986 the overall average was (in nominal terms) a quarter below that of 1980. Prices for some products fell even more steeply. . . . The effect on foreign exchange earnings has often been devastating. . . . For most countries the effects on their terms of trade and balance of payments have been severe, and the repercussions on their development programmes and debt-servicing capacity have been traumatic.

The industrialized countries have of course been very happy indeed to welcome lower commodity prices. At the same time they have resisted bringing into operation the Common Fund, the plan for the stabilization of commodity prices hard-fought for at successive meetings of UNCTAD; they have presided over the collapse of the International Tin Agreement; failed to renegotiate an agreement on rubber; have put a new cocoa agreement in doubt, and so far, as I write, also one on sugar. Sugar is one of the most glaring examples of the tongue-in-cheek approach of the free-market economies towards Third World poverty. The price of sugar has fallen by four-fifths since 1980. It is the main, if not quite the only, export of such countries as Mauritius, Cuba, Fiji, and some of the Caribbean islands. It faces competition from sugar substitutes (on which there is keen new research), which is a trend which will not go away. But the most reluctant to reach a New Sugar Agreement is the EEC which, under the Common Agricultural Policy, pays out vast subsidies to European farmers to grow beet sugars, which compete with Third World cane sugar and lower world sugar prices. It need not happen. It does happen because the EEC has so far shown itself incapable of modifying the self-seeking principles of the free market upon which it is essentially based.

Aid-flows from the DAC countries seem all too sadly settled at 0.35 per cent of GNP: on the one hand, the Scandinavian countries and the Netherlands have moved beyond the 0.7 per cent target. But others, notably Mrs Thatcher's Britain, have cut aid—by almost 20 per cent in our case—on grounds that 'We must put our own house in order'—with a complete rejection of the concept of interdependence and the mutuality of interest. (OPEC aid, despite reduced income from oil revenues, still does well, with an average of 0.6 per cent, and with Saudi Arabia and Kuwait at a level of 2.3 per cent and 2.7 per cent respectively.) As I write, President Reagan has proposed a 'saving of $1,000 million on the US aid budget'.

And all these adversities for the developing countries must be seen within the context of their debt crisis. The facts of this are all too well known. But the political issues it raises for the aid relationship between rich and poor countries are relatively unexplored: yet they present perhaps the most crucial area for any serious consideration of the politics of aid. For what do we have here? Put in its simplest and starkest terms, we see the free-market private banking sector in problems which were of its own creation. The banks made large loans in the expectation of profit, at their own choice and making their own assessment of risk. Certain larger banks, mainly but not wholly in the USA, dangerously overextended their lending. Yet the banking sector, for the most part, has given its support to the very economic policies which have produced the crisis for Third World countries and industrialized countries alike—and, therefore, for themselves.

As for 'official' debt, owed to governments and institutions such as the World Bank, which tends to be the major element in African debt, there has been only one positive initiative. As one who was deeply involved in it, I look back now to see how much more important it was even than it seemed at the time. In 1978, at a special meeting of

UNCTAD, it was proposed and agreed—not without difficulty—that the official debt of the poorer developing countries to donor governments should be written off by converting past loans into grants. As always with international bureaucracy, the exercise was given an incomprehensible description (ministers should always check the fine print of what they do, but usually leave it to the bureaucrats when they have settled the principle). It was called RTA: retrospective terms adjustment. The cost (some $2000 millions to Britain, for example) was largely an accounting cost, with the loss of future income to be set against future aid expenditure, but without real resource costs. What we should have done at that meeting, but did not, was to try to include in the formula the poorer countries' debt to the international and regional financial institutions.

RTA now occupies the dominant role in determining the conditionality applied not only to arrangements for the rescheduling of debt repayment but to new aid for the countries which so urgently need it. The IMF is accepted by the World Bank and major donors as the judge and jury in these matters. The meetings between debtor and creditors, the use of the IMF Compensatory Finance Facility and of special drawing rights, and the measures of 'adjustment' to be adopted in the develoing country as a condition of further lending: all these are dominated by the IMF, which in its turn is the economic international instrument of the major Western industrialized countries, and staffed by economists who, for very many years, have overindulged, unchallenged, in right-wing economic free-market orthodoxy. Their prescriptions for adjustment, and the conditionality they impose, make no distinction between the circumstances of developed and developing countries. Their analysis is in the style of Milton Friedman and the Chicago Boys. It is as though John Maynard Keynes had never existed—let alone Marx.

The formula is unchanging—cut public expenditure, cut purchasing power, deal with the money supply, and devalue, without any regard to its politically destabilizing effects, as the poor become inexorably poorer, and the infrastructure vital for economic growth, which can only be financed by public rather than private spending (simply because there is no profit in a road or a bridge or a hospital), cannot be provided. To these elements of conditionality has been added in the last two or three years the advocacy of privatization of state-owned utilities and agencies, in accordance with the new radical conservative ethos of Reagan, Thatcher, and Chirac.

It is an ethos which has no concern for the democratic principle or for human rights. Not only does the IMF itself condescend merely to hear the voices of the Third World countries along the margins of its meetings, but it self-righteously refuses to discriminate in any way between Chile and South Africa, for example, as against newly democratic Peru and Brazil. Only economic factors are relevant, it says: and these are not allowed to include questions of distributive justice or social and political consequences. Take just three news items of December 1986. In Brasilia, demonstrations involving arrests, the use of tear gas by the police, and the burning of buses followed consumer price increases imposed to reduce the external deficit. Sri Lanka, well known to have achieved remarkable 'quality of life' scores, mainly as a result of steady social welfare provision, is noting a substantial increase in infant mortality following the cuts in food subsidies required by IMF conditionality a few years ago. In Zambia, 96 per cent of whose export earnings are dependent upon copper, the price of which has dropped by one-third since 1980 as a direct result of trends in industrialized countries, and which has a debt burden of $4 billion, the IMF has insisted on a doubling of the price of basic foods. Riots compelled President Kaunda, rightly, to withdraw the increases.

What is new in these later years of the 1980s is that aid, for the major industrialized countries, is, in the case of the many countries overcome by the burden of debt, informally 'tied' to the IMF prescription. Completely abandoning McNamara's World Bank formula of 'redistribution with growth', the Bank now proceeds on new lending for new development projects only when the adjustment policies of the IMF are accepted. And what the Bank does, so do most, if not all, major donors. Thus has oil-dependent Tanzania, for whom the increases in oil prices has meant paying out 60 per cent of its foreign exchange earnings for oil (although it has coal reserves needing only capital for their extraction), and which is one of the poorest countries of Africa, been deprived of new aid commitments—because it refused to accept the social effects of IMF conditionality. Britain, one of Tanzania's traditional main aid donors, resumed new aid only when agreement was finally reached between Tanzania and the IMF—and made no bones about saying so.

Thus is aid full of politics. I would suppose that it always will be, reflecting the political ethos of the powerful as long as the global economy is mainly influenced by the principles of the free market and the politicians who proclaim their virtues.

Governments such as that of Olof Palme can make a contribution which is beyond price. Their criteria for aid can embrace instead of blacklisting the developing countries which seek socialism and self-reliance. They can support liberation movements. They can give more than their fair share of help for refugees from repressive regimes. They can direct their aid to the poorest. They can participate and try to influence the Paris Club meetings when bilateral and multilateral donors decide each year the prospects for growth of individual developing countries. But they, and all of us, must face the reality that even if there were to be, by some miracle of electoral fortunes, a majority of socialist and social democratic governments among the industrialized donor countries, the US Goliath, with its powerful role based on its subscriptions and resulting voting power in the Bank and the IMF, can distort the best of other people's intentions.

That Washington is so blind to the tragedy of so many of the world's people is not wicked. It is just as much a product of history and culture as are most social attitudes in every country. There, in that vast country, with its frequent periods of isolationism, its pride in its capitalism, where not very many people outside New York and Washington read a newspaper with more than the most superficial foreign reporting, and television offers only the most trivial of pursuits, and presidents are elected on the votes of only half the population, but where individuals and families are as good or as bad as anywhere else in the world, it is not at all astonishing. Nevertheless, the fact must be faced that the political debate between left and right no longer knows national boundaries and encompasses the whole world. There is a mutuality of interest of the wrong kind: and interdependence of free-market forces to maximize profit at whatever social cost.

What is needed is so clear and so obvious. It has been spelled out so many times by so many. The world needs a new Bretton Woods, it needs a reformed and democratically accountable IMF; it needs a more enlightened World Bank; it needs poverty criteria for aid; it needs more aid; it needs rational planning of trade and of commodity prices; it needs a formula for relieving and ending the debt burden which will put people before profit; it needs to encourage South–South co-operation; it needs to demonstrate a generous understanding of the refugees who seek a home. Above all, it must take the politics of the cold war out of the politics of aid. (The recent Reagan proposals for cuts in US aid also provide that half of the remaining aid programme will be concentrated on five favoured countries: Israel, Egypt, Pakistan, Eire, and Cyprus; and reduce aid to Africa by one-third.)

But how much longer can we wait for sense and sensibility to prevail? And what alternative could there be?

It seems to me that the time has come when like-minded countries should explore together an agenda of alternatives. Some member countries of DAC, some OPEC members, some private banks, some public-sector banking institutions: they could add up to a formidable enough coalition to offer an alternative approach and alternative international financial institutions—not merely a parallel institution, a concept already advanced, but an alternative. That is an agenda which would put the politics of aid where they should be—in the centre of the world stage. There is no issue more entitled to be there.

18

Swedish Development and Foreign Policy

THORD PALMLUND

Foreign policy is commonly associated with a nation's self-interest and the promotion of its influence and position in the world. These aspects of foreign policy have not been important in forming the Swedish aid programme, which probably explains why there has been a tendency, in presentations of the programme, to play down its relationship to Swedish foreign policy.

A country's programme for development co-operation is inevitably part of its foreign policy, however, and—more interesting than this truism—it stems from specific foreign policy concerns. Sometimes it gives substance to policy intentions better than the words.

It is the purpose of this chapter to explore the aspects of Sweden's foreign policy that have found expression in the aid programme and determined its direction. I will also discuss some of the conflicts that have arisen between foreign policy objectives and those of the programme for development co-operation, or, as it can also be put, between various foreign policy objectives on issues related to the aid programme.

Inspiration from Foreign Policy

Being a minor power, Sweden has not had to relate its aid programme to global strategic concerns—political or military. Sweden has also been spared the sensitive task of transforming colonial relationships into relations of co-operation between independent states. No, the foreign policy concerns of relevance are those of a small, industrialized, and non-aligned country, starting out with a next-to-clean record as regards it relationship to the developing world. Commerce and investments of limited significance, the work of missionary societies in some countries, and the relationships established by individuals, mainly scholars and politicians—these were ties to the Third World existing

228

when Sweden started to develop its aid programme. The absence of strategic interests and this 'clean record' has prompted the image of an aid programme untainted by the egoistic foreign policy considerations. This image has been reinforced by the government's statement in the 'bible of Swedish aid policy'[1] to the effect that moral duty and international solidarity are reason enough for the aid programme: 'The Swedish programme for development cooperation requires no motives in addition to these.'

That, of course, is a foreign policy statement of significance in itself. The foreign policy concerns that have made Sweden an ardent supporter of the UN are to a great extent the same as those giving motivation and direction to its programme for development co-operation. They are the concerns of a small non-aligned country. Support for national independence became one of the goals of the Swedish programme for development co-operation. At the UN Sweden has voted against colonialism and imperialism; it has been an important task for Swedish aid to strengthen the political and economic independence of new nations—in relation to the former colonial powers, to the superpowers, and to regional powers such as South Africa that seek to increase their economic and military superiority at the expense of weak neighbours.

Growing out of our UN policy as the aid programme did, the goal of supporting national independence was present from the beginning, but mainly as a general motive. In the 1950s and the early-1960s, when the aid budget was still small, the only meaningful implementation of that goal took the form of contributions to UN programmes set up with the explicit aim of helping newly independent states to manage their own affairs. In step with the growth of the bilateral progamme the idea that development co-operation should be started with a view to strengthening the national independence of individual countries grew in importance.

In spite of its privileged status as a wealthy and industrialized country, Sweden has seen reason to stress its community of interests with the Third World. Standing outside the power blocs Sweden chose to attach great importance to its relations with the developing world and its many newly independent states.

For a country in Sweden's position, economic interests and political and military security are largely determined by other relationships. Still, Sweden has tried to promote its economic and security interests also by developing its role in the UN and by strengthening its relationship to the Third World. The aid programme has benefited from this ambition. It has also been one of its main tools.

Defence and promotion of democracy and human rights are basic goals for Sweden's foreign policy which also have inspired the aid

programme. Promotion of a democratic development has been
established as one of the tasks of Swedish development co-operation.

The UN Aspect

A determining factor for the initiation and development of the Swedish
aid programme was the fact that the UN occupied such a significant
place in our foreign policy. The intimate interplay between decisions of
the UN, often energetically promoted by Sweden, and actions by
Sweden in the aid field are noteworthy. Sweden made its first
allocations of funds for aid as a loyal member of the world body, and
the expansion of the programme was undertaken in line with our UN
policy.

At an early stage the references to UN positions were a way of
seeking authority to back up policy initiatives on the part of a small
and inexperienced nation. Later, when our programme had grown, our
actions in the UN were those of a spokesman for qualitative and
quantitative improvements in the aid field, by the UN and by the
wealthy countries as a group.

In line with our policy to work for a strengthening of the UN we
advocated a significant role for multilateral aid and made contributions
accordingly. The active policy and the increasing funds gave Sweden,
particularly when in the company of its Nordic neighbours, a platform
and a stronger voice in issues concerning international development co-
operation than followed from our size and economic strength.

In the UN and outside, Sweden has been—and is—a spokesman for
many Third World interests including the work to secure greater
influence in international fora for the nations of the developing world.
In the 1960s and the 1970s when development strategies, global
rounds and North–South dialogues were on the international agenda,
Sweden—normally in concert with like-minded countries—sought to
play the role of bridge-builder, accepting its given membership in the
North, but often with a position closer to that of the South than the
other industrialized countries. Sweden's role in this context was
reinforced by the relative size of our aid allocations and the high level
or our contributions to UN programmes.

In the early-1960s about two-thirds of Swedish aid resources were
contributed to international programmes; now the share is less than
one-third. These funds are still enough to give us a fairly prominent
position as a contributor to multilateral aid programmes. However,
this trend invites an unavoidable question: does the UN now hold a
less prominent place in Sweden's foreign policy than it did in the 1950s
and early-1960s?

From a foreign policy standpoint there has always been a difference between support of UN aid programmes, on the one hand, and, on the other, participation in the World Bank group and co-operation with the regional development banks. The UN, being universal, is fully compatible with Swedish neutrality, while Western domination and the preference for market economies in the banks provoked questioning of Sweden's participation and the banks' positions on specific issues, particularly from the Swedish left.

Such foreign policy reservations have had to be overcome by spokesmen for Sweden's economic and commercial interests, who identified Sweden as a Western market economy. The banks' demonstrated competence and efficiency in the use of funds were also given as motives for Swedish participation and the levels of its contributions. Participation in the Special Fund of the UN, when it started in 1959, met with no foreign policy reservations, while Swedish membership of the IDA of the IBRD had to be defended shortly afterwards against those who saw increased participation in the World Bank as questionable for non-aligned Sweden.

Sweden joined the IDA, however, and accepted a larger contribution than followed from our share of the World Bank and made extensive use of joint financing with the IDA until the beginning of the 1970s. That this co-operation was subsequently reduced can partly be attributed to the growth and different planning methods of the Swedish aid administration. However, a foreign policy motive also played in: Sweden wanted to limit its identification with the US-dominated World Bank at a time when the war in Vietnam and other—at least initially—leftist causes dominated the public debate in Sweden. After 1968 and the orientation to the left of Sweden's aid policy, ideology took the upper hand over pragmatism and imposed limitations on Sweden's co-operation with the IBRD.

When Swedish shares of later IDA replenishments were reduced, the motive for this 'normalization' of Sweden's contribution was mainly financial. But it was a good reflexion of general foreign policy considerations; the Swedish profile should be reduced a little in this Western institution.

In the case of regional banks, foreign policy considerations have played an important part in forming Sweden's attitudes. We have had no foreign policy reservations with regard to the African Development Bank. It was created as the institution of the countries of the region, many of whom received bilateral Swedish aid.

Our attitudes were more reserved with regard to the Asian Development Bank, dominated by Japan and the USA, and the Inter-American Development Bank, dominated by the USA and with clients who are richer than most recipients of Swedish aid. But we participate in both, in the case of the IDB with funds for export promotion, rather than aid. Our interests as an industrialized country highly dependent on exports and our respect for the concerned regional banks as the development institutions have overcome the reservations.

Joint Nordic Activities

Nordic co-operation came to play a significant role for activities of the Nordic countries in the field of international development co-operation. Policy co-ordination in international fora has become a rule. We have joint executive directors in the IMF and the IBRD. In these institutions the Nordic countries present mutually agreed positions. At the UN and its specialized agencies one spokesman at times speaks for all the Nordic countries. Internationally, others see us as a group, an entity.

It is difficult to say to what extent Sweden's positions in international fora have been influenced by Nordic co-ordination and the overriding foreign policy concern that mutually agreed standpoints are desirable. This subject would deserve a study of its own. Sometimes 'noble competition' between the Nordic countries has led to more advanced joint positions than would have been the result without Nordic consultations.

The normal case, however, particularly when it comes to important issues, for instance in the IMF and the World Bank, has been the contrary: most joint Nordic positions on questions regarding international development co-operation have been more conservative and cautious than they might have been, had Sweden spoken for itself alone. The main benefit is, of course, that joint Nordic positions are taken more seriously than the views of an individual country. This collaboration has increased Sweden's capacity, jointly with the other Nordic countries, to exert a progressive influence on issues of international development co-operation.

Ongoing contacts between politicians and civil servants in the Nordic countries and the normal observation of what close neighbours do, have had a profound mutual influence on the policy and administration of the aid programmes of the Nordic countries. In terms of its size, its larger administrative resources, and more progressive policies, Sweden has probably exerted more influence on Nordic neighbours than it has received.

At the Nordic Council and in the national legislative bodies, parliamentarians have since the late-1950s looked for ways to strengthen Nordic co-operation by means of joint Nordic aid projects. Some people went further. Before the national aid administrations had been set up at the start of the 1960s, they asked: Why not one Nordic aid administration? We established national aid administrations, but also joint Nordic projects administered by a Nordic aid office placed in Stockholm. Nordic sentiment was not strong enough, however, to keep this administration alive. Its very existence departed from a cherished principle of Nordic co-operation, namely, that such co-operation should be the responsibility of the regular national administrations. At the same time the strong political demand for joint Nordic projects on the part of parliamentarians in all Nordic countries had to be met. The solution was Nordic projects administered by one or another of the national aid administrations. This became the model for a few joint projects.

The most significant co-ordination of Nordic aid resources in recent years has been under the Southern African Development Co-ordination Conference (SADCC). Here co-ordination is mainly on the policy level: the joint Nordic position that the neighbours of South Africa should be helped to reduce their dependence on the apartheid regime. It is no longer a question of starting new joint Nordic *projects*.

Choosing partners for Development Co-operation

When the bilateral programme began, co-operation with individual countries came about in various ways. Often it was a matter of approving a request for a project without too much thought being given to the country in question. The concern on the Swedish side was initially with projects rather than with countries.

Various sets of criteria for choosing recipients of Swedish aid were discussed in the early-1960s. In the meantime the number of partners grew, and controlling that development became the main Swedish concern. Resources, particularly administrative resources, were insufficient for effective co-operation even with the countries already on the list. As a result a policy of concentration was set forth. In short, it meant that we should concentrate on the countries with which we had co-operation, expand them, and avoid acquiring new partners for development co-operation.

As a whole, this policy was pursued with success. It served the purpose of defending the programme from geographic expansion— except when it suited Swedish policy interests as in the case of Botswana, Lesotho, and Swaziland, to which I will return.

At the end of the 1960s and the beginning of the 1970s there was a marked turn to the left in Swedish aid policy in response to the general radicalization of the intellectual and ideological climate. The 'technical' policy of concentration was not abandoned, but more than before it was challenged by forces seeking to change the direction of the Swedish aid programme. The Government Aid Bill of 1970 stated:

> It is ... natural that Sweden primarily seeks to cooperate with countries, the Governments of which, in their economic and social policies, aim at such structural changes as will create the preconditions for a development towards economic and social justice.

This declaration by the government was accepted by Parliament when combined with a compromise formula, noting that the government did not propose the discontinuation of co-operation with any country and that the goals of the Swedish aid programme could be achieved in countries with different political and social systems.

This compromise formula offered a defence for the co-operation that existed with a number of countries, while the starting up of new programmes of co-operation followed the government's policy intentions. When motivating co-operation with new countries considerable attention was given to a country's stated policy in the economic and social fields. The initiation of co-operation with new countries was also motivated in terms of support for national independence.

It was under this policy that Sweden started to co-operate with Cuba, Chile, Vietnam, Laos, Angola, Mozambique, Guinea-Bissau, and later Nicaragua. In the case of all except Cuba, Chile, and Vietnam, Sweden added these new partners for development co-operation more or less automatically. We had supported their liberation movements and saw no reason to discontinue the co-operation when the movements got into power. The political sympathy that Sweden extended to these countries was based on their struggle for political and economic independence and for their policy of social justice. Sweden's choice of partners for development and its appreciation of the aims of these countries in the social and economic field resulted in an identification of Sweden with progressive forces in the Third World. This did not mean that Sweden abandoned its policy on non-alignment, but it certainly had an impact on how this policy was interpreted, by Sweden itself and by others. With the exception of Chile after the military coup in 1973, where Swedish aid was discontinued, Sweden's new partners for development had good relations with the Soviet Union. Some of them can adequately be described as falling within the Soviet sphere of interest. In an international context, this development of the Swedish aid programme has rightly been seen as a movement to the left, bringing it into obvious conflict with Western, particularly US, positions.

The most controversial issue in this context has been the case of

Vietnam. The starting up of the programme was a diplomatic balancing act, and its development was very much in step with the advancement of our foreign policy position on Vietnam and our criticism of the USA. Briefly, the main steps were as follow: early in 1968 Nordic consultations were held concerning aid to Vietnam. Under the pressure of the public debate in Sweden the government obviously felt a need to move faster than was possible in Nordic company, and plans for joint Nordic action were abandoned. Sweden then started extending humanitarian assistance through the Red Cross, some of which went to the South.

The next step was to increase the allocation to the North and to the Provisional Revolutionary Government (PRG), the ally of North Vietnam in the South. The Red Cross was no longer seen as a necessary channel, and humanitarian aid was provided without intermediary to the North Vietnamese government and also directly to the PRG in the South. The fact that the planning of development projects was initiated even before the war ended represented a further stepping up of Swedish policy. We see here how diplomatic considerations and principles of international law imposed limitations, which by and by were overcome. As public support for the policy in Sweden grew, so did the readiness of the government to challenge the USA.

After the reunification of Vietnam many states were ready to help with reconstruction. Our development co-operation with Vietnam then became less controversial from a foreign policy standpoint. However, when Vietnam intervened in Kampuchea and let its army remain in the country to fight the Khmer Rouge, the situation changed once more. Several Western countries withdrew from co-operation with Vietnam. Sweden stayed on, and after 1982 the Social Democratic government was criticized more and more aggressively, particularly by the Conservative party, for doing so.

While aid and foreign policy had kept in step when the programme of co-operation with Vietnam was developed—even if diplomatic concerns imposed limitations—the situation changed after the Vietnamese intervention in Kampuchea. The provision of aid had now come into conflict with principles vital to Swedish foreign policy. Should Sweden provide aid to a country responsible for grossly violating the UN Charter by military invention and what seemed a long-term occupation of a neighbouring country? I will come back to this problem in my discussion of conflicts between aid and foreign policy.

As described here, Sweden started to co-operate with a number of progressive countries in the 1970s. Old partners of co-operation with progressive policies, like Tanzania, received substantially increased aid from Sweden. Thus, fully in line with the Bill of 1970, increased aid resources were devoted to 'countries, the governments of which, in their economic and social policies aim at such structural changes as will create the preconditions for a development towards economic and social justice'.

This development, which was actively promoted by the Social Democrats and more or less reluctantly accepted by the non-socialist parties, was only marginally modified after the non-socialist parties came into power in 1976. While there was no change of policy, the increases of aid budgets for progressive countries were somewhat smaller, and budgets for less progressive countries were somewhat more generous.

From an international point of view the Swedish aid profile was still very progressive, identifying Sweden to a great extent with the countries in the Third World that resisted Western domination and favoured centralized planning of the economy. Sweden was helping Communist countries like Vietnam and concentrated part of its bilateral aid on countries within the sphere of interest of the Soviet Union. This is to a great extent true, but it has an interesting ironic twist, which is highly relevant to a judgment of the foreign policy implications of this radical orientation of the aid programme. The fact that a good deal of Swedish aid goes to socialist countries with limited relations with Western market economies means that Sweden represents for those countries an alternative to exclusive reliance on resources and technology from the Soviet bloc. It cannot be said that Swedish bilateral aid got its orientation for this very purpose, but this is definitely an effect.

It is easy enough to dismiss the idea of Sweden offering an alternative in this context and, in so doing, of increasing a country's chances to choose its own way. Sweden is too small to be of real significance in many situations. True—but there is still no reason to dismiss totally the role that has become Sweden's because of its aid relationship with countries who have limited contacts with the West.

Take the case of Cuba. When Sweden started its co-operation with Cuba in 1971 we probably helped to break the ice of isolation around Cuba imposed by the USA. This occurred during a period of improving East–West relations. However, the new cold war between the superpowers made it diffucult for Cuba to increase the scope of her independence. Still, breaking the ice was important. Sweden acted, with the aid programme as its main tool, to promote a development that might have given Cuba the possibility of reducing its one-sided foreign dependence.

The role of Sweden's aid presence can be discussed in a similar fashion with regard to several other countries—Ethiopia or Vietnam, for example. Our presence in these and other countries does not compromise Sweden's policy of non-alignment.'Its main significance is that it gives a few countries in the Third World a somewhat better possibility to choose their own way by giving them access to a greater selection of technology and development models.

High Priority for Southern Africa

A substantial part of Sweden's resources for development co-operation goes to Southern Africa. The main factors that have brought this about are political and well in line with Sweden's stand in the UN. Sweden has acted on the basis of UN resolutions condemning the apartheid system in South Africa and South Africa's illegal rule over Namibia. Similarly, actions in the aid field have also followed from Sweden's stand against colonial rule in Africa and a desire to support the former colonies after independence.

From a timid start in 1962–63, when aid resources were first used in response to political assessments of the situation in Southern Africa, the development on the aid side has to a considerable extent been governed by Sweden's reaction to political developments in the area. It started with some scholarships to refugees, then, in 1964, Parliament approved a government proposal for special funds for mainly educational purposes in Southern Africa and the setting up of a special committee to give advice on the development of a programme.

Informal contacts were established with liberation movements, but no aid was provided directly to these organizations. The boldest ingredient in the programme, from the point of view of international law, was support to the Mozambique Institute in Tanzania, which in reality constituted indirect support to Frelimo, the dominant liberation movement in Mozambique. Formally, however, the Institute was a Tanzanian institution, and thus Sweden could claim that this support was no interference in Portugal's internal affairs. Consequently, Sweden was not in conflict with international law.

A new interpretation of what was acceptable from the point of view of international law was given by Parliament in 1969, when it approved a recommendation from the competent committee *Statsutskottet* to the effect that:

Swedish development assistance cannot be allowed to conflict with the rule of international law that lays down that no state has the right to interfere in the internal affairs of another state. As regards liberation movements in Africa, humanitarian aid and educational support do not come into conflict with the said rule of international law, if the UN has taken a clear-cut stand against suppression of peoples who are striving for national independence. This can be considered to be the case regarding Southwest Africa, Rhodesia and the territories in Africa under Portugal's rule. With regard to assistance to the victims of the policy of apartheid, such support can be motivated *inter alia* by the explicit condemnation by the UN of the South African apartheid policy.

Parliament's approval of this recommendation opened the way for direct support to liberation movements. Such support was then provided in increasing measure to movements in all the countries concerned. The definition of humanitarian and educational support was gradually broadened, at times under protest from Conservative party MPs. Thus, departing from a conventional interpretation of what is humanitarian aid, support to liberation movements in Southern Africa came to include development projects, information activities, and administration.

In the mid-1960s educational support to institutions in the British territories in Southern Africa (subsequently Botswana, Lesotho, and Swaziland), mainly for refugees from South Africa and Rhodesia, developed into co-operation with these countries after independence. One of the most important motives for starting regular development co-operation in this case was their extreme dependence on South Africa and the role that international, preferably UN, aid could play to strengthen their limited independence and, by its presence, help to protect their sovereignty.

The small initial allocations to Botswana, Lesotho, and Swaziland were the first country programmes to be motivated with reference to South Africa. During the years to come closeness to South Africa and related motives figured to an increasing extent in decisions concerning aid to countries in Southern Africa. From the mid-1960s on, it was seen as an important task for Swedish aid to help cover costs connected with this geographic position and to reduce the countries' dependence on the apartheid regime.

Among the costs that Sweden was ready to share were expenditures for refugees and other economic burdens following from an anti-apartheid stand. Zambia's costs for loyalty to UN decisions concerning sanctions against Rhodesia after its unilateral declaration of independence similarly motivated extra aid from Sweden. These costs were given considerable weight when the country frame for aid to Zambia was fixed during the 1970s. To a a lesser extent, an increased frame for Tanzania was motivated in terms of the country's costs as a Front Line state and host for refugees.

Many other examples could be cited to show the weight given to the Southern Africa argument in consideration of Swedish aid allocations.

The value of this argument can be well illustrated by the wishful thinking of a frustrated official arguing the case for increased aid to Laos: 'Oh, if only it were in Southern Africa!'

Thus, the priority attached to aid to Southern Africa has been strong and on the whole uncontroversial in Sweden. The political aim to reduce dependence on South Africa now stands as the main purpose of the international programme SADCC, in which the Nordic countries play a major role.

After the Portuguese colonies and Zimbabwe gained independence, the programme for humanitarian assistance to Southern Africa came to focus mainly on people from South Africa and Namibia, the ANC and SWAPO being the single most important recipients of aid.

Considerable resources for humanitarian and educational purposes were, however, also channelled through a number of international and national voluntary organizations. Legal defence of opponents of apartheid and efforts aimed at informing the public and strengthening the international stand against apartheid are also supported under the programme. Some of the funds go to the UN and its humanitarian and educational programmes for people from South Africa and Namibia, placing Sweden at the top of the list of contributors to such programmes.

As Sweden sees it, the apartheid policy of South Africa constitutes a threat to world peace. It is on the basis of this judgement that Sweden, jointly with many other countries, has supported resolutions in the UN calling for mandatory sanctions of South Africa to be imposed by decision of the Security Council.

Sweden's aid effort in Southern Africa should also be seen in the light of this analysis, not only as support for development, human rights, and national independence. What we and other Nordic countries are trying to do, with aid as one of our tools, is to strengthen the chances for an alternative course of development and to reduce the risk of a superpower confrontation, triggered by the consequences of the apartheid policy. One result of our action is a reduction of the dependence of South Africa's neighbours and the liberation movements in the area on Soviet bloc support. This may possibly mitigate the risk of an East–West confrontation, but the crucial decisions on this issue are not taken at the UN in New York or in the Nordic capitals.

Democracy and Human Rights in Latin America

Sweden's aid to Latin America has been—and is—of marginal significance. In this context it is worth noting, however, that Swedish aid initiatives in Latin America have been based more exclusively on foreign policy considerations than aid to Asia and Africa.

Great poverty, over the years becoming a precondition for Swedish aid, tended to exclude Latin American countries. The commercial argument for development co-operation with countries in Latin America, as presented by spokesmen for non-socialist parties and the export industry, was often counterproductive: if the Latin American markets were of interest to Sweden—which they were, as evidenced by substantial Swedish investments and exports—then our relations could be taken care of by business rather than by aid. At times in the 1960s the commercial argument was coupled with a geographic one, urging that Swedish aid ought to have a presence in Latin America. This argument came mainly from Liberals and Conservatives.

The main function of the geographic argument came to be that it strengthened political support in Parliament for the aid initiatives which were taken by the government, based to a great extent on foreign policy grounds. Development co-operation with Cuba starting in 1971 was mentioned above.

Chile was the other Latin American country to become a recipient of Swedish aid around 1970. The first initiatives came from a Conservative member of Parliament, arguing for development co-operation with the government of Christian Democrat Eduardo Frei, as an alternative to aid to Cuba, which at that time was advocated by the left. Aid to Chile became a matter of priority to the Social Democratic government after Salvador Allende became president.

Co-operation with Chile was motivated with reference to the social and economic reforms which were the aims of the Allende regime. But it was primarily a question of supporting a Latin American democracy which aimed at reforms in favour of the mass of the people and which was exposed to the economically forceful displeasure of Washington. The coup by Augusto Pinochet in 1973 resulted in an immediate discontinuation of the aid programme. The reason was given in the language of development co-operation: the Pinochet government did not pursue the development of the Allende government. But, of course, the motive was strictly political. Sweden could not maintain development co-operation with a Chile under Pinochet. Saying so could have been dangerous, however. It would have meant admitting that foreign policy motives dictated aid decision. Who might next call for changes in the aid programme on political grounds? And how would it be possible to dismiss such demands as incompatible with the principles of the programme for development co-operation, if political motives were once admitted?

Basically, aid to the Allende regime was an expression of sympathy for a Latin American democracy trying to achieve reforms. After the Pinochet coup this policy of solidarity with Chile was pursued by way of support to refugees and contributions to human rights work in the country. What became a humanitarian programme for Latin America began with a contribution to what was later called the Vicaria de la Solidaridad of the Roman Catholic Archbishop's office in Santiago.

From this start in 1974 Sweden has developed a programme consisting of contributions to international and national voluntary organizations, mainly religious, for work in the fields of human rights and legal aid in Latin American countries. In recent years the programme has particularly expanded in Central America, where the stress has been on refugee work and efforts to support victims of dictatorial regimes. In the 1970s the Swedish Agency for Research Co-operation with Developing Countries developed a Latin American programme which to some extent fits into the same foreign policy context as the humanitarian programme. Support was offered to research institutions which functioned more or less as protected zones for free research and independent thinking on a continent which at the time was largely under military dictatorships. Some of the research had to do with political and economic alternatives to the regimes of the day. Like a good deal of the rest of Sweden's aid to Latin America, much in this research programme can be seen as support to democratic development in the region.

The present programme of development co-operation in Nicaragua started in 1980 as a logical consequence of earlier Swedish support to civilian work undertaken by the opposition to the Somoza regime. The parallel to the origins of co-operation with the former Portuguese colonies is obvious. Still, there are substantial differences: support for national independence was an essential goal for Swedish aid to the concerned African countries, whereas, in the case of Nicaragua, Sweden's aid was primarily to support a democratic development.

This purpose makes the development of pluralism in Nicaragua an essential precondition for continued Swedish aid to the country. While Sweden's willingness to provide aid to Vietnam, Tanzania, or Mozambique has not been seriously related to a democratic development in terms of pluralistic political and economic structures, in the case of Nicaragua it most definitely is.

This reflects a major development—certainly in the rhetoric, but also in the Swedish attitude towards its partners. In the 1980s there is a greater readiness to set the terms under which Sweden is prepared to co-operate—for reasons of foreign policy and public opinion.

How Immune are Aid Programmes?

How has Sweden reacted to human rights violations committed by its partners in development co-operation? And what has been the major foreign policy concern in that context? Was it not to disturb the good relationship which is a precondition for development co-operation, or was it to promote human rights by criticizing violations?

A primary objective has generally been to protect development co-operation. The first line of defence for the programme of co-operation has been to insist that it should not be used to pressure the recipient government on issues unrelated to the development programme.

Development co-operation has to be seen in a long-term perspective as aid to people, not to any given regime. For that reason aid should not easily be withdrawn or altered—even in the face of human rights violations. The aid programmes should not be used to express displeasure or to punish. Protests, when called for, should take other forms.

Several departures from that line of action have occurred, however. Many decisions about the volume of aid have been affected by information about human rights violations. There have even been cases when complete withdrawal of aid has been contemplated because of the human rights situation.

Ethiopia, some time after the downfall of the emperor, is one example. The regime showed, and tolerated, great brutality, not only towards political opponents, but also towards the population at large. The aid programme was reduced on account of the generally chaotic situation and the war in Eritrea. Most aid personnel were withdrawn for security reasons, but we stayed on as partners, hoping for an improvement. Even in that situation the long-term interests of the development programme gained the upper hand over the political need to dissociate Sweden from a regime responsible for gross violations of human rights.

How would human rights have been helped if we had pulled out? The regime would probably not have cared less at the time. People of goodwill in Ethiopia would have felt abandoned. It would have taken a long time to come back as a useful partner in development had we withdrawn completely. And perhaps there were situations where our presence, and that of other international observers, actually helped save lives and protect human rights.

How, then, is the Swedish foreign policy objective to promote human rights best achieved? Withdrawal of aid is seldom the answer. Experience has rather shown that there often exists a community, rather than a conflict of interests between the provision of aid and the protection of human rights.

Human rights can best be promoted if we insist that the ultimate recipients of aid are the people, not the regime, and that co-operation has to be of a long-term character. The use of the aid programme to express displeasure should therefore be limited. But an active policy of concern for human rights, including criticism of violations, may at the same time be essential if we wish to retain public support for the aid programme among the Swedish electorate.

Are we faced with a quite different sort of situation if a recipient of Swedish aid commits military aggression in obvious violation of the UN Charter? No, apparently not, judging from Sweden's reaction to Vietnam's military intervention into neighbouring Kampuchea and Tanzania's intervention into Uganda (when Tanzanian troops were still stationed in the country, Sweden even provided some additional aid to Tanzania). In the case of Vietnam's intervention into Kampuchea, Swedish political reaction was strong. But in spite of official condemnation and an intense domestic debate there was at first no reduction in the allocation of development resources.

The restraint shown on the aid side from the beginning of the 1980s, however, is partly attributable to the Kampuchea factor. The continued military presence of the Vietnamese army in Kampuchea, combined with information about human rights violations in Vietnam and problems with the implementation of the programme for development co-operation, undermined public support for the sizeable aid to Vietnam, and resulted in attacks on the programme, particularly from the Conservative party. A significant reduction of the aid programme undertaken in 1985 can be read as an expression of criticism. In a situation of dwindling public support the aid programme could not be kept aside. On the other hand the cut in the aid volume is still one of Sweden's most substantial programmes of development co-operation.

Even in this case it was only reluctantly, with an eye on the political situation in Parliament and on public support for the aid programme, that the Social Democratic government brought itself to express political criticism by reducing the aid volume. The non-socialist parties would have gone further.

There is a certain difference in attitude between political parties on the question of aid cuts or aid withdrawals on account of military aggression and human rights violations. Particularly the Conservative party, at least when in opposition, questions the immunity of the aid programme. The Conservatives have advocated reductions of aid on obvious foreign policy grounds. Examples are when Cuba sent troops to Africa, mainly Ethiopia and Angola, and when Vietnam continued to hold troops in Kampuchea. It should be noted that the issue has been raised with regard to socialist states, aid to whom the Conservatives would like to see withdrawn for other reasons as well.

Clearly, the exposure of the aid programme has grown over the years—in step with the growth of the programme and with the more critical focusing on problems in the Third World and on development efforts. Higher priority on the foreign policy agenda for questions of human rights highlights the problems. There is reason to believe that this development will continue and increase the vulnerability of Sweden's programme for development co-operation.

The Impact on Foreign Policy

I have discussed how Sweden's foreign policy has inspired and given direction to the aid programme. To some extent the aid programme has been used as a tool for its implementation. Meanwhile, it has also contributed to the development of our foreign policy. Which are its main contributions? In my opinion, these:

—— It has strengthened our UN policy and given us a platform for more active participation in the world body.

—— It has supported our policy on non-alignment and over the years contributed to a more radical reading of it—thus, in the eyes of many, increasing its credibility.

—— It has given substance to our stress on a community of interests among non-aligned states, which, on the margin, is part of our security policy.

—— It has contributed to co-operation between the Nordic states and strengthened the international image of close Nordic co-operation.

—— It has given substance to essential foreign policy objectives with regard to support of national independence and the promotion of democracy and human rights. In concrete situations (Vietnam, South Africa, Chile) it has been an important way of expressing solidarity and encouraging the struggle for national independence and human rights. It has commanded greater attention to the Third World and questions of human rights in our foreign policy.

Acknowledgement

The author, editor and publisher are grateful for permission to reproduce this chapter which originally appeared in *Swedish Development Aid in Perspective: Policies, Problems and Results since 1952* (ed. Pierre Früling), (Stockholm, 1986).

Note

1. *Government Bill 1962:100*, on International Development Co-operation. This Bill marked the beginning of Swedish development aid as a major official concern. It contained a number of principles and goals and expressed a will to gradually increase the hitherto very modest budget for development aid.

Olof Palme—Liberation and World Peace

19

The Africa of Olof Palme

BASIL DAVIDSON

The inter-island plane from San'Antao, where the Cape Verde archipelago reaches furthest to the west, flies in directly to the airport at the capital of Praia on Santiago Island. If you sit at a left-hand window you can see down there the new national buildings, nicely ranged together, as the plane slides in to land. The largest of these buildings is the People's National Assembly, where the Parliament of the Republic has its sessions. This morning I could see the national flag flying above the building. But it was not flying as usual. It was flying at half-mast.

They told me as soon as the plane had landed and we passengers had disembarked. They told me with gravity of sorrow edged by anger. They had heard the news from Stockholm three hours earlier but were still trying to think that it could not be true. They were long-accustomed to losing comrades by the enemy's assassinating hand: but how could this have come to pass in Sweden? The hours went by and no denial came. Cape Verde mourned the loss of Olof Palme with a direct emotion, as I observed and shared it, that came from losing a strong companion whose voice carried across the world, defending the oppressed and shielding the weak, and whose friendship had been all the dearer because it was the fruit of shared ideas and understandings. Here in this Africa of Olof Palme—in this as in other African countries whose peoples knew Palme as friend and comrade—the loss was felt with a bitter sense of outrage. Better than any other statesman of worldwide influence and vision, Palme had understood what they are trying to achieve. And his interest in this and support had come with a moral solidarity of its kind and perhaps unique in its time, that was worth more, even, than its material sum.

The people of Cape Verde, having emerged from a long colonial night, are trying to build a new life for themselves. They are doing this by the construction of a system of self-government which they call participation, *participacao popular*, 'people's participation'. Human

247

solidarity apart, it was this, I think, that aroused Palme's vivid interest and continuous support. And in my opinion, for two reasons: first because Palme saw the project as being one of singular value in itself, and second because this value might in some degree become exemplary for other peoples. Here was a most profound social and political crisis which was not getting worse, but was getting solved. Exemplary or not, this had to deserve attention.

The case of the Cape Verde Republic is certainly remarkable in the annals of anti-colonial liberation anywhere. These 300,000 people in their nine Atlantic islands, lying some 500 km into the Ocean west of the West African mainland, reached independence in July 1975 in a condition of utter destitution and, for the most part, unrelieved despair. Behind them lay a long history of enslavement, forced labour, misgovernment, more or less complete administrative neglect, and, most recently, six years of total drought and near famine.

Before them, even with the palsied hand of Salazarist Portugal removed, there seemed to lie nothing but continued escape by emigration across the seas to America, the Netherlands, or any other land that would receive them. No other country has had to emerge from colonial rule in so desperate a condition of poverty and weakness.

Amilcar Cabral had launched their party of independence 19 years before it could finally succeed. Amilcar Cabral had fallen to the enemy's assassinating hand in 1973, when independence was at last in sight. What now, with independence gained, could the continuers of Cabral possibly make of that independence, beyond mere survival? Between 90 and 100 Cape Verdean men and women had answered the call of the liberation struggle on the African mainland, in 'Portuguese Guine', Guinea-Bissau as they would call it, and volunteered to fight through that harsh enterprise. All but one or two of them—all of those, that is, who were still alive—came back to their islands as soon as that became possible in August 1974 and in the following months. With Aristides Pereira at their head, Cabral's closest companion and *alter ego* and now soon to be president of the new republic not yet quite born, they joined another small group of the 'continuers of Cabral'. These were political prisoners released from Cape Verdean colonial gaols after the coup in Lisbon which had overthrown the dictatorship. The veterans found overwhelming enthusiasm and support. A few months later a general election—supervised, incidentally, by the Portuguese as well as by themselves—carried the party of Cabral to power.

But their power, in that famous July of 1975, was only in their unquestioned popularity and prestige. Almost literally, nothing else was given them to work with. There was no Cape Verdean state save in the muddled leavings of a meagre and demoralized colonial administration whose local officials, had not departed for Lisbon with the Portuguese governor and his garrisons. They remained without the slightest understanding of what an independent country could be or should expect. There was no money in the till, none at all: the last of the administrative cash had run out the previous September, leaving teachers, nurses, and other vital personnel unpaid and surviving on such credit as they could still find. There were no exports in that period, while the prospect of renewed exports was so poor that they might at best cover some 15 per cent of essential imports: above all, of imported food that could alone fend off famine. There was no economic system. There was no national economy.

Even if food could be found with foreign aid, how was this people to govern itself? Outside the still slender ranks of the party of Cabral, there was no political practice, knowledge, or understanding of any kind: colonial fascism had seen to this with its drastic suffocating hand. Aside from the continuers of Cabral, most of whom were young and inexperienced except for the veterans of the mainland struggle in Guinea-Bissau, there was no 'public opinion' with the least perception of the needs and demands of independence. On the contrary, the despair of joblessness and hunger had long cleared the ground of any perception save that of the need to escape across the seas. Yet the Cape Verde which Olof Palme vividly admired was to become, by 1986, a viable and very different country. Large quantitites of foreign aid had come to the party of Cabral from many parts of the world; but it had not been wasted or misspent. The drought had persisted until 1985 but, unlike all the previous droughts in Cape Verdean history, a history going back as far as the fifteenth century, this drought had not been allowed to bring famine. Foreign aid remained indispensable, but viability was now a sure prospect. Emigration still continued, but no longer as a flight from hopelessness.

Water was still in short supply, but new sources were coming to hand. Cape Verde's barren hillsides still glittered with an arid infertility, but now, for the first time in centuries, were being clothed with drought-resistant trees: with millions of new trees already planted, and more millions on the way, annually, by plan and perseverance. All that, and much else of the same sort, is interesting; and conservationists in particular will take heart from these achievements. But none of it is half as interesting—or as I think, was so for Olof Palme—as the political method and approach by which these things have been begun and made to happen.

The continuers of Cabral have had to build a state and nation from the bare ground; but at least they came back with the knowledge of what to build and how to build it. They brought with them the political and moral lessons of their long struggle on the mainland. They came with a programme of political construction: *participacao popular.* Progress with programme, they considered, was going to form the central test of any success they were going to have.

This programme had tough experience behind it. They had framed and forged it in the wide zones of Guinea-Bissau that armed struggle had taken out of Portuguese control, onwards from 1964 and increasingly after 1968; zones which were used as laboratories of political experiment in the practice of grass-roots self-government. All real progress, in their view, must turn on the degree of personal and group commitment that could be evoked from liberated people. Only by that kind of commitment—partial to begin with, but gradually stronger—were people going to achieve a real control over their lives in community. Only that process, however difficult and fraught with human failings, could build a consciousness of freedom. Only a consciousness of freedom could teach that freedom is also a struggle against oneself, one's shortcomings, as well as against an enemy that denies freedom. This was the sense in which they had learned to understand the process of participation. This was the commitment which Cabral had placed before those who followed him, the central project of his discourse, the measure of his originality.

Much has been written about the mass participation of the liberated zones of wartime Guinea-Bissau. In its mature form, through rural zones such as Cubucare and Como, Kinara and Quitafine, it showed the emergence of a post-colonial society organized in such a way that practically no aspect of community life lay outside its transforming influence: with, however, one crucial exception. That was to count for much later on and help to bring in its wake a crippling setback. Whether for lack of time or personnel or sheer possibility, and because the war pressed hard, nothing was done or perhaps could be done to transform the economic patterns of life in the liberated zones: to move, for example, towards collective or co-operative types of cultivation such as to underpin prosperous farming in the future. Yet the setbacks and reverses which followed the military coup in Guinea-Bissau of November 1980 do not cancel out the major achievements of the liberation struggle.

Those achievements were political and moral. 'Here was the beginning of a true self-determination'—to quote a Cape Verdean retrospective of 1984, looking back on the liberated zones of wartime Guinea-Bissau—'and of a people's acceptance of responsibility for itself: a conquest of an importance without precedent if one considers that Portuguese colonialism, for centuries, was pledged to deprive its colonized peoples of any kind of responsibility for themselves, and rot out from their collective memory any thought of the need to assume the defence of their own interests.'

The structures of participation have become central to the whole political and social scene. Functionally, they are the organs of what we in Britain call local government—parish and district and town councils and assemblies: devolved power—and they stand in contrapuntal influence to the power of central government, of state government, of government at the centre. They are there, one may also say, to ward off and prevent the crisis of state degradation now so often seen in Africa, where more and more schlerotic central powers receive less and less public loyalty. In this respect the structures of mass participation in Cape Verde, as they could be examined in detail in 1986, have gone far to develop the grass-roots initiative and confidence in which Cabral and his companions, from the outset, saw the final justification of their leadership. At the outset they had been obliged to substitute themselves for the will of their people. They had been, as Cabral said, 'nationalists without a nation'. But they had led the peasants of the liberated zones in such a way that these peasants came increasingly to identify the party of Cabral with the embodiment of their own peasant interests, of their own programme, of their hopes of being able to live better and see their lives go forward. Many in the outside world had failed to perceive this truth or believe it when they did perceive it. Like Salazar's generals, they were left with no tenable explanation of the reasons why and how six men who began in 1956 could raise an unbeatable army of peasants. But if the Cape Verdean veterans came home in 1974 with clear notions of what must be attempted, they can have had few illusions about the difficulties they were going to face in attempting it. They had gone through instructive years, and they were acutely aware—as one of them was to recall in 1984—that the project of mass participation 'has to meet the most varied types of resistance, old habits, old ideas, the remnants of distortions of old evils and colonial miseries such as authoritarianism, *caciquismo* [local tyranny], corruption and the trade in influence, bureaucratism etc.: all these tend to take root and reproduce themselves'. The challenge had to be accepted.

It had to be accepted—here in the words of the vice-chairman of the Second National Assembly elected in 1980—because 'there would not be, nor ever was, any national liberation without mass participation'. None of the aims of the party of Cabral were otherwise possible. 'None of our government's objectives in the years ahead can be realized without mass participation. Without this participation, no future can be built, no material foundations which can guarantee the well-being of our people.'

Meeting the challenge called for a complex and co-ordinated process. To reinforce unity and drive behind social construction—to move, in other words, from mere survival in emergency to the firm ground of self-affirmation—there must be a political system and structure. There was none to be overthrown, once the colonial power was removed, for the colonial power left a void behind it. The fact of this void, of course, had its own compensations: there was no system and structure to be removed. Both must be built. This meant that the party of liberation (PAIGC until 1980, when it became PAICV after Guinea-Bissau had broken away from the projected union of the two countries) must be expanded from its few hundred activists of 1975 to many hundreds and then to several thousands. And this party would act as 'the continuer of Cabral', as the creator of the structures and of the practice of mass participation. This new party would be the dynamic force in the new republic and the master of the new state.

By the same line of thought, there could be no plurality of political parties. Any such plurality, even if it could have been achieved, was seen as being bound to introduce the disunities of group or personal ambition, of rivalries backed by external interferences, inducing in one way or another a waste of effort and resources when there was none to spare of either, and threatening an eventual frustration and defeat. The future might provide a different answer, but the future was still far ahead.

This being so, party power would have to be clearly separated, save at the summit of command, from state power. But there must be a one-party state. 'Very well', comments a leading political thinker in 1986, Olivio Pires, 'and the objection is obvious. How to protect the rights and duties of democracy without a plurality of parties?'. He goes on to recall the various African experiments and experiences which they had watched through their wartime years: the degeneration of Senegalese political life, on the one hand; the decline into outright dictatorship, on the other, of (ex-French) Guinea. They had watched much else. They had travelled widely. They had sojourned in many countries. And the spectacle of what could happen to the one-party state, as well as to the multiparty state, had been a chilling one.

'We have been able', continues Olivio Pires, 'to measure the bad as well as the good. Yet I have to say that none of this experience of ours, varied and extremely vivid and enormously discussed among ourselves, has been able to persuade us that the European model of the multi-party state can be workable in Africa.' At the same time their experiences had similarly taught them that the one-party state was not workable without mass participation. 'We thus remain convinced that a living grass-roots democracy is indispensable to progress. And we are just as much convinced that this democracy can be promoted and protected only by the force of mass participation.'

So there were these two imperatives for development. The party of Cabral must be built large and mature. The structures of a system of mass participation must be devised, launched, and made self-sufficient. I have written at length on the ways in which these imperatives have been and are being realised.[1] By 1980 the party of Cabral had expanded to some 4000 men and women who were organized in several hundred *groupos de base*, established throughout the Islands. In 1986 this total stood at rather more than 6000 men and women in a correspondingly larger number of local groups. At between 1½ and 2 per cent of the whole population, this total was evidently regarded as sufficient; efforts were now concentrated on improving the quality and capacity of the members. The leadership of this party, with Aristides Pereira as its secretary-general as well as being President of the Republic, controls the state in its every administrative department and policy; but beneath the summits of this control there is a sharp separation of powers. Party members have been given no authority to control or command anyone or anything outside their own ranks and functions. On the contrary, their principal duty is to 'teach and steer', above all by example, the participatory work of the great majority who are not party members. Only the smallest hand receives a salary or any other payment; the party works by voluntary effort. There can thus be no party dictatorship over the structures and system of participation; equally, the National Assembly has all legislative power, is elected by secret and universal adult suffrage, and is answerable to the electorate and not to the party.

Very well, as Olivio Pires might comment, but what are these structures and system of mass participation? Where is their guarantee against party dictatorship and administrative ossification? The answers began to be provided in 1979. Up to then, the void in political structures outside the central government had been temporarily though very partially filled by 'deliberative councils', which had tried, not very successfully, to take the first uncertain steps towards local self-government. The legal void had began to be filled a little earlier with the formation of local courts or tribunals on the model of those created, six or eight years before, in the liberated zones of wartime Guinea-Bissau. Some of these early local courts had functioned quite well, others barely at all, others again had limped along as well as they could. But by the early 1980s the level of their effectiveness had greatly improved. Much valuable experience was now to hand. In 1980 came the launching of regular forms of local self-government. Local assemblies—consisting of as many persons as local party members could persuade to attend, but, on the whole, assemblies of many people—were asked to elect local councils to which real powers were devolved from central government. Given the utter want of any experience of electing anyone to anything, these early councils were formed with persons nominated by local party groups and then submitted, one by one, to public approval or disapproval in local assemblies. The procedure rapidly became popular, as it was found:

shown the way to begin to govern their community lives, people clearly liked it. Again one has to bear in mind that no such concept of self-government had been as much as thinkable before 1975.

The project of mass participation through local councils—*commissions de moradores*, 'residents' councils'—took life and grew. By the latter part of 1984 a total of 224 local councils had come into existence and were at work, together with 140 local tribunals which had some 1100 male judges, or magistrates as we should call them, and about 220 women judges. The proportion of women to men activists in the whole participatory process was still markedly low, reflecting the traditional male chauvinism of this not untypical African country. It would still need a lot of time and persuasion to get the better of that; and this anti-woman discrimination remains meanwhile the Achilles' heel of the system. At the same time there is much awareness of this discrimination, and of the need to work against it. This is partly the duty of the Cape Verdean Women's Organization, Organiscao da Mulher, which has 9000 activists and a strong sense of mission. A corresponding mass organization for trade unions, and another for the needs and interests of young people (whether male or female), complete the structures of participation.

Mere members, perhaps needless to say, prove little but mere numbers. Behind the numbers are the persons and what they do. Even in relatively brief periods of research it is possible to test the actual existence of these persons and their work, in councils or in tribunals or in party sessions or in other activities; and to gain a measure of their real effectiveness.

This kind of testing gives positive results; the institutions exist, and the institutions work. It is possible to go anywhere you wish; to walk the hill tracks to distant hamlets for as long as you are able; to find motor transport so far as it exists; and the results are impressive. In 1976 I visited the huge crater of the volcano of Fogo, the Fire, not yet quite extinct, and found a few hundred people settled there. The revolution of the party of Cabral had yet to reach them, save as puzzling news from far below. I went back in 1986 and found 400 people who now had a local party group, a local court, a new primary school with a soccer pitch cleared in the jagged lava field, and a co-operative producing red local wine (at some 5000 feet above sea level); and were about to form their local council of self-government. The system and structures of mass participation have become all-pervasive in these islands. Altogether, by 1986, some 60,000 men and women were involved in one way or another in this sytem and structure of mass participatory self-government, or about one-fifth of the total population. They are involved in varying degrees of sincerity and commitment, Cape Verdeans being no less subject to the frailties of human nature than any other people. The right measure of all this is not against some utopian ideal of perfection. The right measure is against the void of 1975. Here is a people, however surprisingly in view of its past and its condition, that has known how to save itself; and has known how to do this from the sources and potentials of its own intelligence and will. Foreign aid has been generous and, one hopes, will continue to be generous; but no amount of foreign aid could have saved this people unless it had known how to save itself. And it may not be claiming too much to think that success of this kind is always likely to breed further success. I think that Olof Palme, who will not be forgotten in these islands and whose optimism was of the tough and tried variety, would have said yes to this.

Note

1. In my forthcoming book, *The Fortunate Isles*.

20

Olof Palme and the Liberation of Southern Africa

OLIVER TAMBO

When the terrible news was announced to the world on 1 March 1986 that Olof Palme had fallen to an assassin's bullet, the peoples of Southern Africa reacted with a stunned disbelief that quickly grew into grief and anger. Accustomed as we have become to the animal savagery of the apartheid system and therefore to swift and unnatural death, yet the passing of this great Swede and the circumstances which caused him to cease to be, evoked among us a sense of horror which recognized that a crime beyond comprehension and forgiveness had been committed.

Olof Palme had come to epitomize for us the commitment of the Swedish people to our cause. He was as well a factor of assurance and encouragement because he demonstrated that we were right to expect that leading politicians and statesmen of the Western world could overcome all constraints, both real and imagined, finally to side with the poor, the oppressed, the exploited, and the brutalized in Southern Africa. When he died, a beacon of hope was extinguished.

Of him, his successor as prime minister of Sweden, Ingvar Carlsson, has written that:

> During more than three decades, Olof Palme consistently argued against the insanity of the apartheid system. He showed that it is incompatible with all basic values of a civilized society, but also that it is a threat to international peace and security. And furthermore he took action, and argued for action, to help abolish the system.

Seven days before he was murdered, Olof Palme spoke in Stockholm at the 'Swedish People's Parliament against Apartheid' in pursuit of these goals. This speech, in which he described apartheid as 'this despicable, doomed system' was his last statement on international affairs. By virtue of these circumstances, it has taken on the nature of a testament.

In this inspiring statement of his own beliefs and convictions, Olof Palme reaffirmed that 'a system like apartheid cannot be reformed; it can only be abolished'. He went on to spell out the role of the international community in the struggle to achieve this objective, and declared: 'the world is directly implicated in the continuance of this system. If the rest of the world decides, if people all over the world decide that apartheid is to be abolished, the system will disappear'.

The programme of action he elaborated included the imposition of mandatory sanctions by the UN Security Council, and, if necessary, unilateral action by member states of the UN. He spoke of the need for a country such as Sweden to encourage others also to take action. He strongly urged the need for support for the ANC, SWAPO, and the Front Line states. Those of us who were present as Olof Palme expressed this firm resolve to act against the apartheid system were particularly moved because we knew that many of the steps he spoke of had already been translated into reality: others would surely be acted upon.

Precisely because of his deep-seated interest to see the world community take action against apartheid, Olof Palme also addressed the question of the forces that are opposed to such action. He pointed out that 'among those with vested economic interests in the survival of this system, there is resistance'. There is also resistance 'from those who regard people's longing for liberty in a country as a potential cause of a global contest between different superpowers'. To overcome this resistance he called for people's action, for 'mobilizing popular opinion in support of human dignity'. The one thousand Swedish delegates at the 'People's Parliament', representing exactly this popular opinion, responded with warmth when Olof Palme said:

> Fundamentally this is a profoundly emotional question and one which goes to the depth of our feelings because it is such an uncommonly repugnant system . . . [It] will be to the discredit of the world for as long as it persists. [We] must live up to our responsibility to bring this repulsive system to an end.

Those who took Olof Palme's life, whoever they might be, are rejoicing that he is no longer with us to play his role in bringing the repulsive apartheid system to an end. Much as they might celebrate, yet they cannot obliterate and reduce to nought the legacy that Olof Palme left behind, an important part of which is the unwavering involvement of the Swedish and other peoples in the struggle for the liberation of Southern Africa, the establishment of a just and lasting peace in this region, and its development as a prosperous zone of free and equal nations. The durability of that legacy of solidarity and its fundamental long-term importance lies in the fact that it is an integral part of the political formation of the Swedish people. Without it, the definition of a Swedish national consciousness is incomplete. Thus it is not an accretion that has been affixed to a fully formed nationhood, as an incidental element imposed on the body politic by the exigencies of the moment.

From the activities of Olof Palme and from representatives of various schools of political thought in Sweden and the people as a whole, we have come to understand that Sweden sees solidarity not as an expression of pity but as an affirmation that the Swedish people are themselves not free if others elsewhere are oppressed—that freedom, independence, democracy, and peace are indivisible.

To act in solidarity is therefore to seek to transform the world so that both those who extend solidarity and those who are the recipients of such support move in consonance to produce a human order which favours both. Thus in the course of extending solidarity to the peoples of Southern Africa, Sweden has contributed to the birth of a world in which the forces of racism, colonialism, fascism, and war have been put to flight and into permanent retreat. The same process further guarantees that these forces will not raise their ugly head in Sweden itself and that their frontiers of operation are restricted universally, for the common good.

During this process there has also emerged a natural system of relations between Southern Africa and Sweden, from people to people. It is a system of international relations which is not based on the policies of any party that might be in power in Sweden at any particular time, but on the fundamental reality that the peoples of our region and those of Palme's land of birth share a common outlook and impulse which dictates that they should all strive for the same objectives.

To write about Olof Palme and the liberation of Southern Africa must necessarily be to reflect on the struggle, especially since the Second World War, to establish a new system of international relations. Central to this system are the end of colonialism and the domination of small by big powers, and thus the restructuring of the world as a community of independent and equal partners all committed to the pursuit of peace and a commonly shared prosperity and social progress. These ideas found their most concentrated and hopeful expression in the establishment of the United Nations organization in 1945 and the adoption of its Charter and the Universal Declaration on Human Rights. It is little wonder, therefore, that Sweden, a neutral country, too joined the UN, and treated action with and through the world organization, in pursuit of its agreed objectives, as a fundamental tenet of its foreign policy.

Consequently it was natural that Sweden moved in 1946 that the complaint lodged by India at the first General Assembly about the racist treatment of the Indian population in South Africa should be referred to the International Court of Justice. This reflected her confidence in this and other international institutions and her desire to see them operate successfully, within a specific context of international law. In the first two decades of its existence, despite the high hopes that were raised when it was founded, the UN was unable to resolve such issues as the rapid escalation of international tension brought about by the cold war, conflict in the Middle East, US invasion of Cuba and Vietnam, the war in Algeria, and the persistence of apartheid and colonialism in Southern Africa.

Two issues of major importance to Olof Palme's contribution to the struggle for the liberation of Southern Africa derive from this situation. The first is that it ultimately became clear to the Swedish people in general that it was vital that popular opinion be mobilized in support of human dignity, as Olof Palme said a week before he was murdered. The second is that to contribute further to the purposes of the UN it was necessary that Sweden and other countries should also act unilaterally and not always restrict themselves by acting according to the lowest common denominator within the UN. Olof Palme emphasized this position when he addressed the Security Council on the question of apartheid in March 1977. He said:

> [The] actions taken in the United Nations, or lack of such actions, cannot serve as an alibi for passivity on the national level. Each country and government, each popular movement, has its own responsibility and its own role to play ... [The] situation in South Africa has progressed to such a point that each country has to consider unilateral prohibitive measures (Nordic Statements).

A point of additional importance in this context is that this outlook, adopted and expressed by an outstanding international figure, such as Olof Palme, put the final nail to the assumption that neutrality implies passivity—that neutral countries, such as Sweden, could only act on major issues of international relations so long as this was within the spirit and letter of decisions of the UN. It also swept aside the argument that smaller countries with less involvement in the direct or indirect perpetuation of racism and apartheid in Southern Africa had, correspondingly, a reduced obligation to act against white minority rule.

But to return to the question of the mobilization of popular opinions: in the mid-1960s the Vietnam solidarity movement burst out in the streets of the towns and cities of Sweden in common with many other countries. From then on it became clear that major issues of international concern would never again be the predominant or exclusive concern of those who debated such questions within the hallowed precincts of national parliament buildings or the UN centres in New York and Geneva.

In truth, it was the extraordinary high level of mobilization of popular opinion on the Vietnam question, and later Chile, which made it possible to develop the massive movement of solidarity with the peoples of Southern Africa that exists in Sweden today. That mass re-awakening not only brought many people into active involvement in world affairs but also united the Swedish people as never before—regardless of party affiliation, class origin, sex, or age—in favour of human dignity. History will never forget the role that Olof Palme played in this process when, as a senior government leader in 1968, he joined these active masses, as well as the Ambassador of the Democratic Republic of (North) Vietnam to the Soviet Union, in a mass demonstration in Stockholm to demand an end to US aggression against the Vietnamese people. Later on, as prime minister, he was to denounce the US bombing of Hanoi in very strong terms, which led to the USA withdrawing its ambassador from Stockholm.

Olof Palme's simple and peaceful march for humanity lent remarkable weight to the solidarity movement, affirmed its character as the voice of all the people of Sweden, and underlined the importance and the necessity for the masses of the people to act as conscious makers of history for the transformation of the world into a just and peaceful patrimony of all peoples.

The principle and objective of solidarity among citizens of one nation-state is an important element that underlies the debate and consensus which led to the establishment of the Swedish system of public welfare. Its extension to the realm of world affairs and its rooting as an international obligation in the making of the consciousness of the Swedish people constitute a development which has benefited the peoples of Southern Africa to the extent that we can today count these people as reliable allies.

In 1961 the USA invaded Cuba at the Playa Giron with the intention of overthrowing the government of that country and installing its own puppets in power. Through their own efforts the Cuban people repulsed these forces of aggression and thus asserted their right to determine their own future. The Swedish government of the day decided to extend material assistance to the people of the new Cuba, in recognition and support of the right of this small nation to decide its destiny, independent of the wishes of any other country, however powerful. Olof Palme summed up these sentiments as he shared a public platform with Fidel Castro when he paid an official visit to Cuba in 1975. 'Long live the solidarity of the peoples!' he said. 'Long live this free and independent Cuba!'

We mention these positions with regard to Cuba and Vietnam also because the fact that a Western country such as Sweden could and did stand up for the cause of national independence and justice, knowing that it would earn the wrath of a country as powerful as the USA, increased the determination of the peoples of Southern Africa to stand up to the alliance of major Western countries which were supporting the white minority regime in our region.

In 1973 Olof Palme stated that it was 'difficult for the Western democracies to dissociate themselves unequivocally from US intervention in Indochina'. As he explained, this was because:

> Criticism of America's involvement in Vietnam has been regarded as anti-Americanism. The demand that the people of Vietnam should be given the same self-evident right to national independence as other people that were formerly colonized has been depicted as support for Communist expansionism.

The fact that Olof Palme and the Swedish people could speak their minds on the Vietnam question, notwithstanding such accusations and despite the timidity of Western governments in general, demonstrated that even in the West which had colonized our peoples the liberation movement of Southern Africa had friends who would not maintain a Western solidarity if it was directed against the right of the peoples to free themselves from colonial and racist domination. We believe that this is of long-term importance in the general struggle against racism and contributed to the strengthening of democratic principles in the structuring of relations among the peoples.

As Cuba was defeating the forces of aggression at the Bay of Pigs in 1961, Tanganyika was attaining its independence from British colonial domination. From the day of its liberation, Tanganyika (later renamed Tanzania after the union with Zanzibar) became, for the peoples of Southern Africa, our Front Line state. Tanzania became a Front Line state not only to the extent that she allowed the liberation movements of Southern Africa to establish a presence on her territory and extended assistance to them; but also because it would, in practice, provide the peoples of our region with experience of how to conduct the business of developing a newly independent state.

Sweden started extending development assistance to Tanzania in 1963. This has continued to the present, with Tanzania being the single largest recipient of Swedish assistance among all the countries which have co-operation agreements with Sweden. Through this extension of solidarity, Sweden has therefore played an important part in helping Tanzania to play its outstanding role as a Front Line state. It is indeed impossible to imagine how the process of the liberation of Southern

Africa would have evolved if Tanzania had not made herself available to our rear base.

When Olof Palme visited Tanzania in 1971, he paid tribute to the country and expressed admiration for the role she was playing in support of the struggles for liberation in Southern Africa. He observed correctly: 'You are making great sacrifices, both political and economic, in aiding the struggle for freedom in South Africa.' Explaining some of the fundamental ideas which inspired Swedish development assistance to Tanzania and other countries. Olof Palme said:

> National liberation does not automatically lead to real national independence. We see examples of former colonies which have been tied again to the metropolitan powers by measures of commercial policy and other steps. It has been a matter of flag independence rather than national independence. National liberation must be reinforced by economic liberation and the overcoming of poverty. Cooperation is needed for this purpose.

It is of interest to note that even before the independence of Tanganyika, Olof Palme played an important role in establishing relations between the two countries. As part of the leadership of the Social Democratic Youth of Sweden, he helped to build up relations with the TANU Youth League. He later observed that 'these contacts became the introduction to a close and far-reaching cooperation between our countries and movements'.

We should also draw attention to the fact that the purposes of development assistance to which Olof Palme referred were in the first instance laid down in legislation adopted by the Swedish Parliament in 1961. Emphasizing anti-colonialism and the promotion of national emancipation, this law was largely drafted by Olof Palme. Though not directed specifically at Southern Africa, it is however clear that the fact of the existence of such legislation has been of enormous assistance to the peoples of our region, which today receives more than 40 per cent of total direct Swedish development and humanitarian assistance.

The point to emphasize in this context is not only the fact and the volume of this assistance but also its orientation, which coincides with the fundamental aspirations of the peoples of our region for the total liberation of Africa and for economic emancipation, including the reduction of economic dependence on apartheid South Africa. Olof Palme has contributed immensely to the attainment of these objectives as Sweden today occupies the same trenches with all the Front Line states which joined Tanzania as each one of them gained its independence. Swedish assistance to the liberation movements of

Southern Africa, the ANC and SWAPO, is today taken for granted. Yet as Olof Palme observed, even as late as 1971 Sweden was being criticized for extending this humanitarian support to the liberation movements. At the time, during his visit to Tanzania, he said that despite this criticism 'we shall continue to follow the demands of solidarity ... [and] the Swedish government is prepared to increase further its assistance to such movements'. He went on to add that 'the European nations must take up a much more active and more decisive action in these questions' of material and political support for the liberation movements.

Olof Palme could and did persist in his determination to assist the liberation movements, in part because, already in his youth, he understood the need to provide the material assistance to the victims of oppression and racism. As his widow, Lisbet Palme, has observed: 'He did not stand to one side as an observer. He took part actively, from the time when he gave his blood as a 20-year-old to collect scholarship money for young blacks of his own age, who had been thrown out of school because of the colour of their skin.'

But in 1968, when Sweden started extending direct humanitarian assistance, in the first instance to the liberation movements fighting Portuguese colonialism, and later to ZANU, ZAPU, SWAPO, and ANC, much of the Western world thought that this was unacceptable. This assistance has been and is of immense and critical importance to the liberation movements and the tens of thousands of people who were and have been forced into exile.

Of importance also has been the political work that Sweden has carried out to educate and persuade the Western countries to recognize the fact that the liberation movements are the genuine representatives of their peoples and indeed ultimately representatives of their liberated countries. Through practical deeds the Swedish people compelled the Western countries to translate their publicly stated support for the right of all peoples to self-determination into actual recognition and support for those who were and are fighting to secure for themselves and their peoples the possibility to exercise this right.

Respect for the right of all peoples to determine their destiny also resulted in Sweden leading the Western world in taking the position that support for the liberation movements should not be conditional on any requirement that these movements should change their politics to accommodate what might be different views of donor countries. The extensive political and material support for the liberation movements, in the terms we have described above, is therefore yet another of the outstanding contributions that Sweden has made and is making to the struggle for the liberation of Southern Africa. Without in any way seeking to minimize the importance of the contribution and commit-

ment of other political forces in Sweden to our cause, we should
nevertheless make the observation that much of the work of
establishing and consolidating relations between the African liberation
movements and the Swedish government was initiated at the time
between 1969 and 1976 when Olof Palme was prime minister of
Sweden. Happily those relations were maintained at the highest level
when other parties took power. The stubbornness of the racist and
colonial regimes in Southern Africa compelled the liberation movements of our region to take up arms. When the time came for us to
take this decision, we stated that the choice before us was 'to submit or
fight'. In recent times many Western governments have demanded that
we cease fighting and renounce the use of arms as an inducement to the
racist regime to enter into negotiations with us. It has been argued that
our resort to arms for political ends cannot find understanding in the
West because it is anathema to 'Western traditions'.

We are of course clear that the import, if not the purpose, of these
arguments is to persuade us to submit and thus put the apartheid
regime in a position in which it has exclusive power to determine the
future of our country. Given the importance of this issue, we have
spared no effort in seeking to get the widest possible Western understanding of our positions.

Olof Palme understood the centrality of this question in the struggle
for the liberation of Southern Africa. He therefore knew that he could
not stand aside from the debate around this question. When he spoke
at a UN conference on Namibia and Zimbabwe in Maputo in 1977, in
customary fashion Olof Palme confronted the cant and hypocrisy on
this question without any equivocation. Here is what he said:

> We all obviously prefer peaceful solutions to violent ones. But those
> of us who are privileged and who have had the good fortune of
> peaceful change should never moralize about it, never try to appear
> virtuous in relation to those who have been forced to take up arms to
> liberate themselves. If we do we have forgotten our own past.

Olof Palme drew attention to the fact that his own party, the Swedish
Democratic party, had once adopted a resolution which stated that it
'must take into consideration the possibility of using organized
violence as the final means of liberating the suffering proletariat'. He
further explained that: 'It is easy to foresee that when people in search
of peace and progress are met only by oppression and exploitation,
they will ultimately resort to violence. The armed struggle becomes the
last possible resort ... And ... once a people has taken up arms to
liberate themselves, they will not give up until freedom has been
achieved.'

Olof Palme returned to this issue when he visited Southern Africa for the third time in 1984. Speaking in Arusha, Tanzania, once more he identified the cause of the violent conflict in South Africa and made important observations which our white compatriots would do well to study carefully. He pointed out that:

The longer the white leaders insist on maintaining the white dictatorship, the harder and more violent the conflict will become. Long-term security and stability are sacrificed for a policy that is in clear contradiction to the long-range interests of the white minority itself. It is really a march of folly.

When he addressed the UN Security Council in 1977 he said: 'How much armed pressure from the nationalists is necessary depends on how much unarmed pressure the Western powers apply in the form of sanctions and the like.' Thus he challenged those in the West who say they are opposed to armed struggle to act to reduce the need for armed resistance by imposing sanctions.

And indeed, at the 'People's Parliament', Olof Palme related sanctions to the issue of a negotiated resolution of the South African and Namibian questions. He pointed out that 'the white people must be aware of their own interests in a peaceful solution, while such a solution is still at all possible'. To raise that awareness to the point where white South Africa is compelled to act for a peaceful solution in its own interests, he said: 'Pressure on the regime must increase. It must be made clear to the minority regime that it has no support in the world around.'

These positions are of course diametrically opposed to those adopted by the proponents of 'constructive engagement' and 'quiet diplomacy'. They signify Olof Palme's principled refusal to enter into any compromises with racism and reaction. They correctly emphasize the point that, in the midst of all the talk about peaceful solutions of the Namibia and South Africa questions, nobody should lose sight of the fact that the task facing the world community is the destruction of the apartheid system through struggle.

As far as Sweden itself was concerned it was in fact popular opinion which took the lead to impose sanctions through the boycott of South African products. This was immediately after the Sharpeville massacre in 1960. By 1963 the government had imposed a voluntary arms embargo against apartheid South Africa. Prohibitions of credit guarantees for exports to South Africa came in 1967. It is also important to note that in 1971 the Palme government piloted an enabling 'Act on Certain International Sanctions' through the Swedish Parliament. This makes it possible for the Swedish government to take swift action if this was called for as a result of decisions or recommendations issued by the UN Security Council. This Act was used to impose sanctions against Rhodesia in the period 1971–79 as well as the mandatory arms embargo against South Africa in 1977.

The government also acted successfully to press the Swedish firm ASEA to withdraw from participation in the construction of the Cabora Bassa Dam in colonial Mozambique. In 1973 the government made a recommendation to the Swedish firms with subsidiaries in South Africa that they should refrain from making new investments in that country.

It would be true to say that in the period from 1963 to 1976 even Sweden moved very slowly in terms of implementation of a vigorous programme of sanctions. Apart from other reasons to which we have referred, Swedish action was slowed down by continued arguments that she had to act as a part of a concerted UN offensive. Yet it was clear that the situation in Southern Africa demanded action—unilateral action, given that the USA, the UK, and France remained committed to thwart all meaningful action by the Security Council.

Once more Sweden sought to get the UN to act. She moved a resolution at the General Assembly, which was approved with an overwhelming majority, urging the Security Council to prohibit new investments in South Africa. But already in August 1976, Olof Palme had urged at a public meeting that Sweden itself 'must seriously consider the question of company representations and new investments in South Africa'. During April 1977 the Swedish Parliament discussed this question on the basis of a motion introduced by the Social Democratic party which was then in opposition. Parliament agreed that it was necessary that Sweden should adopt some unilateral measures against apartheid South Africa.

From this followed the law passed in 1979, prohibiting or restricting new investments in South Africa and Namibia. Other measures have since been adopted, including the cessation of SAS flights to South Africa (taken jointly with other Scandinavian countries) and the prohibition of imports of agricultural produce from South Africa. At the time of writing this chapter, there are expectations that the Swedish government will go further to impose comprehensive sanctions.

The unilateral actions taken by Sweden since 1979 have done a great deal to move the sanctions campaign forward. As Olof Palme said in his speech at the 'People's Parliament' in 1986, to which we have referred:

When in the 1970s, we in Sweden began to pursue the issue of unilateral Swedish sanctions against South Africa, many people shook their heads and said it would have no effect and that no one

would follow suit . . . . The Swedish initiative has now been followed
by many countries. Criticism has died down. More and more people
who were earlier doubtful are now beginning to understand that this
type of action is necessary. Sanctions are not a guarantee that a
bloody settlement can be avoided. But the surrounding world must
take its responsibility and seek every opportunity of actively
contributing.

By imposing comprehensive sanctions unilaterally Sweden would, as
before, break new ground for the Western countries and act in
consonance with this view to which we subscribe, that the surrounding
world must take its responsibility and seek every opportunity of
actively contributing.

Of the Western countries, Sweden had once more to stand alone in
1975–76 in defence of the young People's Republic of Angola when
apartheid South Africa, the USA, surrogate and other forces combined
in their will on the people of Angola.

On the day that Angola attained her independence, 11 November
1975, Olof Palme addressed the UN General Assembly. In welcoming
Angola 'as a new nation in Africa', he said, 'we must reject any foreign
aspirations to limit the right of the Angolan people themselves to
decide their future.' As the second war of liberation raged in Angola,
the Swedish Minister for Foreign Affairs told his parliamentary
colleagues:

> The Government's view is that the MPLA is the political movement
> with roots among the people that has combined the struggle for
> independence with efforts to establish social and economic justice in
> Angola.

In May 1976 the Swedish government announced its decision to
extend economic assistance to Angola, a government delegation having
visited that country during the previous month. But before that,
Sweden had had to take positions within the UN Security Council
which were of historic importance for the future of the struggle for the
liberation of Southern Africa and, indeed, the future of the sovereignty
of all African countries. The question at issue was the situation in
Angola. As the Swedish Foreign Minister explained in a pubic meeting
in Sweden in April 1976:

> The Angola question came up in the Security Council recently . . .
> [The] Western powers emphasized the Soviet-inspired Cuban inter-
> vention in Angola . . . Sweden also criticized the Cuban intervention
> in commitment of Cuban forces in Angola. At the same time it was

clear that the MPLAs decision to invoke Cuban military assistance was mainly prompted by the need to counter South African aggression. The two commitments could not in any way be equally rated.

The Minister went on to explain:

The draft resolution presented by the African states in the Security Council condemned South Africa alone. Following a Swedish initiative, this draft was made to include a reference to the principle that no state is entitled to intervene in the affairs of any other state. After this, we voted for the resolution. Because the Western states all abstained, Sweden's vote decided the adoption of the resolution. If we had abstained and the resolution had been defeated, South Africa would have scored the greatest victory in terms of prestige in the history of the United Nations.

Olof Palme himself was to return to the issue of Angola in August of 1976 when he observed: 'There is particular cause for alarm in the information that is reaching us concerning persistent foreign attempts to sabotage Angola's independence in what is alleged to be a struggle against Communism.' A week before he was murdered, and expressing his opposition to US assistance to the UNITA bandits, he said:

The plans for foreign military and other assistance to the opposition UNITA guerillas in Angola is an example of a measure which can reasonably only obstruct a negotiated settlement and would be perceived as support of South Africa.

Undoubtedly those words and the positions that the Palme government took during the critical days of 1975–76, when independent Angola was fighting for its existence and for the future of the African revolution, rankled with those who think that our mother continent is too important in the matrix of world affairs for us as Africans to settle its future as we see fit.

The struggle for a just and democratic, international, political, economic, and social order, to which Olof Palme dedicated his life, continues. So does the struggle for world peace which Olof Palme, himself a combatant for peace, saw as impossible to realize fully unless all peoples were free to determine their future and free to enter into mutually beneficial co-operation for the creation of conditions of equality, prosperity, and progress for all, across the barriers of colour, nationality, and different social systems.

Olof Palme no longer lives to work with us in pursuit of these objectives. Yet he left us with these as uncompleted tasks—among them the total liberation of South Africa. No rest is possible while Olof Palme's words ring in our ears that 'we must live up to our responsibility for bringing this repulsive (apartheid) system to an end'.

As he insisted throughout his life, the UN has both a special responsibility towards the question of ending the apartheid system and an obligation to act against this system. But as the world is only too aware, those within the Security Council who desire benefits from the continuation of racist tyranny in Southern Africa are determined to thwart all concerted action. This lowers the prestige of the UN and renders it less capable of carrying out the noble tasks that are spelled out in its Charter.

The struggle to get the UN to act in a decisive manner on the question of apartheid is therefore a struggle to re-establish its effectiveness and to restore its character as a world parliament of the peoples, enjoying all the necessary authority to carry out its functions without let or hindrance. Those who do not derive any profit from the apartheid system—the overwhelming majority of the peoples and the nations of our globe—need to act firmly to ensure that the UN lives up to its responsibility. The UN Security Council must impose comprehensive and mandatory sanctions against apartheid South Africa. As Olof Palme said as long ago as 1977, when he addressed the Security Council: 'The oppressed peoples look towards this Council with hope and expectation.' The need continuously to increase pressure on the apartheid regime, for which Olof Palme worked tirelessly, also requires both that popular opinion should be mobilized as never before and that individual countries should act unilaterally, spurned on by the recognition that the apartheid system is a crime against all humanity, a threat to international peace and security.

Our dear friend, Lisbet Palme, addressed the Paris World Conference on sanctions against racist South Africa on the day of the tenth anniversary of the Soweto uprising, three-and-a-half months after her husband and companion had been murdered. She who had known a depth of grief impossible to imagine, transcended the liturgy of politicians and spoke of love:

> In order to justify their own actions or their failure to act, many people do not listen to what is said about apartheid. But those who reach out to others in love and community will be able to stop the haters in whatever form they may appear—as Nazis or fascists or racists or individual fanatics, the men and women of violence: those whose own frustration drives them to destructive attacks on people around them—in the absence of love and community, they get their perverted nourishment from evil forces.

When he spoke at the UN Conference in Maputo in 1977, to which
we have already referred, Olof Palme presented one of those
fundamental truths which mark him out as truly one of our own, one
who was perhaps destined to perish as thousands of his comrades-in-
arms have perished throughout Southern Africa, one who took sides
against the men and women of violence. He said:

> Neutrality towards the existing and coming struggles in Southern
> Africa is impossible. Between the exploiters and the exploited there is
> no middle ground. We cannot escape the question: whose allies do
> we want to be? Which side are we on?

Throughout his life he was on our side, on the side of the liberation of
the peoples of our region and of others beyond the shores of the
African continent; an activist who fought for our emancipation from
colonial and racial domination, from hunger, poverty, deprivation, and
degradation, and from the ravages of war.

As he bid us farewell on 21 February 1986, seven days before he
was murdered, he ascribed to us a degree of importance which others
seek to deny. In the same words he made an appeal for justice, peace,
and an end to the blood-letting:

> It is a legacy of history that the black people of Namibia and South
> Africa have a wide popular movement, a really eminent leading
> stratum which would be a possible interlocutor in a dialogue to
> dismantle this despicable, doomed system. But the regime responds
> there by intensifying oppression and putting the leaders of this people
> in prison. This, then, is a classical example of madness of which
> nothing can come but evil—until the day it disappears and one day
> comes to an end.

We heard him and took his message to heart, as did the thousand
Swedish delegates who attended a solidarity event which was unique in
Swedish history for its magnitude, its representative character, and its
expression of the united view of an entire people. Many years before,
in 1973, Olof Palme had warned: 'Practical solidarity is a thorn in the
flesh of those who believe that egoism and self-assertion are the
mainspring of the future.' We believe he lost his life because these,
whom he despised and opposed, had come to understand how
dangerous the idea and practice of solidarity was to the defenders of
privilege and domination.

Blood and death suffuses the history of Southern Africa, but our
lodestar is a noble hope. Present and future generations of the peoples
of our region, our continent, and our world will forever sing of Olof

Palme as the thorn in the flesh of the forces of reaction that represented a terrible and petrified old order. The poet too evoked his being and told us how to walk in his footsteps when he wrote:

> *And so History teaches with her light*
> *that man can change that which exists*
> *and if he takes purity into battle*
> *in his honour blooms a noble spring*
> (Pablo Neruda; translated by Miguel Algarin).

21

Olof Palme and the Middle East

ANOUSHIRAVAN EHTESHAMI

It seems
There is nothing now.
Neither sun nor moon.
Neither darkness nor dawn.
No Aphrodite in the ocean's eye.
No ship in the harbour of pain.
Perhaps it was all an illusion.
Legend of a tall tree.
The last swirl of desolation.
In the butchered lane.
('Legend of a tall tree', F. Ahmad Faiz.)

In so far as Sweden is a nationwide and an advanced capitalist country inextricably and organically linked to the capitalist world economy, its fortunes and interests cannot be separated from those of other 'imperialist', peripheral, and socialist-style countries of the globe. And yet in attempting to study Sweden's foreign policy and Olof Palme's enlightened role in the world community of states and institutions we are trying to set Sweden aside from the other actors and aside from the internal and external forces that have played a major role in charting the modern history of that country. To establish a balance within this dichotomy, this chapter will critically analyse the substance of Swedish capitalism, and from there attempt to assess Sweden's role in the Third World as a whole, and the Middle East in particular, thus constructing a conceptual niche for understanding Olof Palme's historical position.

Sweden is one of the few industrialized countries in the world that neither fits within the Leninist imperialist model, nor the hierarchical 'world system theory' (WST). Historically, it has not been party to the 'Capitalism that has grown into a world system of colonial oppression and of the financial strangulation of the overwhelming majority of the population of the world',[1] nor an element of imperialism which aimed at 'the partitioning of the world, and the exploitation of other countries . . . [and] high monopoly profits for a handful of very rich countries'.[2]

This is despite the fact that Sweden reached its economic 'take-off stage' some 30 or 40 years after France (1878–1900), Belgium (1833–60), the USA (1843–60), and Germany (1850–73).[3] In other words, for all intents and purposes Sweden should have been regarded as an imperialist state, even at the time of Lenin's *Imperialism*.

So, while Sweden can unanimously be regarded as an advanced capitalist state, it cannot as comfortably be regarded as an imperialist state that competes for domination and political manipulation of the ex-colonial countries of the periphery along with, say, the USA, France, and Britain, or even the Soviet Union. Nor does this Nordic country belong to any political or military power bloc. It is not very penetrating to observe that the USA is the dominant power of the Western world, and the Samsonian pillar of NATO. Most of Western Europe is currently dependent on US patronage for military and ultimate political confidence. In this sense it is true to argue that fairly 'developed' countries may to some extent still be subordinate to other countries in the hierarchy of the world economy.[4] But Sweden is not subordinate to stronger members of the power blocs within the world economy. It is neither a member of the NATO power bloc, nor of the EEC, nor of course the Soviet-dominated Warsaw Pact Treaty. In fact it has charted itself a policy of neutrality, bent on the principles of international law, and in opposition to power-bloc intrigue, conducted by almost all other industrialized countries (East and West). While economically Sweden may be smaller and 'weaker' than some other capitalist countries, politically it wields an independence admired even by her 'potential' adversaries. So, where does Sweden fit in? Now, can an economic member of the metropolis (core) oppose politically the implication of its favoured position, and more often than not ally itself with the oppressed periphery? More crucially, perhaps what is the relationship between Swedish transnational capitalism and the state? It is to an investigation of these issues that we now turn our attention.

In so far as general international comparisons are possible, in my view the well-established Swedish polity has a major common denominator with the young and versatile Nicaraguan regime in Central America. And that is the dichotomy of state–capitalist relations. In Nicaragua the revolutionary socialist ideology of the regime presides over the largely privately controlled capitalist economy. In Sweden, social democracy has, over the last five decades, governed the evolution of the country's transnational capitalist expansion, a blossoming of old and new Swedish firms that increasingly earn their 'livelihood' beyond the boundaries of their home country. Despite the

Sandinista's socialist ideology, the Nicaraguan regime recognizes that 'the socialist model is a solution for contradictions that only exist in developed capitalist countries', further realizing that: 'though we have socialist principles, we cannot affect the transformation of our society by socializing all the means of production . . . [this] could lead to the destruction and disarticulation of our society'.[5] The Swedish state, in view of its internal weaknesses,[6] embarked on a policy of capital protection through the good offices of various international political bodies. Swedish Social Democracy, in order to protect its transnational capital internationally, has internalized the universal principles of international law and justice as the only conceivable vehicle that can adequately guarantee the long-term security of Swedish capital in near and faraway lands. This enlightened outlook and strategy is manifested in Sweden's adherence to internationalist political and economic principles that can best be summed up as 'non-interventionist' or 'neutral' imperialism. Sweden seems dependent on all the factors that are essential for the survival of many other Western states, and yet does not functionally rely on imperialism and neo-colonialism for survival.[7] It has not been involved in any wars since 1814, including the two hot wars of this century, nor in the chilling climate of the cold war since the 1950s. Sweden formulated the basic principles of its policy of neutrality as long ago as the 1830s, when the rest of Europe was ravaged by war and rivalry. To ensure a climate of international stability, Sweden takes 'a great interest in all attempts to create an international legal system to safeguard the integrity and independence of small nations',[8] and thus to promote international stability and conditions congenial to unhampered trade, and free from power intrigue that could ultimately undermine the survival of Swedish transnational capital.

The Swedish economy has not been insulated from the increasingly interdependent condition of the world economy, in particular amongst the industrialized countries themselves. This is reflected in Swedish trade and investment statistics. Exports and imports account for over one-third of the country's GNP, and about 50 per cent of the country's industrial output is exported.[9]

Swedish direct foreign investment in 1982 stood at 2 per cent of the world total, lagging far behind that of say the USA with 48 per cent and Britain with 11 per cent,[10] but in terms of direct foreign investment per capita Sweden is ranked second in the world overtaken only by Switzerland.[11] During the early-1970s, 203 Swedish firms had sales of $25,507 million, or 1.7 per cent of total sales of 4,350 multinational firms surveyed. This put Sweden in the eighth position after the USA, Japan, the UK, the FRG, France, the Netherlands, and Italy.[12] On the other hand the Swedish firms had sales more than the combined sales of the 268 transnationals from those of Denmark, Norway, Finland, Luxembourg, Austria, New Zealand, Ireland, Portugal, and Spain, or 1.5 per cent of total sales for the 4,350 firms surveyed.[13]

Swedish transnationals play a significant role in the Swedish economy, employing almost 50 per cent of the Swedish industrial labour force, and accounting for some 60 per cent of total Swedish exports. The top 20 Swedish transnationals employ over 250,000 people abroad, representing almost half of the 20 companies' total employment.'[14] The bulk of Swedish trade has historically been with her OECD and EEC friends. In 1983, 15 per cent of Swedish exports went to the Third World, and some 12.5 per cent of her imports were from the South. A more important indication of Sweden's 'Northern' trade and investment bias is the pattern of Swedish direct foreign investment. Table 21.1 provides a summary of foreign affiliates of Swedish transnationals in comparison with her major competitors. As readily observable, Swedish firms entertain the highest per cent of affiliates in the West compared with their competitors. And yet the behaviour of successive Swedish governments would give the impression of substantial dependence and historical (colonial) ties with the Third World. Furthermore, they also have the highest European concentration ratio.

Sweden has a history of foreign investment, whereby some 80 per cent of the present direct foreign investment originates from corporations that were well-established and multinational by the second decade of the twentieth century.[15] Table 21.2 gives an impression of the numerical strength of Swedish transnational capital in comparison with two of the leading newly industrializing countries (NICs). In only one of the categories adopted does the total performance of Korean firms outstrip their Swedish counterparts, namely that of 'sales'. In terms of both employment and assets, Swedish transnationals register higher figures.

A tentative conclusion from these indicators is the relative vulnerability of Swedish capitalism to threats not only from corporations of other industrialized countries, but, more crucially, from the burgeoning transnationalism of the fast-developing NICs. Again here, a policy of international stability, open global economic relations, and co-operation with the Third World is likely to benefit and protect Swedish capital abroad. A more commonly used indicator of a country's economic strength is the depth and spread of its automobile industry. Table 21.3 gives a comparison of Swedish automobile firms with some of her major European and non-European competitors. By European and intercontinental standards Swedish firms are rather small, and, as Table 21.4 summarizes, the Swedish automobile industry

Table 21.1 Distributions by regions of foreign affiliates of Swedish and non-Swedish firms, 1980 (percentages).

	Developed market economies				Developing countries					
	North-America	Europe	Other[a]	Sub total	Latin America	Africa	West Asia[b]	South-East Asia[b]	Europe	Sub total
Sweden	9.4	73.1	4.5	87.0	7.1	1.3	0.5	4.0	0.1	13.0
FRG	9.0	68.2	5.2	82.4	9.2	3.0	0.8	4.4	0.9	17.6
UK	14.1	35.2	26.5	75.8	4.7	7.7	0.9	10.4	0.5	24.2
Italy	7.4	63.0	3.5	73.9	15.0	6.7	1.1	2.6	0.7	26.1
France	8.2	58.0	3.3	69.5	7.7	18.7	1.1	2.9	0.1	30.5
USA	12.9	42.6	9.7	65.3	21.4	2.3	0.9	10.0	0.1	34.7
Japan	17.1	19.5	5.2	41.8	13.4	2.2	0.8	41.7	–	58.2
Average	9.2	56.9	9.1	76.1	9.6	4.9	0.9	8.4	0.2	23.9

Source: UNCTC, *Transnational Corporations in World Development: Third Survey*, (UN: New York, 1983).

[a] Australia, Japan, and New Zealand.
[b] Includes the Middle East states.

Table 21.2 Quantitative strength of Swedish, Korean, and Brazilian transnationalism, 1985 (in $ million and 000's of people).

	Sales	Assets	Employment
Sweden			
Volvo	10,014,445	8,479,604	67,857
ASEA	4,670,410	5,476,700	60,979
Electrolux	4,611,041	3,897,550	93,600
L M Ericson Telephone	3,817,493	4,900,594	78,159
Saab-Scania	3,699,268	3,524,109	46,807
SKF	2,295,529	2,876,040	46,582
Stora Kopparbergs Bergbigs	1,501,224	2,349,531	17,718
SSAB (Stanskt Stål)	1,486,087	1,535,842	14,865
Svenska Cellulosa	1,471,913	2,095,050	16,388
Sandrik Group	1,459,249	1,817,030	24,033
Procordia	1,419,050	1,688,185	25,499
Nobel Industries	1,265,050	1,474,099	15,857
Swedish Match	1,245,241	1,083,960	25,300
Oljakensumenternus Förbund	1,228,848	667,630	5,059
Essette	1,187,661	1,076,964	17,177
Alfa-Laval	1,178,739	1,400,251	15,394
Atlas Copco	1,169,026	1,145,149	16,659
AGA	1,133,358	1,645,809	14,441
KP Industri	1,128,490	878,909	14,835
Arld	1,055,810	446,325	7,420
Total	47,037,932	48,765,339	624,629

	Sales	Assets	Employment
Korea			
Samsung	14,193,095	8,221,531	129,039
Hyundai	14,024,594	8,493,891	156,000
Lucky Star	9,859,920	5,958,868	62,000
Dae Woo	8,698,021	8,985,506	92,745
Suakyong	6,436,703	4,480,751	19,454
Ssangyong	3,689,120	2,939,721	13,285
Korea Explosives	2,750,020	2,157,956	16,347
Hyosung	2,390,331	1,988,828	23,000
Pohangtron	2,376,059	3,728,076	17,000
Doosan	1,160,326	1,188,077	14,288
Total	65,578,189	46,955,128	544,158
Brazil			
Petrobras	16,046,448	12,858,595	61,421
Vale do Rio Doce	1,821,704	5,540,818	22,472
Ford Brasil	1,256,926	660,322	22,263
General Motors do Brasil	1,164,636	629,184	23,536
Industrias Votorantin	1,137,287	1,453,397	57,775
USIMINAS	985,987	1,751,242	14,798
Siderúrgica Nacional	984,498	3,574,966	20,839
Total	23,397,486	26,478,524	262,262

Source: Fortune International, 4 August 1986.

Table 21.3   *Swedish and selected leading automobile producers, 1980 (000's of vehicles).*

	Worldwide production	Home production	Foreign production	Firms share of worldwide total %
Sweden				
Volvo	311.5	205.0	106.5	0.9
Saab-Scania	104.6	93.4	11.2	0.3
Total	416.1			1.2
USA				
General Motors	6,712.3	4,753.3	1,959.0	19.2
Ford	4,183.3	1,888.5	2,294.8	12.0
Total	10,895.6			31.2
FRG				
VW-Audi	2,530.6	1,631.8	898.8	7.3
Daimler-Benz	707.4	627.2	80.2	2.0
Total	3,238.0			9.3
France				
Renault	2,136.9	1,713.3	423.6	6.1
Peugeot Citroen	2,019.2	1,647.3	371.9	5.8
Total	4,156.1			11.9
Italy				
Fiat-Lancia	1,569.0	1,349.6	219.4	4.5

Source: UNCTC, *Transnational Corporations in the International Auto Industry,* (New York: UN, 1983).

Table 21.4   *World car production (000's).*

Country	1981	1985	1986	1987	1990
Sweden	227	401	429	448	484
South Korea	69	264	392	540	853
Brazil	586	759	919	937	1204

Source: Financial Times, 14 October 1986.

Table 21.5 *Sweden's net flows of direct foreign investment, 1970–80 ($ million).*

	1970	1971	1972	1973	1974	1975	1976	1977	1978	1979	1980
Outflow	213.0	175.5	263.8	294.5	425.7	435.9	596.9	735.5	415.7	617.6	619.5
Inflow	108.0	83.2	67.3	72.7	75.8	80.1	4.6	80.6	71.4	112.4	251.2
Balance[a]	−105.0	−92.3	−196.5	−221.8	−349.9	−355.8	−592.3	−654.9	−344.3	−505.2	−368.2

Source: UNCTC, *Transnational Corporations in the International Auto Industry*, 1983, Annex Tables II.1 and II.2.
[a] A minus sign indicates net outflow.

is likely to be overtaken by newly built plants and facilities of the advanced NICs.

One response of Swedish capitalism to the structural changes of the world economy has been an increased transnationalization and diversification of markets. This is certainly true of all of the major Swedish transnationals.[16] In fact, as Table 21.5 illustrates, since 1970 Swedish outflow of direct foreign investment has consistently outstripped its inflow into Sweden. Only the USA, Japan, and Britain managed to maintain an annual net outflow of direct foreign investment for the period 1970–80. Undoubtedly this process has further increased Swedish capital's dependence on (calm) international conditions, and as a consequence of its non-interventionist posture (or ideology) the former further relies on the various international agencies to insure 'safety'.

The Swedish policy of neutrality is regarded not only as the best possible defensive posture for the nation; it has further been singularly responsible for giving Sweden a particular profile in the international arena, facilitating the country's independent and progressive policy in a number of fields, including 'development cooperation, environment, laws of war, disarmament.'[17] But to fulfil its national security objectives, Stockholm has maintained a strong non-nuclear defence policy, resulting in high military expenditure and procurement. As Tables 21.6(a) and 21.6(b) show, Sweden's military expenditure per capita was one of the highest in the world, even over a decade ago. And, in effect, in order to maintain strong independent defences, Sweden has had to 'keep up' with the arms race, so that at every level its forces may adequately function against both the major power blocs. Unlike the major weapons manufacturers, however, Sweden does not devote much export emphasis on Third World markets.[18] While such emphasis would undoubtedly reduce the Swedish defence bill, as a result of political considerations diametrically opposed to the policies of other (East and West) weapons' manufacturers, the former has not

Table 21.6(a)   *Total and per capita military expenditure of selected industrialized countries, 1973.*

	Total expenditure ($ billion)	Per capita expenditure ($)
USA	78.4	372
Sweden	2.0	246
FRG	13.3	215
France	9.8	189
UK	9.0	161

Source: IISS, The Military Balance 1976–77, (London: 1976).

Table 21.6(b) Swedish and major Middle East military expenditures (at constant 1978 prices and exchange rates), $ million.

1950	1955	1960	1965	1970	1975	1976	1977	1978	1979
Sweden 1,169	1,763	1,888	2,530	2,696	2,924	2,919	2,933	2,980	3,066
Egypt 206	489	513	974	2,271	5,756	5,004	5,239	[3,325]	[2,840]
Iran 212	291	577	862	1,906	10,168	11,031	8,902	9,506	4,493
Iraq 58	140	313	563	841	2,049	2,010	2,100	1,988	*
Israel 57	49	189	385	2,016	3,160	3,158	2,720	2,377	(3,063)
Kuwait *	*	53	97	393	860	1,073	1,189	1,091	*
Saudi Arabia *	*	*	1,035	2,094	(9,430)	[11,375]	[11,900]	(12,700)	(14,640)
Syria 58	68	170	242	429	1,088	1,086	1,097	1,151	(1,937)
UAE *	*	*	*	*	74	(153)	(904)	(1,066)	(1,195)

Source: SIPRI, 1980.
[ ], rough estimate; ( ), uncertain data or SIPRI estimates; *, information not available.

Table 21.7 *Value of major Swedish weapons exports to the Third World, 1971–82 (at constant 1975 prices), $ million.*

1971	1972	1973	1974	1975	1976	1977	1978	1979	1980	1981	1982
0	5	1	6	21	21	5	16	69	101	36	21

Source: SIPRI, 1983.

Table 21.8 *Rank order of major weapon exporters to the Third World, 1970–79 (at constant 1975 prices), $ million.*

Exporting country	Total value	% of Third World total
USA[a]	27,727	45.0
USSR[b]	16,914	27.5
France[a]	5,894	10.0
UK[a]	3,044	5.0
Italy[a]	1,868	3.0
FRG[a]	1,444	2.3
China	787	1.3
Netherlands[a]	515	0.8
Australia	421	0.7
Canada[a]	323	0.5
Sweden	196	0.3
Czechoslovakia[b]	154	0.2
Spain	110	0.2
Ireland	87	0.1
Poland[b]	80	0.1
Switzerland	55	—
Yugoslavia	47	—
New Zealand	13	—
Belgium[a]	5	—
Japan	3	—
Third World exporters	1,805	3.0

Source: SIPRI, 1980.
[a] NATO.
[b] WPT.

used arms exports as a principal way of gaining political and economic leverage. As Table 21.7 illustrates, only small amounts of Swedish weapons are exported to the Third World. In fact, compared with the other major arms exporters of the 1970s, Sweden comes in twelfth, surpassing only the minor arms manufacturers of the decade (see Table 21.8).

The Swedish policy of restrained arms exports to the Third World is quite evident even in the Middle East, where all the other major and minor arms manufacturers have since the early-1970s attempted to balance their books, and gain political leverage, by exporting sophisticated and high-powered military weaponry to almost all the regimes of the region. Swedish arms exports to the Middle East (including North Africa) accounted for 3 per cent and 5 per cent of the total in the 1950s and 1960s respectively.[19]

But at least two countries of the Middle East (Egypt and Israel) are known to have obtained manufacturing rights of some Swedish weapons' production, both prior to the Camp David Peace Treaty Agreements of the late-1970s. Table 21.9 is a partial list of known major Swedish arms exports to the Middle East.

The Middle East, however, is important for Sweden's non-military trade. In the early-1980s the region accounted for some 8 per cent of Sweden's exports, considerably less than the EEC (20.6 per cent) and EFTA (50.1 per cent), and about 7.5 per cent of the country's imports (see Table 21.10). More importantly, though, a number of Swedish firms and their subsidiaries have established manufacturing and assembly plants in all the major Middle East countries, relying on the political stability of the oil-rich and aid-donating states for prosperity.

Table 21.9   *Major Swedish arms exports to the Middle East, 1952–80.*

Year	Country	Item	Number
1952	Israel	NA F–51 Mustang fighters	4
1953	Israel	NA F–51 Mustang fighters	21
1952	Egypt	M/45 submachine gun	Unknown
1952	Egypt[a]	M/42 Ljungman 7.62 mm rifle	Unknown
1960	Tunisia	Saab 91 Safir aircraft	9
1961	Tunisia	Saab 91 Safir aircraft	6
1980	Bahrain	RBS–70 surface-to-air missile	Unknown
1980	Tunisia	RBS–70 surface-to-air missile	Unknown
1980	UAE	RTBS–70 surface-to-air missile	Unknown

Sources: SIPRI, 1975; Middle East and North Africa, (Europa Publications: 1980–81).
[a] These items were produced under licence.

This reliance is best illustrated by the 1979 Iranian Revolution that transformed the Middle East's most lucrative market into a (temporarily) isolated country in the region. Many Swedish firms have withdrawn from the Iranian market, and Sweden's exports dropped from a high of over 1 billion Swedish crowns (kronor) in 1978 to only about 290 million kronor in 1979, having since recovered to over 900 million kronor by 1981.[20] Saudi Arabia, Iraq, Libya, Egypt, and Algeria, respectively, are currently Sweden's major trading partners in the region. Sweden's neutral foreign policy is likely to have helped its economic fortunes in a number of Middle East states, particularly in Iraq and curiously in post-1980 Iran.

In purely political terms, however, Sweden's Middle East policy, under the premiership of Olof Palme, has verged on the utopian. Sweden's attitude towards the ongoing Arab–Israeli conflict has been based on:

(a) the mutual respect and recognition between Israel's Labour party (ruling uninterrupted from the state's creation in 1948 until 1977) and the Swedish Social Democratic party (ruling uninterrupted from 1932 to 1976, and since 1983) established through long years of association, particularly as two active members of the Socialist International;
(b) pursuing a policy of mutual recognition of the PLO and the Israeli state's right to exist;
(c) close adherence to the UN Security Council resolutions 242 (22 November 1967) and 338 (21–22 October 1973) as the basis for a peaceful negotiated settlement between the Israelis, Palestinians, and other Arab belligerents;
(d) urging Palestinians (PLO) and Israelis to recognize each other as an essential prerequisite to any meaningful peace in the region;
(e) expressing support for a number of Arab–Israeli–Palestinian–Arab peace plans including the Reagan Plan, the Fez Plan, and regional initiatives like the now defunct PLO–Jordan *rapprochement*.

The 1970s brought not only riches to the Middle East oil-producing states and their trading partners. It also marked the era of international recognition and respectability for the Palestinians and their national organization, the PLO, with its climax being Yasser Arafat's historic 'olive branch and freedom-fighter's gun' speech delivered to an engrossed UN General Assembly on 13 November 1974. This speech and its subsequent international reception marked the beginning of the end of the PLO's hitherto 'free hand' and conduct regarding Palestinian, Arab, and international affairs. The price for international respectability was 'conduct' through international means: diplomacy, negotiation, and power-play replaced the rampant application of the

Table 21.10 *Sweden's trade with the Middle East (ME), 1973–81 ($ million).*

	1973	1974	1975	1976	1977	1978	1979	1980	1981
Imports									
Arab countries	715.1	2,413.5	2,243.8	3,337.3	974,575	799,267	1,242.2	2,415.5	1,885.1
% of world	(1.54)	(3.45)	(3.00)	(4.01)	(4.57)	(3.98)	(4.19)	(7.5)	(7.19)
Non-Arab countries	90.3	172.0	357.1	311.0	255,173	312,565	281.6	191.1	41.4
% of world	(0.85)	(1.09)	(1.98)	(1.63)	(1.20)	(1.56)	(0.95)	(0.59)	(0.16)
Israel	19.9	22.3	32.6	40.4	49,761	54,365	66.5	51.7	51.8
% of world	(0.19)	(0.14)	(0.18)	(0.21)	(0.23)	(0.27)	(0.21)	(0.16)	(0.20)
ME total	273.9	738.0	930.1	1,117.6	1,279.509	1,166.197	1,590.4	2,658.3	1,978.2
% of world	(2.58)	(4.68)	(5.16)	(5.85)	(6.00)	(5.81)	(5.63)	(8.24)	(7.54)
World total	10,609.9	15,766.4	18,030.3	19,115.3	21,340,774	20,086,189	29,677.1	32,264.5	26,219.5
Exports									
Arab countries	180.6	348.8	626.8	884.8	860,684	889,535	1,445.2	1,562.9	1,761.4
% of world	(1.48)	(2.20)	(3.61)	(4.80)	(4.25)	(4.18)	(5.07)	(5.24)	(6.79)
Non-Arab countries	90.1	133.0	204.0	221.5	286,161	280,588	280.6	267.0	276.1
% of world	(0.74)	(0.84)	(1.18)	(1.20)	(1.41)	(1.32)	(1.32)	(0.89)	(1.06)
Israel	50.9	64.5	56.5	50.7	53,927	67,164	95.1	57.6	60.6
% of world	(0.42)	(0.41)	(0.33)	(0.28)	(0.27)	(0.32)	(0.33)	(0.20)	(0.23)
ME Total	321.6	546.2	887.3	1,157.0	1,200,772	1,237,287	1,687.9	1,887.5	2,098.0
% of world	(2.64)	(3.45)	(5.12)	(6.28)	(5.93)	(5.81)	(5.92)	(6.33)	(8.09)
World total	12,170.7	15,855.9	17,343.0	18,415.6	20,246,958	21,294,884	28,517.2	29,841.0	28,542.7

Source: Middle East Economic Digest (various issues).

armed struggle. Yasser Arafat's shuttle diplomacy did its utmost to out-perform Henry Kissinger's fateful Middle East missions.

The transformation of the PLO's international image in the early-1970s, from one of a terrorist organization to a respected member of the community of states, is perhaps the greatest achievement of the former's short history of existence. To fulfil its international obligations and to justify this recognition, the PLO has had to forgo an internal transformation as well. At a tragic cost to its internal cohesion and unity, the PLO has been forced to participate in diplomatic ventures whose ultimate aim has had little or no bearing on the resolution of the Palestine/Israeli 'problem'.

Ironically it is largely due to this diplomatic presence of the PLO, rather than its UN status, that it is now respectfully tolerated by the Western European countries. The Swedish state, in its continuous search for international stability and a negotiated resolution of various (Third World) conflicts, has also recognized the value of the PLO's existence and its presence in mainstream politics as a positive gesture towards peace in the Middle East. The Swedish Minister of Foreign Affairs made his country's position clear when he stated: 'The Swedish Government has been interested and gratified to note the PLO's increasingly constructive attitude to·a solution of the Middle East conflict. Talks with representatives of this organization should, therefore, be welcomed'.[21] Stockholm, therefore, regards the PLO's 'constructive attitude' as a first necessary step towards fulfilling the former's recommendation of mutual recognition (see above), thus facilitating a move towards a negotiated peaceful settlement. This policy, formulated by Olof Palme's Social Democratic government, and pursued by the post-1976 centrist government, while admirable, courageous, and far-reaching, is fundamentally idealistic and naïve. Its idealism is embedded in its recommendation that 'the PLO must recognize Israel's right to exist within secured and recognized boundaries . . . [and]Israel must recognize the legitimate national rights of the Palestinians, including their right to establish . . . a State of their own, living side by side with Israel.'[22]

While such proposals may ensure a long-term solution to the conflict as far as Sweden is concerned, they in no way are acceptable to any of the belligerent parties. The PLO rejects entirely the basis of Security Council resolutions 242 (1967) and 338 (1973), and Israel insists on the interpretation of the resolutions in the strictest sense, opposing any political recognition of the Palestinian grievances and their demand for statehood in any part of Eretz Israel. The matter is not helped by the contradictory positions of the external actors in the conflict. While the USA accepts an 'orderly transfer of domestic authority from Israel to the Palestinian inhabitants of the West Bank and Gaza', it firmly rejects 'the establishment of an independent Palestinian state in the West Bank and Gaza', and recommends 'self-government by the Palestinians of the West Bank and Gaza in association with Jordan' as the only solution for a 'durable, just and lasting peace' (Reagan Peace Plan). The Soviet Union, on the other hand, insists that 'the Israeli occupation of all Arab territories captured in 1967 must be ended . . . rights of the Arab people of Palestine must be secured, up to and including the establishment of their own state', and Israel's security and sovereignty ensured (Brezhnev Peace Plan, 1981 and 1982). The EEC regard the ambiguity of resolutions 242 and 338 as foliage enough to cover their lack of decisiveness regarding Israeli security and Palestinian national self-determination. And Jordan, in pursuit of its heady wishes of recovering greater Jordan has put forward the creation of a United Arab Kingdom federation that is meant to incorporate the West Bank and Gaza, and headed by the King of Jordan, thus bringing the Palestinian nation under its control.

Sweden's position is not dissimilar from that of the Israeli Hadash (Communist) Party, which also recommends the establishment of a Palestinian state in the West Bank (including East Jerusalem) and the Gaza Strip as the only available means to a just peace. But as it stands, the PLO cannot recognize Israel (even in pre-1967 borders) if it does not obtain guarantees of negotiations on the basis of Palestinian self-determination (even in the West Bank and Gaza) by all the interested parties, including Israel. And Israel will not recognize the PLO or the political demands of the Palestinian nation so long as it can continue to pursue its Zionist expansionist and irreconciliatory policies unhindered in all of Palestine, including Gaza and the West Bank. So long as this unbalanced status quo prevails, however, the Palestinians will be compelled to use force as the only fruitful avenue for realizing their just and right demands. Sadly though, neither diplomacy nor armed struggle have so far produced results, and even Palme's humanitarian policies and good intentions have failed to grasp the grotesque imbalance of the proposals that they themselves also adhered to. For you need a Palestine; you need the recognition of the injustices committed against the Palestinians; and you need an understanding and rejection of Zionism before you can have peace. And Palestine you cannot have if Israel does not relinquish her; Palestine you cannot have if the USA denies her national identity and leadership, and if the USA continues to need sub-imperialist Israel to fulfil its reactionary and global intentions.[23]

But it is a moral victory for the Palestinians that the PLO has established an information office in Stockholm since 1975, and that the leader of a Western country (Olof Palme) should recognize their plight and their right to a homeland. It is a moral victory that an

international man of peace should condemn Israel's aggressive policies
against its internal and external neighbours. But in concrete terms,
even if the proposals put forward by Palme were the only avenues for
achieving a just and lasting peace, the fact that they are unrealizable (in
the forseeable future) makes them utopian. And if utopian, no matter
how sound and objective, then they must be irrelevant; that is, until the
conditions for their realization are in evidence.

So far as the other Middle East conflict is concerned, however, Olof
Palme's involvement was timely and important. It was an expression of
his international character and an honour for Sweden that Olof Palme,
while out of office, should be chosen as a mediator, on behalf of the
UN Secretary General, between parties of this century's most senseless
bloody conflict. As a man of peace he was respected and received by
both the Iraqis and the Iranians. Iran's ayatollahs had not forgotten
Olof Palme's voice greeting the downfall of the Shah in 1979, while the
rest of the Western world had grappled ways and means of keeping his
throne intact. Although this latest Middle East conflict has acquired
dimensions of complexity and sophistication similar to those of the
Palestinian–Israeli problem, it lacks one fundamental aspect of the
latter: neither side can rightly claim a moral virtue in its deeds. Here
any claim to morality and righteousness, be it Iraq's Ba'athist Arabism
or Iran's Islamic nationalism, is void and amounts to no more than a
tool in the hands of the rulers for justifying warmongering, senseless
aggression, and destruction, as means of monopolizing and ensuring
the retention of internal political power.

Palme's mission, which lasted from November 1980 until February
1981, was the first mediation effort of any external source, coming
only two months after the official declaration of war by Iraq, on 20
September 1980. While the rest of the world sat silently by, only
concerned with the continued passage of oil through the Straits of
Hormuz, the security of the Gulf markets for their investments and
products, and the opportunities for re-arming the two warring parties,
Olof Palme initiated the first international concerns for the resolution
of this senseless conflict. It is tragic that almost in one stroke all the
major powers (USA, Soviet Union, and the EEC) declared their
neutrality in this conflict, thus expressing their lack of concern for the
losses of life and property of the innocent population of both states. It
is, moreover, ironic that amongst this sea of hypocrisy Palme's mission
should be condemned as 'premature and of only marginal significance'.[24]

Its 'prematurity' was surely because of its overwhelming desire for
peace, and its lack of significance due to the disregard of the major
powers. But in attempting to resolve conflicts, peacemakers must not
be concerned with the 'maturity' of a conflict, for death then becomes
the only arbiter, nor with the quantifiable scope of their peacemaking

role. The Palme mission, in its duration, did bring repeated cease-fires between the two parties, thus saving life and property, in addition to its more important role of making the two parties talk, be it indirectly. In fact one can make a case that its failure was based not on the grounds of the mission's prematurity and insignificance, but as being unsuccessful on account of the will of the major powers (regional and global) to keep alight the flames of a (limited) war in the Gulf. It is quite apparent that the continuation of this war has:

(i) caused the annihilation of both countries' internal democratic forces, and the suspension of democracy itself, under the pretext of national emergency;

(ii) destroyed the economic basis for allowing either country to become a regional superpower;

(iii) wasted an enormous amount of resources of each country;

(iv) accelerated the infrastructural disintegration of both states;

(v) caused the diversion of productive resources (labour, capital, and know-how) away from developmental programmes and towards wasteful war-material procurements;

(vi) enabled the arms manufacturers of many states, great and small, Third World and advanced, socialist or capitalist, to test their products and put them into destructive use at astronomical profits;

(vii) resulted in increased dependence of the two countries on external sources of basic and advanced goods and services: Iraq is in heavy financial debt to Western and Gulf countries, and Iran relies more than ever on the importation of foodstuffs and expensive medical care, on top of its increased dependence on imports of goods and spare parts for its flagging economy;

(viii) created the conditions for the long-term dependence of both parties on external powers (mainly Western) for economic recovery and development, military rearmament, and undoubtedly increased demands for security through the purchasing of sophisticated conventional and unconventional weapons of mass destruction;

(ix) meant the loss of at least a whole generation of the able-bodied, young, and committed people of both states;

(x) facilitated the increased high-profile presence of the superpowers in the region;

(xi) diverted attention from the struggle of the Palestinians for self-determination.

It is not the fault of Olof Palme or Swedish foreign policy that peace has not been achieved in the Middle East. In 1967 President Lyndon Johnson said, 'We seem at the edge of progress in achieving stability in the Middle East. . . . We look beyond the current conflict to a new era of greater stability which will permit all the peoples of the area to enjoy the fruits of lasting peace.'[25] Almost 20 years on, there is still no sign of such progress. What ought to be realized is that while the folly of conflicts in the Third World dates back to colonial times, the burden of conflict resolution and international compassion has befallen the neutralist states of Western Europe. This certainly is the case as far as the current two major Middle East conflicts are concerned. The crisis of Palestine today is regarded as having its roots in the British Mandate period prior to 1947. As Yasser Arafat put it: 'All the former British colonies have become independent states, independent peoples, except the Palestinians. We were under a British mandate, but we did not become independent. This is the historical perspective of the Palestinian refugees.'[26]

Similarly, the Iran–Iraq conflict has its historical origins in the post-Ottoman era, when Britain took control of the Arab part of the Persian Gulf and subsequently established Iraq's independence and her geographical boundaries, including the contentious control of the Shatt-al-Arab waterway. So while Britain and other colonizers distance themselves from their historical short-sightedness and mismanagement, and the USA strives to implant its own sense of reality on to the Third World states, with tragic consequences, it is left to the conscientious countries of the West to promote a real sense of peace and stability.

We have said before that Sweden's economy is closely integrated into the capitalist world economy: it is dependent on the West and the Third World as markets and as providers of essential raw materials, consumer and capital goods, and, since the accelerated internationalization of capital, as producers of semi-manufactured goods essential to the nations's industries, assembled in distant lands under the control and auspices of Swedish transnational conglomerates. We have also shown that, as far as basic economic interests are concerned, Sweden's policies cannot be expected to differ drastically from those of other capitalist countries. This is certainly true of the Middle East as well as other regions of the Third World. And yet Swedish governments have often espoused views and positions favouring the plight of Third World nations. In so far as Olof Palme has been instrumental in shaping Sweden's foreign policy in the Middle East and elsewhere, Swedish Social Democracy and the country's strongly pro-UN multilateralist ideology helped him maintain the indigenous base for continuing his prolific international reformist beliefs and posture. And so long as Swedish capital does not 'need' its 'executive arm' to pursue its interests internationally, the Swedish state can afford to be a peacemaker.

Furthermore, the increasingly transnational Swedish capital may actually promote the Social Democrats' beliefs of international political and economic reformism as the best possible means of promoting its capitalist interests. It is not hard to find reasons for Sweden's wishing to resolve the Middle East's conflicts peacefully and amicably. A stable Middle East would expand business opportunities for Swedish firms; it would reduce the interfering potential of outside forces (including the superpowers), and it would eliminate the chances of war spreading from the Middle East to Europe and Scandinavia, thus reducing the threats to Sweden's national security and its international neutrality. But a Middle East peace as envisaged by Olof Palme would also have redressed, at least partially, the injustices suffered by the Palestinian people for decades. Again, peace between Iran and Iraq, as expected by Olof Palme, would not only have saved the two countries' economies and their peoples, it may have also accelerated the internal processes that would have overthrown the oppressions of Ba'athism and Islamic fundamentalism and reaction plaguing the two countries.

It is cruel deception and arrogance to belittle Olof Palme's international role in such words as 'nowadays, far from providing a clear lead to the world, the voice of Sweden is still and small even in its own territorial waters'.[27] Only wise men will realize that with his death 'a world thirsty for peace and justice has become poorer.'[28] It would be in the spirit of Palme's vision to realize his utopia of the Middle East; it would be in his honour to make it just, compassionate, and lasting.

Notes

1. V.I. Lenin, *Imperialism, The Highest Stage of Capitalism*, (Moscow, 1968), p. 9.
2. Ibid., pp. 97–8.
3. W.W. Rostow, *The Stages of Economic Growth: A Non-Communist Manifesto*, (Cambridge, 1962), p. 38.
4. Immanuel Wallerstein, *The Capitalist World Economy*, (Cambridge, 1979), p. 84.
5. Jaime Wheelock, *El gran desafío*, (Nicaragua, 1983), cited in Richard Harris, 'The Revolutionary Process in Nicaragua', *Latin American Perspectives*, issue 45, Spring 1985. Therefore in essence, the revolutionary (socialist) ideology of the state becomes the mainstay and the principal protectorate of private capital and capitalist relations of production.
6. For instance, its heavy dependence on foreign trade, and its reliance on the importation of raw materials, industrial and semi-manufactured goods, and a small population.
7. From the dependency perspectives and the WST, Sweden would be a neo-colonial state in so far as it is a member of the capitalist North responsible for the control and domination of world markets, which consequently lead to the phenomena of economic, social, political, and cultural dependence of the periphery on the former, even through the 'normal' functionings and mechanisms of the market (international, national, and regional).
8. SOU, *Sweden's Security Policy: Entering the 90s*, (Stockholm, 1985, 23), p. 8.
9. Ibid., p. 62.
10. SOU, (Stockholm, 1983, 17).
11. Sweden's direct foreign investment per capita stood at $457 in 1980, compared with $423, $263, and $114 for the USA, the Federal Republic of Germany, and Japan respectively.
12. Their totals were as follows: USA, $680,135 million (46.7%); Japan, $202,178

million (13.9%); UK, $167,248 million (11.5%); FRG, $136,481 (9.4%); France, $74,301 million (5.1%); the Netherlands, $52,302 million (3.5%); and Italy, $36,980 million (2.6%). Source: UNESCO, *Transnational Corporation in World Development; A Re-examination*, (New York: UN, 1978), p. 212.

13. Ibid.

14. SOU, (Stockholm, 1982; 27).

15. Ibid.

16. 'Five years ago the company [ASEA] depended on the miniscule Swedish market for half its sales. Now it does two-thirds of its business abroad, and by the year 2000 [it] wants to push that share to as much as 90%.' *Fortune International*, 16 September 1985, p. 42.

17. Sverker Astrom, *Sweden's Policy of Neutrality*, (Stockholm: The Swedish Institute, 1983), p. 8. Note also the message of the following quotation from the same high-ranking Swedish diplomatic source: 'If we wish to retain the confidence of other countries in our neutrality, we must avoid all engagements that reduce our freedom of action on the international scene and alter our "profile".' Ibid., p. 10.

18. '. . . the Swedish Government has generally applied the principle of refusing all licences for arms exports to countries involved in acute international conflicts and civil wars, or where the international or internal situation is such that disturbances or war can be feared'. Prime Minister Erlander addressing the Riksdag (Parliament) in 1956. See *SIPRI*, 1971, pp. 328–46. However, the export restrictions do not apply to Swedish weapons manufactured under licence abroad.

19. Ibid., p. 330. It is important to note, however, that during the non-Social Democratic Swedish government of the 1976–82 period a tendency of overt arms exports and licensed production rights to Third World countries was more urgently promoted. For some details, see *SIPRI*, 1980.

20. *Middle East Economic Digest*, various issues. Sweden's imports from Iran dropped from a high of nearly 130 billion kronor in 1978 to as little as 30 million kronor by 1981.

21. Reply in the Riksdag by Minister of Foreign Affairs, Mr Lennart Bodstrom, to an interpellation of Mr Hans Goran Frank concerning the Middle East, 3 December 1982.

22. Sweden's representative at the UN (Mr Ullston) addressing the General Assembly (36th Session, 26 September 1981).

23. See my article in the March 1987 issue of the *Scandinavian Journal of Development Alternatives* for an analysis of Israel's existence and its arms industry, and its global role and importance for US foreign policy.

24. John Duke Anthony, 'Regional and Worldwide Implications of the Gulf War', in M.S. El Ezhary, ed., *The Iran–Iraq War*, (Beckenham, Kent, 1984), p. 122.

25. Quoted in the *Daily Telegraph* (London), 9 June 1967.

26. Quoted in a *Time* magazine interview, 8 February 1982.

27. Andrew Brown, 'A Surprising Democrat', *The Spectator*, 8 March 1987.

28. Willy Brandt quoted in *Newsweek* magazine, 10 March 1986.

SECTION EIGHT

On Strategies for Development

22

North–South Dialogue:
Towards a Meaningful Agenda

A.M. BABU

The main thrust of this chapter is the substance of a presentation to the Dag Hammarskjold Seminar on 'The State and the Crisis in Africa: In Search of a Second Liberation' held in September 1986 in Uppsala, Sweden. It is therefore a happy coincidence that it is included in this volume to commemorate the late Olof Palme, who devoted most of his time as leader of his party, in and out of government, to seeking a lasting solution to the problem of poverty in the Third World. He and other leaders of Western social democratic parties, as well as some progressive leaders in the Third World, saw the main causes of the current international economic crisis as emanating from the unjust trade relations between North and South. They thus devoted most of their struggle towards trying to redress the ever growing imbalances that characterize this relationship.

Sweden, under his leadership for most of the post-Second World War era, and the other Scandinavian countries, were the only Western nations to fulfil the UN recommendations for industrialized countries to give 0.7 per cent of their GDP towards aiding developing countries. The Swedish International Development Agency is probably the most active national aid agency in the world and the best known outside the UN agencies. This agency was becoming increasingly influenced by the new approach, shared by Olof Palme himself in the last years of his life, that the best form of aid was of the kind that went into developing structures that would ensure genuine and lasting self-reliance.

I have no doubt that if Olof Palme were alive today he would agree with at least 90 per cent of the views I have expressed in this chapter, and it is for this reason that I feel honoured to be asked to contribute to this collection in the memory of this great man of the people.

Almost the entire continent of Africa is not yet liberated in the real sense of the word. Nowhere was the colonial state eliminated after independence. Nor was the colonial system changed to serve local needs. The traditionally repressive apparatus of the colonial state, far from being dismantled, has been further strengthened, and more repressive measures, in the production and extraction of wealth have led to a massive outflow of capital from Africa. The colonial system has destroyed the old society and hampered the evolution of a new civil society essential for self-sustaining development in a modern nation-state. It has accentuated our lop-sided development, which has resulted in externally integrated economies orientated to the outside world and a lack of development of local infrastructure. The economic mess that was inevitable in this situation has necessitated resort to coercive measures by the state to ensure temporary stability, a state of affairs that has benefited imperialism enormously at the expense of the African people. The extent of this massive exploitation has been starkly revealed by the spectacle of millions of people literally starving to death.

The need for a progressive evaluation of the situation in search of a progressive solution has never been more urgent. We must therefore devise our own liberation theory based on our own concrete experience with the objective of constructing a truly liberated Africa, a truly self-reliant economy; one which, in addition to being self-sustaining is also and primarily one which serves the interests and welfare of the majority of the people. This is the purpose of this chapter. It will approach the topic by first showing that in order to understand the reality of the condition of backwardness and poverty and to seek its genuine and workable solution, we must reject the academism of development studies which, needless to emphasize, have created more confusion and hardly any solution. Having been conceived and implemented primarily for the political ends of the cold war, and by deliberately overlooking or misunderstanding the real nature of the problem, the academism of development has in fact become part of the problem and not part of the solution. In other words we must first liberate ourselves from what might be called 'academic imperialism'—the academism of the West, headed by US academic institutions, and, to a lesser extent, but quite dominant in Africa, the academism of Britain and France.

The chapter will then attempt to introduce a clearer definition of the problem, define its nature and its causes, and propose the way to tackle it, theoretically and practically. It will then show the nature of the colonial and neo-colonial mode of production, and the forces and other obstacles that hamper development.

We will discuss the structures of these economies and their international relations, with specific reference to their *foreign* trade, aid, debt, and investments. We shall look into the doctrine of comparative advantage, its relevance or otherwise to the colonial and neo-colonial conditions, and at who benefits from the advantages. We shall examine the comparative roles of the market economies on the one hand, and the planned and proportionate development of national economies on the other, outlining in the process the essential elements or laws that respectively influence the two systems. We shall attempt to show why the planned and proportionate development strategy is necessary and more relevant at this historical juncture; and how a planned economy can and must to a certain extent utilize the law of value and market mechanisms.

This will be followed by a study of democracy as a precondition for development: the nature of the state as liberator and leading defender of democracy; as the advanced contingent of the oppressed; and its role as 'entrepreneur'. The chapter will also try to identify the necessary order of priorities and the rationale behind it; and finally it will discuss the strategy and tactics of liberating the economy from the status quo and on to a self-sustaining independent national economy.

The Need for Academic Liberation

'Development studies' evolved after the Second World War as part of the discipline of economics. It was conceived, designed, and directed by the West, at the height of the cold war, to control and subvert the economies of the new emerging countries in Africa, Asia, and Latin America. It was intended to counter the development experiences in the socialist countries, the ideological rival of the West, who were viewed as posing a serious challenge to the position of the West in the world balance of forces. On the ideological front development studies were intended to counter the principles of 'planned and proportionate development of national economy', which were then becoming popular in the industrialized economies of the West when left-wing parties were winning political power throughout Europe. It was also anti-Communist, intended to keep the new emerging countries out of the 'Soviet orbit' by means of economic and eventually political domination. Rostow himself, the doyen of development studies, made no bones about his intentions. He subtitled his *Stages of growth* as *An Anti-Communist Manifesto*.

Experience has shown the extent of this crusade and the damage it has wrought. In the 40 years of the crusade's operation, the Third World (excluding the OPEC countries) has borne the brunt of all the crises of capitalism that have occurred without any benefits from its booms. The monetary disasters of the era, exclusively the making of the West and its 'gnomes of Zurich', have evolved into the monster known as the debt crisis, the entire burden of which is heaped on the Third World.

Failure to make a distinction between the academism of the oppressor and that of the oppressed had led to a neglect of evolving a distinctly independent way of enquiry, investigation, and even analysis to reflect the reality of these developing economies. Our local scholars have to a large extent resorted to academic tailism which has prevented them from using their brains and thinking for themselves in order to understand the social and economic trends in their own countries; they parrot the words, concepts, and even thoughts of others, and copy foreign experiences without analysis. This is the heritage of academic imperialism.

In attempts at 'authenticity', many countries have introduced a number of 'isms' without any basis in theory and no grounds in practice. They have turned their countries into huge human laboratories with their people as guinea pigs on whom to experiment with any kind of social, economic, or political theories, most of which make no sense in the first place. The result of this reckless disrespect for the people is the current crisis of 'unmanageable poverty', especially in Africa where the majority of the people suffer the indignity and pain of malnutrition and starvation on a permanent basis. By the turn of the century Africa will have 800 million people to feed, and yet we are not only unable to feed the existing 400 million, but we have not even prepared ourselves to build the economic basis necessary for a minimum survival of the expanding population. As a result natural disasters that afflict us daily and hourly are virtually uncontainable and the human toll is always unbearably high because we have neither the means to control our environment nor the capacity to manage disasters.

This is a great victory for our traditional exploiters and a defeat of harrowing magnitude for Africa. For the last 40 years our scholars and theoreticians have mostly been writing books about books, which are also about books; advancing theories which were constructed purely from the imagination of the writers using information whose rationality is based on experiences such as 'modernization' and 'dependency', whose validity has not been tested anywhere in practice, and which are not taken seriously by the people about whom the theories are advanced. From Latin America to Africa, development scholars have been busy advancing themselves as authorities and winning universal acclaim, but in neither of the continents has any meaningful development taken place. The people's quality of life has continued to deteriorate absolutely to the point of catastrophe.

The academism of development studies has thus proven to be not only unworkable, but a disastrous failure for Africa. And so has its adjunct, the so-called theory of 'rural development'. Africa is paying the price of the cold war with the starving millions of her sons and daughters, while a handful of the proponents of 'development' are either enriching themselves or travelling the world advancing their thoughts.

We must reject all this is if we are seriously seeking a 'second liberation'. We must begin from the beginning, basing our investigation and analysis on the concrete experience of our people; learning from it, analysing and synthesizing it, and cautiously applying it where conditions are ripe. We must also learn from other experiences, especially from agrarian socialist countries like China and North Korea, where people are making progress by leaps and bounds without the assistance of the academism of development.

The Definition of the Problem

We must define 'development' as a process from necessity to freedom, in Hegelian terminology. Africa is closest to the realm of necessity, while the Soviet Union, the USA, Japan, and other industrial economies are comparatively furthest. In the advanced countries the quality of life is higher because they live in better conditions of housing, eat more nourishing foods, are better clad, have reasonable health facilities, education, training, and so on. They live longer with reasonable security from sudden natural disasters and more or less happy for that. Their struggle is to improve this situation either by a fairer distribution of the wealth created by their toil or by creating conditions for greater creation and enjoyment of wealth. This 'developed' condition is brought about by a better understanding of the world around us through science, leading to a greater competence to utilize our environment both to advance the creation and enjoyment of wealth and to minimize natural hazards by means of technology.

The more we advance the greater the pace towards 'freedom'; that is to say, freedom from natural fetters. This freedom is not achieved by building skyscrapers and new cities or owning luxury cars, but initially by damming rivers, controlling floods, digging canals for irrigation, generating electricity, building machine-tools and small-scale iron and steel industries, water-pumping machines, textile, engineering, and construction plants, and so on. These are the factors that will ensure our gradual control over the environment and which will create the basis for future technological innovation and development, and acquisition of skills. They will also contribute towards educating the population and liberating them from the backwardness of the rural life to which 90 per cent of our populations are subjected. This development cannot be achieved by indirect routes, such as developing tourism in order to gain foreign exchange with which to buy imported goods, but rather by means of a frontal attack of investing directly in productive enterprises, minimizing our dependence on external markets, and consciously building up the home market, as will be discussed below.

Colonial and Neo-colonial Economies

The entire African continent was annexed to the European capitalist economy by means of colonialism, and the countries have evolved in a specific historically determined way, with a definite mode of production which serves external interests and the industrial and consumption needs of the metropolitan countries. The penetration of external capital and the subordination of African products to those foreign markets siphon off most of the economic surpluses leaving little for internal accumulation, a precondition for any internally integrated development. To compensate for this massive extraction of surpluses (current estimate: $10 million per hour from all Third World states), foreign countries give aid and credits in infinitesimally small amounts in proportion to what is taken out, at the same time creating conditions for further extraction though servicing their debts. Currently, most African countries are paying more than 60 per cent of their foreign exchange earnings in servicing such debts.

The resultant mode of production does not conform to any other mode, capitalist or feudal; it is an appendage economy which has to be studied as such, without complicating it by introducing alien elements. Neo-colonialism is colonialism's ideological and economic offshoot, necessary for the Western cold war strategy of the 1950s and which has now been transformed into a permanent feature of stagnant economies and the status quo. Our countries have become consumers without internal accumulation. The social classes that have evolved with this mode must also be studied as a unique phenomenon; most of them gravitate externally and do not contribute towards the formation of the civil society as we know it in more integrated economies.

The post-war economic strategy of the West was aimed at making good of what was left after the massive devastation of the war, meanwhile evolving a military strategy against the then rapidly emerging Soviet Union, in order to consolidate the Western hold on Europe and on the new emerging countries of Asia and Africa. All 'international' institutions that were set up—from the Bretton Woods Agreement of 1944 which established the World Bank and the IMF, to the Marshall Plan and the OECD, as well as the European Coal and

Steel Community, and later the EEC and GATT—all were designed to facilitate the achievement of Western domination in these areas, with NATO as the military counterpart of this strategy.

West Germany in Europe and Japan in Asia were to be the anti-Communist bastions in their respective areas and were to be given every opportunity to develop as rapidly as possible. The former, having been deprived of its eastern rural part (after the creation of East Germany), had to be developed at any price, largely at the expense of France and Italy, but mostly at that of the neo-colonies. The colonial structure of exploitation on which Europe was based had to be dismantled, partly because of the colonial revolts of the 1950s and 1960s, but also to allow the USA, as the new Western dominant power, to penetrate into the economies of ex-colonies hitherto highly protected as sources of raw materials and markets.

In East Asia, Japan, now deprived of China as her rural base, was to be developed as the dominant economic power in the area and to that end vast financial and technological resources, until then enjoyed only by the USA, were put at Japan's disposal, including access to the rich US market. Henceforth, the three pillars of the Western international orders were the USA, Europe, and Japan—the 'trilateral strategy', as it later came to be called.

Our academism of development studies wants us to develop within this system by strengthening the institutions in favour of the Third World and by improving trade relations. This is the theme of UNCTAD, of the New International Economic Order, of the Lagos Plan of Action, of the various UN Economic Decades. But any careful investigation can show from past experience that trade and aid relations can never be a viable instrument for economic development if one side is in a position of strength and the other in one of weakness, as is the case now with neo-colonies. These relations are governed by the law of uneven development in which the prosperity of the stronger depends on the impoverishment of the weaker; this law moreover is independent of the human will. This situation leads to external borrowing if only to maintain social welfare and reduce internal social tension. This in turn leads to the notorious debt trap that all of us are currently suffering from, which threatens not only our solvency but also our sovereignty as nations. These economies have developed in the process a social stratum which benefits directly from the chaos that ensues. Their surplus, if not sent abroad, is either invested unproductively, as in building their own mansions, or spent in conspicuous consumption in the midst of universal poverty. Hardly any investment goes to industry or to modernizing agriculture.

The rural stagnation resulting from this mode has led to the theories of rural development which assume that there is a dichotomy between urban and rural economy in which the former is exploiting the latter. Hence the emphasis on rural development. This is a false assumption and we are paying dearly for it. First of all, it is impossible to isolate a part from the whole without creating imbalances; second, you cannot develop one independently of the other without creating serious new unevenness and dislocations. In spite of the many rural development 'strategies', the rural areas have remained stagnant, with youths in their millions flocking to towns and cities in search of jobs. The urban centres in turn are starved because the rural areas are not producing enough to supply them. Most African countries, which before the introduction of 'rural development' used to be food-surplus producing countries, are now importing food, aggravating their balance-of-payments problems and the debt crisis.

Import-substitution industrialization, which worked very well in the early settler colonies in the USA, Australasia, South Africa, Zimbabwe, and Algeria (and Kenya to a certain extent), because they were sustained by growing internal demand, either from the influx of new settlers with new consumption habits or as a result of expanding economies and higher incomes, has not worked in most African neo-colonies whose home demand is shrinking instead of expanding. Unemployment continues to rise as the rural influx aggravates the already diminishing employment opportunties in the cities resulting from industrial decline.

All this is well known to the people in their day-to-day experiences, but has either been ignored or given low priority by our development theorists for reasons that are equally well known. Some, for cold war reasons, deliberately misguided policy-makers by encouraging their prejudices that had led them to believe that development could take place without first changing the very structure of our economies as a necessary precondition. Others, for economic reasons of exploitation, did not want the structure to be changed, only to be 'adjusted', in order to conform to the needs of external interests. And yet others, for purely sentimental reasons which tended to idealize the peasantry as if they were destined to live in the same way for all time, insisted on preserving the old forms on the grounds that failure to do so would destroy the peasantry, their way of life, and old traditions.

However, history has shown us that development must accompany steady elimination of peasant production. In the epoch of rapid capitalist development, mostly in the eighteenth and nineteenth centuries, at a time when capitalism was still a progressive force replacing feudalism and its stagnation, the development of the productive forces was necessarily accompanied by massive destruction of peasant production and the destruction of peasant life. The need for the accumulation of capital also set the stage for the African slave trade and later colonialism, with all their disruption and indeed destruction of the village economy. In *Capital*, Marx remarked that, 'Accumulation for accumulation's sake: by this formula classical economy expressed the historical mission of the bourgeoisie, and did not for a single instant deceive itself over the birth-throes of wealth. But what avails lamentation in the face of historical necessity?'

Socialists, on the other hand, sought to achieve this historical necessity of accumulation by more humane means. One was by eliminating peasant production by the introduction of co-operatives, collectives, and state farms. This facilitated the introduction of technology in agriculture, of large-scale production, and high yield. In other words, whatever the social system, the evidence of history is that if there is no accumulation there is no advancement in agriculture and industry; and accumulation is hampered by the colonial structure of our economies, with its archaic and backward relations and forces of production, both of which perpetuate the existence of old and backward forms.

Comparative Roles of Market and Planned Economies

The development of capitalism and market economies, as is well known, depended on the subjugation of the 'weakest', either nationally or internationally, and the destruction of the latter's economy and way of life. Internationally, Japan was the only non-European country to escape direct domination by Europe, and this was because it started its accumulation of capital and developed its productive forces at about the same time as Europe and when the latter's bourgeoisie was still weak and could not, either physically or economically, bar its entry into the fray.

Once the bourgeoisie, US, European, and Japanese, was consolidated, the road to independent capitalist development in the rest of the world was effectively blocked. Only appendage capitalism was possible; that is to say, only extensions of the US, European, or Japanese economies—extensions or *their* capitalism to our countries. It is instructive to note that since the end of the First World War not a single country in the so-called Third World, outside the socialist camp, has developed an independent, capitalist, national economy. The so-called newly industrializing countries, which are typical appendage economies, cannot claim to be independent capitalist economies. They are national only in name; the real powers behind them are Japanese, US, and European capital, the multinational corporations, and their captive markets the world over where they control not only sales but also production, fixing prices not only of their products but also of the raw materials of the developing countries.

In other words, the Third World has remained as the rural base, or appendages, of the OECD countries and their Japanese and US partners. The only countries that have escaped this pernicious subordination are the socialist countries such as China and North Korea, which have adopted the policy of planned and proportionate development of their national economies; and they have been developing by leaps and bounds. Which is another way of saying that it is no longer possible to develop a viable national economy exclusively via the mechanism of the market economy. That meaningful change must begin with the changing of the entire structure of the economy, its basis and orientation.

If the advanced market economies achieved their highest development by means of plundering the weak, especially the colonies, African countries have no colonies to exploit or plunder, although some African leaders collaborate with external forces to exploit and plunder their own people. The question then arises: How do you accelerate the process of accumulation without exploitation? How do you accelerate the process of rapid development of the productive forces without sacrificing the provision of welfare? What is the role of the state?

The first important precondition for accumulation in these circumstances is that the people must rely on their own diligent labour, on frugality, and on constantly investing in the creation of new wealth by means of extended reproduction. This is achieved by encouraging national unity, and collaboration of classes, guided by the dialectical approach and by observing the law of unity and struggle of opposites. It is wrong to see only contradictions and not to see the unity of the national economy; it is equally wrong to see only the struggle, and not see the collaboration of opposites. This methodology, unlike that of development theorists, recognizes first of all that balance and imbalance are the two sides of a contradiction within which imbalance is absolute and balance is relative. Hence the necessity to use balance and imbalance among the productive forces, the production relations, and the superstructure as a guideline for researching the economic problems of development.

The allocation of scarce resources between alternative and competing ends must be determined by systematic planning in order to establish a proper ratio between accumulation and consumption, and to achieve a balance between production and needs. Whereas in a market economy production is regulated by the law of value, by competition, by demand and supply, and by the maximization of profit, in a planned economy production is regulated by the law of planned and proportionate development. However, a planned economy can and indeed must, in the early stages of development, utilize the law of value for the purpose of regulating exchange, but its use must be put under strict control. In this gigantic task, the state must play a leading role, especially in view of the fact that our private entrepreneurs are either very weak or externally dependent, or both. This does not mean, however, that they have no role to play; far from it.

Whatever our ideological orientation, whether capitalist, socialist, or non-aligned, the basic prerequisites for development are the same, namely the provision of food, clothing, and shelter. To the market-orientated economies, the provision of these basics can be achieved indirectly by obeying the law of supply and demand, by making full use of the principle of comparative advantage; in short, by observing the law of surplus value. To a planned economy, on the other hand, the provision of these basics is the essential first step towards achieving the welfare of the whole society through continuous expansion and perfection of production on the basis of higher technique. And the latter can be attained only by observing the law of balanced, proportionate development of the productive forces.

For a non-aligned country which is hovering between a full-blooded market economy and a socialist planned economy, experience of both systems can be instructive if utilized in a constructive way and with the objective of development rather than mere emulation. Socialists realize that the material conditions for the evolution to socialism have matured within the womb of capitalism, both constituting the evolving human experience in development. The non-aligned must learn from the negative as well as positive experiences of both and from the past as well as existing social formations. But to put such experience to productive use, it must be attuned to the concrete conditions of each country, and it must be relevant to the needs and understanding of the vast majority of the people in the country concerned.

As the economic structure in all African countries is colonial, and continues to divert most of the surplus to the metropolitan countries, the first priority in the new development strategy is to change this structure so that most of the surplus remains in the country and is invested productively for extended reproduction. Naturally it will mean a change from production exclusively for export; it will mean diverting our resources away from export branches and concentrating more on food production, the textile industry, and the construction and engineering industries as a first step towards internally integrated development. This important shift will require a fairly substantial investment programme, in order first to re-activate the existing productive inventory without starving unproductive but essential social consumption and welfare, and second to provide for the expansion and replacement of the above inventory and the introduction of new plants.

The intervention of the state is necessary for this purpose as the policy will entail transferring vast sums and resources from agriculture to industry.

In African countries where land is almost unlimited and under-utilized, the state must create conditions for encouraging the peasants to expand their production thereby expanding both the tax base and the home market. The major constraint in peasant expansion is their exposure to the world market with its systematic diminishing return. Price incentive as a means of expanding rural production is possible only if the state is able to stabilize the price to the final consumer, which is impossible for export commodities. The only alternative, therefore, is to produce for the home market: food, cotton, oil seeds, and the various industrial raw materials, which will ensure steady income to the peasants. Unlike the development of feudalism and capitalism, which achieved their primitive accumulation by exploiting the peasantry, a progressive and planned economy can achieve its accumulation by extending peasant production.

This in turn will entail development of industries as consumers of rural products; and, indeed, the greater the buying power of the peasantry the faster industry develops. Labour-intensive industries such as textiles, the dairy and leather industries, and food-processing, on the one hand, and housing and construction on the other, will act both as consumers and suppliers of the rural areas. But, above all, such industries will create employment opportunities for hundreds of thousands of school-leavers as well as introduce them to the new world of skills and technology. There is no room here to think in terms of a rural–urban dichotomy, or of 'rural development'; the two sectors develop as a single organism.

One of the most attractive aspects of Ujamaa in Tanzania, but that was damaged and lost probably for ever by the adventurism and vulgar practicalism of the leaders in the 1970s, was that, in addition to its obvious economic potential, it could have been politically useful to the urban workers. The moving of peasants to unified and organized units could have led to a dynamic rural–urban complementarity and invalidated the stale outlook of 'rural development' which perpetuates rather than eliminates the peasant's notorious social backwardness and retards development.

In other words, whereas previous modes debased agriculture and destroyed rural life, a scientific and planned approach to development means transformation with rapid expansion of rural life, side by side with the expansion of urban life. A planned economy does not experiment with human life; it takes seriously society's awareness of its historic responsibility. In sustaining and expanding rural–urban complementarity, a planned economy can and must utilize the law of value to regulate the production and exchange of commodities of farm produce for industrial goods, between state-owned and privately owned enterprises, and so on.

Experience has shown that it is a serious error for the state to utilize only planned mechanisms and ignore other forms of exchange; however, to be productive the former must play a leading role and the latter a supportive role. Planning must concentrate on major products, leaving minor ones to private operation. As long as this approach is strictly adhered to the process of structural change will be fulfilled with minimum pain and sacrifice. But the superiority of planned economy over market economy can be realized only if the democratic rights of the people are not thereby undermined, and only if the state which intervenes does so as a liberating instrument rather than as the traditional state of repression.

Democracy and Development

As soon as a planned economy is suggested, the question of democracy is immediately raised, and rightly so. Experience has shown that in most countries that have adopted planned economy, democracy has always been the first victim. But this was not the inevitable outcome of planning; it was the result of serious misinterpretation of socialism and planning, a result of a megalomanic interpretation of socialism which ordained that correct socialist thinking could come from only one source. It introduced the party discipline of 'democratic centralism' into the running of the state, and deliberately confused the difference between voluntary discipline in the party and the coercive powers of the state over the entire population. In other words, whereas individuals join political parties of their own choice and thereby voluntarily abide by its rules or resign, a citizen finds himself or herself under the state, whether she or he likes it or not. However benevolent the state may be, whatever its ideology, socialist or otherwise, the people must have the right to reject it and to seek to change it; they must not be forced to observe the rule of democratic centralism and the wisdom of a handful of political party bureaucrats. That is tantamount to a dictatorship of the worst kind.

Planning must be carried out under the leadership and guidance of a 'planning commission', which must not come directly under the government, although it must work in conjunction with it. It must be a direct instrument of the people and must not be affected by a change of government.

A united front of two or three political parties, with a common strategy but different tactical alliances, is likely to be the future political direction of Africa, which is now already disillusioned by the military regimes and the one-party dictatorships which have reduced Africa to such a pathetic state. The parties will be free to pursue and propagate their separate policies, organize separately, with different alliances, and separately contest elections.

In societies where class antagonisms are acute, the state is used as an instrument of repression by one class over the other. In most African countries the material basis for this kind of acute contradiction has not yet developed fully. The fundamental classes, i.e. landlord versus serf, labour versus capital, are still in rudimentary form and their further development can be arrested wthout the antagonisms of the more developed class societies. Guided by the dialectical law of the unity and struggle of opposites, the state can function as the leading force for liberation, with emphasis on unity.

Its leading role is to initiate the establishment of democratic institutions; to initiate and consolidate by the constitution the 'supreme' institution of the planning commission so that no governing party can abolish or weaken its authority, or interfere with the appointment of its leading cadres, which can only be authorized by agreement of all parties within the united front, and must remain as independent as the judiciary.

Order of Priority and Economic Liberation

As noted above, in the planning of the economy it is essential to use balance and imbalance among the unproductive forces, the production relations, and the superstructure as a guideline for researching the economic problems of development. Proportional relations among various productive sectors can be balanced only by realizing that balance is only temporary and relative while imbalance is permanent and absolute. For instance, imbalance between the advanced and the backward in agriculture, in industry, and between regions, which we have inherited from colonialism's uneven development, can be corrected only through a process of continual changes from balance to imbalance and from imbalance to balance. This implies the breaking down of old production relations as new productive forces outlive them, and the establishment of new production relations at a higher level of development.

This is achieved by being constantly guided by 'experience, theory, practice': evaluate experience, locate it within the context of theory, put the result into practice. The resultant experience is then evaluated and the process repeated, *ad infinitum*. In other words, theory must be accompanied and tested by practice, and practice must enrich theory and be tested by it, otherwise theory without practice ends in a dream world of ultra-leftism, and practice without theory degenerates into vulgar practicalism with most damaging results. The achievement of balance and imbalance, with the evaluation of results through experience, theory, and practice, leads the way to proportional, unimpeded development. As the state takes a leading role in directing the economy, it is essential for it to first identify the leading productive sectors of the economy, give them their proper priority, and mobilize all the forces, state and private, towards achieving the objective. Industry and agriculture are naturally the only two leading productive sectors of the economy and must therefore be acorded top priorty.

To begin with, agricultural policy must play a dominant role in this order of priorities, because, first, 90 per cent of our populations derive their livelihood directly from agriculture, and, second, it is currently the most dominant productive sector. In order to link it with the other productive sector, i.e. industry, the two must be complementary and support each other in their development. Since the colonial structure of these two important sectors has led to our lop-sided and uneven development, in which agriculture is almost wholly for export and industry for import substitution, it is here that the structural change must begin.

If the state is to fulfil its leading role in initiating economic development it must organize the two sectors on the basis of planned and proportional development, in which agriculture is almost wholly for export and industry for import substitution; it is here that the structural change must begin. At the same time it is necessary to observe the principle of balance, imbalance, and proportional relations with the other major sectors of the economy. The *key links* in sector and inter- and intra-sectoral relations must be constantly identified and recognized in: (i) agriculture and industry; (ii) the subsectors within agriculture; (iii) the subsectors within industry; (iv) production and transport; (v) material production and social welfare; (vi) consumption and accumulation; (vii) population growth and output; and (viii) relations between and within various regions of the country.

The relations within agriculture, within industry, and that between agriculture and industry are the three most important relations in the entire national economy and must be given top priority as well as handled with utmost care, with great discipline, and competence. This is because, of all the economic links, i.e. production, exchange, distribution, and consumption, the determining link is *production*.

In the course of maintaining the above relations, imbalances continually present themselves since objective conditions are highly changeable. But by continually recording experience, by investigating and analysing it, and by working closely with the people, planners gradually identify the law of planned development and with experience can plan the national economy more accurately. The objective is to master the overall balance, that is, balance in agriculture, in industry, and balance between agriculture and industry.

The principle that guides overall balance is the recognition of the leading role of industry, while agriculture remains the foundation of the national economy. Industry must produce the means of livelihood as well as the means of production in manufacturing and agriculture. Thus the order of development in a backward economy will be as follows: agriculture, light industry, heavy industry.

To achieve maximum results in as short a time as possible, the state must exercise vigilance by avoiding waste. It must economize in manpower, materials, and funds: since manpower is live labour, material is embodied labour; and funds is live labour and embodied labour manifested in currency circulation. Frugality means, in other words, economizing labour-time. Every waste in labour-time takes it toll. In advanced capitalist countries where labour-time is wasted in chronic unemployment, the penalty is manifested in economic and monetary crises. These economies do not collapse, because developing countries nourish and sustain them throughout their crises while enduring absolute poverty themselves, up to and including starvation on a massive scale.

Neo-colonial relations lead to the exploitation and plunder of developing countries through cheap labour, the plunder of natural resources, and through money-lending at usurious interest rates which has resulted in the debt crisis of the poor countries, all at the expense of the latter's economic development.

It is not the intention or the will of the people directly concerned with it that has hampered development. Most of these people are well meaning and devoted to their cause. The real obstacle is the structure within which they seek to affect development. This political and economic structure is not for development, but for plunder and exploitation, and it obeys its own laws. So first the structure must be changed. This is a political decision and not economic, and therefore theories of development are not helpful in this regard.

If the basic structure changes, then the entire superstructure and all its assumptions which necessarily evolved from within the old structure must also be scraped off and begun again on the basis and premise of the new structure. This is the first point that has been stressed in this chapter.

The second point is that development is not independent of what is taking place in the rest of the world. It must be tackled within the context of imperialism, which caused and continues to cause underdevelopment: the cold war and its objectives, and the evolution of the balance of forces arising directly from this international juxtaposition.

The third point is that in the effort to change the structure in the given conditions, the state must play a leading role, not only in the direction of the economy, but also in safeguarding democracy and championing liberation, which are the necessary conditions under which development can take place. To ensure this the state must be under the control of the oppressed people through their political organizations operating within a united front. This is to safeguard against the predatory military and one-party dictatorships on the one hand, and against the free-for-all but negating and disruptive class- or ethnic-based multiparty system of the 'Westminster model'.

The fourth point is that although the state must play a leading role, there is a necessity to establish an independent institution that will ensure people's democratic control over their economic life, and to safeguard it from the periodic changes in government and political tactics of parties. This institution is the proposed 'planning commission', which, although working in conjunction with the government, is nevertheless independent, in the same way that we aspire for the independence of the judiciary.

Finally, as the structure changes, the order of priorities must also change, and this new order must work from within its own logic, operating through its own distinctly objective course of balance and imbalances, of proportions, of connecting and 'igniting' links, and so on. Above all the scientific method of being directed by 'experience, theory, analysis' is the most important guiding light in the entire process. Only through constant evaluation, shifts, and acquisition of new knowledge, and constant vigilance and readiness to learn from the people's experience, can development take place. This is the way to be cured of aid-addiction, to get rid of aid-pushers and aid-dealers, and to be freed from plunder and exploitation, and to go on to the 'second liberation'.

23

After Olof Palme:
What Needs to be Done?

MICHAEL MANLEY

It is a convenient fiction peddled by the political right that the oil-price explosion of 1973 and the crisis which followed were primary causes of the difficulties which engulf us in the 1980s. Of course the events of the late-1970s were not the primary causes. They were themselves the products of deeper problems which have been at work throughout colonialism and are endemic in the structure of the world economy which evolved during the last three centuries.

The oil-price crisis lends itself to gross misinterpretations of history because it represented a symptomatic reaction on so large a scale as to camouflage the real illness that preceded it and which it is politically convenient for some to seek to mask.

Since the oil-price crisis and particularly in the 1980s two contradictory trends have tended to dominate world events. First, there is a growing consensus among a wide spectrum of thinkers from the centre and throughout the democratic left concerning a broad programme of action which needs to be undertaken in the management of the world economy. This intellectual alliance even includes substantial elements from the centre–right, including as it does men like Edward Heath of the British Conservative Party.

The origin and follow-up work of the Brandt Commission, the studies on disarmament conducted by the Commission headed by Olof Palme, and more recently the work on international economics conducted on behalf of the Socialist International all reflect this growing consensus and a heightened clarity about what needs to be done.

Simultaneously, the problems are getting worse. Third World debt stands at $1000 billion. Arms expenditure is now proceeding annually at the rate of $1000 billion. There are 570 million people in the developing countries who are malnourished; 800 million adults illiterate, and 250 million who do not attend school. There are 1.5 billion persons who have little or no access to medical care. And so one can reel off the figures which measure the social disaster that is creeping across the globe and threatening to engulf the majority of humankind. Each one of those figures, and many others which could be quoted, were substantially smaller five years ago and substantially smaller 10 years ago. As our knowledge of what needs to be done and how we might do it increases, our capacity to translate that knowledge into action seems to decrease.

The second contradiction that can be discerned is important because it largely explains the first. The political process at any epoch of history always reflects a central dynamic. It is the interaction between all those forces which work to preserve the status quo, and those other forces which seek to change it. The essential contest is simple in both origin and nature. At any point in human affairs economic arrangements create appropriate social structures. Within this system there are clear beneficiaries who become the centre of the political forces working for the status quo. Simultaneously, there are those who regard themselves as either disadvantaged by, or more directly the victims of, the present order who become the centre of the forces working for change. Which group has the upper hand in the struggle will vary with place and circumstance and is affected by factors such as the use of force, the capacity to organize, or the ability to persuade.

In the course of the last decade, the forces working against change have had no more than their normal quota of success through the use of force. Pinochet in Chile is a case in point; but the case which he represents must be set against the defeat of Somoza in Nicaragua. It is throughout those powerful and significant sections of the world where the political outcome is determined by organization and persuasion, that is, the industrial democracies, where the forces working against change have had their most striking successes. Even while unemployment in these democracies, which are sometimes loosely described as the First or Developed World, has risen to some 35 million; even while there has been significant contraction in social sectors represented by education and health services, these forces, led by the 'radical right', have maintained firm control of the decision-making process. By contrast, the forces for change throughout much of Western Europe, Britain, Canada, the USA, and Japan are in political disarray and have demonstrated little capacity to influence major decisions affecting the great issues of world economic management, armament spending, and global development. The contradiction is that a worsened social condition has coexisted with a tightening control over decision-making by the forces opposed to change. As the decision-making has remained firmly in these hands, devoted as they are to the global status quo as an extension of national purposes, so have the global conditions deteriorated.

The answer to both sets of contradictions must, logically, be found in the question: Why have the forces for change, particularly in the great industrial democracies, been unable to work with the intellectual consensus reflected in the work of the Third World, which is sometimes described as the New International Economic Order (NIEO), the work of the Brandt Commission, the Palme Commission, and now reflected in the Socialist International's *Global Challenge*, as a basis for persuasive and effective political action?

It is in this context that we must assess the significance of the death of Olof Palme. Palme was at once among the stoutest hearts and clearest minds in contemporary Social Democracy. He was simultaneously a humanist visionary and a superb practising politician. He was immensely courageous, as evidenced by his support of the liberation struggle in Vietnam, his refusal to visit Chile under Pinochet, or his unswerving commitment to the anti-apartheid struggle; and he had an exceptional mind. Two quotations from Palme are both revealing of the man and instructive concerning the challenges which the world faces. He stated in a 1980 interview: 'I have come to the conclusion that one cannot go on building up arsenals without getting into a situation where something will snap sooner or later.' We are now spending $1 trillion a year on those arsenals. On another occasion he stated with succinct relevance:

> The gap between North and South is creating tensions and you cannot have a peaceful world if you have acute poverty in large parts of the world and affluence in the rest . . . in order to work for peace in the present situation, we have to address ourselves to the long-range issues. I have always maintained that disarmament and development are interconnected.

Palme always understood that the cost of producing arms is a deduction from a surplus that could be used for investment or consumption. It was Mary Kaldor, the economist, who put it this way:

> The practice of cost accounting, of awarding fictional profits to the military industry artificially reverse the priorities of capital, shifting the resources from productive to non-productive branches of industry instead of the other way around. In other words, it entrenches and does not overcome the disproportionality between different branches of production that lies at the heart of the crisis.

Paradoxically, from 1977 when NATO decided to increase military spending by 3 per cent in real terms per annum, a decision followed by huge increases in military spending which began under President Carter and have reached lunatic proportions under President Reagan, the world has been busily 'shifting resources from productive to non-productive branches of industry instead of the other way around'. Furthermore, the arms race creates a huge vested interest in the production it requires. This becomes a potent political factor working against a stable world capable of a sustained assault on the problems of underdevelopment. Equally, the gap between the developed and developing world is widened every year, but not even a symptomatic crisis such as Sub-Saharan starvation appeals to more than the marginal conscience of the citizens of the First World. The heart-warming and massive charitable response is reflected in neither government policy nor voting patterns at election time. Even as we mourn the loss of Olof Palme, the vicious act which removed him compels us to ask ourselves: What is next to be done? The truth is that we know what needs to be done. We know, as Palme did, that the problem which we measure with the statistics of suffering is not one of arithmetic. It has to do with the nature and unequal workings of the world economic structure. We have comprehensively analysed:

(i) the structure of unequal trade;

(ii) the international financial institutions, and what they are capable of contributing to the solution of world problems and the ways in which they act in the main to entrench those problems and perpetuate the difficulties associated with them;

(iii) the role of multinational corporations and in particular the extent to which this phenomenon has reduced the concept of the global free market to a myth;

(iv) the protectionism which is applied by the North whenever it is threatened with any form of internal adjustment as a result of the workings of the very kind of global economy which the right claims as its model.

The negotiations between the North and the South concerning these four critical problems are now three decades old, dating as they do from the Bandung Conference in 1955. In the 1970s the Third World formulated the idea of the NIEO, which may have been a tactical error since it tended to disguise a set of highly specific and practical proposals behind the rhetorical cloud represented by the term itself. This has been brilliantly exploited by the right to suggest that the Third World has no specific proposals and is really seeking to hide its own failures behind a dream.

During the last five years the North–South dialogue has broken down completely. Consequently nothing has changed. Inevitably the crisis is now presenting itself in a new form. Third World debt now commands the kind of attention that was given to the terms of trade in the 1970s. In the meantime it is largely forgotten that it is the problems of the terms of trade, which we first recognized in the 1970s and which has in reality been at work throughout this century, which is the fundamental cause of the chronic disproportion between export earnings and import costs. This disproportion is the basic cause of Third World debt.

We understand, as Palme did, that protectionism is relevant because it blocks attempts by the Third World to export its way out of its crisis. We understand, as Palme did, that the multinational corporation system contributes to the overall crisis because it guarantees that large financial flows move from the Third World to the First World in season and out, in a variety of forms as profits, interest rates, royalty payments, technology charges, patent fees, transport costs, and many devices too numerous to mention.

We know as Palme did that armament expenditure is both a cause and a result of social instability in the false search for security or advantage through force. In the absence of equitable social arrangements within and between societies, force has always been employed to underwrite stability. We have no doubt, as Palme did not, that you cannot separate disarmament from development just as you cannot separate both from new types of planned management of the world economy directed towards social ends that have been determined by and for the majority of the world's people.

The recent economic study of social democracy, *Global Challenge*, develops on the Brandt Commission. It first addresses the problem of recovery in the North, arguing that this is vital to a general return to progress. In the section on mutual recovery, the report states:

> This report both strongly endorses and seeks to extend the analysis of the reports from the Brandt Commission on mutual interests in the economic recovery of spending and trade between North and South. In fact, it is especially in recovery and associated means of resolving the debt crisis that the mutual interests between North and South are most pronounced in the global economy.
>
> In those countries in which no action has been taken to generate a sustainable real rate of growth, deliberate action needs to be taken to promote total spending in the economy. The circumstances in which the various countries find themselves are too diverse to allow recommendation of a specific national package of measures to achieve this goal. But it is a policy which can be pursued by governments using well-established methods, for example, expanding public expenditure, cutting taxes or increasing the rate of credit creation. If growth generated by such policies is to be sustainable, it

is essential that cooperative arrangements are established to distribute the economic and social benefits of the recovery. Without such cooperative mechanisms or agreements, the recovery may be diverted into a new inflationary spiral. These mechanisms must ensure the creation of recovery opportunities for developing countries, thus restoring the import capacity they need for growth.

Such recovery in the short term does not solve the more fundamental issues of restructuring trade, finance or international institutions in such a way as to remedy the present imbalance in global power. But it does provide the essential conditions for breaking the stalemate in the North/South dialogue and creating conditions for longer-term development.

The report further states:

General recovery by the European and other OECD economies, adding some $100 billion a year to global net spending. We do not underestimate the scale of the challenge posed by such expansion. But we can express the order of magnitude of such a recovery by setting the objective of creating one-and-a-half to two-million jobs in Europe each year and raising the growth of total production and real income by around three per cent a year. Such growth rates, similar to those in the 1960s and early 1970s, would have to be sustained for a decade before we could say that the economic crisis in the North had been overcome. Certainly, such a general recovery could create, sustain or defend some ten million jobs in the United States (depending on the degree of active or passive US participation in the recovery programme) and more than twenty million jobs elsewhere in Europe and the rest of the OECD.

It continues:

. . . a programme for sustained global recovery would involve new spending to offset the world's deflationary gap. We specified that at a minimum, additional spending of some $100 billion a year would be necessary to achieve an expansion of income and trade, both in North and South, sufficient to inaugurate a decade of genuinely new development.

Such a spending programme is both possible and necessary.

Similarly, one-tenth of arms spending transferred into aid would increase capital flows to the developing countries by the equivalent of 10 per cent of their total external debt. This would simultaneously alleviate the debt crisis and stimulate economic growth.

Global Challenge then turns to North–South issues and proposes in summary as follows:

Firstly, the introduction of an element of management into world commodity trade to provide for stability in commodity prices; a mechanism for maintaining the international purchasing power of commodities; and planned cooperation, leading to greater efficiency and productivity in commodity production and in the development of by-products where possible.

The programme of Common Fund as proposed in UNCTAD remains the best, and still potentially viable, set of mechanisms and arrangements for these purposes.

Secondly, the re-organization of the international financial institutions to ensure that they concentrate on development as well as adjustment; that adjustment programmes are carried out in longer time-frames so as to reduce the terrible social hardships and dislocations which make present IMF policies so agonizing and sometimes disastrous for developing societies; that we create a significant development 'window' so that long-term foreign exchange support can become available for countries with sound development plans and the will to carry them out; that there be incremental resources available to support this more development-oriented approach; that the decision-making process be democratised; finally, that the principles of accountability and prudent management continue to apply.

The third main area for consideration lies in the question of the multinational corporations. This involves the development of a Code of Conduct and some internationally supervised means of ensuring that multinational corporations stay within the bounds of an agreed Code of Conduct and, in particular, deal on a basis of respect with governments, trade unions and other institutions in the countries where they operate.

Fourthly, there is protection. The Third World must have access to the great markets of the North if it is to grow. At the same time, it needs periods of selective and temporary protection if its own infant industries are to have a chance to survive while cutting their teeth.

These, taken together, would significantly alter the net financial flows, trade opportunities and development possibilities of Third World countries. The opportunities for developing countries and the effect upon an enlarged world economy would far outweigh the effects of the small concessions the First World would be asked to make.

In the meantime, the debt crisis itself cries out for planned international response. The international community could do a lot worse than to take as the basis for negotiation the ideas proposed by a group of Latin American experts in an international conference on debt in Cartagena in January of 1985. The ideas involved have been largely adopted by the Socialist International, which proposes in *Global Challenge*:

> Conversion into grants of the debts of the poorest countries, and certainly of the countries of Sub-Saharan Africa, combined with grant conversion of part of the debt of other developing countries. Rescheduling of the remaining debt of Third World countries, through extension of the time period for repayment principal, including, in particular, those Latin American countries whose scale of current indebtedness not only limits their import capacity, but also threatens the security of financial institutions in First World countries.
>
> A ceiling of interest rates at concessionary levels for developing countries. Such a measure would complement extension of the time period for repayment of principal through which, under normal financial criteria, current interest rates, in any event, would be lowered.
>
> A fixing of the ratio of debt repayment to a given proportion of developing countries' export earnings, at a maximum of twenty per cent, which was typical in the early 1970s. Such a measure again would complement extending the time period for repayment of principal and lowered interest rates.
>
> Increasing official development assistance to the 0.7 per cent of GDP recommended by the Brandt Commission and the United Nations. If this were achieved, and if those countries already exceeding 0.7 per cent were to sustain their exceptional contribution, it would not only amount to a significant increase in the resources of the South, but also create an additional two million jobs in the OECD countries of the North.
>
> A complementary increase in the funds of IDA or—pending a change in the willingness of the US administration to the replenishment of IDA funds—action by other countries in the North to provide adequate finance for parallel World Bank initiatives, such as the proposed Fund for Africa. The argument in support of this sixth initiative is elaborated in this report.
>
> An increase of Special Drawing rights over a five-year period, to a US dollar equivalent of approximately 150 billions to support the process of debt readjustment, recovery and development.

In commenting on the work of the Brandt Commission, Olof Palme himself once remarked that the recommendations contained in the Brandt Report would only be implemented as an 'expression of political will'. And this brings us back to the heart of our contradiction: political will. If the forces of change are to be capable of an effective exertion of political will, they must achieve three things: first, clarity of purpose; second, a united effort at persuasion; third, effective political organization as the carrier 'for the first two'. We find ourselves, therefore, in a situation where our problem is not so much what needs to be done as how to do it!

It is foolhardy to attempt to write political prescriptions for societies other than one's own. Indeed, even in the home environment the most carefully considered and elaborated plan of political action is likely to end up as a set of guidelines at best. None the less, it seems that one can isolate certain areas that cry out for action. Three suggest themselves.

If the forces for change are to regain influence and establish momentum—they have to succeed in a substantial section of the industrial democracies. In addition, the democratic forces in the Third World must regain the capacity for strategic planning and action as distinct from the present situation where they are concerned, in the main, with survival. Finally, these forces in both First and Third World must arrive at agreement concerning priorities.

In so far as the industrial democracies are concerned, the democratic left has to learn the importance of co-ordinated action between the governments which are controlled by progressive political parties at any moment of time. The *Global Challenge* analysis is crucial when it indicates how difficult it is for one government of an industrial democracy with its open economy to try to implement change. It is quickly isolated and cut down by the economic forces being led by the financial institutions. Equally, if an industrial democracy tries to spend its way out of a crisis by itself, it tends to produce inflationary pressures within the national economy which quickly undermines its credibility with the people. Even at the level of spending, therefore, industrial democracies under progressive leadership need to co-ordinate their plans since a number of democracies reflating their economies simultaneously would lead to increased trade and general economic activity as a hedge against the danger of inflation. Simultaneously, it is easier for a group of industrial democracies to embark upon forward-looking and expansionist economic policies in their dealings with Third World countries than for any one attempting to do so alone. Hence common-sense demands that both in terms of national and international policies the greater the degree of co-ordinated joint action within the industrial democracies the greater the chances of success, the greater the insurance against failure, and the more rapid the assault upon the common problems which are shaped by First and Third World alike.

If all this is to succeed, there has to be a substantial change in the nature and thrust of political activity. When political parties of change allow themselves to be trapped inside purely national formulation of problems in policy discussions, they play into the hands of the forces of the status quo. What is needed is a vigorous programme of education that begins inside political parties at the level of the leadership, research departments, and the like to sensitize movements to a new perspective for change. This perspective must be firmly international in its focus. The international programme of action must be understood and represented as the extension of national programmes and concerns, because we now occupy an interdependent world and are, consequently, members of a global village.

What is next to be done in so far as the industrial democracies are concerned, therefore, really boils down to a question of reorientation, so that political awareness encompasses the realities of interdependence and how these realities impact upon people's lives and the future they can make for themselves. Furthermore, people must be led to understand how this is subverted by a traditional right-wing perspective which pretends that the national boundaries are also the only horizons of popular hope and expectation.

If political parties are able to develop a new perspective within their own ranks and communicate that to the majority of their respective electorates, they will have a chance to gain control of governments on the basis of mandates for change. On the other hand, if the process does not begin within the political parties, they will end up as they are currently to be seen in the USA. There, political elements normally considered progressive, that is to say, advocating change in the interest of the majority of people, scramble for the political middle ground. In this process everybody ends up dancing to the conservative drums. It is as if there were two boxers who fight each other from time to time. At the start of one fight, however, one of the boxers throws in the towel and proposes to the other that they join forces and attack the referee or, worse, the audience.

In so far as the Third World is concerned, the main challenge lies in the area of political education. This much they share with their brothers and sisters in the First World. As with the industrial democracies, analysis reveals a particular problem which must be overcome. Political parties of the North have to develop an international perspective if they are to create a new dynamic consistent with what they need to do. In the Third World this is also true but there is another problem. Democratic politics in Third World countries tend to suffer from a disabling contradiction. If political action is conceived in terms of the disbursement of benefits without reference to the means of capital accumulation, and development generally, they suffer from a disjuncture. No society can create the means to well-being without going through a continuing investment in capital accumulation and other means to increased production. Early capitalist societies have done this by the simple expedient of gross exploitation. Socialist bloc countries with their rigidly planned economies seek to achieve their objectives by executive orders that determine levels of investment and consumption. On the other hand, Third World democracies come into being in an age of social enlightenment and therefore are philosophically and practically unable to proceed by the route of mass exploitation as an instrument of economic policy. Equally to the extent that they are politically plural and with open economies, they do not have at their disposal the option of rigid planning. Consequently, they are tending to fall between two stools. The political debate is conceived in terms that imply the promise of benefits without addressing the question of how the means are to be mobilized.

To take just one example: foreign exchange is a vital component in any plan to increase production. Machinery for manufacturing or even fertilizer for agriculture will place demands on the foreign exchange budget. If consumer appetites pre-empt all available foreign exchange, however, the plan to increase production will break down. The people, and particularly the better-off citizens, will have to learn to do with less of the luxuries to which they are accustomed and to which they feel they are entitled. This is a challenge to political education and persuasion within the competitive electoral process. Of course it could be argued that increased production through private foreign capital investment would bring its own foreign exchange. This is only partially true, however. Furthermore, if this is the main means to increased production, the strategy will increase rather than reduce dependence on external factors, further entrenching the historic problems.

This kind of problem can only be tackled by coming to grips with the nature of development. This must be followed by internal programmes of party sensitization through education and finally popular mobilization within the existing democratic framework. It is extremely difficult to do, but then we live in difficult times and face difficult tasks. The mobilization of development capacity in terms of human and physical investment is the supreme challenge confronting democratic political processes in the Third World. And it is a task that must be tackled if development is to be achieved and the prized democratic structures maintained.

Finally, there is the question of co-ordination. At present very little effort is directed towards finding the means for progressive forces in the First and Third Worlds to work together to search for common agendas and strategies for implementation.

International conferences involving governments tend to be a prescription for inaction because of the principle of unanimity. Furthermore, even governments which share a broadly progressive outlook are often collectively ineffective because they have no system for hammering out a minimum common programme for change. Only a system of caucusing among like-minded governments and political parties can change this. Once again, this represents a new challenge to be overcome. Yet this, too, is surely not beyond our collective intelligence to accomplish.

The international perspective in the politics of the industrial democracies; the politics of mobilization for development in the Third World; the development of a common agenda for the forces of change in North and South: these would add up to a good start in response to the challenge of what is next to be done.

24

Western Efforts for Change: Sweden's Future Role

INGVAR CARLSSON

When Willy Brandt, together with Olof Palme and others, 10 years ago formed the Brandt Commission, which was to deal with the whole question of the economic relations between North and South, between poor and rich countries, this was done in the realization that a change in these relations might be of decisive importance for the future of mankind. Everyone who has had an opportunity to visit some of the poor parts of the world and has seen the misery, diseases, and starvation can certainly imagine what the Brandt Commission meant.

Despite the fact that 73 per cent of the world's population live in developing countries, these countries account together for only 22 per cent of the world's total GNP, 10 per cent of the world's energy consumption. In Africa the average length of life is just over 50 years. It is true that it is increasing but more than one child in 10 still dies before the age of one in many African countries. Starvation and undernourishment affect perhaps one-fifth of the world population as a result of conflicts, problems in agriculture, and general poverty. In Africa south of the Sahara up to one-third of the children may eat the wrong food or be undernourished.

The developing countries with their frail economies have been particularly badly hit by the economic crisis. Not least their debt burden has increased dramatically. At the end of 1986 their combined foreign debt amounted to more than $1000 billion. Many developing countries are unable today to pay interest and amortizations on their rapidly growing foreign debt. As a result the industrial countries have cut down substantially on their new loans to the Third World. Since 1984 the outflow of capital from the developing countries has exceeded the inflow of new loans. In 1985 there was a net transfer of $22,000 million *from* the developing countries. This must be compared with a net transfer of $35,000 million *to* the developing countries in 1981.

The debt crisis we are facing now was largely unforeseen. No one could know in advance that we would experience at the beginning of the 1980s a combination of sky-high interest rates on loans, an artificially high dollar rate, falling commodity prices, and stagnation in the very markets that are of interest to the developing countries.

For many countries this development meant that the situation changed almost from one day to the next.

From 1984 onwards the world economy certainly improved and the crisis was for a while less acute. Now, however, the future is once again uncertain and the debt problems of the developing countries are being aggravated.

Most of the world's poorest developing countries are located in Sub-Saharan Africa. In six years their debts have increased from 30 to 50 per cent of their combined production. In the case of oil-importing countries in Sub-Saharan Africa the combined foreign debt amounts to 65 per cent of their GNP. Without special efforts from outside they have no chance of extricating themselves from the crisis and restarting their development.

Recent improvements in the economy of many developing countries should be used for a thorough tackling of the debt problems:

—— Through the industrial countries accepting their share of the common responsibility for solving the debt crisis. The markets of the industrial countries must be opened to a greater extent to the exports of the developing countries and we must pull together for a stable growth in the world economy.

—— Through the rich countries increasing their international development assistance. The rich countries have as yet only reached the halfway mark towards the UN assistance target of contributions amounting to 0.7 per cent of their GNP.

—— Through special measures for the very poorest countries. Several of the poorest countries in Africa are implementing readjustment and reform programmes in order to cope with the imbalance in their economies. The aim is to stimulate growth and development, but if nothing is done to alleviate the debt burden, there is a risk that the programmes will only lead to austerity policies with high political and social costs as a result. Sweden has taken the initiative for bringing about co-ordinated international efforts for the poorest debt-ridden countries. A possible measure may be to grant more advantageous terms in the case of debt consolidations. Another may be to increase the flow of resources by means of making new credits available to Africa via the World Bank. Within the framework of its international development assistance budget, Sweden has allocated funds to enable participation in co-ordinated international actions to ease debt burdens. We are also prepared to give special bilateral support to countries receiving Swedish development assistance that have severe debt problems.

Sweden will commit itself seriously in this way to give the poorest countries of the world a real chance of a reasonable development and an improved standard of living for their inhabitants.

Sweden is allocating 1 per cent of its gross national income to international development assistance—and we are doing this, too, when times are hard. Unfortunately there are many industrial countries who allocate considerably less. Percentage-wise, the superpowers do not give more than a third of Sweden's development assistance. If all the industrial countries were to meet the UN target of giving 0.7 per cent of their GNPs in development assistance, the volume of this aid would be more than doubled. In terms of the figures for 1985, this means that a further approximately $35,000 million would be made available to the developing countries. Working for increased international development assistance is and will remain one of the main aims of Swedish development assistance.

Swedish development assistance concentrates considerably on the poorest countries. There has been an emphasis on the development of the rural areas and on the social sectors in the wide sense of the term. Support for liberation and independence is an important feature of Swedish development assistance. It is not a coincidence that Sweden provides extensive development assistance in Southern Africa. We supported the liberation movements at an early stage. After independence it has been natural to continue in the form of regular assistance. It is no coincidence either that we have provided development assistance to Vietnam—this arose from our endeavours to promote a small country's independence and reconstruction after a devastating war. This does not prevent us from later having been critical of the Vietnamese government's foreign policy. We have also chosen to give support to Nicaragua after the revolt against the Somoza regime. Our foreign aid is not least important in a situation when the country has been subjected to aggression from outside.

A growing proportion of Swedish development assistance goes in fact to the countries in Southern Africa. The region receives today more than 43 per cent of our bilateral assistance. The background is the deterioration of the political and economic situation in Southern Africa.

In South Africa the white minority regime has stepped up oppression and has chosen to protect its privileges by increasingly brutal means. At the same time South Africa has escalated its policy of destabilization towards its neighbours. In Angola and Mozambique South Africa supports the anti-government rebel movements UNITA and MNR. South

African raids into Lesotho, Botswana, Zimbabwe, and Zambia have caused innumerable deaths. The supply of goods to several of South Africa's neighbouring countries has been disrupted and there are constant threats of various sanctions. The stream of refugees in the region has increased. The crisis in Southern Africa stems above all from the South African apartheid system. Abolishing this system is not only a moral question, a question of solidarity with South Africa's black population; it is also a question of the possibilities of a peaceful development in the region. As long as the white racist regime remains in power, it will try in every way to keep its neighbours in an economic stranglehold. As long as the aggressive apartheid system continues to exist, peace and stability in Southern Africa will be threatened.

Sweden has long supported the opposition to apartheid. Olof Palme in fact started his political activities with an action against apartheid, in support of some black students who had been thrown out of their schools in South Africa. Today we give economic assistance to South Africa's neighbours and support the opponents and victims of the apartheid regime. We also try in various ways to help isolate the regime in South Africa. Earlier, Sweden stopped its investments in South Africa and imposed a ban on imports of agricultural products. Swedish companies have been firmly requested to refrain voluntarily from trade with South Africa. Municipalities and country councils have obtained the statutory right to carry out boycott actions. All Scandinavian air services to South Africa have been broken off.

Sweden has now decided to go a step further by introducing a total trade boycott of South Africa. A trade boycott is a very far-reaching measure, which Sweden, for reasons of principle and on account of its policy of neutrality, only takes after a decision by the UN Security Council. Despite the fact that an overwhelming majority of the UN member countries today support the demands for a boycott of South Africa, the Security Council has time and again failed to reach a decision on effective economic sanctions against South Africa. Against this background and on account of the apartheid system's wholly unique nature, Sweden has decided as a non-recurring measure to deviate from its traditional line and unilaterally impose a trade boycott. We have no illusions about this decision being able to shake the apartheid regime to its foundations. We hope, however, that it will soon lead to other countries following suit and that it may be a contribution to the efforts aimed at bringing about an effective decision on sanctions in the UN Security Council.

The apartheid system would not be able to survive unless it was supported, accepted, or tolerated in various ways by the rest of the world. It is for this reason that we all have a responsibility for abolishing the system. We who live outside South Africa are under an obligation to take action to bring an end to apartheid and the ascendancy of racism. Sanctions is the best chance available today of bringing about the overthrow of apartheid by peaceful means. For one thing is certain: if the international community does nothing, there is danger of developments in South Africa ending in a violent explosion with serious international repercussions.

The regime in South Africa must be isolated. The opposition in South Africa wants this—and the neighbouring states would like to see it—despite the fact that sanctions would hit them hard. An increasing number of countries subscribe to the idea of economic sanctions against the apartheid regime. Now it is a question of ensuring that the sanctions obtain as broad-based a support as possible.

Equally important, however, as subjecting South Africa to greater international pressure is an increase in assistance to the Front Line states. Several of these are today greatly dependent on South Africa for their vital supplies and would be very badly hit by sanctions against the white minority regime. The international community therefore has a joint responsibility for helping to ensure that the injurious effects on these countries are limited as much as possible. In the autumn of 1986 the Swedish government presented an extensive development assistance package with extra efforts in Southern Africa. The package included, for example, assistance to the ports, roads, and railways of the countries in order to improve the opportunities for transporting goods along alternative routes other than via South Africa, as well as measures in the energy sector to reduce the dependence of these countries on energy from South Africa. In addition the package also included emergency assistance to Angola and Mozambique, which are the countries that have been hardest hit by South Africa's aggression, and increased support to the liberation movements ANC and SWAPO. We did this in order to show solidarity with Southern Africa but also to try to persuade other donor countries to increase their efforts. We have also requested the UN to see whether it could play a co-ordinating role in approximately the same way as it did when it provided relief for Africa's famine disasters some years ago.

However, it is not only the crisis in Southern Africa that has made the collective responsibility of the world community stand out increasingly clearly. Many development problems cannot be solved in any way other than through co-ordinated international efforts. It may be a question of environmental problems, new energy sources, research, or food production. Quite simply, there is no alternative to improved international co-operation, primarily through the UN.

By tradition Sweden makes large contributions to the UN and multilateral development assistance. Close on 30 per cent of our development assistance goes that way. In several organizations Sweden is among the very biggest donors of assistance.

Development assistance through the UN system has considerable advantages. It is a way for a state to demonstrate its support for international co-operation and its confidence in the UN as an instrument for peace and security. Developing countries are also given resources which are not linked to any individual donor country's political or economic conditions. Instead, the developing countries are given a greater chance of influencing how the funds are used by the UN bodies and other multinational organizations.

For Sweden the support for the UN has long been one of the cornerstones of our foreign and development assistance policies. It is for this reason that we take a very serious view of the crisis experienced by the UN today. It is not only a question of acute liquidity problems and of demands for a more efficient UN. It is also a question of a profound political crisis for the whole of the UN as a means of co-operation and for the fundamental principles of multilateral co-operation. The US cut-backs in contributions to the UN reflect the critical attitude of the US Congress to the UN and to multilateral co-operation. The Soviet Union, too, has at different times demonstrated its disapproval of UN decisions by not contributing its share.

Sweden believes in the UN as an idea, as a peacekeeping body, as an important channel for development assistance, and not least as a guarantee for the rights and security of the small states. We therefore want to safeguard and stand up for the UN. This is best done by making progress on the many unsolved issues on the agenda and by means of realistic reforms improving its efficiency.

There is certainly much within the UN that can be improved. The Secretary-General should actively work for the implementation of necessary reforms of the administration and programmes. The Secretariat needs to be streamlined and made more efficient. Member countries that owe debts to the organization must fulfil their pledges. The present maximum contribution of 25 per cent for an individual member country should be lowered. This was a line of thought that Olof Palme presented when he addressed the UN General Assembly on the occasion of the commemoration of the Fortieth Anniversary of the UN in October 1985. He said that:

Selective withholding of assessed contributions and refusal to participate in the financing of certain United Nations activities do not reflect an economic necessity but a political consideration on the part of some countries. Ideas have been put forward to reduce the maximum share of the assessed contributions that any one member state is required to pay. A more even distribution of the assessed contributions would better reflect the fact that this Organization is the instrument of all nations and make it less dependent on contributions from any single member state. In that case the rest of us would have to shoulder a somewhat greater financial responsibility. Sweden, for its part, is ready to participate in discussions to explore these ideas.

It is important that the current crisis within the UN is not only resolved but also turned into something positive. We must not hesitate over the many difficult decisions that will have to be taken if the UN is to be in a position to play an even more important role in the future, with increased trust and support on the part of all member countries. For Sweden it will be a very important task to contribute to improvements of this kind during the next few years.

Long-term measures to tackle the debt crisis, increased development assistance to the countries in Southern Africa, a purposeful support for the UN, and an international co-operation—those are some of the central features of Swedish development assistance policy. Our efforts are not only an expression of international solidarity. They are also to a large extent based on the realization of a mutual interdependence between North and South, of the fact that a successful economic development in the developing countries will also benefit the rich, industrial countries. Increased transfers of resources to the poor countries would in the long run be beneficial to us all. If the rich countries shirk their responsibility and let developments move in the opposite direction, this may constitute a serious threat to stability in the world and ultimately to international peace and security.

SECTION NINE

Olof Palme: The Man

25

Olof Palme: A Portrait

GUNNAR FREDRIKSSON

Olof Palme was an unusually colourful political personality by Swedish standards. Although perpetually controversial, he was in the mainstream of Swedish and Scandinavian Social Democracy, and his political ideas cannot be termed startling in any way. Olof Palme's gradual rise to eminence in the mid-1950s did not imply any ideological change, any more than his sudden demise entailed any disturbing uncertainty or unanswered questions.

But he had the knack of presenting a traditional social democratic view of society with an unusual keenness of mind and a certain rhetorical aggressiveness. For the same reason, his international activities attracted worldwide attention.

Born on 30 January 1927, Olof Palme came of an upper–middle-class family whose members included leading civil servants, army officers, and insurance executives. As a child he suffered from poor health, received a great deal of his education at the hands of private tutors, studied at one of Sweden's few residential high schools, and matriculated with high marks at the exceptionally early age of 17. With equal rapidity he took a law degree in Stockholm and then, in two years, a BA at Kenyon College in Ohio, USA, in political science.

It is not uncommon in the Swedish labour movement for intellectuals with middle-class backgrounds to become Social Democrats, and, moreover, to achieve prominent positions. In the course of 100 years the Social Democratic Party has had only four leaders, a sign of unusual stability. The first of them, Hjalmar Branting, came from the upper class of the closing years of the nineteenth century; his successor, Per Albin Hansson, came from the working class, and Tage Erlander was a graduate of middle-class origins. The fifth in succession, Palme's successor, Ingvar Carlsson, is also a graduate but comes of a working-class family. And yet Palme's upper-class background was frequently quoted against him, seldom by his fellow Social Democrats but all the more so by his opponents in the non-socialist, 'bourgeois' parties (the Moderate Party, the Liberals, and the Centre). It is sometimes argued that the unusual antipathy he encountered, above all in conservative quarters, was due to his being regarded as something of a traitor to his class.

Starting off in student politics Palme made an early debut and became chairman of the Swedish National Union of Students. He had already acquired a fair amount of international experience during his travels abroad, and as a student politician he concentrated on international affairs. His observations in other countries did a great deal to radicalize his convictions. Already as a student in the USA, he was struck by the great inequalities between rich and poor, an experience which was intensified during a long journey through the country which also took him to Mexico. He had previously visited Prague in the spring of 1949 and he returned there as a Swedish student representative at a meeting convened by the Communist-controlled International Union of Students. As a student politician in 1953, he spent almost three months touring poor countries of South and South-East Asia.

At this stage, already, one can identify three factors which helped to shape Olof Palme's radicalism and reformism: familiarity with the US policies of the New Deal, anti-Communism based on his experiences in Czechoslovakia following the 1948 coup, and an anti-colonial attitude which was intensified during his Asian journey.

Palme joined the Social Democratic Student Club in Stockholm in 1951, which also made him a member of the Party. After a brief period at the Defence Staff, where he was employed in a subordinate capacity on international affairs and intelligence activities, he was hand-picked by Prime Minister Tage Erlander, becoming his Personal Secretary in the late summer of 1953.

Olof Palme did not have a political base in the labour movement, but in 1955 he became Director of Studies in the Social Democratic Youth League. At the same time as he became an increasingly prominent and close assistant of Prime Minister Erlander, he retained this comparatively subordinate appointment for six years, until 1961. As a result of constant travelling, frequently at the weekends, he made a name for himself during this period with a generation of young Social Democrats as a popular and original lecturer and debater.

The Discontent of Rising Expectations

The political ideas which Palme evolved during these years were fashioned through interaction with Erlander and in the course of discussions in the labour movement at large, and they were eventually summed up in the slogan 'the discontent of rising expectations'. These words expressed a view of the welfare state which was completely in line with a Swedish Social Democratic tradition and perhaps can be taken to characterize what has been termed the Swedish model. But, typically of Palme, there was also a measure of US inspiration.

While still a student at Kenyon College, Palme had written an essay criticizing the ultra-liberal economist Friedrich Von Hayek, today the Nestor of the so-called neo-liberals.

During the 1950s in the USA, John Kenneth Galbraith put forward critical ideas, in the tradition of the New Deal, about 'private wealth and public misery'. Galbraith soon came to be well known and quoted by Swedish Social Democrats, many of whom regarded him as a latter-day John Maynard Keynes. Translated into Swedish, these ideas generated a positive attitude towards the discontent which implied growing demands on the public sector.

From 1951 onwards, the Social Democrats held office together with the Agrarian Party (now the Centre Party) in a coalition which gradually became less and less workable. During these years there was talk of 'the death of the ideologies'—another US term, proclaimed by 'neo-conservatives' in the USA and at this time popular with non-socialists in Sweden. In 1956, Tage Erlander made a speech in the Lower Chamber of the Riksdag (Parliament) and Olof Palme a speech in the Upper Chamber, referring to 'the discontent of rising expectations', growing impatience and heightened expectations, concerning people's justified demands for reforms. This coincided with the appearance of a publication entitled *Framstegens politik* (*The Politics of Progress*), of which Olof Palme was the principal author.

The Social Democratic defeat in the 1956 local elections led to the break-up of the coalition in 1957. Meantime a radical ideological debate was in progress within the Party, and the Social Democrats won in the 1958 Riksdag election in connection with a thoroughgoing, highly controversial pension reform which established a national supplementary pensions scheme.

In opposition to the liberal–conservative principle of encouraging private saving and private initiatives in pension insurance, as well as for other kinds of social security, the Social Democrats asserted the ideas concerning the tasks of the public sector which are still dominating our political debate.

Olof Palme vigorously argued that the second of these two lines, entailing high taxation, did not mean any restriction of individual liberty but, on the contrary, its augmentation. He also asserted that the system referred to by the non-socialists as a 'social safety net' for people who were worst off, 'basic security' or a guaranteed 'minimum standard', was not a fair one.

Standards of medical and other care, like educational standards and pension benefits, ought as far as possible to be the same for everybody. He developed his ideas of the role of the state in a dynamic society. Unlike his opponents, he argued that the state was not an inhibiting factor but was instrumental in providing employment, security, better housing standards, better communications, and other infrastructure from which private enterprise could also benefit.

In contradistinction to the society of yesteryear, poverty and unemployment were not the causes of widespread discontent. Instead it was insufficient opportunities of education, cramped housing conditions, and insufficient care amenities, for example, that were provoking equally justified discontent, and Olof Palme spoke of the 'strong society' which would measure up to people's demands, and rejected the argument that this would mean bureaucracy and procrustean constraint. In 1962, the Social Democratic Party published a book whose very title—*Valfrihetens samhalle (The Elective Society)*—manifested this approach. Palme was its main source of ideas and probably its author as well.

International Affairs Around 1960

During these years Olof Palme also concerned himself with international affairs; for example, international development co-operation, the question of Swedish nuclear arms, and relations with the EEC.

Palme had been interested in development co-operation ever since his student days, and he now became one of the architects of Sweden's international development policy. That policy became emphatically anti-colonial: development assistance was to promote national emancipation as well as economic development.

In this way, international development policy came to be interconnected with other forms of official Swedish support to national liberation movements. There was also a frequently quoted government bill, passed by the Riksdag in 1962, stipulating democratic development, or at least the hope of such development, in the new independent states. That bill was to a great extent drafted by Olof Palme.

Decolonialization was proceeding in various ways in Asia and Africa, wars were being fought in Vietnam and Algeria, an outright revolution took place in Cuba, and many people feared that the new regimes would prove to be hostile to the Western world. As a friend of the USA, Olof Palme was perturbed at the tendency shown by the Americans to come out against the new states.

Perhaps Palme and the active body of Swedish opinion during these years did tend to see things through rose-coloured spectacles. He wanted to see the Third World following a middle way between the neo-colonialism of Western capitalism and Communist dictatorship. Perhaps he saw at least a partly applicable model in Scandinavian reformism and democratic socialism. But he was probably less optimistic in his mind than in his rhetoric.

Olof Palme always advocated a powerful defence establishment for Sweden, as a necessary prerequisite of our policy of neutrality, defined as non-participation in alliances in peacetime aiming at neutrality in the event of war. If the rest of the world did not believe in our ability to defend ourselves, our non-participation in alliances would soon lose its credibility. But the question of nuclear weapons for Sweden remained a controversial one for a long time, even within the Social Democratic Party.

During this debate Palme helped to secure the postponement of a decision long enough to keep the Party more or less united until the anti-nuclear opinion had completed gained the upper hand in Sweden. Subsequently he agitated for a general reduction of nuclear armaments with a view to their complete worldwide prohibition.

Towards the end of the 1950s there were growing demands from influential non-socialist circles, not least in private enterprise, for Swedish entry into the Common Market. The Social Democrats found Swedish membership incompatible with the policy of non-participation in alliances, considering the important foreign policy aims which the EEC represented.

In a controversial speech at the 1961 Congress of the Swedish Metalworkers' Union, Prime Minister Erlander enlarged on the reasons for the Social Democratic standpoint. One of the authors of that speech was Olof Palme, and the line of policy which it indicated proved to be a lasting one. Most observers agree that Sweden has secured a favourable settlement with the EEC without becoming a member.

Entering the Government

Olof Palme became Minister without Portfolio in 1963, Minister of Transport and Communications in 1965, Minister of Education and Cultural Affairs in 1967, and, in 1969, on succeeding Tage Erlander as Party Chairman, he became Prime Minister of Sweden.

He proved to be an efficient administrator and cabinet minister. His most conspicuous achievement as Minister of Transport and Communications was the change-over to driving on the right, a really complex organization of achievement.

Palme attached particular strategic importance to education policy as a means of achieving greater social equality. He administered and defended a series of reforms which had already been prepared previously, and he had a great deal of heated debate with students during these years of unrest in higher education. The reforms of compulsory and upper secondary schooling were aimed at reducing early differentiation and in this way counteracting the social bias of recruitment for higher education employment. Palme banked on adult education and on more regular, vocationally oriented programmes of university studies. At the universities in 1968 he was confronted with a radical anti-capitalist body of opinion which accused Social Democracy of working hand in glove with capitalism.

The most vehement opposition of all came from those who demanded fewer restrictions on study programmes in the arts and social sciences. The social spectrum of student recruitment was not broadened as much as Palme and others had hoped for, and it seems fair to say that these problems have not yet been solved—at all events, not as Olof Palme envisaged.

The 1960s became a more ideological decade in Swedish politics than the 1950s, just as in other parts of the Western world. The 1969 Party Congress which elected Palme Party Chairman also adopted a programme for greater equality in a number of fields—education, employment, welfare, and between the sexes. The committee which drafted the programme was chaired by Alva Myrdal (1902–86), who had been a leading Social Democrat since the 1930s, had undertaken several UN assignments, and had served as Ambassador and Head of the Swedish Delegation at the Geneva Disarmament Talks.

Radical as it was, the programme was fully in line with the 1956 programme concerning the role of the state and expansion of the public sector. It represented the pragmatic emphasis of the labour movement on egalitarian policies, in contradistinction to the much-publicized student radicalism. It was an optimistic Party Congress that elected Palme Chairman and Prime Minister.

Palme and the Vietnam War

By that time Olof Palme had already begun to acquire an international reputation, mainly in connection with the Vietnam question. He had been swift to condemn US policy in Vietnam, and he had already made a controversial speech to this effect in the summer of 1965, at a congress of Christian Social Democrats.

Palme was essentially an anti-colonialist, and, as he saw it, the US way of taking over an old colonial war that had been lost by the French was doomed to failure and, moreover, morally reprehensible.

He also maintained that efforts to prop up one corrupt military dictatorship after another in Saigon were a futile, repellent way of counteracting Communism, which was the professed aim of US policy.

Once again there is a tie-in here with the US debate, for the arguments used by Palme and other Swedes taking part in these discussions were frequently taken from or agreed with what was being said at the same time in the USA. All the same, Palme's activities led to acrid exchanges with the US administrations during these years, and, on occasions, with the US Embassy in Stockholm.

It was as Minister of Education that Palme joined the demonstration march in Stockholm in February 1968 together with the North Vietnamese Ambassador to Moscow. The photograph of that demonstration march made Palme a household name over night and aroused strong feelings, both for and against. He himself professed that he had not known the North Vietnamese Ambassador would be taking part and that he was surprised to see him but was unable to cancel the demonstration on that account. However this may be, Palme continued his activity on the Vietnam question along the same lines. At Christmas 1972, when the USA bombed Hanoi, Palme made a statement comparing the attack with Fascist and Communist atrocities—Guernica, Lidice, Katyn, Treblinka. This earned him wrath and indignation in some circles, and appreciation and tributes in others. He became particularly well known in Third World countries. Efforts to achieve greater equality during these years were mainly channelled into reforms of working life. Employees' powers of co-determination were augmented by giving the unions a greater share of influence. The new legislation on workers' control and co-determination was combined with even more controversial ideas of wage-earner funds in which employees, through their union representatives, would exert majority control.

The Social Democrats had won a big electoral victory in 1968. Olof Palme's first election in 1970 brought a slight reverse; his second election, under a new constitution in 1973 (with a unicameral Riksdag and a three-year term of office), brought further reverses although still on a small scale. The result was a hung Riksdag, with Social Democrats and Communists controlling exactly the same number of seats as the three non-socialist parties together.

Olof Palme stayed on as Prime Minister and for the most part made deals with one or more of the non-socialist parties, less frequently with the Communists. But governmental power was weak and it was more difficult now for the Social Democrats to carry through reforms and, after 44 years in power, the 1976 election obliged the Party over to a non-socialist coalition. Olof Palme now became Leader of the Opposition.

The Years in Opposition and the Return to Power

This turn of events was connected not only with the new constitution, which facilitated changes of government, but also with a completely new issue, that of nuclear power. The non-socialist opposition now acquired a leader in Centre Party, Chairman Thorbjörn Palldin, who acted as the uncompromising opponent of nuclear power. This was a winning issue. But the new tripartite coalition also included the liberal–conservative Moderate Party, which was for nuclear power. The government broke up on this issue in 1978, as the non-socialists scored a new election victory in 1979, but only by the skin of their teeth. A new tripartite coalition was formed, but it broke up in 1982, this time foundering on the rock of taxation policy, and the Social Democrats, headed by Palme, returned to office in 1983. The 10 years between 1979 and 1983 had seen a process—unusual in modern Swedish politics—whereby governmental power had lost ground to the Riksdag and its standing committees. Meanwhile Sweden, like other Western countries, had been hit by the oil crisis and other economic difficulties.

The nuclear power issue was settled by referendum, the outcome of which favoured a slow phase-out. The question of wage-earner funds was resolved by a substantial lowering of socialist aspirations, which made the reform innocuous. The problems of the economic crisis were gradually solved through a combination of international upturn, falling oil prices, and competent financial administration. There was a great deal of optimism in Social Democracy and Olof Palme was involved in an enthusiastic campaign against 'neo-liberalism' in Sweden and abroad when his political career was suddenly brought to an end.

Olof Palme was gunned down on the street in Stockholm on the night of 1 March 1986 while he was walking home, unescorted, together with his wife after a visit to the cinema. His successor was appointed within a few hours and the new government issued a declaration which did not involve any policy changes whatsoever. The course of events serves to show how not even the blow thus dealt against the open society in Sweden was capable of disrupting political stability.

International Commitments

In all probability, the great majority of Swedish people remained unaware of Olof Palme's international stature until he died and we heard the testimony of international statesmen, as well as seeing a remarkably large number of them at the funeral. On the contrary, some sectors of the non-socialist opposition had for a long time asserted that Palme was a nonentity on the international scene and that suppositions to the contrary were naïve and provincial.

This, like so many other questions, will have to be answered later on. But, at all events, Palme did play a definite part in the so-called Socialist International, consisting of Social Democratic Parties, which underwent a resurgence from the early-1970s onwards, engineered above all by the West German Chancellor Willy Brandt, the Austrian Chancellor Bruno Kreisky, and Olof Palme. Palme also took part in the Brandt Commission which wrote a widely observed report on development assistance, and he personally headed the Palme Commission which put forward proposals on disarmament. He also mediated on behalf of the UN Secretary-General in the war between Iran and Iraq. He was also on good and close informal terms with the leading personalities of the non-aligned countries, for example Indira Gandhi and Rajiv Gandhi.

The Socialist International embodies ideas by which Palme was guided throughout his active career: democratic reformism, anti-colonial independence, and anti-Communism. He has been particularly active in the Third World and has served as an intermediary link between national movements there and Social Democrats in the West.

In keeping with Social Democratic ideas, trade-union organizations have also been involved in this co-operation. It has been argued that an active trade-union movement must be built up to support democratic developments in Third World countries, and the movement had condemned those who, for example, obstruct trade unions in Latin America but readily encourage it in Poland.

The leading idea of the Brandt Commission was that economic developments in the affluent and poor worlds were necessarily interconnected. An attempt is being made to show that the advanced industrialized countries have a vested interest in rapid economic development for the Third World, and the Commission's report ends with an extensive list of practical recommendations to this end. The Palme Commission similarly argues that both East and West have legitimate security needs, and its report, very appropriately, is entitled *Common Security*. It can never be possible, the Commission argues, to demand unilateral security for one bloc, based on superior military resources. On the contrary, every ideological offensive in this direction is a threat to universal security, in a world of incomprehensibly destructive nuclear potential.

Perhaps these ideas of partnership between rich and poor, and *détente* between East and West, could be regarded as a global version of the ideas of solidarity and promotion of common interests which

Olof Palme represented on his home ground, in a small, homogeneous country like Sweden. This seldom met with very enthusiastic approval from the leaders of the superpowers, but it was more favourably received by the small nations of the world.

Defender of the Welfare Society

Palme saw neo-liberalism as a form of egoism, arrogance on the part of the well-situated, the smart people, those who felt no need of solidarity. He regarded neo-liberalism as a threat to the welfare society which he had been wanting to build up and improve, piece by piece, for more than 30 years.

In a speech at Harvard University, one of the last he made to an international audience, Olof Palme said that unemployment was not only an economic waste and social problem resulting in impaired health, elevated mortality, rising suicide rates, more broken families, increased crime, prostitution, and drug abuse: it was also, he said, a threat to the open, democratic society. If large groups of people, and young people especially, are denied work, experience will tell them that they are not needed and that they can contribute towards overcoming the crisis by going without work. This generates distrust, a feeling of exclusion, and hostility towards democratic institutions. It undermines solidarity.

On these grounds Palme also defended the policy of economic and social equality. No gaps are wider than those existing between people in work and people out of it, and it is the least privileged who are in danger of unemployment. It was also on these terms that he attacked the attempts of neo-liberalism and neo-conservatism to allow freer play to the mechanisms.

He pleaded for a strong trade-union movement and governmental power which was capable of pursuing an active policy of employment and welfare, strengthening job security, reforming the conditions of working life, and improving the occupational environment. He argued that his was the only possible basis on which trade unionism could help to bring about a necessary renewal and rationalization of industry, thereby sustaining international competitive strength.

Welfare, he argued, must be universal. If the people paying tax did not participate in welfare themselves but looked for private solutions, at the same time as taxation revenue went on so-called safety nets for the least privileged, this would undermine social solidarity and encourage taxpayers' revolts. Palme spoke of the importance of popular participation and of a welfare policy without any profit motive.

And so his last major contribution to the international debate was an apologia for the Swedish model in the world of the 1980s. Contrary to what the critics alleged, Palme argued that his model did not represent a threat to economic efficiency and individual liberty. On the contrary, it meant preserving the dynamism of private enterprise and incentives for individual creativity, with the support of a high level of popular participation in politics, trade unionism, and other activities. In this way, 'social engineering' could be undertaken without producing a bureaucratic society of top–down governments. Fundamentally, this is an optimistic view of society in the tradition of the Enlightenment, rationalism, and progressivism. Palme was an optimistic thinker and perhaps his rhetoric was more optimistic still. His optimism was concerned with the potentialities of democracy and with the prospects of creating social justice in a world threatened by growing economic and social inequalities and all manner of political oppression.

The murder of Olof Palme did not only result in party-political sorrow and anger in the ranks of Social Democracy. It also provoked a national manifestation on behalf of the open society and against violence, terror, and war. Although Palme was always a supremely controversial politician, after his death public opinion rallied around his ideas of non-violence, peaceful negotiations, and *détente*. This is what dominated the image of Olof Palme during the months following his death, and this too is the way in which Swedish people like to see their own society.

Acknowledgement

The author, editor, and publisher are grateful to the Swedish Institute for kind permission to reproduce this chapter.